WHO'S WHO ON TELEVISION

ITV BOOKS
in association with Michael Joseph

WHO'S WHO ON TELEVISION

**A fully illustrated guide to 1,000
best known faces on British Television**

Compiled and produced by ITV Books and TVTimes

Editors: Alan Curthoys (Research, *TVTimes*), *John Doyle (ITV Books)*
Assistant Editor: Julie Payne
Designer: Jeremy Dixon

published by

Independent Television Books Ltd
247 Tottenham Court Road
London W1P 0AU

In association with Michael Joseph Ltd

First published 1980

© Independent Televison Books Ltd, 1980

Set in Helvetica 7/8pt by Yale Press, Norwood, London

Cased edition: ISBN 0 900727 71 3
Paperback edition: ISBN 0 900727 72 1

CONDITIONS OF SALE

Printed in Great Britain by
Hazell Watson & Viney Ltd
Aylesbury, Bucks.

After nearly two years in preparation – involving many thousands of telephone calls, quires of questionnaires and hours of persistence and patience – this Who's Who on Television makes its bow.

It would not be here at all were it not for the helpful advice and co-operation of the Press Offices of the BBC and of all the ITV Companies along with most of the numerous theatrical agents. The Entries themselves provided invaluable help in the first round of information-gathering and then again in checking and revising their copy during the closing stages of compilation.

Somehow our original questionnaires found themselves as far afield as America, South Africa and Java. Indeed one of the major problems in producing this book has been in actually contacting the Entries directly. Some have requested, often after hours of tracking, that they should not appear in Who's Who On Television and we have respected their wishes accordingly. Others will complain inevitably that they have been unjustly omitted. We have selected the best known faces, from *all* regions and channels, who have been seen on British Television during the last year of compilation. In this way we feel that we have provided the most up-to-date work possible.

The reference material here has been painstakingly checked and rechecked, however we have been rewarded with many surprises in the 'unfulfilled ambition' section in most entries. In the majority of cases we have reported these ambitions in the words of the Entries themselves.

A

ABRAMS, John
Horticulturalist b. 11.6.05 London. Trained in private gardens in the Isle of Wight and Buckinghamshire and did advisory work before becoming Horticultural Officer for Bristol Corporation, a position he held for 18 years until retirement in 1970. HTV West's gardening expert since 1971, his gardening programme being televised from his own garden and woodland just outside Bristol. Holds RHS Senior General Certificate and RHS Teacher's Certificate and in 1978 was made an Associate of Honour by the RHS, a rare honour awarded for distinguished services to his profession. Education: school and technical college, Hackney. m; 1. s. Address: Backwell Hill, Bristol. Starsign: Gemini. Hobby: gardening.

ACKLAND, Joss
Actor b. 29.2.28 London. Started in brewery, then dairy farming before stage training at Central School of Speech and Drama. After 10 years in the theatre went to Africa and

ABINERI, John
Actor b. 18.5.28 London. Trained at the London Old Vic School. Films incl: Diamonds Are Forever; Pope Joan; Operation Daybreak; McKenzie Break; Soft Beds; Hard Battles. TV incl: Last of the Mohicans; Flambards; The Moon Stallion; Henry V; Blake's Seven; The Onedin Line. Education: 'Well educated', he says, 'from the age of five to eighteen.' Address: c/o Tod Joseph, London W1. Starsign: Taurus. Hobby: riding. Unfulfilled ambition: to be a success as a writer.

became a tea-planter. Hundreds of stage and TV appearances including many classical and modern roles. Stage incl: Captain Brassbound's Conversion; Jorrocks; A Little Night Music; Three Sisters; Death of a Salesman; Taming of the Shrew; Madras House; Evita. TV incl: The Crezz; Enemy at the Door; Tinker, Tailor, Soldier, Spy; Constance Kent. Films incl: Royal Flash; The Little Prince; Silver Bears; S-P-Y-S; Silver Bears; Too Many Chefs; Saint Jack; The Apple. m. Rosemary, 5 d. Melanie, Antonia, Penelope, Samantha, Kirsty, 2 s. Paul, Toby. Address: c/o ICM, London W1. Starsign: Pisces. Hobbies: painting, writing. Unfulfilled ambition: to become a successful writer.

ADAMS, Tom
Actor b. 3.9.38 London. From army service he went to London Unity Theatre and a number of rep companies. His first TV role was as a villain in Dixon of Dock Green. He has since appeared in Emergency – Ward 10; Spy Trap; General Hospital; The Onedin Line; Enigma Files. Education: Cooper's School, Bow, London E3. Address: c/o BBC, London W12. Starsign: Virgo. Hobbies: golf, tennis, cricket, cycling and the cinema.

ADAMS, Tony
Actor b. 11.12.40 Anglesey, North Wales. Trained at the

Italia Conti School. TV incl: Kiss Me, Kate (one of BBC2's opening programmes); The Two Ronnies; Crossroads; For Your Eyes Only; Dr Who; Court Martial; Crown Court; Bristol 600; General Hospital. Education: Hillgrove, Bangor, North Wales. Address: c/o David White Associates, London W1. Starsign: Sagittarius. Hobby: sailing.

ADAMS, Tony
TV reporter/ interviewer/ independent film producer b. 25.9.38 Salisbury, Rhodesia. Parliamentary reporter. Experience with news agency, newspapers, radio and TV Rhodesia, Zambia, South Africa and UK before joining Westward TV 1968-76 and then Anglia TV 1976. Education: Ruzawi and University of South Africa. m. Sally Ann, 1 d. Toinette, 5 s. Carl, Mark, Simon, Jonathan, Richard. Address: c/o Douglas Fisher Productions, Essex. Starsign: Libra. Hobby: ocean sailing. Unfulfilled ambition: to cast off, not just metaphorically.

ADAMSON, Peter
Actor b. 16.2.30 Liverpool.

Started as an amateur, trained at LAMDA with Fortescue Players, Bury, Lancs 1949-1954. Actor/ manager/ producer rep companies 1954-60. TV: Skyport; Knight Errant; Len Fairclough in Coronation Street since 1961. Several stage tours. Education: elementary schools. m. Jean, 2 s. Michael, Greig. Address: Ramsbottom, Bury, Lancs. Starsign: Aquarius. Hobbies: swimming, cooking, writing and social work. Unfulfilled ambition: to retire from the business at the age of 96.

ADARE, Elizabeth
Actress b. 3.6.49 Newcastle upon Tyne, but lived in Sierra Leone until she was eight. Mother was a teacher; her father deputy Attorney-General of Ghana. Studied acting at Mountview Drama School and Guildhall School of Music and Drama. Has since appeared with the National Theatre, the Young Vic, Citizen's Theatre, Glasgow and Coventry and toured and went to London in Banana Box, the play which was adapted for TV as Rising Damp. Also worked with various black theatre groups. Films incl: Father, Dear Father. Radio incl: numerous programmes for African Service of the BBC and The Archers. TV incl: Within These Walls; Crossroads; The Tomorrow People; Crown Court; The Expert; Something for the Time Being; Mandog; Sweeney Agonisties; Angels; General Hospital; Rising Damp; Mind Your Language; Enemy at the Door. Education: Ghana and Freetown; Clemence Cave School for Girls, London, and University Tutorial College, London. m. journalist Allan, 1 d. Kibibi. Address: London. Starsign: Gemini. Hobbies: gardening, reading, dancing. Unfulfilled ambitions: to work on a major feature film in a demanding role and to take a play on a tour of East and West Africa.

ADCOCK, Sally
Actress b. 11.5.49. Trained at Leeds Arts Centre and wanted to be a singer. Stage training with Harrogate and York reps. TV: Tom Gratton's War; Jane Smith in Crossroads. Address: c/o Beryl Seton, London WC2. Starsign: Taurus. Hobbies: reading, writing, making jewellery, camping.

AINLEY, Anthony
Actor b. 20.8.37 London. Started as an insurance clerk but gave it up to go to the Royal Academy of Dramatic Art. Plenty of stage experience before going into television and since in

London, New York and Rome. TV incl: It's Dark Outside; The Avengers; Whodunnit?; Spyder's Web; Warship; The Pallisers; Nicholas Nickleby; Lillie; Elizabeth R; Hassan; Brett; Upstairs, Downstairs. Films incl: Oh What A Lovely War; The Land That Time Forgot; Inspector Clousseau; A Man For All Seasons; The Devil's Claw. Education: America and England. Address: c/o Garrick Club, London WC2. Starsign: Leo. Hobbies: swimming and Greek literature. Unfulfilled ambition: to play with Faye Dunaway.

AITKEN, Maria
Actress b. 12.9.45 Dublin. Began in OUDS, then rep in Coventry, Manchester, Northampton and Cambridge. Other stage incl: Far East tour for British Council; Travesties (RSC); A Little Night Music; Blithe Spirit (National Theatre); Man of Destiny; Bristol Old Vic. Films incl: Some Girls Do; Mary Queen of Scots. TV incl: Murder; The Gold Robbers; The Exiles; Manhunt; Counterstrike; Codename; Take Three Girls; The

Regiment; The Three Marias; The Edwardians; Scotch on the Rocks; Moths; Quiet as a Nun; Company and Co. Education: Riddlesworth Hall, Norfolk; Sherborne School for Girls and St Anne's College, Oxford.
m. (1st) Richard Durden (dis), (2nd) actor Nigel Davenport, 1 s. Jack. Address: c/o Leading Artists, London W1. Starsign: Virgo. Hobbies: pig-breeding, goose-rearing. Unfulfilled ambition: to win a pig-breeding prize while starring in London's West End.

AITKEN, Tony
Actor b. 20.6.46 Solihull, Warwicks. Trained in reps incl: Hornchurch and Northampton. Also been in many pantomines. Joined Bristol Old Vic Company 1974 and Regent's Park Open Air Theatre 1975. Other stage incl: Billy. Presenter of Listen With Mother on BBC radio. TV incl: London Belongs to Me; Dick Emery shows; Porridge; Open All Hours; Miss Jones and Son; Prince William of Orange; Quincey's Quest; Tommy Steel's Christmas Show; End of Part One. Education: Belmont Abbey School, Hereford, St Mary's College, Strawberry Hill. m. Adrienne Cross. Address: Richmond, Surrey. Starsign: Gemini. Hobbies: squash, music, renovating Morgan sports cars. Unfulfilled ambition: to drive a Formula One car.

ALAN, Ray
Ventriloquist b. 18.9.30 Greenwich, London. Taught ukelele by George Formby at 13 while call boy/lime boy at Lewisham Hippodrome. Started entertaining at 13 doing impersonations and magic, and won a talent competition when he was 18 with his ventriloquist act. Famous for his Lord Charles creation which was first tried out at a charity show at Wormwood Scrubbs Prison. Since made many TV appearances: The Good Old Days; Check-Mates!; Britain by Jove!; Where in the World; Magic Circle and many guest appearances. Education: Morden Terrace School, Lewisham, London.
m. Barbie. Address: c/o Peter Prichard, London SW1. Starsign: Virgo. Hobbies: model railways and old films. Unfulfilled ambitions: 'too many to list!'

ALBERGE, Betty
Actress b. 27.1.22 Manchester. Experience in rep (Colwyn Bay), ENSA and radio before TV incl: The Verdict is Yours; Knight Errant; Florrie Lindley in Coronation Street for four and

a half years; The Ken Dodd Show; Crown Court; and You've Made Your Bed, Now Lie on It (play). Education: Fallowfield Central School for Girls, Manchester.
1 d. Christine. Address: RKM Ltd, London W1. Starsign: Aquarius. Hobbies: no time for them. Unfulfilled ambition: to keep working.

ALDA, Alan
Actor b. 28.1.36 New York City. Nurse-chasing hero Hawkeye in TV series M*A*S*H. Wanted to be a nightclub comic and though he grew up in Hollywood and was stage trained, his father, actor Robert Alda, tried to persuade him to become a doctor. Professional debut at 16, serving as a theatrical apprentice. Broadway appearance in The Owl and the Pussycat marked the turning point in his career. Films incl: Paper Lion; The Mephisto Waltz; To Kill a Clown; Same Time Next Year; California Suite. Education: high school and Fordham University, New York. m. clarinetist Arlene, 3 d. Eve, Beatrice, Elizabeth. Address: Leonia, New Jersey. Starsign: Aquarius.

ALDERTON, John
Actor b. 27.11.40 Gainsborough, Lincs. Started stage career with York rep. Many plays and films. TV incl: Dr Moon in Emergency-Ward 10; Bernard Hedges in Please, Sir!; Upstairs, Downstairs; No, Honestly; The

Wodehouse Playhouse; The Upchat Line; Thomas and Sarah. Education: Kingston High School, Hull.
m. (1st) actress Jill Browne (dis), (2nd) actress Pauline Collins, 1 d. Catherine, 2 s. Nicholas, Richard. Address: c/o Nems Management, London SW3. Starsign: Sagittarius. Hobbies: golf and cricket (Lord's Taverners).

ALDRIDGE, Michael
Actor b. 9.9.20 Glastonbury, Somerset. Rep in Nottingham and Birmingham, then Embassy Theatre, London, 1938, and Old Vic in London and Bristol. Many TV plays and series incl: The Perfect Friday; Birds in the Wilderness; Love and the Penguins; The Man in Room 17; Raven. Education: Gresham's School, Holt, Norfolk. m. scenic designer Kirsten Rowntree, 3 d. Charlotte, Harriet, Emma. Address: Greenwich. Starsign: Virgo. Hobbies: sailing, carpentry.

ALEXANDER, Kay.
Announcer/presenter/reporter b. 4.6.50 Hawley,

Surrey. Joined BBC almost immediately after University (1973). Radio: worked for Woman's House; You and Yours; Checkpoint on Radio 4. Became a continuity presenter for BBC Midlands, which included reading the news, 1974. At present reporting for and co-presenting Midlands Today. Education: Frensham Heights, Farnham, Surrey, University of Birmingham (English BA Hons). m. Frank Wibaut, 1 d. Chloe, 1 s. Alexander. Address: c/o BBC, Pebble Mill, Birmingham. Starsign: Gemini. Hobbies: music, dressmaking, cooking, reading and sunbathing.

ALEXANDER, Terence
Actor b. 11.2.23 London. Started with the White Rose Players, Harrogate when he was 16, followed by wide rep experience before coming to London. Has appeared in many plays incl: Move Over Mrs Markham; Two and Two Make Sex; There Goes the Bride; Fringe Benefits. Films incl: League of Gentlemen; Magic Christian; Waterloo; Run a Crooked Mile; The Day of the Jackal; Internecine

Affair. Radio incl: several plays as well as Law and Disorder and two series of The Toff. TV incl: Codename; Forsyte Saga; The Pallisers; Churchill and the Generals; Les Dawson; Dick Emery; Devenish, etc. Education: Ratcliffe College. m. (1st) Juno, (2nd) actress Jane Downs, 2 s. Nicholas, Marcus (from 1st m). Address: Fulham, London. Starsign: Aquarius. Hobby: golf. Unfulfilled ambition: to fly on Concorde at someone else's expense.

ALLEN, Patrick
Actor b. 17.3.27 Malawi. Came to England as a child and was evacuated to Canada during the war. Returned to England in 1953 after local radio station experience. Has worked with the Royal Shakespeare Company. Films include Dial M for Murder; High Tide at Noon; I Was Monty's Double; Dunkirk; The Night of the Generals; The Trouble shooters; The Gold Robbers; Codename; Puppet on a Chain; The Wilby Conspiracy. TV incl: Crane; Brett; Hard Times; Kidnapped. The voice behind countless TV commercials and has big business interests. Education: McGill University, Montreal. m. actress Sarah Lawson, 2 s. Stephen, Stuart. Address: c/o ALS Management Ltd, London. Starsign: Pisces. Hobby: fishing. Unfulfilled ambition: to make his video business a success.

ALLISS, Peter
Golf commentator b. 28.2.31 Berlin. Started career as a professional golfer 1949. Played for England as an amateur and followed his father, Percy, into the Ryder Cup team for which he was chosen eight times. Played in World Cup for England 10 times. Left competitive golf to join BBC as golf commentator in 1969. Recent TV series: Around With Alliss. Education was 'very private'. m. Jacqueline, 2 d. Sara, Victoria, 1 s. Simon. Address: Shadwell, Leeds. Starsign: Pisces. Hobbies: TV, books and wine-tasting. Unfulfilled ambition: to play the trumpet.

ALLNUTT, Wendy
Actress b. 1.5.46 Lincoln. Lived for some time in Pakistan where she learned Indian dancing before returning to England and joining the Elmhurst Ballet School and Central School of Speech and Drama. After a spell in rep she got a number of TV parts incl: Bel Ami; Time Lock; The Regiment; Love Story; Rough Justice; Doctor in Charge; Call My Bluff. Films incl: When Eight Bells

Toll; All Coppers Are; Oh What A Lovely War; Tales From Beyond The Grave. Education: St Mary's, Lincoln; St Margaret's, Bushey. m. actor Colin McCormack. 1 d. Katherine; 1 s. Andrew. Address: Kingston, Surrey. Starsign: Taurus. Hobbies: bric-a-brac, sewing.

ALLSOP, Malcolm
Political editor b. 9.9.50 London. Experience on newspapers, BBC local radio and BBC TV before joining Anglia TV. TV presenter and editor of weekly political magazine programme, Probe, and of debate series, Cross Question. Education: Highbury Grammar School, London. m. Elaine, 1 s. Timothy. Address: c/o Anglia Televison. Starsign: Virgo. Unfulfilled ambition: to become very rich.

ANDERSON, Christine
Actress/presenter b. 9.5.56 Wallsend. Drama training with a community theatre. TV roles in Days of Hope and When the Boat Comes In, both from BBC, and presenting Saturday Shake-up for Tyne Tees TV.

Education: Wallsend Grammar, Willington High and Newcastle College of Art and Technology. Address: c/o Tyne Tees TV, Newcastle upon Tyne. Starsign: Taurus. Hobbies: music, playing ukelele and guitar, singing, dancing, darts, sewing, knitting, playing games/sports, music hall memorabilia. Unfulfilled ambition: 'there are so many things I haven't achieved ranging from small to enormous.'

ANDERSON, Jean
Actress b. 12.12.08 Glasgow, but brought up in Guildford. Originally wanted to be a concert violinist and for years played the violin in the Guildford Orchestra. Show business career started in the 1930's, and covers every facet, including musicals. Kept the old-time music hall going at London's Players' Theatre during the war while Leonard Sachs was in the army. Now a member of The National Theatre (For Services Rendered). TV incl: Maigret; Dr Finlay's Casebook; Paul Temple; Kate; Jackanory; Bachelor Father and The Brothers. Education: private school in Guildford. m. theatre director Peter Powell (dis), 1 d. Aude. Address: c/o Julian Belfridge, Leading Artists, London SW1. Starsign: Sagittarius. Hobbies: antique porcelain theatrical figures, gardening. Unfulfilled ambition: to work in the USA.

ANDERSON, Moira OBE
Singer b. 5th June Kirkintilloch, Scotland. Music Teacher in Ayr before becoming a professional singer. Started with Kirkintilloch Junior Choir when she was six. Made her first radio broadcast for BBC in Scotland when she was eight and her first professional broadcast in White Heather Club 1960. Since then she has toured abroad, has had her own radio and TV series, sung in and introduced Stars on Sunday, appeared in summer shows, cabaret, pantomine and other stage shows. Two Royal Variety performances. Education: Ayr Academy; Royal Scottish Academy of Music, Glasgow. m. Dr Stuart Macdonald. Address: Kilmacolm, Renfrewshire. Starsign: Gemini. Hobbies: reading, music, gardening, golf.

ANDREWS, Anthony
Actor b. 12.1.48 London. Started stage career at Chichester Festival Theatre. TV play A Beast With Two Backs led to a long line of TV appearances incl: Doomwatch; Dixon of Dock Green; Follyfoot; The Fortunes of Nigel; The Pallisers; David Copperfield; Upstairs, Downstairs; The Duchess of Duke Street; French Without Tears; London Assurance; The Country Wife; A Superstition; Romeo and Juliet; Danger UXB; Brideshead Revisited. Recent stage appearances incl: The Dragon Variation. Films incl: War of The Children and Operation Daybreak. Education: Royal Masonic School, Herts. m. former actress Georgina, 1 d. Jessica, 1 s. Joshua. Address: c/o ICM, London W1. Starsign: Capricorn. Hobby: riding. Unfulfilled ambition: to have peace of mind.

ANDREWS, Eamonn CBE (Hon)
Commentator/ interviewer/ presenter b. 19.12.22 Dublin. Started as a boxing commentator on radio 1939, Radio Eireann 1941-50, BBC radio 1950, BBC TV 1951. TV incl: What's My Line?; Crackerjack; World of Sport; This is Your Life; Today; Time For Business; The Eamonn Andrews Show. Extensive business interests. Former All-Ireland Amateur Junior Boxing Champion (middle weight). Books: This is My Life; Surprise of Your Life. Education: the Irish Christian Brothers, Synge St, Dublin. m. Grainne, 2 d. Emma, Niamh, 1 s. Fergal (all adopted). Address: c/o Thames TV, London. Starsign: Sagittarius.

Hobbies: walking and talking. Unfulfilled ambition: to play a private eye on television who always gets his man, and who in the process meets at least half a dozen sumptuous ladies.

ANDREWS, Harry CBE
Actor b. 10.11.11 Tonbridge, Kent. Stage debut at Liverpool Playhouse 1933. Has since toured the world in a succession of roles. Served throughout the War in the Royal Artillery after which he joined the Old Vic 1945 and the Royal Shakespeare Companies 1949. Film debut in 1952 in The Red Beret. Other films: The Hill; Entertaining Mr Sloane; Moby Dick; Devil's Disciple; Charge of the Light Brigade; Nicholas and Alexandra; The Prince and the Pauper; Candleshoe; Equus. Many TV appearances incl: Clayhanger; Edward the Seventh. Education: Wrekin College. Address: Robertsbridge, Sussex. Starsign: Scorpio. Hobbies: cricket, sailing, riding, tennis, gardening.

ANDREWS, Julie
Actress b. 1.10.35

Walton-on-Thames, Surrey. Singing potential spotted by her stepfather who gave her singing lessons when she was six. First solo appearance on stage when 12 at London Palladium in Starlight Roof. Royal Variety Show following year. Touring in variety and in pantomine next few years. Then came The Boy Friend; My Fair Lady; Camelot. Film debut in Mary Poppins. Other films: The Americanisation of Emily; The Sound of Music; Thoroughly Modern Millie; Star. Many TV appearances. m. (1st) stage designer Tony Walton, (2nd) producer/director Blake Edwards, 4 d. Emma (from 1st m), Jennifer (step-d from 2nd m) plus 2 adopted, 1 Step-s. Geoffrey (from 2nd m). Address: Beverley Hills, California. Starsign: Libra.

ANGERS, Avril
Comedienne b. 18.4.22 Liverpool. First stage appearance was as a Tiller girl at the age of 14. Later gave up dancing for comedy and joined Fol-de-Rols concert party of which her mother was an original member. Wide experience in all branches of show business, including writing. Was with ENSA for five years during the war. First BBC broadcast was in 1944, followed shortly after by West End appearance in Keep Going. First comedienne in this country to have her own TV series, Dear Dotty. TV also incl: Dawson's Weekly; No Appointment Necessary;

Bright's Boffins; Dad's Army; The More We Are Together; How Do You View?; Friends and Neighbours; The Songwriters; Coronation Concert; The Millionairess; All Creatures Great and Small. Stage incl: Little Me; The Mating Game; Not in the Book; Cockie; Norman, Is That You?; Murder at the Vicarage; Love For Love; Jeannie; She Stoops to Conquer; Mary Had a Little . . .; Hobson's Choice; Blithe Spirit; Also Funny Fairy Godmother in panto. Films incl: The Family Way; Girl in My Soup; Confessions of a Driving Instructor. Education: Chalk Hill House, Wembley Park, and other schools all over England and Australia while on tour with parents. Address: c/o Richard Stone, London WC2. Starsign: Aries. Hobbies: cooking, domestic do-it-yourself, watching TV, writing music and lyrics, photography. (The picture illustrating this entry is a self portrait.) Unfulfilled ambition: to be ambitious and less lazy.

ANHOLT, Tony
Actor b. 19.1.41 Singapore. Evacuated to Australia, then South Africa and arrived in London aged four and a half. Had a variety of jobs before becoming an actor – tea taster, teaching Latin and English at a boys' school, travel courier, insurance, teaching English in Spain and Paris. Was a night watchman while studying drama privately and at the Royal Court Theatre, London. Rep in Folkestone, touring with the Century

Theatre Co, and more rep at Oxford. West End stage incl: Boys in the Band; The Gentle Hook; Sleuth. Also Night and Day in South Africa. TV incl: Court Martial; A Family at War; Jason King; Kate; The Protectors; The Strauss Family; Napoleon and Love; The Fell Sergeant; Wilde Alliance; The Copyist; Turtle's Progress; Seasons; Crown Court; Space 1999; Thriller. Education: Akeley Wood, Bucks, and Cranleigh, Surrey. m. Sheila, 1 s. Christien. Address: c/o Barry Burnett Organisation, Piccadilly, London W1. Starsign: Capricorn/Aquarius. Hobbies: music, reading, swimming, athletics. Unfulfilled ambition: to be discovered!

ANNIS, Francesca

Actress b. 14.5.44 London. Trained for ballet at the Corona Academy but switched to drama after appearing in an Armchair Theatre play. Since been in rep at Richmond, Oxford and Leicester and with the RSC. Stage incl: The Sun and the Wind; Ophelia to Nicol Williamson's Hamlet in America. Films incl: Cleopatra; Run With the Wind; The Walking Stick; Macbeth. TV incl: The Human Jungle; Heritage; Danger Man; Dr Finlay's Casebook; Great Expectations; View from the Bridge; The Family is a Vicious Circle; Edward the Seventh; Lillie (TV Times Best Actress on TV 1978-79); Why

Didn't They Ask Evans? 1 d. Charlotte. Address: c/o ICM Ltd, London W1. Starsign: Taurus. Hobby: travel.

ANTHONY, Patrick

Presenter/ announcer/ actor b. 20.4.45 Dublin. Trained in restaurant management before joining Chesterfield rep for the 1970-1971 season. Station announcer for HTV 1973-1976, then moved to Anglia TV. Stage incl: comedian/ compere in northern clubs, plays at Chesterfield and Shanklin reps, old-time music hall chairman. Radio: school plays for Radio 4. TV incl: presenter for Anglia's The Next Week Show and About Anglia, various haute cuisine programmes, Sports Report and newsreader, interviewer on Christmas in Action. Education: De La Salle College, Dublin. m. Vanessa, 1 d. Francesca. Address: c/o Anglia Television. Starsign: Aries. Hobbies: TV, theatre, books, haute cuisine, squash. Unfulfilled ambition: to be 80 years old and still working in the business.

ARCHER, Geoffrey

TV news reporter b. 21.5.44 London. Formerly a solicitor's articled clerk. Worked as researcher, reporter and producer for Southern 1964, Anglia 1965, and Tyne-Tees TV before joining ITN in 1970 for which he has reported widely in Europe, Africa, the Middle East and Britain. Education: Highgate School,

London. m. Eva, 1 d. Alison, 1 s. James. Address: Richmond. Starsign: Taurus/Gemini. Hobbies: gardening, cooking and eating, sailing.

ARNESS, James

Actor b. 26.5.23 Minneapolis, USA. Started in school plays and operettas. Served in Italian campaign in Second World War and was injured on the Anzio beach-head. Discharged in 1945, tried radio announcing; radio dramatic roles made him decide to make acting his career. To Hollywood and his first role in The Farmer's Daughter, then Battleground and 20 films in next three years. Other films incl: Island in the Sky; Hondo; Her Twelve Men; Many Rivers to Cross; Them; The Sea Chase and Hellgate. (Hellgate led to his part as Marshal Matt Dillon in Gun Law, perhaps his most famous role, which he played for 20 years, and which he first turned down.) Then took role of Zeb Macachan in How the West Was Won. Education: Beloit College, Wisconsin. m. (1st) actress Virginia Chapman (dis),

(2nd) actress Janet Surtees,
1 d. Jenny (dec) (from
1st m), 2 s. Craig, Rolf (from
1st m). Starsign: Gemini.

ARTHUR, Toni
Singer/actress b. 26.12.41
Oxford. Originally trained as
a nurse but went into show
business, touring the world
with her husband as a folk
music duo in the early 1960's.
Never happier than when
entertaining children and
between TV appearances
devotes a lot of her time to
voluntary work with young
people. Her stage show, Toni
Arthur's Music Box, designed
to develop children's
appreciation of music, was
designed by her husband, an
authority on British folklore.
TV incl: Play School;
Playaway; Take a Ticket
To . . .; Seeing and Doing;
What Do You Watch?
Records incl: Play-A-Way;
Bang on a Drum; Sing a
Story; and songs from Seeing
and Doing. Education: Mary
Datchelor's Girls' School,
Camberwell, and Royal
Academy of Music. m. Dave
Arthur, 2 s. Jonathan,
Timothy. Address: Oxted,
Surrey. Starsign: Capricorn.
Hobbies: studying women's
lore, making cosmetics,
learning any new strange
musical instrument that
comes along (she owns 14
musical instruments and can
play every one). Unfulfilled
ambition: to go on finding life
as exciting as it is now.

ASKEY, Arthur OBE
Comedian/entertainer

b. 6.6.1900 Liverpool. On
leaving school became a
Liverpool Corporation clerk.
Started professional career
1924 with a touring concert
party. Summer seasons; –
after dinner entertainer in
London; Palladium; revues;
musical comedies;
comedies; Royal Command
Performances. Radio from
1938: Band Wagon; Forever
Arthur; Big Time; Arthur's Inn;
Hello; Playmates. Films:
Band Wagon; Charlie's Aunt;
The Ghost Train; I Thank You;
King Arthur Was a
Gentleman; Miss London Ltd;
Ramsbottom Rides Again.
Stage: The Love Racket;
Follow the Girls; The Kid from
Stratford. TV: started in the
early days of TV and has
since appeared in almost
every major programme,
including reading the lesson
in the Epilogue; Before Your
Very Eyes; Living It Up; The
A A Show; Raise Your
Glasses; Comedy Bandbox;
Jokers Wild; The Blackpool
Show. Education: Liverpool
Institute. m. Elizabeth (dec),
1 d. actress Anthea.
Address: Kensington,
London. Starsign: Gemini.
Hobbies: golf (ex-captain
and president, Stage Golfing
Society), motoring.
Unfulfilled ambition: 'to be
shot by a jealous husband
when I'm 98.'

ASPEL, Michael
Broadcaster/Writer
b. 12.1.33 London. Worked
in publishing house before
his National Service with the
King's Royal Rifle Corps, and

after a brief business career
became a radio actor with
BBC repertory company in
Cardiff 1954. BBC TV
announcer and reader in
London 1957-68 when he
switched to freelancing, both
on radio and TV. Radio incl:
Today; Family Favourites;
daily programme on Capital
Radio. TV incl: Ask Aspel;
Come Dancing; Miss United
Kingdom; Miss World;
Crackerjack; Aspel and
Company; Give Us a Clue;
Starsigns. Book: Polly Wants
a Zebra. Education: Emanuel
School, London.
m. (1st) domestic science
student Dian (dis),
(2nd) production secretary
Ann (dis), (3rd) actress
Elizabeth Power,
2 s. Gregory, Richard (from
1st m), twins Edward and
Jane (from 2nd m). Address:
c/o Bagenal Harvey
Organisation, London W1.
Starsign: Capricorn.
Hobbies: cinema,
letter-writing. Unfulfilled
ambition: to work in America.

ATTENBOROUGH, David
CBE
Broadcaster and traveller
b. 8.5.26 London. After
service in the Royal Navy,

worked for a firm of educational book publishers. Joined BBC TV as trainee producer 1952. Two years later he made the first of his famous Zoo Quest programmes. Is now an acknowledged expert on the world's wildlife and his TV has incl: The Tribal Eye; Wildlife on One; Eastward with Attenborough and the mammoth 13-part series, Life on Earth. For that series he and his team travelled a million and a half miles, visited more than 30 countries and shot one and a quarter million feet of film. Controller of BBC2 1965-68 and as such saw the channel into colour. Director of BBC TV programmes 1969-72, resigning from that post to return to programme-making. Many awards and honours incl: Hon DLitt, Leicester; Hon DSc Liverpool; Hon LLD Bristol; Hon Fellow Manchester Polytechnic; Special Award, Society of Film and TV Arts (1961); Silver Medal, Zoological Society of London (1966); Silver Medal, Royal Television Society (1966); Desmond Davies Award, Society of Film and TV Arts (1970); Cherry Kearton Medal and Award, RGS (1972). Books incl: Zoo Quest to Guiana; Zoo Quest for a Dragon; Zoo Quest in Paraguay; Quest in Paradise; Zoo Quest in Madagascar; Quest Under Capricorn; Tribal Eye; Life on Earth. Education: Wyggeston Grammar, Leicester; Clare College, Cambridge (hons degree in natural sciences). m. Jane, 1 d. Susan, 1 s. Robert. Address: c/o BBC, London W12. Starsign: Taurus. Hobby: collecting almost anything. Unfulfilled ambition: to play the piano well.

AUSTIN, Wendy
Reporter b. 19.11.51 Belfast.

Journalistic background, starting on a Thomson Training Course. After working on the East Antrim Times and Belfast Telegraph, joined Downtown Radio before moving to the BBC in Belfast. Education: Victoria College and Queen's University, Belfast. Address: c/o BBC, Belfast. Starsign: Scorpio. Hobbies: motor racing, watching TV, gardening and pot plants, decorating. Unfulfilled ambition: to fly round the world – first class.

AVILA, Kay
TV reporter b. 5.2.46 Whitstable, Kent. Research in newspapers, House of Commons, radio and TV incl: Westward and Thames where she is working on After Noon Plus. Education: Winchester County High and Surrey University (BSc Human Relations). Address: Downderry, Cornwall. Starsign: Aquarius. Hobbies: cooking, gardening, painting, playing piano. Unfulfilled ambition: to play the piano well, cook like a dream and to be half as good at everything as I want to be.

AYRES, Pam
Writer/entertainer b. 14.3.47 Stanford-in-the-Vale, Berks. Was a Civil Service clerk, spent four years in the WRAF, was then a secretary before becoming a full-time entertainer. First TV appearance in Opportunity Knocks 1975. Then The Black and White Minstrel Show; What's On Next?; The World of Pam Ayres; Royal Variety Performance 1977; Pam Ayres' Hong Kong Christmas. Best-selling books of poems and LP's. Education: Farringdon Secondary Modern School. Address: c/o Dolphin Concert Productions Ltd, Oxfordshire. Starsign: Pisces. Hobbies: squash, mountaineering, swimming, drawing, walking.

AYRES, Rosalind
Actress b. 7.12.46 Birmingham. Three year teacher-training course specalising in drama at Loughborough College of Education, before becoming an actress. TV incl: Nearest and Dearest; Coronation Street; The Lovers; Home and Away; Suspicion;

General Hospital; Country Matters; Father Brown; Hindle Wakes; Affairs of the Heart; Within These Walls; The Limbo Connection; Holding On; Public Eye; Warship; Two's Company; Dick Emery Show; Rings On Their Fingers and many plays. Appeared at Windsor and Nottingham and in London's West End (I Claudius; Dracula). Films incl: That'll Be The Day; Stardust; Little Malcolm; The Slipper and the Rose. Radio incl: Evan Harrington; Pickwick Papers; The Circle; Room With a View; As You Like It. Education: George Dixon Grammar School for Girls, Birmingham. m. actor Martin Jarvis. Address: c/o CCA Personal Management, London SW6. Starsign: Sagittarius. Hobbies: interior decorating, sewing. Unfulfilled ambition: to keep working.

B

BAILEY, Robin
Actor b. 5.10.19 Hucknall, Nottingham. Began his working life in the Post Office, then moved to the War Office and became interested in amateur dramatics. Joined Nottingham Theatre Royal as an actor in 1938. Also in rep at Newcastle on Tyne, Birmingham, Worthing before coming to London. Appeared in many plays since. Films incl: Private Angelo; Catch Us If You Can; Blind Terror. Served during the war in the RASC. Appeared in many TV programmes, incl: compering The 64,000 Challenge. Recent TV incl: The Pallisers; Upstairs, Downstairs; North and South; Punch Revue; A Legacy; I Didn't Know You Cared. Education: Henry Mellish School, Nottingham. m. Patricia, 3 s. Nicholas, Simon, Justin. Address: c/o Derek Glynne Ltd, London SW1. Starsign: Libra. Hobbies: gardening, cricket.

BAINBRIDGE, Hazel
Actress b. 25.1.11 Whitby,
Yorks. Born into a theatrical
family and had much
experience in rep incl:
Worthing, Oxford and
productions at Guildford and
Plymouth. Other stage work
incl: Salad Days; Jockey
Club Stakes; Gentle Hook
and tours of I Am a Camera.
Also worked on radio for CBC
in Montreal, Canada. Films
incl: Term of Trial; The Family
Way; Twisted Nerve. TV incl:
Middlemarch; David
Copperfield; Cranford;
Wodehouse Playhouse;
Z Cars; Walking the Dog;
Some Mothers Do 'Ave 'Em;
Michael Crawford's
Christmas Show; Feet First;
Chalk and Cheese.
Education: Woodford Private
Boarding School, Southsea,
Hants. m. J. F. Carrol,
2 d. actresses Kate O'Mara,
Belinda Carroll. Address: c/o
Bernard Gillman Ltd,
Tolworth, Surrey. Starsign:
Aquarius. Hobbies: reading
biographies, collecting
theatrical books and
playbills. Unfulfilled ambition:
to be a syncopating pianist.

BAKER, Hylda
Comedienne/actress
b. 4th February Bolton,
Lancs. Started as a single
variety act when she was 10.
Starred with her father,
Harold Baker, in revue Whirls
and Girls. After leads in
revues and touring the
provinces, she spent 15
years developing, writing,
directing and appearing in
her own shows. Instant

success in Good Old Days
with Cynthia ('She knows
y'know'). Other TV incl:
Z Cars; Emergency-Ward 10;
Our House; Seeing a Beauty
Queen Home; Best of
Friends; Nearest and Dearest
(also play and film of the
same name); Not On Your
Nellie. Other films incl:
Saturday Night and Sunday
Morning; Oliver!; Up the
Junction. West End stage
appearances: Fill the Stage
with Happy Hours; Mr and
Mrs and the London
Palladium. Eldest of seven
children. Education: St
Hilary's College Eastbourne.
Address: c/o London
Management Ltd, London.
Starsign: Aquarius. Hobbies:
do-it-yourself, football –
especially Bolton Wanderers.
Unfulfilled ambition: to be a
champion golfer.

BAKER, Richard OBE
Newsreader/presenter
b. 15.6.25 Willesden,
London. Cambridge ADC
and Footlights; actor
1948-49; joined BBC 1950;
radio announcer 1951-54. TV
since 1954, newsreader on
BBC 1 and 2, commentator
on major events, particularly
royal visits and concerts such

as The Proms, panelist on
BBC 2's Face The Music.
Hon LL.D, Strathclyde
University. Education:
Kilburn Grammar,
Peterhouse, Cambridge
University (MA). m. Margaret
Martin, 2 s. Andrew, James.
Address: c/o BBC London.
Starsign: Gemini. Hobbies:
music, sailing. Unfulfilled
ambitions: to command a
ship and conduct an
orchestra.

BAKER, Susie
Actress b. 9.2.46 London.
One of the Baker Twins who
started as child models at
age of three. Trained at Aida
Foster Stage School. Stage
incl: Stop the World I Want to
Get Off; cabaret in Las
Vegas, Mexico City, London,
Italy. Films incl: A Funny
Thing Happened On The
Way To The Forum; Casino
Royale; Kaleidescope.
Numerous TV shows incl: The
Basil Brush Show; The Dick
Emery Show; Dave Allen at
Large; Les Dawson Show;
Revolver; Vienna 1900;
Prowling Offensive; The Star
Maidens; Beryl's Lot; Swap
One of These for One of
Those; Middlemen; Hazell.
Education: Aida Foster Stage
School. Address: c/o Aida
Foster Ltd, London NW8.
Starsign: Aquarius. Hobbies:
riding, swimming, driving,
dress designing,
needlework, designing
knitwear.

BAKER, Tom
Actor b. 20.1.36 Liverpool.
Was a novice monk for seven

years before deciding he had no vocation. National Service in the army and troop shows set him on the acting road via Rose Bruford Drama School and several reps before joining the National Theatre. First big part was as Rasputin in the film Nicholas and Alexandra. Then came Dr Who on TV in 1974. Other TV incl: The Millionairess; The Author of Beltraffio; Call My Bluff; The Book Tower. m. Anna Wheatcroft, 2 s. Address: c/o London Management, London W1. Starsign: Aquarius.

BAKER, Tony
Reporter/presenter b. 26.3.47 Northampton. Experience with Northampton Chronicle and Echo, Coventry Evening Telegraph and BBC Radio Leicester before joining Border TV. Concerned with TV programmes Lookaround and Border Month. Freelance since January 1979, mainly with BBC Radio Carlisle and TV. Education: Northampton Grammar. m. Susan, 2 d. Kathryn, Rosemary. Address: c/o BBC Radio Carlisle. Starsign: Aries. Hobbies: writing, travel.

Unfulfilled ambition: to get rich quick.

BAKEWELL, Joan
Interviewer b. 16th April Stockport, Cheshire. Started as studio manager for BBC radio. Most recent radio: PM on Radio 4. TV incl: Sunday Break; Home at 4.30; Meeting Point; Late Night Line-up; Holiday 75,76,77; The Brontë Business; The Shakespeare Business; Reports Action. Education: Stockport High for Girls and Cambridge University (economics, history). m. (1st) TV director Michael Bakewell; (2nd) Jack Emery, 1 d. Harriet, 1 s. Matthew (both from 1st m). Address: c/o A D Peters, London WC2. Starsign: Aries. Hobbies: travel and theatre.

BALL, Bobby
Comedian b. 28.1.44 Oldham. Half of the comedy partnership, Cannon and Ball. Former workmates in a Lancashire engineering factory by day and a singing duo, The Harper Brothers, at night. Changed names to Cannon and Ball nine years ago and are now major club and theatre attractions.

Voted clubland's top comedy duo 1975. Summer seasons in Bournemouth, Jersey, Cleethorpes and Great Yarmouth and pantomine in Bradford, Leeds, Stockport and Liverpool. TV incl: Wheeltappers and Shunters' Social Club; Bruce Forsyth's Big Night; and their own series, Cannon and Ball. Education: High Crompton Secondary, Shaw, Oldham. m. Yvonne, 1 d. Joanne, 2 s. Darren, Robert. Address: c/o Kennedy Street Artistes Ltd, Manchester. Starsign: Aquarius. Hobby: fishing. Unfulfilled ambition: to reach No 1 in the TV ratings with own show.

BALL, Kenny
Trumpeter/band leader b. 22.5.31 Ilford, Essex. Formed jazz band in 1958 with debut at Southend. TV debut in BBC's New Faces in 1959. Many stage, radio and TV shows with such artists as Frankie Vaughan; Morecambe and Wise; Englebert Humperdinck; Les Dawson. Also Royal Variety Shows, foreign tours, jazz festivals, Sunday Night at the London Palladium; Saturday Night at the Mill; London Night Out. Many recording hits incl: Teddy Bears' Picnic; Samantha; Midnight in Moscow. Education: Mayfield Comprehensive, Ilford. m. Betty, 2 d. Gillian, Jane, 1 s. Keith. Address: c/o Kenny Ball Entertainments, London W1. Starsign: Gemini. Hobbies: squash, horse racing, cooking exotic

dishes. Unfulfilled ambition: to be a good musician.

BALL, Nicholas
Actor b. 11.4.46 Leamington, Warwicks, but brought up in Hastings. Always wanted to be an actor. Trained at Bristol Old Vic Theatre School and while there made his professional debut on radio and in The Queen's Traitor on TV. Other TV incl: The Gunpowder Plot; The Elusive Pimpernel; The Black Tulip; The Gold Robbers; Softly, Softly; A Story to Frighten the Children; The Crezz; Dorian Gray; Rogue Male; Hazell; Thicker Than Water. Founder member of the Portable Workshop Co, a co-operative formed to provide an outlet for new drama; toured Britain and Europe with the outfit. Left in 1974. Stage incl: Izabel's a Jezebel (musical); The Natural Cause; Echoes from a Concrete Canyon; Moving Clocks Go Slow; The Soul of the White Ant. Films incl: Overlord; Someone is Killing the Great Chefs of Europe. Education: Yes. Address: c/o William Morris Agency, London W1. Starsign: Aries. Unfulfilled ambition: see starsign.

BANNISTER, Trevor
Actor b. 14.8.36 Durrington, Wilts. Drama school at 16, two years in the army, then rep at Torquay, Bath, Bedford, Worthing, Wolverhampton, York and Birmingham (total of six years). London West End plays: The World of Suzie

Wong; Billy Liar; Move Over Mrs Markham. Many radio and TV plays incl: Five Finger Exercise. Series incl: Tickets Please; Travelling Light; The War of Darkie Pilbeam; Coronation Street; The Dustbinmen; Are You Being Served?; Voyage Around My Father; Cider With Rosie. Education: private school. m. actress Kathleen Cravos, 3 s. Simon, Timothy, Jeremy. Starsign: Leo. Hobbies: antiques, riding, swimming, golf, tennis.

BARCLAY, Campbell
Broadcaster b. 8.7.29 Greenock, Renfrewshire. Worked as research chemist in industry 1951-66 and was a local councillor in Greenock 1961-64. Joined BBC Glasgow as a freelance reporter 1966 and was political/industrial reporter 1967-73. TV: BBC's Scottish Industrial Correspondent since 1973. Education: Greenock Academy and Paisley Technical College (HNC Chemistry). m. Elma, 2 d. Susan, Gillian. Address: c/o BBC, Glasgow. Starsign: Cancer. Hobbies: politics, trad jazz, golf. Unfulfilled

ambitions: too numerous to mention!

BARKER, Katharine
Actress b. 3.10.41 Sedbergh, Yorks. Trained at Central School of Speech and Drama. Stage debut in Out of the Crocodile, Phoenix Theatre, London. Other stage incl: Two seasons with Royal Shakespeare Company; Royal Lyceum, Edinburgh, Belgrade Theatre, Coventry, Hampstead Theatre Club, Stables Theatre Club, Manchester. TV incl: Thirty Minute Theatre, D H Lawrence; Emmerdale Farm. Education: Jamaica and Trinidad, The Mount School, York. Address: c/o Yorks TV, Leeds. Starsign: Libra. Hobbies: music, films. Unfulfilled ambition: to go to Peru.

BARKER, Ronnie OBE
Actor/comedian b. 25.9.29 Bedford. Started as an amateur; Aylesbury Rep 1948, then Manchester and Oxford. Films incl: Futtocks End; Home of Your Own; Robin and Marian; Porridge. Radio incl: Floggitts, The Navy Lark. TV incl: I'm Not

Bothered; Frost Report;
Foreign Affairs; The Ronnie
Barker Playhouse; Frost On
Sunday; Hark at Barker; 6
Dates With Barker. His
Lordship Entertains;
Midsummer Night's Dream;
Seven of One; The Picnic;
The Two Ronnies; Porridge;
Open All Hours; Going
Straight. Education: City of
Oxford High School. m. Joy
Tubb, 1 d. Charlotte,
2 s. Larry, Adam. Address:
c/o Peter Eade Ltd, London
W1. Starsign: Libra. Hobby:
collecting Victoriana
(postcards, books and
prints).

BARKWORTH, Peter
Actor b. 14.1.29 Margate.
Trained at RADA and, after
rep at Folkestone, was called
up for the army. Returned to
more rep at Folkestone and
Sheffield. West End
successes incl: Roar Like A
Dove; Crown Matrimonial
(and on TV); Donkey's Years;
Can You Hear Me at the
Back? TV incl: The Power
Game; Manhunt; A Death in
the Family; Rasputin; The
Passenger; The Rivals of
Sherlock Holmes; The
Company Man; Intent to
Murder; Melissa; The Country
Party; The Saturday Party;
Professional Foul; Secret
Army; Telford's Change.
Education: Stockport.
Address: Hampstead,
London. Starsign: Capricorn.
Hobbies: looking at the
countryside, and at
paintings, listening to music,
walking, gardening,
entertaining. Unfulfilled
ambitions: to see my first

book, 'Tricks of the Trade',
published, and to write my
second, 'An Actor's Diary'.

BARLOW, Thelma
Actress b. 19th June
Middlesbrough, Yorks.
Secretary in Huddersfield
before joining Joan
Littlewood's Theatre
Workshop in East London.
Then in rep before joining
Coronation Street as Mavis in
1974. Education: in
Huddersfield. m. drama
lecturer Graham Barlow,
2 s. Clive, James. Address:
c/o Granada TV, Manchester.
Starsign: Gemini. Hobbies:
yoga, cookery, growing
herbs, wine-making, making
her own clothes. Unfulfilled
ambition: to play in a TV
situation comedy.

BARNES, Carol
TV journalist b. 13.9.44
Norwich. One-time public
relations officer at London's
Royal Court Theatre. Before
joining ITN was in radio (BBC
and LBC) where she was also
a reporter, and production
manager on Time Out
magazine. Education: St
Martin in the Fields High
School; South West London
College; Sheffield University

(BA in Languages and
teaching diploma). Address:
c/o ITN, London W1.
Starsign: Virgo. Hobbies:
ski-ing, good food. Unfulfilled
ambition: to be a musician.

BARNES, Greg
Film reporter b. 15.7.47
Essex. Trained on
newspapers, principally daily
evening papers. Since
entering TV has worked as
film reporter on regional news
and current affairs
programmes incl: About
Anglia; ATV Today.
Education: grammar school.
m. Chris. Address: King's
Lynn, Norfolk. Starsign:
Cancer. Hobbies: sailing and
the cinema. Unfulfilled
ambition: to sail round the
world in his own boat.

BARNES, Paul
Broadcaster b. 31.7.39
Coventry. Many years in the
advertising and
documentary film business,
ultimately as a director (Black
Five; King George V; Tanker)
before becoming contributor
and presenter for numerous
radio and TV programmes
which incl: Today; World at
One; Woman's Hour; In
Vision; Parents and Children;

The Winners; The Book
Programme; Six-O-One
(Granada); ATV Today.
Presently working on About
Anglia and as presenter of
the forthcoming Portrait of a
Village. Education:
Leamington College;
Coventry College of Art.
m. Jean, 2 s. Matt, Dan.
Address: Hatfield, Herts.
Starsign: Leo. Hobbies: early
transport (railways in
particular), preserving old
vehicles (he owns a
steam-roller and a
single-deck bus), jazz
(especially big bands),
riding. Unfulfilled ambition: to
stop being told he looks like
other people, and to start
hearing that other people are
being told they look like him.

BARRATT, Michael
Commentator/interviewer
b. 3.1.28 Leeds. Began in
journalism. Films incl: Magic
Christian; Percy's Progress.
Radio incl: Nigerian
Broadcasting Service; BBC
Overseas; BBC Midlands. TV
incl: Panorama; 24 Hours;
Nationwide (1968-77); Songs
of Praise. Education: Rossall;
Paisley Grammar; Aberdeen
University (LL D).
m. (1st) Joan, (2nd) Dilys,
3 d. (from 1st m), 4 s. (3 from
1st m), Oliver (from 2nd m).
Address: London W1.
Starsign: Capricorn. Hobby:
golf. Unfulfilled ambition:
breakfast TV host.

BARRON, John
Actor b. 24.12.20
Marylebone, London.
Trained at RADA, then rep at

Croydon, Leicester and
Brighton. Apart from war
service in Royal Navy, has
been an actor all his working
life. Films incl: Jigsaw. TV
incl: Fly Away Peter;
Emergency-Ward 10; Softly,
Softly; All Gas and Gaiters;
Doomwatch; Crown Court;
Timeslip; Ace of Wands; The
Fall and Rise of Reginald
Perrin; The Foundation;
Potter; Bernie; Spooner's
Patch; Shelley; The Glums.
Education: Portsmouth
Grammar. m. actress Joan
Peart, 1 step-d. Address: c/o
Green and Underwood,
London W3. Starsign:
Capricorn. Hobby: collecting
wine. Unfulfilled ambition: to
be an accomplished pianist.

BARRON, Keith
Actor b. 8.8.34 Mexborough,
Yorks. After working in the
family wholesale provision
business, started acting
career with Sheffield Rep.
Small parts on TV and
appearances at Bristol Old
Vic led to The Odd Man and
Lucky Jim series. Other TV
incl: My Good Woman;
A Family at War; Let's Get
Away From It All. Education:
Mexborough Technical
College. m. stage designer

Mary Pickard, 1 s. Jamie.
Address: East Molesey,
Surrey. Starsign: Leo. Hobby:
recovering from visits to the
dentist. Unfulfilled ambition:
to live by the sea.

BASS, Alfie
Actor b. 8.4.21 Bethnal
Green, London. Started as an
amateur with Unity Theatre.
First professional
appearance 1939, resuming
his acting career, after war
service in the army, with
documentary films, plays and
revues. Stage incl: season at
Stratford-upon-Avon;
Finian's Rainbow; The Punch
Revue; Mr Bolfry; Fiddler on
the Roof. Films incl: Alfie;
Help; The Sandwich Man;
A Funny Thing Happened on
the Way to the Forum; The
Bespoke Overcoat; A Tale of
Two Cities; The Vampire
Killers; Death on the Nile;
Revenge of the Pink Panther;
Moonraker. TV incl: The Army
Game; Bootsie and Snudge;
Six of the Best; Gideon's
Way; Robin Hood; Till Death
Do Us Part; Daughter of the
House; Our Mutual Friend;
A Roof Over My Head;
Legend of Dick Turpin;
Danger UXB; Return of the
Saint. Education: Elementary
School, Bethnal Green.
m. actress Beryl Bryson,
1 d. Gillian, 1 s. Julian.
Address: c/o Pamela
Simmons, London WC2.
Starsign: Aries. Hobbies:
fishing, making furniture (his
father was a cabinet-maker),
football.

BASSEY, Shirley
Entertainer b. 8.1.37 Cardiff.
Started her stage career as a
chorus girl in two touring
revues. Spotted by
impressario Jack Hylton and
signed to appear at London's
Adelphi Theatre in Such Is
Life (1955), then followed a
long term TV contract. First
major stage appearance at
the old London Hippodrome
1957. Has since appeared in
cabaret all over the world and
made numerous TV
appearances both as guest
artist and in her own shows.
Britannia Award for the Best
Female Solo Singer in the
Last 50 Years of Recorded
Sound 1977; American Guild
of Variety Artists voted her
Best Female Entertainer
1976; TVTimes Award as
Best Female Singer 1972,
1973. Began making records
1956, incl: Banana Boat
Song; As I Love You; Kiss Me
Honey Honey, Kiss Me; As
Long As He Needs Me;
Goldfinger. Numerous silver
and gold discs, Royal Variety
appearances and invited by
President John F. Kennedy to
sing at the White House.
m. (1st) film producer
Kenneth Hume (dis),
(2nd) hotel manager, later
her manager, Sergio Novak,
2 d. Sharon, Samantha.
Address: Lugano,
Switzerland. Starsign:
Capricorn. Hobbies: keep-fit,
cooking, cinema. Unfulfilled
ambition: to take a leading
role in a major film.

BASTABLE, Tony
Presenter/writer b. 15.10.44

Hexham, Northumberland.
Former schoolmaster and
reporter before breaking into
TV with Southern TV's Three
Go Round. Has since worked
on numerous television
series incl: Magpie; Drive-in
and Money-Go-Round.
Education: University
College School, Hampstead.
m. Jacqueline Colkett,
1 d. Kate. Address:
Chertsey, Surrey. Starsign:
Libra. Hobbies: cricket,
reading history.

BASTEDO, Alexandra
Actress b. 9.3.46 Hove,
Sussex. Drama training at
Worthing and Brighton
Schools of Drama. Film debut
in Hollywood at the age of 16
after winning a personality
contest in 1962. Then
returned to school in
England. British films since
1966 incl: Casino Royale;
Doctor in Clover. TV incl: The
Count of Monte Cristo; The
Champions; The Flying
Swan; Compact; The Man
Who Never Was; The Saint;
The Scobie Man; Aren't We
All?; The Aphrodite
Inheritance. London stage:
Don't Just Lie There, Say
Something. Education:

Brighton and Hove High.
Address: London W1.
Starsign: Pisces. Hobbies:
travelling, scuba diving.
Unfulfilled ambition: to be a
marine archaeologist.

BATE, Anthony
Actor b. 31.8.29 Stourbridge,
Worcs. Chose acting in
preference to working in a
bank, staying in the Royal
Navy (in which he served
after the war), or running his
father's hotel on the Isle of
Wight. Trained at the Central
School of Speech and
Drama. Rep at Worthing,
Shanklin, Bournemouth and
with the Royal Shakespeare
Company. Films incl: Act of
Murder; Davy Jones's
Locker; Destination Treason;
Ghost Story. TV incl: The
Idiot; Macbeth; Les
Miserables; Angel Pavement;
Spindoe; Treasure Island;
Julius Caesar; The Main
Chance; Ivanhoe; Grady;
Intimate Strangers; Couples;
Murder; Beasts; Philby,
Burgess and Maclean; The
Dutch Train Hijack; An
Englishman's Castle;
Scorpion Tales; Crime and
Punishment; Tinker, Tailor,
Soldier, Spy. Education: King
Edward VI School,
Stourbridge, Worcs.
m. Diana Fay, 2 s. Gavin,
Mark. Address: c/o Al Parker
Ltd, London W1. Starsign:
Virgo. Hobbies: music,
cooking. Unfulfilled ambition:
to go skin-diving for amphora
off the Greek Islands.

BATEY, Derek
Compere/presenter b. 8.8.28 Brampton, Cumberland. Trained as accountant before going into broadcasting, first with BBC. Joined Border TV when it began 1961 and now Assistant Controller of Programmes. Presented and produced hundreds of current affairs, sport and light entertainment programmes for Border. Regular appearances on Celebrity Squares and Open House; producer and host of Mr and Mrs and Look Who's Talking. Education: White House, Brampton. m. Edith, 1 d. Diane. Address: c/o Border TV, Carlisle. Starsign: Leo. Hobbies: golf, tennis, family, travel. Unfulfilled ambitions: to compere a show at the London Palladium; to top the national TV ratings with one of my shows.

BAXTER, Stanley
Actor b. 24.5.28 Glasgow. Revues and pantomimes in Scotland after three and a half years with Glasgow Citizens' Theatre. Moved to London 1959. TV revues for BBC then London Weekend TV. West End shows incl: The Amorous Prawn; On the Brighter Side; What the Butler Saw; Phil the Fluter. TV incl: The Stanley Baxter Picture Show (Parts I – III); Stanley Baxter's Christmas Box (1976); Merrie Old Christmas (1977); Stanley Baxter on Television (1979). Education: Hillhead High School, Glasgow; CSE Singapore. m. Moira. Address: David White Associates, London W1. Starsign: Gemini. Hobbies: swimming, cycling, reading. Unfulfilled ambition: to direct a feature film and not botch it.

BAYLDON, Geoffrey
Actor b. 7.1.24 Leeds. Amateur theatricals before training at Old Vic Theatre School. First professional appearance in Cochrane's Tough at the Top. Shakespeare Memorial Theatre; Birmingham Rep and Glasgow Citizens'. Films incl: Casino Royale; A Night to Remember; To Sir With Love; King Rat; Dandy in Aspic; 55 Days in Peking; Otley; The Slipper and the Rose; The Pink Panther Strikes Again. Extensive radio and TV. TV incl: An Age of Kings; The Massingham Affair; The Victorians; Nicholas Nickleby; Under Western Eyes; Catweazle; The Avengers; The Saint; Devenish; Alice Through The Looking Glass; Abide with Me; Edward the Seventh; Worzel Gummidge. Education: Bridlington School; Hull College of Architecture. Address: c/o Joy Jameson Ltd, London SW1. Starsign: Capricorn. Hobbies: gardening, walking, painting. Unfulfilled ambition: to understand elementary mathematics.

BAYLER, Terence
Actor b. 24.1.30 Wanganui, New Zealand. Trained at RADA and London University (Diploma in Dramatic Art). Numerous reps and West End plays. Films incl: Polanski's Macbeth. Monty Python's Life of Brian. TV incl: Renoir My Father; The Light Princess; Rutland Weekend Television; Law and Order; The Snow Queen; The Rutles. Education: Wanganui Technical College. Divorced, 1 d. Lucy, 1 s. Michael. Address: c/o Bernard Gillman Ltd, Tolworth, Surrey. Starsign: Aquarius. Hobbies: attending jumble sales, light gardening. Unfulfilled ambition: to be ambitious.

BEAVIS, Ivan
Actor b. 22.4.26 Liverpool. Gave up career as accountant to become an actor. Twelve years with amateur companies. Stage

incl: Royal Shakespeare Company, productions at Mermaid, Shaw and Prince of Wales Theatres, reps at Bristol, Chesterfield, Harrogate, Liverpool, Watford, Nottingham, Westcliffe, Worthing. In spite of wide experience, still best known as Harry Hewitt in Coronation Street. Other TV incl: Skyport; Biggles; Knight Errant; The Verdict is Yours; The Army Game; Famous Trials; Crown Court; Liver Birds; Six Days of Justice; Z Cars; The Onedin Line; Kids of 47a; Freewheelers; Black Arrow; No, Honestly, and a number of plays. Also stage, TV and radio in New Zealand. Education: Liverpool Collegiate and Christ's College, Finchley. Separated, 1 d. Hilary, 1 s. Michael. Address: c/o CCA, London SW6. Starsign: Taurus. Hobbies: fluctuating, none abiding. Unfulfilled ambitions: to work with National Theatre and to do more work in films.

BEENY, Christopher
Actor b. 7.7.41 Bristol. Wanted to be a dancer. Joined Ballet Rambert 1949 while attending stage school. First acting appearance was Peter Pan 1951. First TV series, The Grove Family, when he was 12; appeared regularly on TV in Dixon of Dock Green; Emergency-Ward 10; The Plane Makers and Armchair Theatre. Then took a course at RADA, but quit acting because of lack of work and started a building

firm. An episode of Softly, Softly in 1970 brought him back to acting – Upstairs, Downstairs; Miss Jones and Son; The Rag Trade; In Loving Memory. Education: XIV School, Bristol. m .(dis), 1 d. Joanne, 1 s. Richard. Address: LWT, South Bank TV Centre, London SE1. Starsign: Cancer. Hobbies: photography, swimming, relaxing in the sun, water ski-ing. Unfulfilled ambition: to play Buttons in a London Palladium pantomime.

BELL, Martin
BBC TV News North America Correspondent b. 31.8.38 Redisham, Suffolk. News assistant to BBC Norwich 1962 and joined BBC TV News, London two years later. BBC TV News North America Correspondent since 1977. Royal Television Society's award as Reporter of the Year 1977. Education: The Leys School and King's College, Cambridge. m. Nelly Luciene Gourdon, 2 d. Melissa, Catherine. Address: c/o BBC, Washington DC 20036. Starsign: Virgo.

BELL, Tom
Actor b.1932 Liverpool. Started in local rep at 15 and trained at Bradford Civic Theatre School. After a spell in the army, rep and tours took him to Ireland, Swansea, Morecambe, York and Cheltenham before going to London. Stage work incl: Progress in the Park; The Ring of Truth; Royal

Shakespeare Company. Formidable list of films incl: The L-Shaped Room; A Prize of Arms; HMS Defiant; Ballad in Blue; He Who Rides a Tiger; Straight on Till Morning; Lock Up Your Daughters; All the Right Noises; Concrete Jungle; Bent. TV incl: A Night Out; Cul de Sac; No Trams to Lime Street; Angels Are So Few; Be Lucky; The Virginian; The Frighteners; Hedda Gabler; Straight on Till Morning; The Samaritan; A Man Without Friends; Sea Song; Death of an Informer; Out. Education: secondary school. m. Lois Daine (dis), 1 s. Aran. Address: c/o Chatto and Linnit, London W1. Hobby: growing sunflowers.

BELLAMY, David
Botanist/ writer/ broadcaster b. 18.1.33 London. Had several jobs when he left school because he had no idea what he wanted to do until he became a lab assistant at Ewell County Technical College, Surrey. Within five years (in 1960) he was a lecturer and then senior lecturer in Botany at Durham University.

'Discovered' by radio and TV in 1967 through his views on pollution at the time of the Torrey Canyon oil tanker disaster. Popularised wild life in TV programmes for adults and children on both BBC and ITV. TV incl: Life In Our Sea; Bellamy on Botany; Bellamy's Britain; Animal Game; What on Earth Are We Doing?; Bellamy's Europe; Don't Ask Me; It's Life; It's More Life; Botanic Man (three times round the world to collect material); Looks Natural; Bellamy on Heathland. Books incl: Bellamy on Botany; World of Plants; Bellamy's Britain; It's Life; Bellamy's Europe; Life-giving Sea; Botanic Man; Botanic Action; Half of Paradise. Awards: Duke of Edinburgh Prize for Underwater Research 1969; British Association Certificate of Merit (for Fox in the Mire) 1973; Karl-Foerster-Stiftung Award (for Bellamy on Botany) 1973; BSAC Diver of the Year 1974; BISFA Bronze Medal 1978; Golden Ear Award at Berlin Agricultural Film Festival (for Bellamy on Heathland) 1978; Richard Dimbleby (BAFTA) Award 1978; Radio Industries Club Award (best science-based programme) 1978; TVTimes Special Award (for Botanic Man) 1978-79. Education: London University; Chelsea College of Science and Technology (BSc); Bedford College (PhD). m. marine biologist Rosemary, 3 d. Henrietta, Brighid, Iseabal, 2 s. Rufus, Eoghain (all adopted). Address: c/o Thames TV London. Starsign: Capricorn. Hobbies: children, ballet.

BELLINGHAM, Lynda
Actress b. 31.5.48 Montreal, Canada. Came to England as a child. Trained at the Central School of Speech and Drama, then rep at Crewe, Coventry and Oxford. Stage

incl: Bordello; Norman; pantomime. Films incl: Confessions of a Driving Instructor; Stand Up Virigin Soldiers; Waterloo Bridge; Handicap. TV incl: Cottage to Let; Yes – Honestly; Second Opinion; The Pink Medicine Show; Don't Forget to Write; Hazell; Funny Man. Education: convent and Aylesbury High School. m. producer Greg Smith (dis): Address: c/o CCA, London SW6. Starsign: Gemini. Hobbies: wining and dining, travelling. Unfulfilled ambition: to score a goal in a Cup Final.

BENHAM, Joan
Actress b. 17.5.18 London. Theatrical background with mother a singer and father an actor and theatrical manager. Decided she wanted to be an actress when she was four. Trained at RADA and went into rep and has since been seen in a vast number of TV programmes, especially as aristocratic ladies (the Doctor series; Upstairs, Downstairs; The Duchess of Duke Street). Other TV incl: Take My Wife; Within These Walls; Melissa;

The Upchat Line; Just William; Happy Ever After; Jackanory; Three Piece Suite; Father Brown; Six Dates With Barker; Present Laughter; Never a Cross Word; Dr Finlay's Casebook; Mrs Thursday; My Wife and I; Whodunnit?; Pig in a Poke; Tarbuck's Luck; It's a Whacky World; etc, etc. Education: Kensington High School. m. Martin Lingen Case, 1 s. Antony. Address: c/o Fraser and Dunlop Ltd, London W1. Starsign: Taurus. Hobbies: theatre-going, coin collecting. Unfulfilled ambition: to be a great actress.

BENJAMIN, Christopher
Actor b. 27.12.34 Trowbridge, Wilts. Trained at RADA and rep seasons at Salisbury and Bristol Old Vic. West End stage incl: A Severed Head; Maigret and the Lady; Artuo Ui; The Licentious Fly. Films incl: Brief Encounter. TV incl: Churchill's People; Private Affairs; Dick Turpin; Donkey's Years. Education: Warminster School. m. actress Anna Fox, 2 d. Kate, Emilia, 1 s. Sebastian. Address: c/o Scott Marshall, London W3. Starsign: Capricorn. Hobbies: music, cricket, gardening.

BENNETT, David
Announcer/newsreader/presenter b. 18.2.53 Leeds. Trained with Nancy Day, LGSM and Jonathan

Tremayne. Experience with BBC Radio Leeds, Anglia TV, BBC2, ATV and HTV and commercial radio voice-over work before joining Grampian TV. Contributions to The Electric Theatre Show; About Britain; By Appointment; and a schools' programme, Mathman. Education: Church School, Leeds and Park Lane College, Leeds. Address: c/o Grampian TV, Aberdeen. Starsign: Aquarius. Hobbies: cycling, music, theatre, cinema, TV, travel within Britain, chess, gourmet dining, pubs with atmosphere. Unfulfilled ambitions: to learn to swim and play the bagpipes!

BENNETT, Hywell
Actor b. 8.4.44 Garnant, South Wales. Family moved to London when he was five. Spent five years with the National Youth Theatre which he joined at the age of 14 to play Ophelia. Went to RADA on a scholarship and was in plays in London's West End, Edinburgh Festival and TV before big break in his first film, The Family Way, with Hayley Mills. Other films incl: Twisted Nerve; The Virgin

Soldiers; Loot; Percy; Endless Night; It's a 2 ft. 6 in. Above the Ground World; The Buttercup-Chain. Stage incl: Night Must Fall; Otherwise Engaged; Julius Caesar (Young Vic). TV incl: Redcap; The Sweeney; Pennies from Heaven; Strangers; Malice Aforethought; Tinker, Tailor, Soldier, Spy; Shelley. Education: grammar school, Clapham. m. former TV personality girl Cathy McGowan (dis), 1 d. Emma. Address: c/o Thames TV, London NW1. Starsign: Aries.

BENNETT, John
Actor b. 8.5.28 London. Trained at Central School of Speech and Drama followed by wide rep experience incl: Dundee, Bromley, Watford, Bristol Old Vic and Edinburgh Festival before London's West End. Latest stage appearance in The King and I. TV incl: The Forsyte Saga; Special Branch; Ryan International; Softly, Softly; The Main Chance; Honey Lane; Strange Report; The Avengers and more recently, Pews; The Dybbuk; Return Fare; I Claudius; Dr Who; Anna Karenina; Blake's Seven; Tales of the Unexpected; Lillie; Depart in Peace. Education: Bradfield College, Berks. Address: c/o St James's Management, London SW1. Starsign: Taurus. Hobbies: gliding, do-it-yourself.

BENNETT, John
Commentator/presenter

b. 12.7.42 Belfast. From singer/guitarist to current affairs to sport. Full-time teacher. TV and Radio: Commentated on most of Northern Ireland's international soccer matches over the past nine years and covered the Queen's Silver Jubilee tour of Northern Ireland for Radio Ulster. Has also been involved with various series on folk music on radio and TV. Education: Royal Belfast Academical Institution and Stranmillis Teacher Training College. m. Joan, 1 d. Siobhan, 1 s. Mark. Address: Sports Department, BBC, Broadcasting House, Belfast. Starsign: Cancer. Hobbies: squash and walking. Unfulfilled ambition: to walk from Land's End to John O'Groats.

BENTINE, Michael
Writer/actor/ comedian b. 26.1.22 Watford, Herts. Show business career started in Cardiff 1940 playing juvenile lead in Sweet Lavender; then with Robert Atkins's Shakespearian company in Regent's Park, London, until called up for

service in the RAF. After the war Windmill Theatre, revues (Starlight Roof) and variety. Founder member of The Goons. Two years in Australia (1954-55) after TV in America. Radio incl: Round the Bend. Films incl: The Sandwich Man; Bachelor of Arts. TV incl: Quick On the Draw; The Bumblies; The Cathode Ray Tube Show; It's A Square World; Potty Time; Celebrity Squares. Autobiography: The Long Banana Skin. Education: Eton. m. (1st) (dis), (2nd) ex-ballet dancer Clementina Stuart, 3 d. Elaine (from 1st m), Fusty, Suki (from 2nd m), 1 s. Peski (from 2nd m). Address: c/o John Carlsen, London SW19. Starsign: Aquarius. Hobbies: sailing, fencing, archery, guns, Egyptology. Unfulfilled ambition: to use my training in the Arts and Sciences to make people happier.

BERGMAN, Anna
Actress b. 5.5.49 Sweden. Former model and au pair, daughter of Swedish filmmaker Ingmar Bergman. Studied drama in Sweden. Films incl: Penelope Pulls It Off; All Change; Fantasy; Click; Hazell Pays The Piper; Queen Kong; Come Play With Me; What's Up Doc? No. 2; Licence To Love and To Kill; Wild Geese; In the Sign of the Scorpio; In the Sign of Sagittarius. TV incl: Tomorrow's World; Parrot 76; The Balcony; Mind Your Language (8 episodes).

Education: Sweden; England. m. former policeman Peter Brown, 1 s. Mikael. Address: c/o Aida Foster Ltd, London NW8. Starsign: Taurus. Hobbies: swimming, riding, skating. Unfulfilled ambition: to appear in a stage show.

BERNETTE, Shelia
Actress/comedienne b. 30.3.41 London. Started training for ballet at two and a half with the Italia Conti School, gave it up at seven and concentrated on acting. Stage incl: The King's Mare; The Players' Theatre (London and New York); The Boy Friend; Something's Afoot; London Palladium pantomime and Royal Variety Show 1971. Films incl: Sons and Lovers; The Wild Affair. TV incl: Black and White Minstrel Show; The Good Old Days; Hugh and I; Milly Martin Show; Candid Camera (also in US); Upstairs, Downstairs (US); The Saturday Crowd. Many TV commercials, notably Extra Strong Mints. Address: c/o CCA, London SW6. Starsign: Aries. Hobbies: gardening in my growbag, cooking, bio-chemical medicine. Unfulfilled ambitions: finding a diet I can live with, doing a film with Mel Brooks.

BERRY, Lynda
Reporter b. 24.5.51 brought up in Scotland. Started in local radio, various documentaries incl: a profile of the Marchioness of Tavistock; Format V; and

Breathing Space, a film series for BBC Scotland. Other TV incl: Pebble Mill at One and film series, plus short spell on Tomorrow's World before joining ATV. Education: in Edinburgh, Lausanne and Italy. Address: c/o Bank of Scotland, Edinburgh. Starsign: Gemini. Hobbies: riding, tennis, music, cinema. Unfulfilled ambition: to make 90-minute documentary on the life and loves of Miss Peaches Laverne.

BERRY, Mary
Cookery presenter b. 24.3.35 Bath. Cookery expert on After Noon Plus since 1974. Trained at Bath College of Domestic Science and Paris Cordon Bleu. Teacher of cookery, caterer and cookery editor and consultant of national magazines. Also presenter of new products and author of 12 books with a two million sale. Education: Bath High School. m. Paul Hunnings, 1 d. Annabel, 2 s. Thomas, William. Address: c/o Thames TV, London. Starsign: Aries. Hobbies: ski-ing, cooking, antiques, gardening,

arranging flowers – without fuss. Unfulfilled ambition: to have an evening TV programme.

BEWES, Rodney
Actor b. 27.11.38 Bingley, Yorks. First became interested in acting (at 12 years old) when BBC advertised for boys for a production of Billy Bunter. Rodney didn't get the part but was put into two other plays and recommended for PARADA, a preparatory to RADA. After a year at RADA went into RAF for National Service for two years. Returned to RADA, was expelled after one term, then went into rep at Stockton-on-Tees, Hull, York, Watford, Eastbourne, Morecambe and Hastings. First break in the 1960's in Harold Pinter's A Night Out. Decided to concentrate on TV (both BBC and ITV), which led to the successful series The Likely Lads; Whatever Happened to the Likely Lads?, and the series he wrote and produced, Dear Mother . . . Love Albert. Stage incl: The Loudest Tears in Town. Films incl: Billy Liar; Decline and Fall; Spring and Port Wine; Dance to Your Daddy; Whatever Happened to the Likely Lads? Other TV incl: Love Story; Z Cars; Albert; Jonah and the Whale. Education: nil. m. fashion designer Daphne Black, 1 d. Daisy, 3 s. Joe, Tom, Billy (triplets). Address: Barnes, West London, and Cornwall. Starsign: Sagittarius. Hobbies:

antiques and children. Unfulfilled ambition: to finish RADA.

BIG DADDY
(Shirley Crabtree)
Wrestler b. 14.11.36 Halifax, Yorks. One of the three brothers who are all in wrestling (one, Brian Crabtree, is a referee). Trained at gyms and YMCA's all over the country. Taught wrestling at University of Vienna in 1972. Weighs 24st 2lb. Education: secondary modern. m. Eunice, 1 d. Jane, 1 step-s. Paul. Address: Joint Promotions. Ltd, Leeds. Starsign: Scorpio. Hobbies: reading, music, walking, training, everything appertaining to sport. Unfulfilled ambition: to visit America and wrestle at Madison Square Garden.

BIXBY, Bill
Actor b. 22nd January, San Francisco. Dr David Barber in The Incredible Hulk. After army service went to Hollywood to pursue an acting career, but his first job was as a hotel clerk, later becoming lifeguard at the pool. While there he was

approached to make industrial films – in Detroit. Shortly after returned to Hollywood to appear in such films as Lonely Are the Brave; Irma La Duce; The Apple Dumpling Gang. TV incl: The Danny Williams Show; The Andy Griffith Show; The Joey Bishop Show; My Favourite Martian (1963); Courtship of Eddie's Father; The Magician. Education: San Francisco City College and Berkeley. m. actress Brenda Benet, 1 s. Christopher. Address: Brentwood and Malibu, Calif. Starsign: Aquarius.

BLACK, Cilla
Entertainer b. 27.5.43 Liverpool. Began her career at The Iron Door Club, Liverpool, 1959. Became a professional entertainer in 1963 when the late Brian Epstein launched her as a recording artist with a single record, Love of the Loved, written for her by Lennon and McCartney. First West End season London Palladium 1964. Other stage incl: Way Out in Piccadilly; Cilla at the Palace; pantomimes at the London Palladium, Wimbledon (twice) and Liverpool; summer seasons; tours of Europe, Far East and Australia as concert, cabaret and TV performer. TV incl: Juke Box Jury; Thank Your Lucky Stars; Top of the Pops; Sunday Night at the London Palladium; Cilla; Cilla's World of Comedy. Films incl: Ferry Across the Mersey; Work is a Four-letter Word. Many hit

records incl: Anyone Who Had A Heart; You're My World; Alfie; Step Inside Love. Voted Top TV Personality for five consecutive years by the Sun newspaper. Education: St Anthony's Secondary, Liverpool. m. Robert Willis (now her manager), 2 s. Robert John, Benjamin. Address: c/o Tony Barrow International, London SW15. Starsign: Gemini. Hobbies: music, golf. Unfulfilled ambitions: to become a Dame and to be a star in America.

BLAIR, Isla
Actress b. 29.9.44 India. Trained at RADA at 19, straight into West End production of A Funny Thing Happened on the Way to the Forum. Much stage and TV. Stage incl: The Rivals; Popkiss; Man of Mode; Subject to Fits; The Grand Tour. Films incl: The Blood of Dracula; The Battle of Britain. TV incl: The Dickie Henderson Show; The Doctors; The Regiment; The Crezz; When the Boat Comes In; Forgotten Love songs: Wilde Alliance. Education: private boarding school, Sussex. m. actor Julian Glover, 1 s. Jamie. Address: Barnes, London. Starsign: Libra. Hobbies: tennis, reading historical novels.

BLAIR, Lesley
Presenter b. 24.11.44 Northern Ireland. Started work as a secretary but was fired after three months.

Taught at a girls' school in Aberdeen; started working for Grampian TV at 17, presenting Romper Room. After three years moved to Scottish TV as announcer, but was soon presenting her own children's show, Lesley, and Cartoon Parade. Presented STV's first colour TV programme, Lesley with Oscar. Has done news reporting, continuity announcing for ATV and run her own quiz programme for Grampian, Win a Word With Lesley. Other TV incl: Top Score; Finding Out; Right Now and The Better Sex. Recently spent six months in America talking about Scottish life on many TV stations. Also does schools radio broadcasting and gives poetry readings. Education: Mosely College; Oriol College, Cheltenham. Address: Pollockshield, Glasgow. Starsign: Sagittarius. Hobbies: reading and writing poetry, riding, international cooking. Unfulfilled ambition: to keep in varied work.

BLAKE, Christopher
Actor b. 23.8.49 London.

Trained for three years at Central School of Speech and Drama. Then played juvenile lead in BBC children's series Anna of Avonlea; Yorkshire TV's Death or Glory Boy; The Trials of Oscar Wilde, at Oxford and the film Aces High. Recent TV incl: Love For Lydia; Mixed Blessings; Mill on the Floss; The Lost Boys. Education: Fitzherbert Secondary Modern, Brighton, Sussex. m. Wendy, 2 d. Charlotte, Louise, 1 s. Sean. Address: c/o LWT, South Bank TV Centre, London SE1. Starsign: Virgo. Hobbies: cricket, photography. Unfulfilled ambition: to work in America.

BLAKE, Peter
Actor b. 8.12.51 Selkirk, Scotland. Started career as a pop singer when he was 15. Trained at the Scottish Royal Academy of Dramatic Art. Rep in Edinburgh, Sheffield and Chichester. Stage incl: Hair; Jesus Christ, Superstar; Joseph and the Technicolour Dreamcoat; The Rocky Horror Show. TV incl: his familiar Fonz spoof in the Pepsi commercial, Z Cars; Plays For England; Out; The Songwriters; Dr Finlay's Casebook; The Brothers; Agony; Penmarric; The Racing Game. Also a singer and guitar player of some ability. Records incl: Lipsmackin Rock 'n' Roll; Boogie Breakout. Education: grammar school. Address: c/o Barry Brown Management, London SE11.

Starsign: Sagittarius. Hobbies: riding, sailing. Unfulfilled ambition: to retire young.

BLAKISTON, Caroline
Actress b. 13.2.33 London. After training at RADA, rep experience at Liverpool, Worthing, Coventry, Hornchurch and then London. Films incl: The Idol; Magic Christian; Sunday, Bloody Sunday; TV incl: The Avengers; Emergency–Ward 10; The Saint; The Forsyte Saga; The Caesars; Wives and Daughters; Saturday, Sunday, Monday; Kids; Raffles; The Racing Game; The Prince Regent; The Mallens. m. actor Russell Hunter (dis), 1 d. Charlotte, 1 s. Adam. Address: c/o Fraser and Dunlop, London W1. Starsign: Aquarius. Hobbies: sun, music, cooking.

BLESSED, Brian
Actor b. 9.10.37 Mexborough, Yorks. Many jobs – steeplejack, plasterer, undertaker's assistant – before two years' National Service in RAF Parachute Regiment where amateur theatricals heightened his

ambition to be an actor. Studies at Bristol Old Vic Theatre School and did four years in rep before TV fame in Z Cars. TV also incl: The Double Agent; Jackanory; Arthur of the Britons; Justice; Lorna and Ted; The Recruiting Officer; Boy Dominic; The Three Musketeers; Hadleigh; Public Eye; Brahms; Cold Comfort Farm; Churchill's People; I Claudius; The Aphrodite Inheritance; Lamb to the Slaughter (Roald Dahl's Tales of the Unexpected). Films incl: Man of La Mancha; Country Dance; The Trojan Women; A Last Valley; Henry VIII. Theatre incl: Incident at Vichy; The Exorcism; State of Revolution. Holder of a Black Belt in judo and does his own stunts. m. (1st) American actress Anne Bomann (dis), (2nd) actress Hildegard Neil, 2 d. Catherine (from 1st m), Rosalind (from 2nd m). Address: Chobham, Surrey. Starsign: Libra.

BOARDMAN, Stan
Comedian b. 7th December Liverpool. Ran his own haulage business before winning a holiday camp competition which set him on the showbiz road. TV incl: Opportunity Knocks; Celebrity Squares; Seaside Special; Runaround; The Comedians. m. Vivien, 1 d. Andrea, 1 s. Paul. Address: c/o Bernard Lee Management, Warlingham, Surrey. Starsign: Sagittarius. Hobbies: football and all

sports. Unfulfilled ambition: to play for Liverpool football team.

BOBIN, David
Sports reporter b. 15.11.45 London. Trained on local newspapers 1960-70. With local radio 1970-74 when he joined Southern TV's Day By Day team. Education: Roysses School, Abingdon, Oxon. m. Susan, 2 d. Joanna, Victoria, 1 s. James. Address: Titchfield, Hants. Starsign: Scorpio. Hobbies: listening to music, horse racing, motor racing, relaxing at home, football, squash. Unfulfilled ambitions: to present World of Sport and visit South America.

BOND, Sue
Actress b. 9.5.45 Aylesbury, Bucks. Singer in the 1960's. Stage incl: Love Thy Neighbour; George and Mildred; Leave Him to Heaven; Stop the World, I Want to Get Off; Tommy. TV incl: George and Mildred; Love Thy Neighbour; Leave Him to Heaven; On The Buses; Benny Hill Shows; Mike Yarwood Shows; Spring

and Autumn; Dr In Charge; Golden Shot; Mother Makes Five. Education: Tottenham Technical College.
m. merchant banker David Bond. Address: c/o Bernard Gillman Ltd, Tolworth, Surrey. Starsign: Taurus. Hobbies: singing rock 'n' roll, dining out or cooking something exotic. Unfulfilled ambitions: to play Nellie Forbush in South Pacific, and to write a successful novel.

BOND-OWEN, Nicholas
Actor b. 13.11.68 Ashford, Middlesex. Never acted before gaining the part of Tristram in George and Mildred. Other TV incl: Jamie in The Park Ranger; Celebrity Squares. Also Kevin in Confessions From a Holiday Camp (film). Education: Hengrove Middle School. Address: c/o Magnus Management, Teddington, Middx. Starsign: Scorpio. Hobbies: football (avid Liverpool supporter), drawing. Unfulfilled ambitions: to play for Liverpool football team and to star in a James Bond film.

BOSANQUET, Reginald
Newscaster b. 9.8.32 Surrey. Joined ITN as a sub-editor when it began in 1955. Since reported from almost every part of the world. Diplomatic correspondent for four years and anchorman for Dateline for eight years, newscaster on News at Ten 1967 – 1979. Father was England cricketer B J T Bosanquet. Member of Wildlife Fund

Administrative Panel. Education: Winchester and New College, Oxford (read History). m. (1st) Caren (dis), (2nd) Felicity (dis), 2 d. (one from each m). Address: c/o ITN London W1. Starsign: Leo. Hobby: tennis.

BOUGH, Frank
Sports commentator b. 15.1.33 Fenton, Stoke-on-Trent. Started in industry as organisation and methods expert. Radio football reports BBC Newcastle 1962, then news magazine and sports TV Newcastle and London, incl: Sportsview (1964); commentator Tokyo Olympics (1964); linkman Grandstand and Mexico Olympics (1968); World Cup, Mexico 1970; Commonwealth Games, Edinburgh. Anchorman of Grandstand since 1972. Education: Oswestry High, Merton College, Oxford (soccer blue and degree in history). m. Nesta, 3 s. David, Stephen, Andrew. Address: c/o Bagenal Harvey, London EC1. Starsign: Capricorn. Hobbies: music, gardening.

BOWERS, Lally
Actress b. 21.1.17 Oldham, Lancs. Was a secretary before walking-on and understudying at the Shakespeare Memorial Theatre, Stratford-upon-Avon. Has since been in hundreds of stage productions, films, and TV programmes and in rep at Manchester, Sheffield, Southport, Guildford, Liverpool, Birmingham and Bristol Old Vic. Her London debut was in 1944 and her many West End successes since incl: Dinner With The Family (Clarence Derwent Award 1957); Difference of Opinion; The Killing of Sister George; Dear Octopus. Recent films incl: The Slipper and the Rose and TV incl: The Duchess of Duke Street; Mr Axelford's Angel; My Name is Harry Worth; The Life and Death of Penelope; The Importance of Being Earnest; Pygmalion; Fallen Angels; John McNab; You're Only Young Twice; Tales of the Unexpected Education: Hulme Grammar School, Oldham. Address: Barnes, London SW13. Starsign: Aquarius. Hobby: counting the calories. Unfulfilled ambition: to drive my own car round Hyde Park Corner.

BOWKER, Judi
Actress b. 6.4.54 Shawford, Hants. Spent her childhood in Zambia where her father was a lawyer. Shot to fame when chosen by Zefferelli to play St Clare in his film Brother Sun and Sister Moon. Other films

incl: East of Elephant Rock and Clash of the Titans. Theatre appearances incl: The Important of Being Earnest; The Prince of Homburg; The Rivals (Manchester Exchange); Much Ado About Nothing (Nottingham); The Cherry Orchard; Don Juan comes Back From the Wars; Macbeth and The Double Dealer (National Theatre). TV incl: Black Beauty; Dr Jekyll and Mr Hyde (musical for US TV); Crimes of Passion; South Riding; In This House of Brede; The Picture of Dorian Gray; The Saturday Party; The Glittering Prizes; The Country Party; Hindle Wakes; Silver Lining; Count Dracula. Education: Dominican Convent, Ndola, Zambia; Broken Hill Convent, Salisbury, England, and Salisbury Art College. Address: c/o William Morris Agency, London W1. Starsign: Aries. Hobbies: drawing and painting, riding, cooking, walking, reading.

BOWLER, Norman
Actor b. 1.8.32 London. Former deckboy on an oil tanker, he travelled the world before becoming an actor. A

spell in rep led to films in America, incl: Tom Thumb; Naval Patrol; Von Ryan's Express. Other films incl: Julius Caesar. Switching to TV, probably best known as Det Chief Inspector Harry Hawkins in Softly, Softly, a part he played for 11 years. Other TV incl: Harpers West One; Deadline Midnight; The Ratcatchers; Letters from the Dead; Park Ranger; Jesus of Nazareth. Education: grammar school and City Literary Institute.
m. (1st) (dis), (2nd) Berjouhi (dis), (3rd) Diane,
2 d. Caroline (from 1st m), Tamara (from 2nd m),
2 s. Joshua (from 1st m), Simon (from 3rd m).
Address: c/o ICM, London W1. Starsign: Leo. Hobbies: sailing, walking, pottery, travelling. Unfulfilled ambition: to sail the Atlantic.

BOWLES, Peter
Actor b. 16.10.36 London. Trained at RADA and by the age of 18 was a professional actor. Went to Old Vic for a year, then into rep. His break came with his part in Happy Haven at Bristol Old Vic, which he repeated in London 1960. Plays more rogues than heroes and is in constant work on stage, films, and TV. Stage incl: Absent Friends; Dirty Linen. Films incl: Charge of the Light Brigade; The Informer; Live Now, Pay Later; Yellow Rolls-Royce; Blow Up; Joe Egg. TV incl: The Avengers; The Saint; The Prisoner; Take Three Girls; A Thinking Man

As Hero; Napoleon and Love; The Survivors; Churchill's People; Only on Sunday; The Crezz; A Ghost Story for Christmas; Rumpole of the Bailey; To the Manor Born; Only When I Laugh. Education: Nottingham High Pavement Grammar School. m. Susan, 1 d. Sasha, 2 s. Guy, Adam. Address: Hammersmith, London. Starsign: Libra. Hobby: modern British art. Unfulfilled ambition: to still be working at the age of 80.

BOYD, Tommy
Presenter b. 14.12.52 Chiswick, London. While training as an English teacher, took job with Radio Brighton and at 19 was producing and presenting his own phone-in show. He was also a dolphin trainer at Brighton Dolphinarium. After getting his teaching qualifications he worked as a news producer with LBC. Then he joined the Magpie team in September 1977. Education: Tudor Grammar School; Feltham Comprehensive; Brighton College. Address: Teddington, Middx. Starsign: Sagittarius. Hobbies: helping to run local youth club, playing football, cricket, tennis, golf (badly), buying records, keeping fit, driving to Brighton and collecting jokes. Unfulfilled ambition: to write the world's greatest joke.

BRAGG, Melvyn
Writer/broadcaster
b. 6.10.39 Carlisle, Cumbria.
Monitor 1962-65; 2nd House;
editor and presenter of Read
All About It 1974-77.
Documentaries incl:
Barbarolli; Debussy; John le
Carré; Tennessee Williams.
TV also incl: Tonight 1976-77;
editor and presenter of The
South Bank Show from 1978.
Novels incl: The Silken Net;
The Hired Man; Josh Lawton.
Non-fiction incl: Speak for
England. Writing also incl:
Mardi Gras (musical);
Isadora; The Music Lovers;
Jesus Christ, Superstar (all
films). Education: Wigton
Nelson-Thomlinson
Grammar School; Wadham
College, Oxford (MA Hons
modern history). Fellow of the
Royal Society of Literature.
m. Catherine Mary,
2 d. Marie Elsa, Alice Mary.
Address: London NW3.
Starsign: Libra. Hobby:
walking.

BRAKE, Patricia
Actress b. 25.6.42 Bath.
Trained at Bristol Old Vic
School, then rep at Salisbury
and Royal Shakespeare
Company. Better known on
TV than for stage work,
though she did appear in The
Odd Couple; Play It Again
Sam, with Dudley Moore, and
A Murder is Announced. TV
incl: Home Tonight; Z Cars;
Emmerdale Farm; The
Ugliest Girl in Town; Forget
Me Not; Second Time
Around; Call My Bluff;
Porridge; Nicholas Nickleby;
Going Straight; A Sharp
Intake of Breath; The Glums.
Education: City of Bath Girls'
School. m. actor Robert
McBain (dis), 1 d. Hannah,
2 s. Jonathan, Angus
(step-s). Address: c/o Scott
Marshall, London W3.
Starsign: Cancer. Hobbies:
gardening, reading, cats.
Unfulfilled ambitions: too
many to mention.

BREAKS, Jim
Wrestler b. 25.3.40 Bradford.
Started as amateur and was
British amateur champion,
Northern Counties
champion, Yorkshire
champion, European
lightweight champion.
Education: secondary school
in Bradford. m. Carole,
2 d. Karen, Stacey,
1 s. Gary. Address: c/o ATS,
Leeds. Starsign: Aries.
Hobbies: football and
running a pub. Unfulfilled
ambition: to be world
lightweight champion.

BRIGGS, Johnny
Actor b. 5.9.35 London. Italia
Conti Stage School pupil
1947-53. Films incl: Cosh
Boy; Hue and Cry; Perfect
Friday; Best Pair of Legs in
the Business. TV incl: No

Hiding Place; The Young
Generation; The Saint; The
Avengers; Crime of Passion;
Danger Man; The
Persuaders; Softly, Softly;
Mike Baldwin in Coronation
Street and many more too
numerous to mention.
Education: Schools'
Certificate standard.
m. (1st) Carole,
(2nd) Christine, 2 d. Karen,
Jennifer, 1 s. Mark. Address:
Marina Martin Management,
London W1. Starsign: Virgo.
Hobbies: golf, squash,
snooker. Unfulfilled ambition:
to work on a TV series in
America.

BRIERLY, Alison
Reporter/presenter
b. 23.10.47 Huddersfield,
Yorks. With Granada as
production office assistant
1971, followed by
researcher/ script-writer for
pre-school programme, then
with HTV as light
entertainment researcher.
Researcher for BBC
Nationwide 1974 and
following year joined
Southern TV as consumer
reporter for Day By Day.
Turned freelance reporter/
presenter 1978 and since

then TV has incl: People Rule and Your Men at Westminster (Southern TV), Home-made for the Home and Toy Craft (Tyne Tees TV). Education: Church of England Convent, North Yorkshire, and Edinburgh University (MA in History and Fine Art). m. Michael Carmichael, 1 s. Jamie. Address: Broughton, Nr Stockbridge, Hants. Starsign: Scorpio. Hobbies: ski-ing, painting, avoiding housework. Unfulfilled ambitions: to be thinner and blonder and able to get up in the morning without groaning. But much more important to present and report on as varied a number of programmes as possible.

BRIERS, Richard
Actor b. 14.1.34 Merton, Surrey. Started as a clerk, RADA 1954-56. Rep at Liverpool, Leatherhead, Coventry. London debut 1959. Plays incl: Present Laughter; Arsenic and Old Lace; Cat Among the Pigeons. Films incl: Fathom; All The Way Up. Radio series incl: Brothers in Law; Doctor in the House; Marriage Lines. TV plays and series incl: Brothers in Law; Marriage Lines; Ben Travers farces; Norman Conquests; The Good Life. Education: Wimbledon. m. actress Ann Davies, 2 d. Katy, Lucy. Address: c/o International Famous Agency, London W1. Starsign: Capricorn. Hobbies: theatre history, golf.

BRITTEN, Barry
Comedian/compere/impressionist b. 8.10.53 Eltham. Trained to be a chef but became a Butlin Redcoat, then entertainments manager. Has played all the top northern clubs, pantomime, South Africa tour with Lena Zavaroni, West End show with Fiona Richmond. TV incl: Opportunity Knocks; Charlie Drake Show. Education: Eltham High School. m. Deborah. Address: c/o Patricia Mackay, Wembley Park, Middx. Starsign: Libra. Hobbies: doing as little as possible, has vast record collection of American TV shows and is an avid fan of Al Jolson. Unfulfilled ambition: to appear on TV with The Muppets.

BRITTON, Tony
Actor b. 9.6.24 Birmingham. First worked in estate agents and aircraft factory at Weston-super-Mare. Joined amateur dramatic group. First professional appearance in Weston-super-Mare. After war service in army, rep in Manchester, season at Stratford-upon-Avon, Old Vic, toured 1964-66 in My Fair Lady. Wide stage, film and TV experience. Stage incl: Move Over Mrs Markham; No, No, Nanette; The Dame of Sark. Films incl: Sunday, Bloody Sunday; There's a Girl in My Soup; The Day of the Jackal. TV incl: Romeo and Juliet; The Six Proud Walkers; Melissa, The Nearly Man; Father, Dear Father; Robin's Nest. Education: Edgbaston Collegiate, Birmingham; Thornbury Grammar, Glos. m. (1st) Ruth (dis), (2nd) Danish sculptress Eve Birkefeldt, 1 d. Cherry (from 1st m), 1 s. Jasper (from 2nd m). Address: c/o International Creative Management Ltd, London W1. Starsign: Gemini. Hobbies: golf, cricket, gardening, photography, wine. Unfulfilled ambition: to play more Shakespeare with the RSC.

BROADHURST, Topline
Gardening expert, Westward TV b. 9.10.19 London. Learnt by experience at a rose nursery and on a farm since serving in RNVR during the war. Got the nickname Topline because it was his call-sign when serving in MTB's. Gardening expert with Plymouth Sound Radio. Weekly syndicated gardening column. Education: Charterhouse. m. Kitty, 1 d. Sarah, 1 s. Christopher. Address: Torquay, Devon. Starsign: Libra. Hobbies: roses, gardening, photography.

painting, good food and wine. Unfulfilled ambitions: not to have to work, and to have the time to breed a world-famous rose.

BROCKLEBANK, Ted
Broadcaster b. 24.9.42 St Andrews, Fife. Training on local newspapers and in Fleet Street. With Scottish Television before joining Grampian Television where he is now Head of News and Current Affairs. TV: presenter and producer of news, current affairs and political programmes and network documentaries incl: What Price Oil? (presenter); Highland One, Black Water – Bright Hope. Cinderella from the Sea (producer); A Tale of Two Cities (producer/presenter). Education: Madras College, St Andrews. m. Lesley Beverly, 2 s. Andrew, Jonathan. Address: c/o Grampian Television. Starsign: Libra. Hobbies: making television programmes, reading, music, sketching. Unfulfilled ambition: to see the Loch Ness monster.

BROOK, Faith
Actress b. 16.2.22 York.

Trained for the stage under Kate Rorke, Dame May Whitty and at RADA. Stage debut in California 1941; in London 1942 in Aren't Men Beasts? Served in the ATS during the war and appeared with Stars in Battledress. Joined Bristol Old Vic 1946 and has since had distinguished theatrical career in London and New York. TV incl: The Mark Two Wife; The Main Chance; So It Goes; War and Peace; Mary and Louisa; Angels; Crown Court; After Julius. Education: California; Switzerland; England. m. (1st) Dr Charles Moffett (dis), (2nd) Michael Horowitz (dis), 1 s. Brook (from 2nd m). Address: c/o Boyack and Conway Ltd, London W1. Starsign: Aquarius. Hobby: cooking. Unfulfilled ambition: painting.

BROOKE-TAYLOR, Tim
Actor/scriptwriter b. 17.7.40 Buxton, Derbyshire. Has a law degree, but started his career in Cambridge Footlights Revue, followed by the successful Cambridge Circus revue in London and Broadway. Then came the radio show, I'm Sorry I'll Read That Again followed by At Last The 1948 Show; Marty; Broaden Your Mind and The Goodies, all on TV. Other TV incl: On the Braden Beat; His and Hers; Hello Cheeky (and radio); The Rough With The Smooth; Shades of Greene. Theatre incl: The Unvarnished Truth. Films incl: Twelve Plus One; The

Statue. Records incl: Funky Gibbon; The Least Worst of Hello Cheeky; The Seedy Sounds of Hello Cheeky; The New Goodies LP; The Goodies' Beastly Record. Education: Winchester and Pembroke College, Cambridge. m. Christine, 2 s. Ben, Edward. Address: c/o Jill Foster, London SW3. Starsign: Cancer. Hobbies: travel, ski-ing, golf, watching all sport, films and TV. Unfulfilled ambition: to score the winning goal for Derby County – with a broken leg – in extra time.

BROWN, Janet
Comedienne b. Glasgow. Began doing impersonations while still a teenager. After serving with the ATS during the war, went to London and worked on a radio show which led to a summer show in Scarborough in which she met her husband. More radio and TV, followed by a stage play with Alistair Sim, Mr Gillie. TV incl: Rainbow Room; Where Shall We Go?; Friends and Neighbours; Who Do You Do?; Mike Yarwood in Persons. Education: Rutherglen Academy. m. comedian Peter Butterworth (dec), 1 d. Emma, 1 s. Tyler. Address: Sussex. Hobbies: collecting antiques, cooking, sitting in the sun by the sea. Unfulfilled ambition: 'Just to do everything to the best of my ability.'

BROWN, Peter
Industrial correspondent,
BBC West b. 8.7.27
Longhope, Glos. Started as a
freelance broadcaster on
radio and TV for both BBC
and ATV. Experienced in
industrial, agricultural and
political matters and BBC
West's Industrial
Correspondent since 1965.
Education: Lord Wandsworth
College, Hants. m. Heather,
2 d. Victoria, Catherine,
2 s. William, James.
Address: c/o BBC, Bristol.
Starsign: Cancer. Hobby:
walking. Unfulfilled ambition:
more walking.

BROWNE, Angela
Actress b. 14.6.39
Walton-on-Thames, Surrey.
Trained at RADA, then rep at
Worthing, York, Windsor
before West End and films.
TV incl: Armchair Theatre;
Wednesday Play; Thirty
Minute Theatre; The Saint;
The Prisoner; Danger Man;
The Avengers; General
Hospital; The Hanged Man;
Paul Temple; Père Goriot;
Call My Bluff; Against the
Crown; Love Story; Upstairs,
Downstairs. Recent stage:
Cause Célèbre at Her
Majesty's Theatre.

Education: St Maur's
Convent, Weybridge and
Arts Educational School.
m. actor Francis Matthews,
3 s. Paul, Dominic, Damien.
Address: c/o Essanay Ltd,
London W14. Starsign:
Gemini. Hobbies: reading,
growing vegetables.

BRUCE, Mona
Actress/writer b. 3.12.24
Birmingham. Trained in rep
theatres, incl: Liverpool
where she met her husband.
Multifarious roles in the
theatre and on TV, but her
break came with the part of
the chief prison officer Mrs
Armitage in Within These
Walls, for which she and her
husband wrote some of the
episodes. Other TV incl: the
Mind of Mr J G Reeder; Sam
Education: Loughton High,
Essex and Tiffins Girls
School, Kingston. m. actor
Robert James, 1 d. Clare.
Address: London and
Suffolk. Starsign: Sagittarius.
Hobbies: swimming,
gardening.

BRUNSON, Michael
Journalist b. 12.8.40
Norwich. Formerly with BBC
radio and TV, joined ITN
1968. US Correspondent

1973-77, covering
Watergate, US Bicentennial
and US Presidential election.
Has since been reporter/
newscaster and was with Mrs
Thatcher throughout her
1979 election campaign.
Now ITN's European
Correspondent. Education:
Bedford School and Queen's
College, Oxford. m. Susan,
2 s. Jonathan, Robin.
Address: c/o ITN, London
W1. Starsign: Leo. Hobbies:
'Don't have time.' Unfulfilled
ambitions: to go to Russia; to
interview the Queen.

BRYANT, Michael
Actor b. 5.4.28 London.
Served in the Merchant Navy
and the army before studying
for stage at Webber Douglas
Academy of Dramatic Art.
First part was in touring
production of A Streetcar
Named Desire. Rep at
Worthing and Oxford, then
West End debut in The
Iceman Cometh 1958,
followed by Five Finger
Exercise (London and
Broadway); Ross; Royal
Shakespeare Company;
National Theatre (State of
Revolution; The Lady From
Maxim's; Brand). Films incl:
The Ruling Class; Nicholas
and Alexandra; Life for Ruth;
The Mindbenders; Goodbye,
Mr Chips. Has been a
National Theatre actor since
1977. TV incl: (plays and
series) The Stone Dance; The
Paradise Makers; The Big M;
The Explorer; Three Sisters;
Talking to a Stranger;
Anniversary; Rain; The
Roads to Freedom; Willow

Cabin; Mr Axelford's Angel;
Duchess of Malfi. Education:
Battersea Grammar.
m. actress Josephine Martin,
2 d. Sarah, Josephine,
2 s. Kerrigan, Simon.
Address: Longfield, Kent.
Starsign: Aries. Hobbies:
none. Unfulfilled ambition:
has none. Takes life as it
comes.

BUCKMAN, Dr Robert

Presenter/comedian /writer
b. 22.8.48 London. Trained
as a doctor but appearances
with Cambridge University
Footlights gave him a taste
for entertainment. Radio incl:
The Soppy Legends; Start
the Week; Marks in His Diary.
TV incl: Don't Ask Me; Don't
Just Sit There; The Pink
Medicine Show. Record: The
Pink Medicine Show Album.
Contributor to Punch;
Cosmopolitan; View, etc and
written a book: Out of
Practice. Education:
University College School,
Cambridge University,
University College Hospital
Medical School. m. Dr
Joan-Ida Van Den Ende,
1 d. Joanna. Address: c/o
Fraser and Dunlop, London
W1. Starsign: Leo/Virgo (and
Aston Villa according to
some). Hobbies: collecting
books, inventing filing
systems, avoiding
astrologers. Unfulfilled
ambition: to be mistaken for
Robert Redford (preferably
by Katherine Ross).

BULLEN, Sarah

Actress b. 3.10.50
Charmouth, Dorset. Little

training for an acting career
except for some private
coaching at Webber Douglas
Academy of Dramatic Art.
Rep at Dundee and
Edinburgh. Films incl:
International Velvet; The
Sandbaggers. TV incl: two
series of Space 1999;
Darling, I'm Home; The XYY
Man; The House of Caradus;
Dick Turpin. Education:
Westwing School, Thornbury,
Nr Bristol. Address: c/o Jean
Diamond, London
Management, London W1.
Starsign: Libra. Hobbies:
riding, water ski-ing, opera,
ballet, films, theatre,
sketches, water colours,
good television and meeting
people who make me laugh.
Unfulfilled ambition: to create
a so far undiscovered
heroine on film or in the
theatre.

BURDIS, Ray

Actor b. 23.8.58 London.
Trained at Anna Scher
Theatre. TV incl: Diaries;
Scum; The Vanishing Army;
Marya; Mary's Wife; Four Idle
Hands. Film incl: Music
Machine; Panic; Scum.
Education: Islington Green
School, London. Address:
c/o Anna Scher Theatre

Management, London N1.
Starsign: Leo/Virgo.
Hobbies: girls, cars, physical
training. Unfulfilled ambition:
to win the pools.

BURKE, Alfred

Actor b. 28.2.18 Peckham,
London. Started as a
14-year-old office boy in the
City of London. After being a
club steward and working in
a silk warehouse, joined a
local amateur dramatics
group before moving to
Morley College and winning a
scholarship to RADA 1937.
Acting career started two
years later at Barn Theatre at
Shere, Surrey. London debut
at Watergate Theatre where
in the 1950's he worked in the
kitchen during a lean spell.
Worked with both Young and
Old Vic and other
companies. Later on stage:
Sailor Beware. Films incl: The
Angry Silence; Touch and
Go; Yangtse Incident;
Interpol. TV series incl: Public
Eye; Marker; Enemy at the
Door. TV plays incl: The Tip
and Treasure Island.
Education: Leo St Boys'
School; Walworth Central
School. m. Barbara, 2 sets of
twins, Jacob and Harriet,
Kelly and Louisa. Address:
Barnes, London. Starsign:
Pisces. Hobbies: football,
music.

BURN, Christine

Newsreader b. 8.8.45
Birmingham. Holder of Poetry
Society Gold Medal for Verse
Speaking (1966), Associate
of the London Academy of
Music and Dramatic Art

(1962). Licentiate of Guildhall School of Music and Drama (1963). Attended many courses for speech, drama, teacher training and modelling before teaching for ILEA and Richmond Education Authority 1967-70 and 1972. Acted with Argyle Theatre For Youth, Birkenhead, 1970; Stan Stennett Productions, South Wales 1970-71. Also TV presenter in Amsterdam and teacher/actress at Greenwich Theatre for Youth. Joined Grampian as announcer/newsreader/presenter/actress for religious, music and children's programmes, 1973. Same year joined BBC in Manchester as TV announcer/newsreader. TV announcer for BFBS, 1976-77. Education: Edgbaston College Prep School; Bartley Green Grammar, Birmingham. m. Christopher Dunston, 1 d. Anya, 1 s. Timothy. Address: c/o Presentation Dept, BBC Manchester. Starsign: Leo. Hobbies: poetry recitals, rock climbing and mountaineering. Unfulfilled ambitions: to read the News at Ten and to join the Royal Shakespeare Company in Stratford.

BURNET, Alastair
Newscaster b. 12.7.28 Sheffield. Worked on The Glasgow Herald and The Economist before joining ITN (1963). Anchorman for General Elections 1964, 1966, 1970 and 1979, and associated with This Week and News at Ten, of which he was one of the original newscasters. Editor of The Economist 1965, won Richard Dimbleby Award for work in TV 1966 and 1970. With BBC 1972-74 as presenter of Panorama and anchorman for both General Elections 1974. Editor Daily Express 1974, returned to ITN 1976 to present News at 5.45 and then News at Ten. Education: Leys, Cambridge, and Worcester College, Oxford. m. Maureen Sinclair. Address: Kensington, London. Starsign: Cancer.

BURNS, Gordon
Producer/presenter b. 10.6.42 Belfast. Reporter East Antrim Times and Belfast Telegraph. Sports department of BBC Radio. TV: Ulster – UTV Reports; Gordon Burns Hour; Granada – Reports Politics; Granada Reports; The Krypton Factor; World in Action. Commentator at political party conferences, Blackpool. Education: Dulwich College, London; Campbell College, Belfast. m. Sheelagh, 1 d. Anna,

1 s. Tristun. Address: c/o David Anthony Promotions, Warrington. Starsign: Gemini. Hobbies: too busy to have any! Unfulfilled ambitions: to be less busy and to play soccer for Northern Ireland.

BURR, Raymond
Actor b. 21.5.17 New Westminster, Canada. Stage debut at 12. Summer theatres all over Canada and England by the age of 19, cafe singer in Paris, Broadway musical, radio series and more than 90 films. Films incl: Pitfall; A Place in the Sun; Rear Window; A Cry in the Night; Desire in the Dust; A Man Whose Name Was John. Has also worked in 1,000 radio shows, 200 plays and 100 TV shows but is best known for title role in TV series Perry Mason (1957-67) and A Man Called Ironside (1967-74) and recently Centennial. Education: San Rafael Military School. m. (1st) Annette Sutherland (dec), (2nd) Isabella Ward (dis), (3rd) Laura Andrine Morgan (dec), 1 s. Michael (from 1st m, dec). Address: the Fijian island of Naitumba which he bought in 1965. Starsign: Taurus.

BURTON, David
Sports reporter/presenter b. 29.9.49 Dulwich, London. BA (Hons) in Law, graduate trainee for Tyne Tees (1974). TV: Reporter/presenter on weekly sports magazine Sportstime since joining Tyne Tees. Co-presenter of

football programme Shoot, for season 1977-78. Introduced bowls series Carpet Bowls, 1976. Education: Cheltenham College, Gloucestershire; St John's College, Cambridge. m. Northern Life reporter, Anne Avery. Address: c/o Tyne Tees Television, Newcastle upon Tyne. Starsign: Libra. Hobbies: all sports, particularly golf (Cambridge Blue, 1972) and squash (Northumberland County Champion, 1976, 1978-79), current affairs, music, theatre, crosswords, good food and social drinking. Unfulfilled ambition: to win the treble chance.

BURTON, Humphrey
Presenter/ producer/ executive b. 25.3.31 Trowbridge, Wilts. Began as radio effects boy with BBC Radio, then studio manager and music producer. BBC TV 1958-67, then he joined London Weekend TV as founder member. Edited and introduced Aquarius 1970-75 then he returned to BBC as Head of Music and Arts and introduced Omnibus. He has also worked freelance on

programmes in Austria, Germany and America. Other TV incl: In Performance; Opera Month. Education: Long Dene, Chiddingstone; The Judd School, Trowbridge; Fitzwilliam House, Cambridge University (BA).
m. (1st) Gretel (dis), (2nd) photographer Christina, 2 d. Clare (from 1st m), Helena (from 2nd m), 2 s. Matthew (from 1st m), Lukas (from 2nd m). Address: c/o BBC TV, London W12. Starsign: Aries. Hobbies: tennis, ping-pong, playing duets, travel. Unfulfilled ambition: to conduct at the Royal Opera House.

BUTLER, Blake
Actor b. 22.10.24 Barrow-in-Furness, Cumbria. Trained at RADA and rep in Manchester and Bristol Old Vic, before London. Stars in Battledress, radio and theatre in Australia. Wide TV experience in plays and series incl: Last of the Summer Wine; Mind Your Language; God's Wonderful Railway; Danger UXB; Rings on Their Fingers; George and Mildred; Rumpole of the Bailey; Grange Hill; Sharp Intake of Breath; Première. Education: Huyton Hill School, Ambleside. Address: London W4. Starsign: Libra. Hobbies: archeology and gardening. Unfulfilled ambition: to do a world tour.

BUTLER, Kenneth
Race commentator b. 29th October, London. First worked in the family firm before commentating on sport for ITV since 1963. Education: Rugby. m. Muriel, 3 step-d. Linda, Janette, Nicola, 2 s. Neil, Christopher (step-s). Address: Lingfield, Surrey. Starsign: Scorpio. Hobby: wine. Unfulfilled ambition: to win the Derby with a home bred colt.

BYGRAVES, Max
Singer/actor/ entertainer b. 16.10.22 Rotherhithe, London. Won a talent contest at 13. West End debut at London Palladium 1949 after service in the RAF. Countless stage and TV shows and hit records. Autobiography: I Wanna Tell You A Story. Novel: The Milkman's On His Way. Films incl: Charlie Moon; A Cry From The Streets; Spare the Rod. Radio incl: Educating Archie. TV incl: Max Bygraves; Max; Singalongamax; Lingalongamax. More Royal Variety Performances than any other artist. Education: St Joseph, Paradise Street, Rotherhithe. m. Gladys

(Blossom), 2 d. Christine, Maxine. 1 s. Anthony. Address: Bournemouth. Starsign: Libra. Hobbies: golf, vintage cars. Unfulfilled ambition: to make a dramatic film.

BYRNE, Peter
Actor/director b. 29.1.28 London. Trained at Italia Conti Stage School. Stage incl: Double Edge; Boeing-Boeing; There's A Girl in My Soup; Underground; There's a Small Hotel; Move Over Mrs Markham (Toronto). Films incl: Large Rope; Reach for the Sky; Carry on Cabby. TV incl: Mutiny at Spithead; The New Canadians; Whodunnit?; Looks Familiar and hundreds of appearances in Dixon of Dock Green since it started in 1955. Education: Finchley Grammar. Address: c/o Renée Stepham, London SW1. Starsign: Aquarius. Hobbies: squash, swimming, riding, golf, cars. Unfulfilled ambition: to direct a film.

planned to take a degree, but gave it up in favour of acting and won a scholarship to the Old Vic Theatre School. It was wartime and she was called up to work as a censor for the Ministry of Information. After the war came her acclaimed part of a mad nun in the film Black Narcissus. Other films incl: A Matter of Life and Death; Small Back Room; Prelude to Fame; Madness of the Heart. Came into TV 1957 incl: Emergency–Ward 10; The Avengers; Who is Sylvia?; Countercrime; That Woman is Wrecking Our Marriage; Emmerdale Farm. m. writer Alaric Jacob, 1 d. Harriet, 1 s. Jasper. Address: c/o RKM Ltd, London W1. Hobbies: collecting cookery books.

BYRON, Kathleen
Actress b. Wanstead, Essex. Studied languages and

C

CAIN, Shirley
Actress b. 30.4.35 West Midlands. Rep and London theatre experience before TV appearances in Upstairs, Downstairs; Double Echo; North and South; Victoria's Scandals; Crown Court; Love for Lydia; Rebecca of Sunnybrook Farm; People Like Us; Malice Aforethought; Thomas and Sarah; God's Wonderful Railway; Pride and Prejudice. Education: Halesowen Grammar School; Birmingham Theatre School and RADA. m. assistant controller, educational broadcasting, BBC, John Cain, 2 d. Charlotte, Susannah. Address: c/o Roger Storey Ltd, London W1. Starsign: Taurus. Hobbies: sewing, gardening, collecting pictures. Unfulfilled ambition: 'To have a marvellous part specially written for me – different from anything I've ever done before.'

CADELL, Simon
Actor b. 19.7.50 London. Trained at Bristol Old Vic Theatre School, then joined the Bristol Old Vic Company. Many theatre appearances. TV incl: Hadleigh; Hine; Love Story; A Man from Haven; Love School; Glittering Prizes; Wings; Space 1999; She Fell Among Thieves; Play For Today; Enemy at the Door; Edward and Mrs Simpson and many radio appearances. Education: Bedale's, Petersfield, Hants. Address: c/o MLR Ltd, London SW5. Starsign: Cancer. Hobby: travelling. Unfulfilled ambitions: too many to list.

CAINE, Marti
Comedienne/vocalist b. 26.1.45 Sheffield. Wanted to be a singer but gradually built up the comedy in local working men's clubs. First big show business break in New Faces in 1975. Since then she has appeared at the London Palladium; three series for ATV; a series for BBC; and numerous TV specials; Wheeltappers and Shunters Social Club; Celebrity Squares; Las Vegas. m. manager Malcolm Stringer (dis), 2 s. Lee, Max. Address: c/o Johnnie Peller Enterprises, Sheffield. Starsign: Aquarius. Hobbies: housework, photography, listening to records.

CAMPBELL, Patrick
TV Panelist/ columnist/ author b. 6.6.13 Dublin. Third Baron Glanavy. Call My Bluff panellist since 1962. In Irish Marine Service 1941-44; columnist Irish Times, Sunday Dispatch and, since 1961, Sunday Times. Books incl: A Long Drink of Cold Water, Life in Thin Slices, Patrick Campbell's Omnibus, Brewing Up in the Basement, Rough Husbandry, My Life and Easy Times, 35 Years on the Job. Education: Rossall and Pembroke College, Oxford. m. (1st) Sylvia (dis); (2nd) Cherry (dis); (3rd) Mrs Vivienne Orme, 1 d. (from 2nd m). Address: Le Rouret 06, France. Starsign: Gemini. Hobbies: golf and pleasure.

CANNON, Tommy
Comedian b. 27.6.38 Oldham. The other half of the comedy partnership, Cannon and Ball. Former workmates in a Lancashire engineering factory by day and a singing

duo, The Harper Brothers, at night. Changed names to Cannon and Ball nine years ago and are now major club and theatre attractions. Voted clubland's top comedy duo 1975. Summer seasons in Bournemouth, Jersey, Cleethorpes and Great Yarmouth and pantomime in Bradford, Leeds, Stockport and Liverpool. TV incl: Wheeltappers and Shunters' Social Club; Bruce Forsyth's Big Night and their own series, Cannon and Ball. Education: Henshaw Secondary, Oldham. m. Margaret, 2 d. Janette, Julie. Address: c/o Kennedy Street Artists Ltd, Manchester. Starsign: Cancer. Hobby: golf. Unfulfilled ambition: to reach No. 1 in the TV ratings with own show.

CAPPER, David
Reporter b. 19.11.32 Belfast. Journalistic background on newspapers in Canada and Northern Ireland. In Canada for Thomson Newspapers and while there gained experience of commerical radio in Vancouver. Returned to Ireland 1956 and worked on a number of papers before joining BBC radio and TV in Northern Ireland 1961. Education: Campbell College, Belfast. m. Sandy, 1 d. Samantha, 2 s. Chris, Diarmit. Address: Bangor, Co Down. Starsign: Scorpio. Hobbies: golf and wine tasting. Unfulfilled ambition: to get my golf handicap down to below 10.

CARBY, Fanny
Actress b. 2nd February, Sutton Coldfield, Warwicks. Originally wanted to be a dancer but gave it up for acting, spent eight years with Joan Littlewood at Theatre Workshop where she was in such productions as Ned Kelly; Sparrers Can't Sing and Oh! What a Lovely War (also in Paris and New York). Also in rep at Watford and Sheffield. Other stage work incl: Look After Lulu; The Threepenny Opera; and Billy's mum in Billy. Vast amount of TV incl: Nearest and Dearest; Both Ends Meet; Who's Your Father?; three series with Spike Milligan; Angels; The Fuzz; The Cost of Loving; and many TV plays. Education: private school and ballet school. Address: Hampstead and Hertfordshire. Starsign: Aquarius. Hobbies: gardening, antiques. Unfulfilled ambition: to have an Elizabethan knot garden.

CAREY, Joyce
Actress b. 30.3.1898 London. Studied for stage under Kate Rorke at the Florence Etlinger Dramatic School. Now one of our most distinguished and experienced actresses. Stage debut with her mother (Dame Lilian Braithwaite) when she was 15, has since played Shakespearian and other parts, particularly in Noël Coward productions – Blithe Spirit; This Happy Breed; Tonight at Eight; Quadrille; South Sea Bubble and Nude With Violin. Films incl: Way to the Stars; Brief Encounter; Cry the Beloved Country; A Nice Girl Like Me. TV incl: Father, Dear Father; The Shopper; Coffee and Lace; Edward the Seventh; Barchester Towers; The Cedar Tree. Address: c/o Essanay Ltd, London W14. Starsign: Aries. Hobbies: reading and crosswords.

CARGILL, Patrick
Actor b. 3.6.18 London. After service in Indian Army, started acting career in rep at Bexhill. Returned to army during the war, then returned to rep at Buxton and Windsor.

West End Stage incl: Dear Delinquent; Boeing-Boeing (three years); Say Who You Are; Two and Two Makes Sex; Blithe Spirit; Sleuth. Wrote Ring for Catty, the West End play which became first Carry On film, Carry on Nurse. Many film appearances incl: Help; Countess from Hong Kong; Magic Christian; Every Home Should Have One; Inspector Clouseau; Father, Dear Father; The Picture Show Man. TV incl: Top Secret; Father, Dear Father; The Many Wives of Patrick. Education: Haileybury and Sandhurst. Address: East Sheen. Starsign: Gemini. Hobbies: tennis, pet animals, writing plays.

CARMICHAEL, Ian
Actor b. 18.6.20 Hull. Schoolboy ambitions were for an acting or musical career (he ran his own band during the hols). Acting won and he went to RADA. First professional tour was in the Farjeon revue, Nine Sharp, which began his training in comedy. Called up during the last week of the tour, joined the Royal Armoured Corps and then to Sandhurst and a commission in the 22nd Dragoons. Resumed his career at the end of the war in She Wanted a Cream Front Door. Other theatre work incl: The Lilac Domino; Wild Violets; Lyric Revue; Globe Revue; High Spirits; Simon and Laura (also the film); Tunnel of Love; The Gazebo; Critics' Choice.

Films incl: Private's Progress; Brothers in Law; Lucky Jim; I'm All Right Jack; Heavens Above; Happy is the Bride; The Lady Vanishes. TV incl: The Girl at the Next Table; The World of Wooster; The Importance of Being Earnest; Bachelor Father; Lord Peter Wimsey. Has also directed light entertainment shows on radio and TV. Education: Scarborough College and Bromsgrove School. m. Pym, 2 d. Lee, Sally. Address: c/o London Management Ltd, London W1. Starsign: Gemini. Hobbies: cricket, gardening and reading. Unfulfilled ambitions: to learn to relax, and to acquire peace of mind.

CARPENTER, Harry
Sports commentator b. 17.10.25 London. Former Fleet Street sports journalist. Presenter of BBC's weekly Sportsnight programme and former Grandstand linkman. Commentator at world heavyweight title fights since 1955 and every Olympic Games since 1956. Joined BBC full-time in 1962. Also presenter of Wimbledon Lawn Tennis and Open Golf Championships. Other sports he has covered incl: greyhound racing and the Oxford-Cambridge boat race. Book: Masters of Boxing. Education: Selhurst Grammar, Croydon. m. Phyllis, 1 s. Clive. Address: c/o BBC TV Centre, London W12. Starsign: Libra. Hobbies: golf, classical music. Unfulfilled ambition: to

upstage Mohammed Ali.

CARROTT, Jasper
Comedian b. 14.3.45 Birmingham. Before turning professional (1969) had a variety of jobs incl: trainee buyer in a dept. store, carpet and car seat cover salesman, window cleaner, clerk, builder's labourer, tote operator, barrow-boy, kitchen porter. Started in a club where he was host and compere, also in 1969. Became an all-round entertainer in clubs, universities and at concerts. Had own show, Folk Club (1972). TV debut in The Golden Game. Also, for BBC Midland (1975), An Audience with Jasper Carrott. Education: Acock's Green Primary; Moseley Grammar. m. Hazel, 3 d. Lucy, Jennifer, Hannah. Address: DJM Records, London WC1. Starsign: Pisces. Hobbies: football, squash, socialising with his best friends. Unfulfilled ambition: to manage the England football team.

CARSON, Frank
Comedian b. 6.11.26 Belfast.

Was a TV favourite in Ireland before coming to England to try his luck in clubland. After The Good Old Days, Opportunity Knocks, and The Comedians, he has become one of this country's leading performers who is much in demand and much televised. Other TV incl: The Melting Pot; Celebrity Squares. Education: St Patrick's Elementary, Belfast. m. Ruth, 1 d. Majella, 2 s. Tony, Aiadan. Address: Blackpool. Starsign: Scorpio. Hobbies: golf, collecting money.

CARSON, John
Actor b. 28.2.27 Colombo, Sri Lanka. After gaining a law degree at Oxford and service in the Royal Engineers, experience with the New Zealand Broadcasting Service drama dept both as actor and producer. Came to England 1955 and after some time in rep got his first break in Emergency–Ward 10. Has since had vast experience on TV and his is a familiar voice on commercials. Stage incl: A Man For All Seasons; A Day in the Death of Joe Egg (London and New York). Films incl: Capt Kronos; The Plague of the Zombies; The Man Who Haunted Himself. Recent TV incl: The Lie; Dombey and Son; Emma; Shades of Green; Raffles; The Troubleshooters; The Flaxborough Chronicles; Children of the New Forest; Send in the Girls; Secret Army; 1990; Kidnapped; The Professionals; Telford's Change; After Julius.

Education: mainly in Sri Lanka, but prep school in England, and Oxford University. m. Lvanshya Greer, 2 d. Kate, Suzanna, 4. s. Richard and Christopher (twins), Harry, Ben. Address: c/o Joy Jameson, London SW1. Starsign: Pisces. Hobbies: fishing, golf. Unfulfilled ambition: to be an artist.

CARSON, Violet OBE
Actress b. 1.9.05 Manchester. Can't remember when she actually started in showbusiness, but played piano for silent films. Also concerts, private engagements and broadcasts as singer and pianist. Introduced Northern edition of Woman's Hour for BBC and was pianist for Have a Go. Appeared in many TV plays before taking up residence in Coronation Street as Ena Sharples in 1960. Also many appearances as singer in Stars on Sunday. Education: 'Ordinary elementary – and very good too!' m. George Peploe (dec). Address: c/o Granada TV, Manchester. Starsign: Virgo. Hobby: gardening. Unfulfilled ambition: to grow old gracefully . . . eventually.

CARTER, Lynda
Actress b. 1952 Phoenix, Arizona. Miss USA in the Miss World contest 1972 and voted the most beautiful girl in the world by the International Academy of Beauty in London 1978.

Became a professional singer after leaving school and toured America. Rave reviews for her cabaret debut at Cesar's Palace, Las Vegas. Film: The New, Original Wonder Woman. Record: Portrait. TV in Britain: Wonder Woman; Up Sunday; Top of the Pops. Address: Beverly Hills, California. Hobby: music. Unfulfilled ambition: to write and sing more songs.

CARTHEW, Anthony
ITN reporter specialising in coverage of the Royal Family. b. 2.4.27 London. Started in journalism as a graduate trainee reporter on the Sheffield Telegraph. Was on the Daily Herald and the Sun before joining the Daily Mail as a foreign reporter. Also wrote for New York Times. Reporter of the Year 1965, 1968. Moved to ITN in 1971. Education: Birmingham University (BA Hons French and Italian). m. Olwen, 2 d. Rachel, Henrietta. Address: c/o ITN, London. Starsign: Aries. Hobbies: cooking, cricket. Unfulfilled ambition: to have more time to make better films.

CARTNER, Allan
Announcer b. 13.12.33
Carlisle. National Service
Officer in Royal Artillery, BBC
TV outside broadcast
cameraman 1957-61. Film
commentator and voice-over
for commercials. Senior
announcer, Border TV since
1962. Education: Carlisle
Grammar; University of
Durham (BA). m. Terri,
1 s. Kimble. Address:
Broadwath, Carlisle.
Starsign: Sagittarius.
Hobbies: wildlife
photography, sound
recording, fell-walking.
Unfulfilled ambition: to have a
daughter.

CASTLE, Roy
Entertainer/actor b. 31.8.32
Scholes, near Huddersfield.
Started in amateur concert
party. Turned pro 1953.
Stooge for Jimmy James and
Jimmy Clitheroe. Learned to
dance and can play any
musical instrument.
Breakthrough came on
Dickie Valentine Show on TV.
Other TV incl: New Look; The
Roy Castle Show; Roy Castle
Beats Time; The Record
Breakers; Show Castle;
guests spots on most variety
shows; 32 TV shows in
America. Radio incl: Castle's
on the Air. Stage incl:
Pickwick (in America). Films
incl: Dr Terror's House of
Horrors; Dr Who and the
Daleks; Carry on Up the
Khyber; The Plank; The
Intrepid Mr Twigg.
Education: Scholes Council
School; Honley Grammar
School. m. Fiona, 2 d. Julia,
Antonia, 2 s. Daniel,
Benjamin. Address: c/o
London Management.
Starsign: Virgo. Hobbies:
gardening, squash, golf,
charity cricket, sleep.
Unfulfilled ambition: to get a
pension.

CAUNTER, Tony
Actor b. 22.9.37
Southampton. Formerly a
regular in the Royal Air Force.
Trained at LAMDA. Stage
incl: Chips With Everything
(London and New York).
Films incl: The Hill; Ipcress
File; Cromwell; SOS Titanic.
TV incl: Stockers Copper;
Hunchback of Notre Dame;
Pennies From Heaven;
Sporting Club Dinner; Willy;
Beryl's Lot; The Sweeney; The
Professionals; The Vanishing
Army; Waterloo Sunset;
Rumpole of the Bailey.
Education: Worthing High;
Westcliff High School.
m. schoolteacher Frances,
1 d. Sarah, 3 s. Nicholas,
William and James (twins).
Address: c/o CCA, London
SW6. Starsign: Virgo.
Hobbies: watching old
movies, reading biographies,
making home movies,
cruising on the inland
waterways of Great Britain.
Unfulfilled ambition: to fly in a
Spitfire or Lancaster
(preferably both).

CAZENOVE, Christopher
Actor b. 17.12.45
Winchester. Always wanted
to be a film star, though his
father wanted him to be an
officer in the Coldstream
Guards. Ironically, it was his
role in The Regiment on TV
that made his name. Trained
at Bristol Old Vic Theatre
School and rep in Leicester,
Leatherhead, Windsor and
Pitlochry before arriving in
London's West End. Stage
incl: Darling Daisy; The Lionel
Touch; The Winslow Boy;
Joking Apart. Films incl: East
of Elephant Rock; The Girl in
Blue Velvet; Zulu Dawn. In
addition to The Regiment, TV
incl: The Freewheelers;
Rivals of Sherlock Holmes;
The British Hero; Affairs of the
Heart; Jennie, Lady
Randolph Churchill; The
Duchess of Duke Street; East
Lynne. Education: Eton.
m. actress Angharad Rees,
2 s. Linford, Rhys William.
Address: c/o Chatto and
Linnit, London W1. Starsign:
Sagittarius. Unfulfilled
ambitions: 'Too many to
name.'

CHALMERS, Judith
Presenter b. 10th October, Manchester. Always wanted to be a broadcaster and asked BBC Manchester for an audition when she was 13. Started on Northern Children's Hour, had her own radio programme at 17; first TV appearance was Northern TV announcer. Now one of TV's busiest women, introducing After Noon Plus and Wish You Were Here. Radio incl: regularly chairing Radio 4's Tuesday Call phone-in. Also commentates on special events for BBC radio OB's, incl: Grand National; Derby; Ascot and Royal occasions (Princess Anne's wedding; Silver Jubilee; State Opening of Parliament). Education: Withington Girls', Manchester; Miss Wilkinson's Secretarial School. m. commentator Neil Durden-Smith, 1 d. Emma, 1 s. Mark. Address: c/o Thames TV, London. Starsign: Libra. Hobbies: photography, cooking, gardening, watching cricket. Unfulfilled ambitions: to be a successful pianist and a top-notch tap dancer.

CHAMBERLAIN, Richard
Actor b. 31.3.35 Los Angeles. Was studying dancing when he was offered the lead part in Dr Kildare, which made him famous. Other TV incl: Gunsmoke, Portrait of a Lady; The Woman I Love; Centennial. Stage in England: Hamlet (Birmingham rep and on TV);

Chichester Festival. Films incl: Julius Caesar; The Lonely Heart; The Mad Woman of Chaillot; The Music Lovers; Lady Caroline Lamb; The Count of Monte Cristo; The Slipper and the Rose; The Man in the Iron Mask; The Last Wave; Jack the Ripper. Education: Vista Grammar School and High School, Beverly Hills; Pamona College, Claremont, Calif. Address: c/o ICM Ltd, London W1. Starsign: Aries. Hobby: painting. Unfulfilled ambition: to sing and dance in a big film musical.

CHAMBERS, Julia
Actress b. 27.2.56 Bristol. Trained at Bristol Old Vic Theatre School and was with the Contact Theatre before going into TV incl: Rogue Male; Silver Blaze; Jackanory Playhouse (Big Little Pete); Going to Work; Accident; Sally Ann; The Mallens. Education: Brislington Comprehensive, Bristol; Warblington Comprehensive (Hants); Chichester College of Further Education. Address: c/o Carol James Management, Richmond, Surrey. Starsign: Pisces.

Hobbies: swimming, horse riding, knitting the family clothes during rehearsals. Unfulfilled ambition: 'on the way to fulfilling my ambition as an actress.'

CHAMPNEY, Clive
Announcer/newsreader b. 12.4.29 Wokingham, Berks. Entered broadcasting in Australia 1949. Since 1960 has produced language laboratory tapes; made talking books for the blind (1961-72); was Carlisle Historical Pageant narrator; and has written and presented (with wife) daily radio serial for children (1975-76). Also actor/reader BBC plays; Woman's Hour. Annnouncer/newsreader with Border TV since 1963. Education: Ranelagh School, Berks. m. Jo, 1 d. Julia, 5 s. Gerard, Jonothan, Adrian, Matthew, Edmund. Address: Warwick on Eden, Carlisle, Cumbria. Starsign: Aries. Hobbies: music, crosswords. Unfulfilled ambitions: 'Several – but nothing important.'

CHARLES, Maria
Actress b. 22nd September,

London. Trained at RADA, she was one of the stars of the original play The Boy Friend. Wide stage experience incl: The Matchmaker; Annie. TV incl: Within These Walls; Six Days of Justice; Seven Faces of Woman; Fast Hands; She; The Secret Army; Barmitzvah Boy; Agony. Education: Grammar School. m. Robin Hunter (dis), 2 d. Samantha, Kelly. Address: c/o Barry Brown Management, London SE11. Starsign: Virgo. Hobby: crashing her car. Unfulfilled ambitions: too numerous to mention.

CHARLTON, Jack
TV football commentator/manager Sheffield Wednesday FC. b. 8.5.36 Ashington, Northumberland. Started playing with Leeds United as an amateur 1950; joined them as a professional two years later. England International player, being capped 35 times 1965-70 and a member of the World Cup winning team 1966. Manager of Middlesbrough FC 1974; joined Sheffield Wednesday FC in same capacity 1977. Football commentator on TV since 1974 World Cup. Education: Hirst Park Modern School, Ashington. m. Patricia. 1 d. Debra, 2 s. John, Peter. Address: Worsborough, Barnsley. Starsign: Taurus. Hobbies: shooting, fishing, gardening.

CHARLTON, Michael
Presenter/commentator b. 1.5.27 Sydney, Australia. Started his broadcasting career 1942 in commercial radio in Perth and Melbourne and subsequently with the Australian Broadcasting Commission, establishing himself as one of Australia's best-known cricket commentators. Was the first face to be seen on Australian TV when it started in 1956. Came to England 1956 to join BBC's Panorama team and has been here ever since. One of his first reporting assignments was President Kennedy's assassination. Books incl: Many Reasons Why, the story of American involvement in Vietnam. Education: Scotch College, Perth, W Australia; University of Perth, W Australia. m. Isabelle, 1 d. Anne, 2 s. Timothy, Jeremy. Address: c/o BBC TV, London W12. Starsign: Taurus. Hobbies: carpentry and joinery, golf.

CHARLWOOD, Veronica
TV journalist b. 2.2.42 Croydon, Surrey. 12 years with ITN as secretary/

production assistant/film organiser/researcher. Documentary researcher Southern TV, then journalist on Day By Day; Southern Report; People Rule. Education: Croydon High School for Girls. m. Lionel Charlwood. Address: Bishops Waltham, Hants. Starsign: Aquarius. Hobbies: dog showing, tennis. Unfulfilled ambitions: to be a TV war correspondent and to be thin.

CHASE, Lorraine
Actress b. 16.7.51 South London. Former model who became better known as the girl in the Campari commercials. TV appearances in Max Bygraves Show, Celebrity Squares, Blankety-Blank. Also in film Love and Bullets. Address: c/o Peter Charlesworth Ltd, London SW7. Starsign: Cancer.

CHASEN, Heather
Actress b. 20.7.27 Singapore. Trained at RADA, then rep, touring and provincial and West End theatres. First London stage appearance in Blood

Wedding 1954.
Broadcasting in the Navy
Lark since 1959. TV incl: The
Newcomers; Danger Man;
Call My Bluff; General
Hospital; Marked Personal;
Waste; Traveller in Time.
Education: Princess Helena
College. m. John Webster,
1 s. Rupert. Address: c/o
Richard Jackson, Personal
Management, London SW1.
Starsign: Cancer. Hobbies:
collecting junk and sending
postcards. Unfulfilled
ambition: to afford to be
selective.

CHEGWIN, Keith
Presenter b. 17.1.57
Liverpool. Attended a
London stage school for six
years, but from the age of 11
sang in working men's clubs
in the north as a member of a
family trio. Stage shows incl:
The Good Old Bad Old Days;
Tom Brown's Schooldays.
Films: Polanski's Macbeth;
and, for the Children's Film
Foundation, Eggheads
Robot; Elspeth's Double;
Robin Hood Junior. TV incl:
Swapshop; Cheggers Plays
Pop; Ronnie Barker Show;
Liver Birds; The Chester
Mystery Plays; Wackers; My
Old Man; Black Beauty;
Armchair Theatre; Village
Hall; Celebrity Squares; It's a
Knockout; Star Turn; All Star
Record Breakers. Radio:
presents a regular Sunday
morning show on Radio
Liverpool and contributes to
Radio 1. Used to sing with the
Kenny pop group. Address:
Rainford, St Helens, Lancs.
Starsign: Capricorn.

Hobbies: horse riding,
reading, skating, playing
guitar and piano. Unfulfilled
ambition: to compere a Miss
World contest.

CLARK, Ernest
Actor b. 12.2.12 London.
Always wanted to be an actor
but was first a reporter in
Croydon. When offered a job
at the local rep he jumped at
the chance. Acting has been
his career ever since; except
for six years in the army. First
stage appearance at Festival
Theatre, Cambridge.
Appeared in many plays in
London and New York, but
best known as Professor
Loftus in the Doctor TV series.
Also in Gilbert and Sullivan
serial; All Gas and Gaiters.
President of Equity
1969/1973. Education: St
Marylebone Grammar.
m (1st) actress Avril Hillyer,
(2nd) actress Julia
Lockwood, 1 d. Lucinda (by
2nd m), 3 s. Andrew (by
1st m), Timothy, Nicholas (by
2nd m). Address: Barnes.
Starsign: Aquarius. Hobby:
his family. Unfulfilled
ambition: to be a good and
successful actor.

CLARK, Paul
Presenter b. 4.12.54 Belfast.
Newspaper experience and
reporting on Ulster situation
for BBC. TV incl: a series of
programmes on Irish history,
reporting on the situation in
Northern Ireland and special
programmes and reports
from Australia in 1978.
Education: St Mary's, Belfast

and Belfast College of
Business Studies. Address:
Dunmurry, Co Antrim, N.
Ireland. Starsign: Sagittarius.
Hobbies: squash, tennis,
model railways, Irish history.
Unfulfilled ambitions: there
are many.

CLARK, Peter
Journalist/newscaster
b. 8.7.37 Nottingham.
Newspaper experience with
Nottingham Evening Post
and in Fleet Street. Created
and presented awardwinning
documentary, Take It From
Us. Lectures to national
police college students.
Education: Nottingham.
m. Valerie, 2 s. Jeremy,
Nicholas. Address: Hedge
End, Southampton. Starsign:
Cancer. Hobbies: soccer
(former vice-chairman of
Portsmouth), relaxing at
home, writing, thinking.
Unfulfilled ambition: to build,
as editor, a successful
current affairs programme.

CLARK, Petula
Singer/Actress b. 15.11.32 Epsom. Began career when seven years old and in radio when she was nine, incl: It's All Yours and Pet's Parlour. Entered films when 12 in Medal for the General; other films incl: London Town; Vice Versa: the Huggett films; Made in Heaven; The Card; Finian's Rainbow; Goodbye Mr Chips; First record when 17. Starred in stage, cabaret and TV shows all over Europe and America. Education: Moor Lane, St Bernard and Romanoff schools. m. Claude Wolff, 2 d. Barbara, Catherine, 1 s. Patrick. Address: c/o BBC, Wood Lane, London W12. Starsign: Scorpio. Hobbies: skiing, swimming, guitar, antiques. Unfulfilled ambition: to appear in an original stage musical.

CLEESE, John
Actor/writer b. 27.10.39 Weston-super-Mare. Started in the Cambridge Footlights Revue. Went to America with it and stayed on to play in Half a Sixpence. Returned to make Frost Report; I'm Sorry, I'll Read That Again; At Last the 1948 Show; Monty Python's Flying Circus; Fawlty Towers, for which he won TVTimes Award as Funniest Man on TV (1978-79). Education: Clifton; Cambridge (studying Law). Was married to actress Connie Booth, 1 d. Cynthia. Address: c/o Roger Hancock Ltd, London SW1. Starsign: Scorpio. Hobby: filling in questionnaires. Unfulfilled ambition: to have a baby.

CLIVE, John
Actor/author b. 6.1.38 London. Started as a child actor: Casey's Court; The Winslow Boy; Young Woodley; Life With Father; until National Service in Royal Air Force. Then rep and London for revue at the Poor Millionaire. Other stage work incl: Absurb Person Singular; The Real Inspector Hound (for the Young Vic); Wizard of Oz. Films incl: Smashing Time; The Italian Job; Yellow Submarine (Lennon's voice); Clockwork Orange; Carry on Abroad; Great Expectations. TV incl: Perils of Pendragon; Robert's Robots; How Green Was My Valley; The Government Inspector; The Dick Emery Show; Tropic. Books: first novel, KG 200 (international best-seller); The Last Liberator. Education: London; Wales; Liverpool. m. Carole, 1 d. Hannah, 1 s. Alexander. Address: c/o CCA, London SW6. Starsign: Capricorn. Hobbies: football, boxing, films, Second World War aircraft. Unfulfilled ambitions: to have appeared with Errol Flynn in Robin Hood, to age as creatively as Walter Matthau.

CLYDE, Jeremy
Actor b. 22.3.41 Dorney, Bucks. Trained at Central School of Speech and Drama. Part of partnership, Chad and Jeremy, with several hits in the Sixties before big acting break on stage in Conduct Unbecoming. TV incl: The Pallisers; The Darkwater Hall; Mystery; Strife; How Green Was My Valley; The Marrying Kind; Sexton Blake and the Demon God; Disraeli. Films incl: The Silver Bears; Esther, Ruth and Jennifer. Education: Ludgrove and Eton. m. Vanessa, 1 d. Lucy, 2 s. James, Matthew. Address: c/o Joy Jameson, London SW1. Starsign: Aries.

COFFEY, Denise
Actress/writer/ director b. 12.12.36 Aldershot, Hants. Trained at Royal Scottish Academy of Music and College of Drama, Glasgow. Rep and variety in Edinburgh and interviewing for BBC

radio before London West End appearances which incl: High Spirits; The Beggar's Opera; Let's Get a Divorce, and numerous productions at the Mermaid Theatre. With the Young Vic Company in various capacities 1970-78. Many TV appearances, notably in Stanley Baxter Shows; Do Not Adjust Your Set; Girls About Town and End of Part One. Education: mainly Scottish. Address: c/o Beryl Seton Agency, London WC2. Starsign: Sagittarius. Hobbies: picnics, the sea. Unfulfilled ambition: to direct in film and television.

COLE, George
Actor b. 22.4.25 London. Discovered in 1940 by Alastair Sim to play a Cockney evacuee in the West End play, Cottage to Let, and became a star overnight; also appeared in the film version. After three years' service in the RAF he was in such films as My Brother's Keeper; Quartet; Morning Departure; Lady Godiva Rides Again; Laughter in Paradise. Other films incl: Top Secret; Will Any Gentleman; The Belles of St Trinians; The Green Man; Blue Murder at St Trinians; The Great St Trinians Train Robbery; One Way Pendulum. Stage incl: Flare Path; Mr Bolfy; Dr Angelus; The Anatomist; Too True to be Good; The Three Sisters; The Philanthropist; Banana Ridge; Deja Revue; Brimstone and Treacle. On radio he was a household name in a Life of Bliss, for 15 years; more recently, Don't Forget to Write. On TV he had another success in A Man Of OurTimes. Other TV incl: Out of the Unknown; The Gold Robbers; Sex Game; Murder; The Good Humoured Man and many plays. Education: Morden Council Secondary. m. former actress Penny Morrell, 1 d. Tara, 1 s. Toby. Address: c/o Joy Jameson Ltd, London SW1. Starsign: Taurus.

COLE, Julie Dawn
Actress b. 26.10.57 Guildford, Surrey. Acting experience while still at school. Debut in Peter Pan 1969, then Willy Wonka and the Chocolate Factory; And Mother Makes Three; The Intruders. Stage incl: The Wizard of Oz; Charley's Aunt; City Sugar; Love's Labour's Lost. Films incl: That Lucky Touch. Radio incl: Westward Ho. TV incl: Angels; Poldark; The Many Wives of Patrick; Within These Walls; People Like Us; Emmerdale Farm; The Mill on the Floss; Company and Co; Dick Turpin; In the Confessional; My Old Man; Bernie. Education: Bushy Park Primary; Italia Conti Stage School; Barbara Speak School of Acting. Address: c/o CCA, London SW6. Starsign: Scorpio. Hobbies: riding, dress designing and doing anything I've never done before. Unfulfilled ambition: to make a free fall parachute jump.

COLEMAN, David
Reporter/interviewer b. 26.4.26 Alderley Edge, Cheshire. Started as newspaper journalist, Editor of Cheshire County Express at 23. Freelance radio contributor before joining BBC in Birmingham and later in London. TV incl: Match of the Day; Grandstand; Sportsnight with Coleman. m. Barbara, 3 d. Anne, Mandy, Samantha, 3 s. David and Dean (twins), Michael. Address: c/o Bagenal Harvey, London EC1. Starsign: Taurus. Hobby: golf.

COLERIDGE, Kate
Actress b. 22.9.43 Inverness, Scotland. Trained at RADA then rep incl: Farnham, Chesterfield, Leicester. Also worked for Mermaid Theatre, Young Vic and National Theatre, Prospect Company and Ludlow Festival. Much radio incl: Book at Bedtime, and TV incl: Oil Strike North; Upstairs, Downstairs; Blake's Seven; The Cedar Tree; Heartland; The Dancing Years; Armchair Thriller – Dying Day. Education: Pax Hill, Bentley, Hants, and self taught. m. writer/ stunt

co-ordinator Frank Maher.
Address: c/o Roger Carey,
London WC2. Starsign: Virgo
and Libra cusp. Hobby:
having Sunday lunch and
witty conversation with my
friends in a good restaurant
from 2 till 7. Unfulfilled
ambition: to have Saturday as
well as Sunday lunch with my
friends.

COLLINGS, David
Actor b. 4.6.40 Brighton.
Started as a sculptor but after
appearing in a few small
stage productions was
offered a job by Liverpool
Repertory Company and his
acting career took off. Has
since appeared in many
plays on stage and TV. Also
rep at Chichester, Oxford,
Edinburgh. His work at
Liverpool led to the lead in
Crime and Punishment on TV.
Other TV incl: The Fall of the
Sparrow; Moving On; The
Mind of Mr J G Reeder;
Elizabeth R; The Regiment;
Point Counter Point; Sinister
Street; Midnight is a Place.
Education: grammar school.
m. Diedre (dis), 1 d. Kate,
1 step-d., 1 s. Matthew
(dec). Address: c/o Essanay
Ltd, London W14. Starsign:
Gemini.

COLLINS, John D.
Actor b. 2.12.42 London.
Trained at RADA. TV incl: Get
Some In; Secret Army; Flesh
and Blood; Bernie Winters
Show and Spike Milligan's Q7
and Q8. Education: Harrow
School. m. Caryll Newnham.
Address: Wimbledon,
London SW19. Starsign:

Sagittarius. Hobbies: music,
chess. Unfulfilled ambition: to
play the Ravel Concerto For
The Left Hand with both
hands.

COLLINS, Lewis
Actor b. 26.5.46 Birkenhead.
Started as a ladies'
hairdresser, then played
drums and guitar in pop
groups and had a number of
jobs before deciding to
become an actor. Trained at
the London Academy of
Music and Dramatic Art
followed by rep at
Chesterfield and Glasgow,
touring with Prospect Theatre
Company and London's
West End. Also tours in
America and Canada. Stage
incl: City Sugar; The
Threepenny Opera. TV incl:
Warship; Z Cars; Rooms;
Marked Personal; The New
Avengers; The Cuckoo
Waltz; The Professionals;
Must Wear Tights. Expert rifle
and pistol shot and driver of
fast cars and motor-cycles;
trained in judo and karate.
Education: Bidston Primary
and Grange School,
Birkenhead. Address: lives in
a converted, still mobile,
ambulance. Starsign:

Gemini. Hobbies: squash,
tennis, weight training,
swimming, target shooting,
motor-cycling, judo, writing
stories and songs, reading,
cooking, playing musical
instruments and driving very
fast at night down country
lanes. Unfulfilled ambitions:
to have a happy wife and
family, to gain recognition as
a versatile actor.

COLLINS, Pauline
Actress b. 3.9.40 Exmouth,
Devon. Trained at Central
School of Speech and Drama
before making her
professional debut at Theatre
Royal, Windsor, 1962. Other
stage incl: Passion Flower
Hotel; The Happy Apple; The
Importance of Being Earnest;
The Night I Chased the
Women With an Eel; Come As
You Are; Judies; Engaged;
Confusions. Many plays and
TV series, TV incl: Upstairs,
Downstairs; No, Honestly,
Thomas and Sarah. Voted
TVTimes Most Compulsive
TV Character 1978-79.
Education: Convent of the
Sacred Heart, Hammersmith,
London. m. actor John
Alderton, 1 d. Catherine,
2 s. Nicholas, Richard.
Address: c/o Nems
Management, London SW3.
Starsign: Virgo. Hobbies:
writing, armchair travel with
the atlas. Unfulfilled ambition:
to sail round the world.

CONRAD, Robert
Actor b. 1.3.35 Chicago.
Started as a singer and still
has a night club act. Had jobs
as deck-hand and milkman,
but always wanted to be an
actor. After small parts, he
was given more substantial
roles in Lawman; Maverick;
77 Sunset Strip; and a star
part in Hawaiian Eye. Other
TV incl: Wild, Wild West;
Centennial. Education:
public schools, and
Northwestern University in
Chicago where he studied
drama. m. Joan, 2 d. Joan,
Nancy. Address: Hollywood.
Starsign: Pisces. Hobbies:
boxing, music, Spanish ballet
and studying Spanish.

CONTI, Tom
Actor b. 1942 Glasgow.
Originally hoped to be a
classical pianist, but became
an actor after studing drama
at the Glasgow College of
Drama, followed by rep in
Glasgow and Edinburgh.
Stage incl: Savages; Let's
Murder Vivaldi; Don Juan;
Devil's Disciple; Whose Life
Is It Anyway? (also in America
where he won the Broadway
Tony award for best actor).
Films incl: The Duellists; Full

Circle; Eclipse; Galileo;
Flame. TV incl: Adam Smith;
The Glittering Prizes;
Madame Bovary; The
Norman Conquests.
m. actress Kara Wilson,
1 d. Nina. Address: c/o
Chatto and Linnit, London
W1.

COOK, Tony
TV Journalist b. 6.9.45
Ashton-under-Lyne, Lancs.
Experience in newspaper
journalism, radio and TV
reporting before becoming
youngest-ever BBC news
editor, youngest BBC
producer and 'oldest-feeling'
ITV reporter/ presenter.
Presenter of Tyne Tees TV
documentaries and
interviewer on political
programmes, regular
presenter Northern Life and
Where the Jobs Are.
Education: 'Very little.'
m. Lynne, 1 d. Emily-Jo,
1 s. Edward. Address:
Haydon Bridge,
Northumberland. Starsign:
Virgo. Hobbies: cooking,
parapsychology, talking,
politics, finding good beer.
Fulfilled ambition: to appear
in Who's Who on Television.

COOKE, Peter
Actor/writer b. 13.11.37
Torquay. Started career while
at Cambridge University in
Footlights Revues. Wrote and
starred in Beyond the Fringe
in Edinburgh, London and
New York. Started The
Establishment Club 1961.
Other theatre incl: Behind the
Fringe. Films incl: The Wrong
Box; Bedazzled; Derek and

Clive (Live); The Hound of the
Baskervilles. TV incl: many
guest appearances; Tonight;
Juke Box Jury; Line Up; On
the Braden Beat; Not Only . . .
But Also; Revolver. Records:
Once more with Cook; Derek
and Clive (Live); Derek and
Clive Come Again.
Education: Radley School.
m. (1st) Wendy (dis),
(2nd) actress Judy Huxtable,
2 d. Lucy, Daisy (by 1st m).
Address: c/o CCA, London
SW6. Starsign: Scorpio.

COOMBS, Pat
Actress b. 27.8.30
Camberwell, London. First
job was teaching at a
kindergarten. Scholarship to
LAMDA and after training
stayed on to teach. Then rep
at Scunthorpe and with
companies all over England.
First came to fore as Nola
(with Irene Handl in Hello
Playmates on radio). In
constant demand for TV
series – Lollipop Loves Mr
Mole; Beggar My Neighbour
and other Reg Varney shows;
Dick Emery's series; Don't
Drink the Water; Celebrity
Squares; third series of
You're Only Young Twice.
Recent films: Oooh . . . You

Are Awful; Adolph Hitler – My Part In His Downfall. Education: County School for Girls, Beckenham, Kent. Address: Harrow-on-the-Hill, Middlesex. Starsign: Virgo. Hobbies: writing letters, driving, reading, puss-cats! Unfulfilled ambition: 'To play electronic organ properly! To say nothing of wishing I had learned to play the piano.'

COOPER, Del
Reporter/presenter
b. 20th September, Essex. Journalistic training in Fleet Street on daily and Sunday papers and was magazine editor. TV incl: Westward Diary; The Chasing Game; Challenge; The Great Clipper Race; The Loneliness of the Long Distance Sailor, etc; Single-handed trans-Atlantic Race 1976; Catch 1976 series. Education: Wanstead School; University of Nottingham. m. Ann, 2 d. Vanessa, Samantha, 1 s. Ashley. Address: Millbrook, Nr Torpoint, Cornwall. Starsign: Virgo. Hobbies: sailing, golf, horse-racing. Unfulfilled ambitions: to play scratch golf, to breed a Gold Cup winner and to produce a feature film.

COOPER, Tommy
Comedian b. 19.3.22 Caerphilly. Childhood spent in Exeter and Southampton where he joined the army, serving in the Horse Guards for seven years. Became an entertainer on leaving the army 1947. Cabaret, music

hall, revue, TV, Windmill Theatre London, summer seasons, pantomime, own shows, appearances before royalty, visits to USA – he's done them all and is now one of the country's highest paid entertainers. Specialises in tricks that go wrong, but in fact is a fine straight magician and a member of the Inner Magic Circle. His TV shows have been screened abroad, e.g. Europe and Australia. He is extremely popular in those countries as a result. Education: Mount Radford School, Exeter. m. Gwen, 1 d. Vicky, 1 s. Thomas. Address: c/o Miff Ferrie, London SW1. Starsign: Pisces. Hobbies: boxing, judo, swimming, show business and magic. Unfulfilled ambition: to participate in a really first class film.

COPLEY, Paul
Actor b. 25.11.44 Denby Dale, Yorks. Many jobs before becoming an actor and Yorkshire TV presenter – clerk, lorry driver, despatch manager, student, secondary school teacher. Stage incl: For King and

Country; German Skerries; Sisters; Whose Life is it Anyway? Films incl: Alfie Darling; A Bridge Too Far; Zulu Dawn. Considerable TV in plays and series incl: Cries From a Watchtower; After Julius; Christmas Carol; Treasure Island; Dear Harriet; Secret Army; Strangers; Glad Day; Travellers; Mucking Out; The Turkey Who Lives on the Hill; Days of Hope; Trinity Tales; Some Enchanted Evening; Stepping Stones. Education: Northern Counties College of Education. m. actress Natasha Pyne. Address: c/o Kate Feast Management, London NW1. Starsign: Sagittarius. Hobbies: motor-cycling, swimming. Unfulfilled ambition: to direct a film.

COPLEY, Peter
Actor b. 20.5.15 Bushey, Herts. Wanted to go into the Royal Navy when he left school, but became interested in the theatre through his housemaster. Trained at the Old Vic School and later joined the Old Vic Company. Rep at Bexhill, Leeds and Dublin before London. First appearance was as a footman in Viceroy Sarah 1935; many plays since return to the Old Vic 1945-50; National Theatre. Films incl: Jane Eyre; Troopship; King and Country. TV incl: The Gold Robbers; Hadleigh; Big Brother; Forsyte Saga; Paul Temple; The Regiment; Manhunt; Father Brown; Survivors;

Sutherland's Law; Bill Brand; The New Avengers; You're Only Young Twice; Bless This House; The Foundation; Anna Karenina; Churchill and the Generals. Education: Westminster.
m. (1st) actress Pamela Brown, (2nd) actress Ninka, (3rd) writer Margaret Tabor. 2 d. Fanny, Emma (step-d), 1 s. Gideon (step-s). Address: c/o St James Management, London SW1. Starsign: Taurus. Hobby: reading law (called to the Bar at Middle Temple 1973).

CORBETT, Harry OBE
Entertainer b. 28.1.18 Bradford, Yorks.
Apprenticed in electric motor manufacture and spent five years as an engineer surveyor. Part-time amateur magician and pianist, before becoming full-time entertainer 1952. Created Sooty 1949 from a teddy bear bought while on holiday in Blackpool. Sooty TV shows, first on BBC then ITV, TV's longest running children's programme. Associate Member of the Institution of Electrical Engineers, Life Governor of the National Children's Home, Member of the International Brotherhood of Magicians. Education: high school to age of 16.
m. Marjorie, 2 s. David, Peter (Matthew). Address: Child Okeford, Dorset. Starsign: Aquarius. Hobbies: woodwork, pianoforte, making theatrical props.

CORBETT, Matthew
Entertainer b. 28.3.48 Yorkshire. Trained as an actor at Central School of Speech and Drama, and in rep at Bristol, York, Chelmsford, Dundee and Richmond. TV incl: Magpie; Rainbow; Matt and Gerry Ltd; and The Sooty Show which he took over following his father's (Harry) heart attack. Education: Woodhouse Grove Public School, Bradford, Yorks. m. Sallie, 1 d. Tamsin, 2 s. Benjamin, Joe. Address: c/o Vincent Shaw Associates, London W1. Starsign: Aries. Hobbies: music (writing and recording), photography, squash, poultry keeping. Unfulfilled ambitions: to get The Sooty Show on major foreign TV, to play the London Palladium, to launch another children's TV show separate from Sooty.

CORBETT, Ronnie OBE
Actor/comedian b. 4.12.30 Edinburgh. Started amateur dramatics at 16. Many TV shows incl: Crackerjack; Dickie Henderson Show. Spotted in Danny La Rue's nightclub by David Frost, then Frost Report; No – That's Me Over Here; Frost on Sunday; The Corbett Follies and The Two Ronnies.
m. Anne Hart, 2 d. Emma, Sophie. Address: c/o Kavanagh Entertainments, London W1. Starsign: Sagittarius. Hobbies: football, golf, horse-racing.

CORNWELL, Judy
Actress b. 22.2.42 London. Trained as a dancer and singer, was initially a student dancing teacher. Untrained as an actress except for a period of coaching by Sybil Wise. First stage appearance in pantomime at Brighton when 15; London debut in Oh, What a Lovely War! Stage also incl: Mr Whatnot; Don't Let Summer Come; Old Flames and 1972 season with RSC at Stratford. Films incl: Every Home Should Have One; Wuthering Heights. TV incl: Younger Generation series; Feydeau farces; Call Me Daddy (Emmy Award 1967); Relatively Speaking; Cork Moustache; Man of Straw; The Chinese Prime Minister; Night of the Tanks; Moody and Peg; London Assurance; Cranford (musical); Bonos; Mill on the Floss; Good Companions; Brothers Grimm (Omnibus); A Case of Spirits. Also children's programmes, story reading, panel games, plays and light entertainment shows. Education: Inglethorpe Prep, Norfolk; Convent of Mercy, Australia; and Lewes Grammar for Girls, Sussex. m. John Parry,

1 s. Edward. Address: c/o Larry Dalzell, London WC2. Starsign: Pisces. Hobbies: writing, cooking, community involvement, psychology, gardening. Unfulfilled ambitions: to have a book pubished and make a Western film.

COWAN, Barry
Presenter/interviewer
b. 1.2.48 Coleraine, N. Ireland. All forms of freelance writing and broadcasting for Radio Telefis Eiran; CBC; British Forces Broadcasting Service and BBC in Belfast where he is a presenter and interviewer on Nationwide. Education: Ballymena Academy; Queen's University, Belfast. Address: c/o BBC, Belfast. Starsign: Aquarius. Hobbies: show-jumping, flying, playing with all kinds of toys. Unfulfilled ambitions: to write a best-selling novel, ride for the Irish national show-jumping team and live to a ripe old age.

COWIE, Alan
Reporter/presenter
b. 28.4.48 Aberdeen.
Trained at Central School of Speech and Drama; Jordanhill College of Education; BBC and Grampian TV. Presented 12 Noon and Northbeat 1972-75 on Radio 4 Scotland. Presenter/ reporter Grampian TV since 1975, also commentator for Grampian documentaries Blowout at Bravo, and Cinderella from the Sea. Education: Aberdeen Grammar School. m. Evelyn, 1 d. Fiona. Address: Newburgh, Aberdeenshire. Starsign: Taurus. Hobbies: gardening, fishing. Unfulfilled ambition: to interview Gordon Williams.

COWING, Ronnie
Journalist b. 1.5.52 Carlisle. Worked with freelance news agencies before joining Border TV. Education: Caldecote Primary and Carlisle Grammar. m. Anne, 1 d. Sarah, 1 s. Paul. Address: Upperby, Carlisle. Starsign: Taurus. Hobbies: music, snooker, football, cinema, pantomime. Unfulfilled ambitions: to appear as the Straw Man in The Wizard of Oz; to win the world heavyweight boxing championship.

COWPER, Gerry
Actress b. 23.6.58 London. Stage school for five years. TV incl: Forget-Me-Not Lane; Do As I Say; Double Echo; Country Party; Eustace and Hilda; Two People; Telford's Change. Address: c/o Roger Carey, London WC2. Starsign: Cancer. Hobbies:

bargain hunting, collecting old movie books and pictures, playing swingball. Unfulfilled ambitions: to work in America and to be able to fill in forms neatly and correctly.

COYNE, Tom
Presenter/interviewer
b. 15.4.35 South Shields. Started out as an engineer, but became a professional actor with rep companies at Newcastle, South Shields and Worcester. Was in The Archers on radio before joining Tyne Tees TV as compere/ interviewer, appearing on the station's first programme, January 1959. Switched to BBC Midlands 1964. More than 20 years in television and always associated with a daily programme that does not have a summer break. Also has his own production company which is largely concerned with the making of TV commercials. TV incl: North East Roundabout; Top Gear; Midlands Today; Nationwide. Education: Corby Hall, Sunderland. m. Patricia, 1 d. Elizabeth, 1 s. Michael. Address: c/o

BBC, Pebble Mill, Birmingham. Starsign: Aries. Hobby: writing. Unfulfilled ambition: to win the pools.

CRABTREE, Shirley
See Big Daddy.

CRAIG, Andy
Announcer b. 5.12.54 Cumbria. Always wanted to work in some branch of entertainment and began as freelance in commercial radio. Joined Metro Radio 1977 and Tyne Tees TV 1978. Recently cut his first disc, Bad Dream. Education: The Grammar School for Boys, Barrow in Furness and Newcastle University (Hons degree in Agriculture). Address: c/o Tyne Tees TV, Newcastle-upon-Tyne. Starsign: Sagittarius. Hobbies: music, art, motor vehicles. Unfulfilled ambition: to present a live chat/feature programme.

CRAIG, Michael
Actor b. 27.1.29 Poona, India. Served in the Merchant Navy 1944-49 when he started acting at the Castle Theatre, Farnham. Rep at York, Windsor and Oxford

when he was given a film contract with the Rank Organisation 1954-61. Appeared in 42 films incl: Passage Home; House of Secrets; Yield to the Night; The Angry Silence (also the writer); Doctor in Love; Life at the Top; Star!; The Royal Hunt of the Sun; The Virgin and the Gypsy. Stage incl: season at Stratford 1963-64; A Whistle in the Dark; Funny Girl; The Homecoming (in New York). On TV has appeared in 48 plays and series, incl: Tiger Trap (also the writer); The Talking Head; Husbands and Lovers; Second Time Around; Saint Joan; The Foundation; The Danedyke Mystery. Educated in Canada. m. Susan, 1 d. Jessica, 2 s. Stephen, Michael. Address: c/o ICM, London W1. Starsign: Aquarius. Hobbies: sport, golf, snooker, reading. Ambition: continued survival.

CRAIG, Wendy
Actress b. 20.6.34 Sacriston, Co. Durham. Won first acting award at the age of three. Later trained at London's Central School of Dramatic Art before going to Ispwich Rep. Chosen by J B Priestley for the role of Monica Twigg in Mr Kettle and Mrs Moon. Leading stage appearances since, incl: George Dillon; The Sport of My Mad Mother; Ride A Cock Horse; I Love You Mrs Patterson; Peter Pan. Films incl: Room at the Top; The Mindbenders; The Nanny; I'll Never Forget

What's His Name; Joseph Andrews; The Servant. TV incl: Candida; Wings of a Dove; Not in Front of the Children; And Mother Makes Three; And Mother Makes Five; Butterflies. Voted Funniest Woman on Television 1972/73/74 by TVTimes readers. TV Actress of the Year (Drama) BAFTA 1968. Variety Club TV Personality of the Year BBC 1969, ITV 1973. Education: Durham and Darlington High Schools; Yarm Grammar. m. showbiz journalist Jack Bentley, 2 s. Alaster, Ross. Address: c/o William Morris Agency, London W1. Starsign: Gemini. Hobbies: music and horticulture.

CRAVEN, Gemma
Actress b. 1.6.50 Dublin. Won a singing contest when she was three and has been interested in a career as a singer and actress ever since. Trained at the Bush Davies School in Romford, Essex. Professional debut in pantomime at Westcliff-on-Sea followed by summer season at Blackpool and pantomime at Watford. Joined Fiddler on the Roof company and has since done extensive stage work in London (Trelawney) and the provinces including: Bristol Old Vic, and two seasons at Chichester. Latest stage: Songbook. Films incl: The Slipper and the Rose; Why Not Stay For Breakfast?. TV incl: Hey Brian; The Harry Secombe Show; The Late, Late Show; The Russell Harty

Show; Pebble Mill; So You Think You Know About Love?; Saturday Scene; Emily; Stars on Sunday; Call My Bluff; Celebrity Squares; Whose Baby Are You?; Perry Como Christmas Special; Pennies From Heaven; Must Wear Tights; She Loves me; Blankety Blank; Song by Song. Evening News Film Award for Most Promising Actress and Variety Club Award for Film Actress both in 1976. Education: Loretta College, St Stephen's Green, Dublin; St Bernard's Convent, Westcliff-on-Sea. Address: c/o Stella Richards Personal Management, London SW3. Starsign: Gemini. Hobby: crochet. Unfulfilled ambitions: to continue a varied acting career and perhaps work for the National Theatre and the Royal Shakespeare Company.

CRAWFORD, Michael
Actor b. 19.1.42 Salisbury, Wilts. One time St Paul's Cathedral choirboy, he performed in Benjamin Britten's Let's Make an Opera. Left school at 15 and appeared in some 400 broadcasts, mostly for schools. Joined the Belgrade Theatre, Coventry when he was 18 and later, Nottingham Playhouse. Was in such early TV programmes as Probation Officer; Emergency–Ward 10; Billy Bunter and Sir Francis Drake. While appearing in his first West End play (Come Blow Your Horn) he was spotted by Ned

Sherrin and subsequently appeared in Not So Much a Programme . . . on TV. Other TV incl: The Policeman and the Cook; The Move After Checkmate; Some Mothers Do 'Ave 'Em; Sorry; Chalk and Cheese. Stage incl: No Sex Please – We're British; Billy; Same Time Next Year; Flowers for Algernon. Films incl: The Knack; Two Left Feet; The Jokers; How I Won the War; A Funny Thing Happened on the Way to the Forum; The Games; Hello and Goodbye; Hello Dolly; Alice's Adventures in Wonderland. m. Gabrielle (dis), 2 d. Lucy, Emma. Address: c/o Chatto and Linnit, London W1. Starsign: Capricorn.

CROMPTON, Colin
Comedian b. 22.6.33 Manchester. Radio appearances (Variety Fanfare) led to his deciding to become a professional comedian. Was a northern clubs' comic for years before appearing in The Comedians and later as chairman of the Wheeltappers and Shunters Social Club. Other TV incl: The Good Old Days; Second City Firsts; Paul Daniels' Blackpool Bonanza. Films incl: Confessions From a Holiday Camp. Education: North Manchester High School. m. (1st) Jean (dis), (2nd) Valerie, (3rd) singer Carole, 2 d. Cheryl, Erica (from 2nd m), 1 s. John (from 3rd m). Address: Mere, Cheshire. Starsign: Cancer. Hobby: piloting light aircraft.

Unfulfilled ambition: not got one. Quite happy!

CROWDEN, Graham
Actor b. 30.11.22 Edinburgh. Started as trainee assistant stage manager at Stratford-upon-Avon followed by rep experience at Dundee, Nottingham, Bristol Old Vic and Glasgow Citizen's Theatre. Has appeared in many productions at the Royal Court London, and was a member of the National Theatre Company at the Old Vic, and the RSC. Large number of plays and series on TV incl: The Last of Mrs Cheyney; Twelfth Night; MacAdam and Eve; Nil Carborundum; The Enemy; The Soldier's Tale; Ten Commandments; Trelawney of the Wells; Long Lease of Summer; The British Hero; On the Highroad; Bellamira; Shades of Greene; Porridge; The Island; Raffles; The Camerons. Education: Edinburgh Academy. m. Phyllida Hewat, 3 d. Lucy, Sarah, Kate, 1 s. Harry. Address: c/o Peter Browne Management, London SW9. Starsign: Sagittarius. Hobbies: music, tennis, cooking. Unfulfilled ambition: to climb Everest.

CROWTHER, Leslie
Actor/comedian b. 6.2.33 Nottingham. Originally intended for a musical career and studied piano seriously for a number of years. During this time he appeared in schools broadcasts for BBC

Drama School, then rep at Regents Park Open Air Theatre. Accent on Youth (radio) led to High Spirits in the West End and six seasons with the Fol-de-Rols. Other stage appearances incl: Let Sleeping Wives Lie; Palladium Pantomime; summer seasons; Royal Variety Performance. TV incl: High Summer; Crackerjack; The Black and White Minstrel Show; The Saturday Crowd; Crowther's in Town; My Good Woman; Big Boy Now; Hi Summer; Leslie Crowther's Scrap Book. Education: Nottingham High School; Thames Valley Grammar School; Arts Educational School, London. m. Jean, 4 d. Lindsay and Elizabeth (twins), Caroline, Charlotte, 1 s. Nicholas. Address: Corston, Bath. Starsign: Aquarius. Hobbies: cricket (Lord's Taverners), collecting pot-lids. Unfulfilled ambition: to make a film.

CRYER, Barry
Comedian/writer b. 23.3.35 Leeds. Professional debut at Leeds City of Varieties when he was at Leeds University. Calls himself a failed comedian; started writing comedy scripts for something to do while ill. Has since written for Les Dawson, Tommy Cooper, The Two Ronnies, Bruce Forsyth, Morecambe and Wise and numerous TV and radio shows, in some of which he also appears – A Degree of Frost; Those Wonderful TV Times; Hello Cheeky; Jokers Wild; Who Do You Do?; What's on Next? Education: Leeds University (studying English literature).
m. showgirl Terry Donovan, 2 d. , 2 s. Address: c/o Thames TV, London NW1. Starsign: Aries.

CUDDIHY, Bob
Journalist/broadcaster b. 11.9.46 New York City, New York, USA. Came to England to go to school 1962. Since leaving university has been a freelance journalist and editor of a small newspaper circulating among Scottish islands. Joined STV six years ago and is local government and education correspondent for Scotland Today. Other TV inc: Ways and Means; Scotland Today Reports. Education: various schools in America; Kilquhanity House, Castle Douglas, Scotland; Napier College, Edinburgh; University of Edinburgh (MA with hons.). m. Liz, 2 d. Aimee, Kate, 1 s. Patrick. Address: c/o STV, Glasgow. Starsign: Virgo. Hobby: the study of real ale.

CUFF, Susan
TV hostess b. 21.7.53 Broxburn, Scotland. Became Mr and Mrs Hostess after a year as Miss Great Britain 1975, and a year's teaching at her old school in Manchester. Qualified teacher in dress design, still does some designing and at one time designed and made all the dresses she wore on the programme. Other TV incl: Happy Families. Education: Moorclose Senior High, Manchester, and Bath College of Home Economics. m. TV journalist and presenter David Davies. Address: Sale, Cheshire. Starsign: cusp of Cancer and Leo. Hobbies: macramé, water skiing, dress design, squash. Unfulfilled ambitions: to have a large family and maybe present a TV programme for children.

CULLEN, Sarah
TV reporter b. 6.10.49 Newcastle upon Tyne. Joined ITN as a graduate trainee after graduating (BA Hons) from University College, London. Address: c/o ITN, Wells St, London W1. Starsign: Libra. Hobbies:

politics, French cooking, medieval literature. Unfulfilled ambition: to go to China.

CUTHBERTSON, Iain
Actor b. 4.1.30 Glasgow. First break as an actor was on radio while studying at Aberdeen University. At one time aimed at a job in the Foreign Office. After two years' National Service in the Black Watch became a radio journalist with the BBC in Glasgow. Started acting at Glasgow Citizens' Theatre of which he became General Manager and Director of Productions 1962; three years later he became Associate Director of London's Royal Court Theatre. Distinguished career both on the stage and in TV. TV incl: The Borderers; Diamond Crack Diamond; Budgie; The Onedin Line; Tom Brown's Schooldays; Scotch on the Rocks; Black Beauty; Sutherland's Law; The Ghosts of Motley Hall; Duchess of Duke Street; The Mourning Brooch; Z Cars; Dr Who; Danger UXB; Casting the Runes; Charlie Endell; McPhee the Mother and Me. Films incl: The Railway Children; Up the Chasity Belt. Education: Glasgow Academy; Aberdeen Grammar; University of Aberdeen (MA Hons French and Spanish). m. actress Anne Kirsten. Address: c/o French's, London W1. Starsign: Capricorn. Hobbies: sailing and fishing.

CUNNINGHAM, Lyn
Announcer b. 21st February, Aberdeen. Trained as a commercial artist and fashion model. Panelist in Who Are You? quiz. Scottish winner of GPO's Interflora Personality Contest – Girl with the Golden Voice. Now with Grampian TV. Education: Convent of Sacred Heart, Aberdeen; secretarial college; Gray's School of Art, Aberdeen. m. Gerald, 1 d. Lyndy, 2 s. Paul, Michael. Address: c/o Grampian TV. Starsign: Pisces. Hobbies: sketching, French cooking, interior design, TV. Unfulfilled ambition: to have dinner with Roger Moore.

CURRY, Tim
Actor b. 19.4.46 Cheshire. Graduated from Birmingham University with honours in Drama and English Literature. Joined the London cast of Hair. Then came After Haggerty, with the Royal Shakespeare Company, seasons at the Royal Court, London, and Glasgow Citizen's Theatre. Also The Rocky Horror Show (London, Los Angeles and New York). Films incl: The Rocky Horror

Picture Show. TV incl: The Policeman and the Cook; Napoleon in Love; Veritee; Three Men in a Boat; Rock Follies of '77; Will Shakespeare; City Sugar. Records: Read My Lips; Fearless. Address: c/o Clodagh Wallace, London W6. Starsign: Aries. Hobby: writing songs.

CURTHOYS, Ann
Actress b. 16.2.42 Clevedon, Somerset. Dancing and drama school training before RADA and rep at Salisbury and Royal Shakespeare Company. Many TV plays and series incl: Return to Yesterday; You Can't Win; 1990; Public Eye; Rainbow; Rooms. Films incl: The Magnet; A Man For All Seasons. Education: Waterloo Secondary, Liverpool. m. (1st) actor Tim Wylton (dis), (2nd) musician Roger Walker, 1 d. Emma, 1 s. Huw (both from 1st m). Address: c/o Carole James Management, Richmond, Surrey. Starsign: Aquarius. Hobbies: walking and cycling. Unfulfilled ambition: to drive to India.

D

London W1. Starsign: Virgo. Hobbies: sketching, reading, embroidery, flower arranging. Unfulfilled ambitions: a continuing happy marriage and successful record career.

DANEMAN, Paul
Actor b. 26.10.25 London. Studied for the stage at RADA and after some time in rep joined the Old Vic. First appearance on stage was as the front legs of a horse in Alice in Wonderland. Was the original Vladimar in Waiting For Godot at the Arts Theatre in London. Other stage work incl: Camelot; Hadrian VII; Don't Start Without Me; Who Do They Think They Are? (one-man show); Double Edge; Pygmalion; Shut Your Eyes and Think of England. TV incl: Our Mutual Friend; Emma; Persuasion; An Age of Kings; Not in Front of the Children; Never a Cross Word; Spy Trap; Waste; Arnold. Education: Haberdashers' Aske's, London; Sir William Borlase's, Marlow; and Reading University (Fine Arts). m. (1st) Susan (dis), (2nd) Meredith, 2 d. Sophie, Flora. Address: c/o Chatto and Linnit, London W1. Starsign: Scorpio. Hobby: painting.

DANA
Singer b. 30.8.51 London. Wanted to be a music teacher, but while still at school won the Eurovision Song Contest 1970 in Amsterdam with All Kinds of Everything and became an overnight singing star. Other records since incl: Who Put the Lights Out; Please Tell Him That I Said Hello; It's Going to be a Cold, Cold Christmas; Fairytale; Something's Cooking in the Kitchen; The Girl is Back. Since the Eurovision Song Contest she has travelled the world, made a film (Flight of Doves), been in pantomime, cabaret, appeared with Frankie Vaughan in Canada and with Tom Jones at the London Palladium and appeared in countless TV programmes incl: Stars on Sunday; Golden Shot; When Irish Eyes Are Smiling; Celebrity Squares; They Sold a Million; A Day With Dana; Wake Up, Sunday. Has twice overcome throat surgery in the past couple of years. Education: convent school, Londonderry. m. hotelier Damien Scallon. Address: c/o MAM Agency Ltd,

DANIEL, Jennifer
Actress b. 23.5.39 Pontypool, Gwent. Trained at Central School of Speech and Drama, rep experience at Dundee and Oxford. Leading roles on West End

stage and in films. TV incl: Hamlet; Great Expectations; Coriolanus; Barnaby Rudge; The Lie; The Vortex; General Hospital; Public Eye; Rooms; Van Der Valk; The Duchess of Duke Street; People Like Us; Young Merlin; Thomas and Sarah. Education: Badminton. m. actor Dinsdale Landen. Address: Filmrights Ltd, London W1. Starsign: Gemini. Hobbies: reading, antiques, going to the theatre and cinema, old buildings and pottering in the garden. Unfulfilled ambition: many.

DANIELS, Paul
Comedian/magician
b. 16.4.39 Middlesbrough. Became interested in magic when he was 11. First job on leaving school was junior clerk in the treasurer's office, Redcar Borough Council. After a spell in the army, returned to office work but did part-time entertaining. Ran a grocer's shop before becoming an entertainer full-time. His father makes his apparatus. TV debut on Opportunity Knocks. TV incl: Be My Guest; Wheeltappers and Shunters Social Club;

The Paul Daniels Show; Fall In The Stars; Blackpool Bonanza. Education: grammar school. Divorced. 3 s. Paul, Martin, Gary. Address: Buckinghamshire. Starsign: Aries. Hobby: photography. Unfulfilled ambition: to fly a helicopter.

DANNATT, Adrian
Boy actor b. 29.8.63 Wrote in for the plum part of William in Just William and won it in competition from 2,000 other hopefuls. Education: Westminster School. Address: London. Starsign: Virgo. Hobbies: keenly interested in military history and admits to being 'rather cheeky'. Collects modern 1st editions and 1920's detective novels. Unfulfilled ambitions: to visit Florence and Venice; to have a novel published to wild intellectual and popular acclaim; direct a thriller with intellectual pretensions; become a horribly influential film critic; meet Oscar Wilde or Max Beerbohm.

DANTON, Graham
Writer/presenter b. 29.5.31 Eltham, Kent. Merchant Navy officer for 12 years. Master

Mariner and Extra-Master Mariner. Two Royal Society of Arts Silver Medals. New York Film Festival gold medal for documentary, Loss of the SS Schiller. Five times South-West TV Personality of the Year. Education: grammar school, HMS Worcester Training Ship. Address: c/o Westward TV, Plymouth. Starsign: Gemini. Hobbies: hand-gun target shooting, music/hi-fi, model making. Unfulfilled ambition: to cross the Sahara Desert.

DARRAN, John
Actor/newsreader
b. 24.12.24 Mountain Ash, Glamorgan. Joined BBC in 1946 and has worked as actor, light entertainment, newsreader, author. Written and read mid-morning stories on radio. Book: Counterspy. Education: Duffryn House Grammar School, Oriel College, Oxford (MA Hons, History). m. Joan, 2 d. Andrea, Elizabeth, 1 s. David. Address: Cardiff. Starsign: Capricorn. Hobbies: swimming, writing, food and wine. Unfulfilled ambition: to be cook of the year.

DAVENPORT, Nigel
Actor b. 25.5.28 Shelford, Cambridge. Decided to become an actor while reading English at Oxford University where he was a member of the Oxford University Dramatic Society. Military service in the RASC during the war and worked as an Army radio disc jockey in

Hamburg. First theatre job was as understudy in a Noel Coward play. Seasons at Stratford, Chesterfield and Ipswich and one of the first members of the English Stage Company at London's Royal Court Theatre. First success in A Resounding Tinkle. Other stage incl: A Taste of Honey (and in USA). Notes on a Love Affair; Three Sisters. Film debut in 1952 in Peeping Tom. Other films incl: A Man For All Seasons; Sebastian; Sinful Davy; Play Dirty; The Royal Hunt of the Sun; The Virgin Soldiers; The Mind of Mr Soames; Villain; Living Free; Mary, Queen of Scots; Charlie One-Eye. TV incl: An Affair of Honour; Sharing the Honours; Goose With Pepper; The Apple Cart; South Riding; Oil Strike North. Education: St Peter's, Seaford; Cheltenham College; Oxford (MA). m. (1st) Helena (dis); (2nd) actress Maria Aitken, 1 d. Laura, 1 s. Address: c/o Leading Artists, London SW1. Starsign: Gemini.

DAVID, Joanna
Actress b. 17.1.47
Lancaster. Trained at

Elmhurst Ballet School and Webber Douglas Academy of Dramatic Art. Rep at Ipswich, Canterbury, Guildford. Films incl: A Smashing Bird I Used to Know; All Neat in Black Stockings; The Mind of Mrs Soames; One Plus One. TV incl: John Brown's Body; When Johnny Comes Marching Home; Sense and Sensibility; Last of the Mohicans; War and Peace; Colditz; Duchess of Duke Street; Softly, Softly; Ballet Shoes; Dancing Princesses; Jennie; Just William; Within These Walls; Two's Company; Affront; Lillie; Rebecca. 1 d. Emilia. Address: c/o Peter Browne Management, London SW9. Starsign: Capricorn.

DAVIDSON, Jim
Comedian b. 13.12.54
London. ITV's New Faces gave him his big chance after a variety of jobs, including window cleaner, fork-lift truck driver. TV incl: What's On Next?; Night Out; Tiswas; Make 'em Laugh; The Jim Davidson Show. Education: secondary modern school. m. Susan (dis), 1 d. Sarah. Address: c/o Thames TV, London NW1. Starsign: Sagittarius. Hobbies: golf, fishing, football. Unfulfilled ambition: to play football for Scotland.

DAVIES, Barry
Sports commentator
b. 24.10.40 London. Began broadcasting with BFBS in Cologne and spent a year

with Sports Report on BBC radio. Joined The Times 1963 and made his debut as football commentator in Feb 1966. Covered the World Cup for ITV. Football commentator for ABC TV 1966-68 and Granada 1968-69. Joined BBC 1969 and TV since incl: Match of the Day, Grandstand, Sportsnight. Has commentated and/or introduced football, athletics, badminton, water skiing, tennis. Education: Cranbrook School and London University. m. Penny, 1 d. Giselle, 1 s. Mark. Address: c/o Bagenal Harvey Organisation, London W1. Starsign: Scorpio. Hobbies: family, theatre, sports. Unfulfilled ambitions: many.

DAVIES, David
TV journalist/presenter
b. 28.5.48 London. A reporter for BBC Wales and lobby correspondent for the London Broadcasting Company, before joining BBC in Manchester. A regular contributor to Look North and Nationwide; Nine O'Clock News; Grandstand; BBC religious programmes

and sports programmes on Radio 2. Is also a trained teacher. Education: Royal Masonic School; Sheffield University (degree in politics). m. Mr & Mrs hostess Susan Cuff. Address: c/o BBC TV News, Manchester. Starsign: Gemini. Hobbies: tennis, reading (mainly politics). Unfulfilled ambition: to produce a film in Peking.

DAVIES, Deddie
Actress b. 1938 Bridgend, South Wales. Trained at RADA and soon found work with reps and on radio and TV. Stage work has taken her to the Northcott (Exeter); The Orange Tree (Richmond); The Royal Exchange and The Mermaid Theatre (London); and to the West End in Lady Frederick. Films incl: The Railway Children; The Amazing Mr Blunden. TV incl: The Forsyte Saga; Vanity Fair; Clochemerle; Pin to See The Peep Show; Jennie; Some Mothers Do 'Ave'Em; Upstairs, Downstairs; Just William; The Rag Trade; The Mayor of Casterbridge. Education: Howells School, Llandaff, Wales. m. actor Paddy Ward. Address: Kingston-upon-Thames. Starsign: Pisces. Hobbies: reading, classical music, walking, Victorian architecture. Unfulfilled ambition: to travel much more.

DAVIES, Dickie
TV presenter b. 30.4.33 Wallasey, Cheshire. Entertainments purser on

Queen Mary and Queen Elizabeth 1 before joining Southern TV as announcer/newscaster. Then to World of Sport (1968). Education: various elementary and grammar schools. m. Liz, 2 s. Daniel and Peter (twins). Address: Over Wallop, Hants. Starsign: Taurus. Hobbies: real family and unreal golf. Unfulfilled ambitions: to share with World of Sport a greater international involvement in big time sport, and to explore other areas of television.

DAVIES, Freddie (Mr Parrotface)
Comedian b. 21.7.37 Brixton, London. Started as holiday camp entertainer and turned professional 1964. Appeared in cabaret in clubs and every major theatre in the country in summer shows and pantomime. Also guest spots on many TV series and panel games. Stage incl: London Palladium with Cliff Richard. TV debut in Opportunity Knocks. Other TV incl: Sunday Night at the London Palladium and own series, The Small World of Samuel Tweet. Education: Salford,

Lancs. m. Jacqueline, 1 step-d. Jennifer, 1 s. Kent. Address: Greenford, Middlesex. Starsign: Cancer/Leo. Hobbies: reading, eating good food, watching good entertainment well performed. Unfulfilled ambition: to stage a production at the London Palladium.

DAVIES, Geoffrey
Actor b. 15.12.41 Yorkshire. Commercial artist before becoming an actor. Harrogate and Sheffield reps before taking a two year course at RADA. Then filming in Oh, What a Lovely War; 1917; and Vault of Horror. Dick Stuart-Clarke in the Doctor TV series. Went to Australia with Doctor On The Go, came back to England to appear at Windsor and the Old Vic (The Ghost Train), and recently completed a second tour of the Far East, Australia and New Zealand which included a series called Doctor Down Under. Education: grammar school, art college. m. Ann, 1 d. Emma-Kate. Address: Crouch Associates, London W1. Starsign: Sagittarius. Hobbies: Tinkering with cars, riding. Unfulfilled ambitions: 'Many – but not for publication!'

DAVIES, Lynette
Actress b. 18 October Tonypandy, South Wales. Trained at RADA, then rep before the Royal Shakespeare Company and a few small TV parts. TV incl:

The Ghosts of Motley Hall; Clayhanger; Will Shakespeare; The Foundation. Education: Our Lady's Convent School, Cardiff. Address: c/o Bryan Drew Ltd, London W1. Starsign: Libra. Hobbies: reading and travelling abroad. Unfulfilled ambition: to visit South America.

DAVIES, Robin
Actor b. 16.1.54 Merionethshire, North Wales. Started as a child actor and trained at the Aida Foster Stage School. Films incl: If . . ; The Magnificent 6½. TV incl: Catweazle; Newcomers; Doomwatch; And Mother Makes Three; And Mother Makes Five; Warship; The Saturday Party; Forget-Me-Not-Lane; The Country Party; Spearhead. Education: Gladstone Park School. Address: c/o Aida Foster Ltd, London NW8. Starsign: Capricorn. Hobbies: music, films, arts and drama. Unfulfilled ambition: to make films my own way in my own time and not to have to worry about the cost.

DAVIS, Philip
Actor b. 30.7.53 Grays, Essex. First job in the theatre was with Joan Littlewood's Theatre Workshop. Theatre incl: The Hostage (Stratford); Gimme Shelter (Soho Poly and Royal Court). Films incl: Mister Quilp; Quadrophenia. Radio incl: several plays, Waggoners Walk. TV incl: The Professionals; Orson Welles' Mystery Stories; People Like Us; Sexton Blake; Play For Today (Gotcha, Mayor's Charity, Who's Who). Education: Ockendon Courts Secondary School. Address: c/o Duncan Heath Assoc., London SW10. Starsign: Leo. Hobbies: golf, football, tennis, reading, rock music, writing. Unfulfilled ambitions: to have a novel published, to keep acting for another 50 years and improve all the time.

DAVISON, Peter
Actor b. London. After school plays and amateur dramatics, trained at Central School of Speech and Drama. First job was season at Nottingham Playhouse. After appearing at Edinburgh Festival he went into TV series, The Tomorrow People. Big TV break was in Love for Lydia, followed by All Creatures Great and Small. Other TV incl: Print-Out; Once Upon a Time. Also writes songs, incl: the theme song for Mixed Blessings. Made his singing debut on Pebble Mill at One. m. actress Sandra Dickinson. Address: c/o John Mahoney Management, London W1.

DAWBER, Pam
Actress/singer b. Detroit. Has a four-octave soprano voice and began singing in musical productions while still at high school. Did some modelling and TV commercials before taking up an acting career. First professional performance was the leading role in Sweet Adeleine. Also appeared in A Wedding and Sister Terri, before Mork and Mindy. 'Home' is a rustic cabin on the Delaware River in upstate New York. Hobbies: canoeing, cooking, skiing, horse-riding, swimming, surfing and water skiing.

DAWSON, Les
Comedian b. 2.2.34 Manchester. Began as jazz pianist with Manchester band, Cotton City Slickers. Worked in clubs and pubs as solo comic before successful appearance in Opportunity Knocks 1967. Appearances in such shows as Big Night Out; Sunday Night at the London Palladium before his own series, Sez Les. Other TV incl: This is Your Life; Holiday

With Strings; The Loner; also specials and his own series for ITV and BBC. Writer of comedy material and author of books; A Card for the Clubs; The Spy Who Came; Smallpiece Guide to Male Liberation; British Book of Humour. Education: elementary school and technical college.
m. Margaret, 2 d. Julie, Pamela, 1 s. Stuart. Address: c/o Norman Murray, London Management, London W1. Starsign: Aquarius. Hobbies: golf, writing, gardening. Unfulfilled ambition: to be a clown in a circus.

DAY, Robin
Interviewer/presenter
b. 24.10.23 London. Started career as barrister 1952. Served in the army during Second World War and after being called to the Bar served with British Information Services, Washington, 1953-54. Freelance journalist 1954-55 and BBC radio talks producer before ITN newscaster and parliamentary correspondent 1955-59. Joined Panorama 1959 and introduced the

programme 1967-72. Other TV incl: Roving Report; Tell the People; The Parliamentarians and many abrasive interviews. Radio: The World at One. Books: Television: A Personal Report; The Case for Televising Parliament; Day By Day: a dose of my own hemlock. BAFTA Richard Dimbleby Award for Factual TV 1974. Education: Bembridge School, St Edmund Hall, Oxford University (BA). President of the Oxford Union Society 1951. m. Katherine, 2 s. Alexander, Daniel. Address: c/o BBC, London. Starsign: Scorpio. Hobbies: reading, talking, skiing.

DAZE, Charlie
Comedian b. 10.5.38 Scotland. Comes from showbiz family; father was a conjuror and mother was a singer/comedienne. Appeared in school concerts from the age of seven. Started professional career at 17. TV incl: Opportunity Knocks; Seaside Special; The Comedians. Education: St Colomba's School, Portadown. m. Patrice, 1 s. Carl. Address: c/o Roy Hastings, Tyldesley, Lancs. Starsign: Taurus. Hobbies: football, snooker, table tennis. Unfulfilled ambition: to have appeared with the old time 'greats' like Groucho Marx and the Three Stooges.

DEACON, Brian
Actor b. 13.2.49 Oxford.

Window cleaner, butcher's van driver while member of the Oxford Youth Theatre. Webber Douglas School training in London. Rep seasons at Bristol; Coventry (Belgrade); Leicester; Soho Poly. Other stage incl: Curse of the Starving Class. Films incl: Triple Echo; Il Bacio; Vampyres; Jesus. TV incl: First Sight; The Guardians; Public Eye; Love and Mr Lewisham; Ghosts; The Emigrants; Lillie. Education: primary and secondary modern until 17. m. actress Rula Lenska. Address: London SW19. Starsign: Aquarius. Hobbies: tennis, squash, football, bridge, reading, cinema, gardening, entertaining friends.

DEAS, Maxwell
Producer/presenter religious programmes b. 27.12.16 Sunderland. Experience in commerce, the army, industry, the stage and public relations before venturing into TV production. Has since produced more than 7,500 nightly Epilogues nearly all of which he has presented. Has also been responsible for many TV

'firsts' – the Royal Maundy Service; and Network Morning Services from a prison, quarter deck of one of H M ships, a railway station, a ship repair yard, a holiday camp and a reservoir among others. Licentiate of the Guildhall School of Music (Speech and Drama) and Poetry Society medallist. Education: St Peter's School, York. m. June Larson (actress Joy Merlyn), 1 d. Maxine, 1 s. Richard. Address: c/o Tyne Tees TV, Newcastle upon Tyne. Starsign: Capricorn. Hobbies: theatre, music, football (soccer and rugby), cricket (Scarborough). Unfulfilled ambition: to be an established actor.

DeCOURCEY, Roger
Ventriloquist b. 10.12.44 London. Went into the Stock Exchange on leaving school but studied opera in the evenings. After a season as holiday camp sports organiser, he turned professional. Was with the Fol-de-Rols at Worthing before going into Sweet Charity in London. TV programme New Faces turned him into overnight success after 10 years in show business. Education: Henry Thornton, Clapham, London. m. Cheryl, 1 s. Jamie. Address: c/o International Artistes, London W1. Starsign: Sagittarius. Hobbies: golf, squash. Unfulfilled ambition: to get a hole in one.

DEEKS, Michael
Actor b. 18.4.56 Farnham Royal, Bucks. First part was Jim Hawkins in Treasure Island at the Crucible Theatre, Sheffield. Has also had a spell at the National Theatre. TV incl: Armchair Theatre; Hunter's Walk; The Boys and Mrs B; Champions; Dick Turpin. Education: Reading Blue Coat School, Sonning; Licensed Victuallers, Slough. Address: c/o Plant and Froggett, London W1. Starsign: Aries. Hobbies: music, nature and being pampered. Unfulfilled ambition: to be in Who's Who for normal people.

DELANEY, Frank
Presenter b. 24.10.42 Ireland. Has been broadcasting regularly on radio and TV since 1966 and writing for magazines and newspapers (Cosmopolitan, Sunday Times, Telegraph and Observer magazines) since 1970. Newsreader RTE Radio and TV. Current affairs and documentaries presenter/ reporter for RTE Dublin and BBC Northern Ireland (incl: weekly programmes such as

Bookshelf). Education: to A-level standard. Separated, 3 s. Frank, Bryan, Owen. Address: London W3. Starsign: Scorpio. Hobbies: running, squash, food. Unfulfilled ambition: to breed a pedigree herd of Charolais cattle on a farm in the heart of Ireland.

DELANEY, Pauline
Actress b. 8th June, Dublin. Trained at the Brendan Smith Academy of Acting, Dublin then rep in the North of England and the Dublin Globe Theatre. Appeared in the 1962 O'Casey season at London's Mermaid Theatre and in the West End in The Poker Session and The Hostage. Films incl: Nothing But the Best; The Young Cassidy; Percy; Brannigan (with John Wayne); and Rooney. Her numerous TV appearances incl: Public Eye; The Dead; The Achurch Letters; Crime of Passion (in the Detective series); The Seagull; The Playboy of the Western World; The Expert; The Avengers; Z Cars; Fallen Hero; Mixed Blessings and various plays. Education: convent schools in Dublin. m. Gerry Simpson, 1 d. Sarah. Address: c/o Green and Underwood, London W3. Starsign: Gemini. Hobbies: reading, listening to music. Unfulfilled ambition: to have a cottage in the country.

DENCH, Judi OBE
Actress b. 9.12.34 York. Wanted to be a designer and

attended art school for a year before training at the Central School of Speech and Drama. Made her professional debut as Ophelia in Hamlet at Liverpool in 1957 with the Old Vic; London saw her in the same part a week later. She has since played a wide variety of roles during four seasons at the Old Vic, several seasons with the RSC, rep at Oxford as well as cabaret, The Good Companions and London Assurance, in which she played opposite the actor who was to become her husband. Her range has been equally wide on TV incl: Hilda Lessways; Village Wooing; On Giant's Shoulders; Langrishe, Go Down; Macbeth; Comedy of Errors; The Teachers; Z Cars; The Age of Kings; Love Story; The Funambulists; Parade's End; Talking to a Stranger; The Morcambe and Wise Show. Education: The Mount School, York. m. actor Michael Williams, 1 d. Tara. Address: c/o Julian Belfrage, London SW1. Starsign: Sagittarius. Hobbies: sewing, painting, tapestry.

DERBYSHIRE, Eileen
Actress b. 6th October, Manchester. Trained at the Northern School of Music (now Royal Northern College), LRAM. Speech and drama teaching before rep and radio work. Emily in Coronation Street since 1961. Education: Manchester High.

m. Thomas Holt, 1 s. Oliver. Address: c/o Richard Stone, London WC2. Starsign: Libra. Hobbies: concerning the Arts, the countryside and the home. Unfulfilled ambition: to catch up.

DICKINSON, Angie
Actress b. 30.9.31 Kulm, North Dakota. First gained attention as a dance hall girl in Howard Hawk's film Rio Bravo with John Wayne. Other films followed incl: Lucky Me; The Bramble Bush; Rachel Cade; Captain Newman MD; Ocean's 11; The Killers; The Chase; Point Blank; Pretty Maids All In A Row; Big Bad Mama; Labyrinth. Only accepting smaller roles so that she could devote more time to her family, a part in Police Story led to her taking the Police Woman role, encouraged by her husband. Education: Immaculate Heart and Glendale Colleges. m. composer Burt Bacharach, 1 d. Nikki. Address: Beverly Hills, California. Starsign: Libra.

DICKINSON, Sandra
Actress b. Washington DC. Came to England with her English husband whom she met and married while both were studying at Wisconsin University. Trained at Central School of Speech and Drama. Probably best known as the dumb blonde in the St Bruno commercials, but has an impressive list of TV credits that incl: The Tomorrow People; Rainbow; It's Sandy; Money; What's On Next?; also appearances in Des O'Connor; Tom O'Connor and Max Bygraves shows. Chosen to play Marilyn Monroe in stage play, Legend, which toured but did not come into London. m. (1st) biology lecturer (dis); (2nd) actor Peter Davison. Address: c/o London Management, London W1.

DIMBLEBY, David
Interviewer/TV presenter b. 28.10.38 London. First job was with BBC in Bristol as news reporter 1961, reporting for Enquiry 1964, but left TV (1965) to concentrate on family newspapers when his father

Richard Dimbleby died. After six months in America for CBS, he joined Panorama 1967 as a freelance, then 24 Hours (1969); Yesterday's Men; Reporter at Large; Dimbleby Talk-in; Panorama 1975-77; General Election Results programme; The White Tribe of Africa; Person To Person. Education: Glengorse; Charterhouse; Paris Sorbonne; University of Perugia; Oxford University. m. Josceline, 2 d. Liza, Kate, 1 s. Henry. Address: Barnes. Starsign: Scorpio. Hobby: sailing.

DIMBLEBY, Jonathan
Broadcaster/journalist/writer b. 31.7.44 London. Thought of becoming a farmer, but discovered journalism while at University. Younger brother of David Dimbleby. Joined BBC in Bristol (1969) reporting for Points West, then World at One. Switched to ITV's This Week 1972. To Yorkshire TV for own series 1979. BAFTA's Richard Dimbleby Award 1974; coverage of Middle East, South Africa and British politics. Books: Richard Dimbleby; The Palestinians. Education: Charterhouse. and London University (philosophy). m. journalist Bel Mooney, 1 s. Daniel. Address: c/o David Higham Associates Ltd, London W1. Starsign: Leo. Hobbies: reading, music, sailing.

DINENAGE, Fred
Presenter b. 8.6.42 Birmingham. Originally

wanted to be a journalist, but after spells with the Birmingham Mail and Evening Argus, Brighton, joined Southern TV 1964 to help introduce Three Go Round. Since then his TV appearances have included Day By Day; Afloat; Weekend; Miss Southern Television; Calendar Sport; Sunday Sport; World of Sport; Gambit; How; Miss Great Britain; Southsport; Pro-Celebrity Snooker; Pro-Celebrity Darts; Miss Anglia TV; Reflections; Cuckoo in the Nest; Showjumping. Education: Birmingham. m. Beryl, 1 d. Caroline. Address: c/o Southern TV, Southampton. Starsign: Gemini. Hobbies: squash, football, working. Unfulfilled ambition: to retire (rich).

DOBIE, Alan
Actor b. 2.6.32 Wombwell, Yorks. Trained at Barnsley School of Art and the Old Vic Theatre School. Began his career at the Old Vic in September 1952 as Paris's Page in Romeo and Juliet. Joined Bristol Old Vic the following year where he was

The Tramp in the original production of Salad Days. Has since played every kind of part from a pantomime cat to Macbeth. His films incl: The Charge of the Light Brigade; Doctor Syn; White Bird. Radio work incl: My Cousin Rachel; Morning Departure; Love on the Dole; Look Back in Anger. More recently, An Inspector Calls; Dial a Poem; What's Your Pleasure; and Hello, Hello, Hello, Here We Are Again. First impact on TV was in The Planemakers. Other TV incl: Dance of Death; The Corsican Brothers; The Siege of Manchester; Why Aren't You Famous?; Conquest; Resurrection; Danton; Diamond Crack Diamond; The Troubleshooters; War and Peace; Double Dare; Our Young Mr Wignal; Hard Times; The Dick Emery Show; Waxwork; The Death of Ivan Ilyich; Wobble to Death; Detective Wore Silk Drawers; Mad Hatter's Holiday; Invitation to a Dynamite Party; Abra Cadaver, and Sergt. Cribb in a series of plays from the novels of Peter Lovesey. m. (1st) actress Rachel Roberts (dis), (2nd) singer Maureen Scott, 2 d. Millie, Natasha, 1 s. Casey. Address: c/o Vernon Conway Ltd, London SW11. Starsign: Gemini. Hobbies: farming, painting. Unfulfilled ambitions: to appear in a good new play in London and to make a major film.

DODD, Ken
Actor/comedian b. 8.11.27

Liverpool. Always wanted to go on the stage; Christmas presents of a Punch and Judy set and a ventriloquist's doll helped him in his decision. Professional comedian since 1954. Inventor of the Diddymen. Many summer and variety shows and his own TV and radio programmes. TV incl: Ken Dodd Show; Doddy's Music Box; The Good Old Days; Thank Your Lucky Stars; Funny You Should Say That; Look Who's Talking; Ken Dodd's World of Laughter; Seaside Special; Stars on Sunday. Theatre: Malvolio in Twelfth Night; Ha Ha – A Celebration of Laughter (both in Liverpool); Ken Dodd's Laughter Show (London Palladium and provinces). Records incl: Love is Like a Violin; More Than Love; Let Me Cry on Your Shoulder; Tears; Tears Won't Wash Away My Heartache; Happiness; When Love Comes Round Again; This is Our Dance; Just Out of Reach. Education: Holt High, Liverpool. Address: Knotty Ash, Liverpool. Starsign: Scorpio. Hobbies: watching racing and reading science fiction and psychology. Unfulfilled ambition: to go to America.

DONNELLY, Elaine
Actress b. 22.3.48 Cheltenham. Started as assistant stage manager at the Everyman Theatre, Cheltenham, then rep at Cheltenham, Salisbury,

Nottingham, Liverpool, Leatherhead and the Shaw Theatre in London. Also toured in Spring and Port Wine. TV incl: Fraud Squad; Hunter's Walk; Thriller; General Hospital; Please Sir; The Fenn Street Gang; Doctor at Large; Doctor in Charge; The Train Now Standing; People Like Us; Upstairs, Downstairs; Mixed Blessings; Rooms; Hadleigh; Follyfoot; Emmerdale Farm; Village Hall; Cuckoo Waltz; The Expert; The Regiment; Ronnie Corbett Show; The Brothers; Z Cars; Softly, Softly; Dixon of Dock Green; Angels; All Creatures Great and Small; Casanova; Lovely Couple; Billy. Education: Gloucester Road Primary, Cheltenham; Bishop's Cleve Junior, Cheltenham; Pate's Grammar School, Cheltenham. Address: c/o Joseph and Wagg, London W1. Starsign: Aries. Hobby: supporting Tottenham Hotspur Football Club. Unfulfilled ambitions: to visit Disneyland and watch Tottenham Hotspur from the directors' box.

DOODY, Pat
Announcer b. 11.11.38 Birmingham. After short service commission in the Royal Signals, went into British Forces Broadcasting Service and BBC radio before joining Border TV. Education: Fernden, Haslemere, Surrey and King Alfred's, Wantage, Berks. m. Jill, 2 d. Pippa, Helenne. Address: Wetheral, Cumbria.

Starsign: Scorpio. Hobbies: study of wild life, wine making, researching unusual recipes, being a life-boat crewman. Unfulfilled ambition: to have first book published.

DOONICAN, Val
Singer b. 3.2.29 Waterford, Ireland. Originally worked in a steel foundry and orange-box factory before his first professional engagement in 1946. Radio work in Ireland, joined The Four Ramblers 1951 in Riders of the Range. Later went solo. First radio show, Your Date With Val, 1959. The famous chair and sweaters arrived with TV show in 1964. Will be in 18th own TV show 1980. Many variety shows and own series incl: The Val Doonican Show; The Val Doonican Music Show; Sunday Night at the London Palladium; Stars on Sunday. Hit records incl: Walk Tall; Elusive Butterfly; Paddy McGinty's Goat; No Charge; Rafferty's Motor Car; Special Years; Morning; If the Whole World Stopped Lovin'; What Would I Be? Education: De La Salle College, Waterford. m. former cabaret and revue star Lynette Rae, 2 d. Sarah, Fiona. Address: Seer Green, Bucks. Starsign: Aquarius. Hobbies: golf, oil painting, archery.

DORNING, Robert
Actor b. 13th May, St Helens, Lancs. Studied music in Liverpool but stage fright so marred his professional debut that he decided to take

up dancing. Studied ballet and joined the Dolin/Markova company. The war ended that career and after five years in the RAF, chose musical comedy for his return to the stage. That career was curtailed by an attack of synovitis in both knees, so he settled on an acting career in rep at Leatherhead and late night revues in London. Two years in Canada with the London Theatre Company and he returned to parts in films, They Came by Night and The One That Got Away. Other films incl: Live Now, Pay Later; The Human Factor. Stage incl: The Great Waltz; Something's Afoot. He is also a TV comedy veteran from the days of Hancock's Half Hour; Tommy Cooper and Spike Milligan shows; The Army Game; Bootsie and Snudge; Pardon the Expression; and more recently, No Appointment Necessary; Big Deal at New York City; Clubs; Hogg's Back; P G Woodhouse. Education Cowley, St Helens. m. actress Honor Shepherd, 2 d. actresses Stacy Dorning and Kate Dorning. Address: c/o CCA Personal Management, London SW6. Starsign: Taurus. Hobby: golf. Unfulfilled ambition: to sing a duet with Cleo Laine.

DORNING, Stacy
Actress b. 11.5.58 London. Wanted to be a nurse, but after appearing in the Black Beauty series, became dedicated to show business. Parents are actor Robert

Dorning and actress Honor Shepherd and sister is actress Kate Dorning. Stage incl: Peter Pan; toured in Little Women and While the Sun Shines; Romeo and Juliet and Mary Rose at Worthing. Films incl: Cromwell; Frankenstein. TV incl: Space 1999; Just William; Keep It in the Family. Education: Hazelhurst School, Wimbledon. Address: c/o CCA Personal Management, London SW6. Starsign: Taurus. Hobbies: riding, spanish guitar, interior decorating, gardening.

DORS, Diana
Actress b. 23.10.31 Swindon. Studied at RADA and at 16 was under contract to the Rank Organisation. Many films incl: Shop at Sly Corner; Good Time Girl; Here Come the Huggetts; Worm's Eye View; A Kid for Two Farthings; Yield to the Night and, more recently, The Amazing Mr Blunden; Steptoe and Son Ride Again. Stage incl: Man of the World; Three Months Gone. TV incl: The Lovely Place; A Nice Little Business; Queenie's Castle; Just William;

Celebrity Squares, many chat shows. Education: Colville House, Swindon. m. (1st) Dennis Hamilton (dec); (2nd) comedian Dickie Dawson; (3rd) actor Alan Lake, 3 s. Mark, Gary (from 2nd m), Jason (from 3rd m). Address: Sunningdale, Berks. Starsign: Scorpio. No time for hobbies. Unfulfilled ambitions: to have own chat show and to write best-selling books.

DOTRICE, Michele
Actress b. 27.9.48 London. Been on the stage all her life; carried on when three weeks old, Royal Shakespeare Company at 12; many stage and TV dramas since. Probably best known for her part as Betty, Michael Crawford's screen wife in Some Mothers Do 'Ave 'Em. Stage incl: Odd Girl Out; The Male of the Species; Twelfth Night; Same Time Next Year; Romeo and Juliet. Films incl: And Soon the Darkness; The Devil's Touch; Not Now Comrade. TV incl: Emma's Time; A Kind of Bonus; The Morecambe and Wise Show; Nobody Does It Like Marti; Celebrity Squares; I'm Bob – He's Dickie; I'm Dickie; That's Show Business; Henry IV. Education: grammar school, Corona Academy. Address: Banbury, Oxfordshire. Starsign: Libra. Hobbies: collecting antique fans, riding.

DOUGALL, Robert MBE
Former BBC newsreader/
author/ broadcaster
b. 27.11.13 Croydon. Started
in BBC accounts dept.
Announcer Empire Service
1934, served with the RNVR
during the war, returned to
the BBC 1946, and
successfully held
appointments in European
Service, and Far Eastern
Broadcasting Service in
Singapore. Light Programme
announcer before becoming
TV newsreader 1954. Retired
1973 and same year won
Radio Industries Club award
for Top Newsreader. Awards
for clearest speaking voice
on TV 1963, 1965, 1967.
President of the Royal
Society for the Protection of
Birds. TV incl: This is Your
Life; Generation Game;
Russell Harty Show; Celebrity
Squares; Nationwide;
Thames at Six; Survival; Stars
on Sunday. Books: In and Out
of the Box (autobiography);
Now For the Good News; A
Celebration of Birds.
Education: Whitgift School,
Croydon. m. Nan, 1 step-d.
Michele, 1 s. Alastair.
Address: c/o Essanay Ltd,
London W14. Starsign:
Sagittarius. Hobbies:
ornithology, gardening,
riding, walking dogs.
Unfulfilled ambition: to ride
the winner of the Grand
National.

DOUGLAS, Alton
Comedian b. 22.1.40
Birmingham. Began career
as leader of own jazz band.
Progressed to comedy and

as a solo comic has
appeared in summer shows
and pantomimes.
Sophisticated cabaret, hotel
and theatre comedian. Writes
comedy material and scripts.
TV: has appeared as a
warm-up comic on over 800
shows including New Faces;
Happy Ever After; Citizen
Smith; The Generation
Game; The Golden Shot.
Appearances in:
Crossroads; A Soft Touch;
The Golden Shot. Own BBC
show The Original Alton
Douglas.'Several
appearances and series for
BBC TV Midlands.
Education: Saltley Grammar.
m. Jo. Address: c/o George
Bartram Enterprises,
Birmingham. Starsign:
Aquarius. Hobbies: pet dog,
Groucho Marx (Old English
Sheepdog), jazz records,
books on the theatre and
comedy, paintings, models,
all information on clowns,
keep fit. Unfulfilled ambitions:
to have his own series and
meet George Burns.

DOUGLAS, Jack
Comedian/actor b. 26.4.27
Newcastle-upon-Tyne.
Pantomime producer at 14

before joining small combo
playing drums. Acting debut
at 21 in Dick Whittington.
Partnered Joe Baker for nine
years, then went solo,
created Alf Ippititimus and
was with Des O'Connor for
five years on stage and TV.
Pantomimes, summer
seasons, farces, musicals
and films. Hosted TV shows
in Britain, America, Canada
and Australia and appeared
on Ed Sullivan Show. TV
acting debut in The Reluctant
Juggler. Own cookery/chat
show for Channel TV. Also for
ITV, Red Saturday; The
Shillingbury Blowers and
The Alan Stewart Show.
Established member of the
Carry On team. Writer of cook
books. Education: St
Joseph's College, Beulah
Hill, London. m. Susan,
2 d. Deborah, Sarah,
1 s. Craig. Address: c/o
Richard Stone, London.
Starsign: Taurus. Hobbies:
painting, antiques,
photography, cooking,
shooting, driving. Unfulfilled
ambitions: to live next door to
Bernard Delfont and to have
my own cookery/chat show
on TV.

DOUGLAS, Colin
Actor b. 28.7.12 Newcastle.
Emigrated to New Zealand
when 16 but came back after
five years and went to RADA.
Spell in rep then Catterick
and Sandhurst, became
captain and adjutant in the
Border Regiment and served
in First Airborne Division.
Was appearing in Alan
Plater's mining play, Close

the Coalhouse Door when he was chosen for part of Edward Ashton in A Family at War. Other TV incl: Dick Barton – Special Agent; Follyfoot; The Seventh Juror; Love Story; The Flockton Flyer; The Sweeney; Headmaster; The Greenhill Pals; Thicker Than Water; Even Solomon; The Night People; Omega Factor; Telford's Change; Eleanor. Education: farm school, Cumberland. m. actress Gina Cachia, 1 d. Amanda (dec), 4 s. Timothy, Angus, Blaise, Piers. Address: Battersea, London. Starsign: Leo. Hobbies: fishing, golf, cooking. Unfulfilled ambition: to die in harness!

DOUGLAS, Michael
Actor/producer b. 25.9.44 New Brunswick, New Jersey. Never wanted to be an actor and for a while lived in a commune. A visit to his father, Kirk Douglas, then filming Heroes of Telmark in Norway, gave him the taste for a screen career. Studied for a drama degree at the University of California and parts in TV series before sharing starring honours in The Streets of San Francisco. Left the series to go into production and his first effort One Flew Over The Cuckoo's Nest won five Oscars. Films in which he has appeared incl: Hail Hero!; Adam at 6am; Summertree; Coma. m. Spanish-born student Diandra Zucker. Address: Hollywood, Calif. Starsign: Libra. Hobbies: reading, music, skiing, botany.

DOYLE, John
Freelance journalist b. 9.8.34 Coventry. Started as reporter in Sevenoaks, Kent and Exeter. TV with TWW in Cardiff and Bristol 1961-67, then Westward. Freelance since 1968. Also regular contributor to ITN. Education: private and grammar schools; Exeter University (reading Law). m. Suzi, 3 d. Sarah, Penelope-Jane, Melanie (step-d.), 1 s. Guy. Address: Plymouth, Devon. Starsign: Leo. Hobbies: flying, riding, railway modelling. Unfulfilled ambition: to parachute!

DRINKWATER, Carol
Actress b. 22.4.48 London. Three years' training at the Drama Centre, London, then wide experience in rep. Stage appearances incl: Stoke, Bristol Old Vic, Glasgow Citizen's Theatre, Open Space, Hampstead Theatre Club, Birmingham and Leeds reps, National Theatre, Dublin, Edinburgh and Malvern Festivals. Also appeared at Northern Italian Theatre Festival and toured South East Asia. Films incl: Clockwork Orange; The

Dawn Breakers; Mondo Candido; Queen Kong; Joseph Andrews; The Shout. TV incl: Public Eye; Bill Brand; Softly, Softly; The Sweeney; Raffles; Sam (third series); Bouquet of Barbed Wire (two series); All Creatures Great and Small (three series) for which she shared 1979 Variety Club Award for BBC TV Personality. Education: Holy Trinity Convent, Bromley, Kent. Address: London. Starsign: Taurus. Hobbies: scuba diving, swimming, writing, music, travelling, walking. Unfulfilled ambitions: many, including to play Cleopatra.

DRUETT, Geoffrey
Reporter/interviewer b. 8.5.44 Wendover, Bucks. Graduate trainee with Tyne Tees TV 1966, political correspondent Anglia TV, 1974-77, presenter of Yorkshire TV's Calendar since 1977. Education: Taunton School, Somerset, and Exeter College, Oxford. m. Judith Brook, 1 d. Vanessa, twins Jonathan and Hannah. Address: c/o Yorkshire TV, Leeds. Starsign: Taurus. Hobbies: music, theatre, gardening, caravanning. Unfulfilled ambition: to grow a lettuce before the slugs get it.

DUCKENFIELD, Richard
TV journalist b. 5.2.45 Anston, Yorks. Training on local and daily newspapers and radio before becoming BBC reporter on Merseyside.

m. Barbara. Address: c/o BBC, Liverpool. Starsign: Aquarius. Hobbies: supporting Tranmere Rovers and Huyton Rugby League Football Club, snooker, bananas and orange ice cream. Unfulfilled ambition: to own a bicycle.

DUDLEY, Peter
Actor b. 21.6.35 Manchester. Trained in rep before TV work, but regularly appears at Manchester Library Theatre. Five previous parts in Coronation Street before becoming Bert Tilsley. TV incl: Strangers; Siege of Golden Hill; Against the Crowd; Shabby Tiger; A Raging Calm; Crown Court. Education: secondary school. Address: c/o Peter Campbell, London W1. Starsign: cusp of Gemini/Cancer. Hobbies: painting, cooking. Unfulfilled ambition: to act at the National Theatre.

DUFF, Lesley
Actress b. 25.4.52 London. Voice and drama training with Beryl Cooke, then ASM Birmingham, and wardrobe on tours and rep at Watford,

Derby, Colwyn Bay, Leicester, Stratford East. West End: The Philanthropist; Happy as a Sandbag (and on TV and radio); The Bells of Hell; Beyond the Rainbow. Films incl: Carry On Camping; Hamlet (Ophelia). TV incl: Up the Workers; Emu's Christmas Adventures; People Like Us; Leave Him to Heaven; The Ink-smeared Lady. Education: Bishop Simpson C of E School for Girls. Address: c/o LM Agency, London W2. Starsign: Taurus. Hobbies: reading, ice-skating, gardening. Unfulfilled ambition: to go overland to Australia by Land Rover on her own.

DUFFY, Patrick
Actor b. 17.3.49 Townsend, Montana. Moved to Seattle when he was 12 and his high school drama teacher recommended him for a drama course at the University of Washington in Seattle, where he later joined the Washington State Theatre Company as their first 'actor in residence' performing with touring groups. He also met his future wife who was a

dancer. Experience with the Seattle Rep Co and on Broadway before going to Hollywood where his first job was driving a truck. Small parts in TV films before acting with the San Diego Old Globe Shakespeare Company. More TV appearances then, in 1976, he won the title role in Man From Atlantis and subsequently Dallas. Member of Nichiren Shocshu Academy, a Buddhist organisation. m. dancer Carlyn Rosser, 1 s. Padriac Terence. Address: Santa Monica, Calif. Starsign: Pisces. Hobbies: collecting children's books and antique toys.

DUNCANSON, John
Reporter/interviewer b. 14.4.40, Prestwick, Ayrshire. After a BBC course in broadcasting, spent four years as presenter on BBC TV and 14 years as newsreader/ announcer with various TV companies. Also producer/ presenter of radio shows. TV incl: About Women (Anglia TV); Reporting Scotland (BBC); Grampian Today (Grampian TV). Education: Barlborough Hall, Waid Academy, Royal High School, Edinburgh. m. Norma, 1 d. Eilidh, 1 s. John. Address: c/o Grampian TV, Aberdeen. Starsign: Aries. Hobbies: sailing, boat building, learning Gaelic, folklore, music, cooking. Unfulfilled ambition: to have enough money not to worry about unfulfilled ambitions.

DUNHAM, Joanna
Actress b. 6.5.36 Luton,
Beds. First ambition was to
be an artist, and with this end
in view studied at the Slade
School for two years. A part in
the school's play decided her
on an acting career and she
studied at RADA for a further
two years. Won Daily Mirror
award as most promising
actress in I Remember
Mama. Other plays incl: Lady
From the Sea; Romeo and
Juliet (also on tour, in
America and Europe); The
Formation Dancers; A Month
in the Country etc. Films incl:
The Greatest Story Ever Told;
A Day on the Beach. TV incl:
Arms and the Man; Blithe
Spirit; Love Story; Sanctuary;
Wicked Women; Platanov;
The Passenger; The Voice;
Van Der Valk; The Other One.
Education: Bedales,
Petersfield, Hants.
m. architect Harry Osbourne
(dis); 1 d. Abigail,
1 s. Benedict. Address: c/o
Plunket Green Ltd, London
W1. Starsign: Taurus.
Hobbies: gardening,
cooking, sewing. Unfulfilled
ambition: to write a book.

DUNHAM, Rosemarie
Actress b. 13th December,
Leuchars, Scotland.
Repertory training. Films incl:
Get Carter; Something to
Hide; Sarah; Lady Oscar; In
Search of Eden. TV incl: The
Avengers; Public Eye; Kisses
at 50; Crown Court; Late Call;
Village Hall; Angels; Anna
Karenina; The Return of the
Saint; Rosie. 1 s. Paul
Address: c/o Peter Browne

Management, London SW9.
Starsign: Sagittarius. Hobby:
growing roses. Unfulfilled
ambition: to appear in a
Western – preferably with
Robert Mitchum.

DUNN, Clive OBE
Actor b. 9.1.22 London. Third
generation of his family in the
theatre. Trained at Italia Conti
School and first professional
debut in Where the Rainbow
Ends. Best known for his old
men roles on TV, especially in
Bootsie and Snudge and
Dad's Army (also on stage).
Other TV incl: It's a Square
World; The World of
Beachcomber; Ooh, La La;
Jokers Wild; My Old Man.
Records: Grandad; Senior
Citizen. Appeared with the
English National Opera
Company as Frosch in Die
Fledermaus. Education:
Sevenoaks, Kent. m. actress
Priscilla Morgan, 2 d. Polly,
Jessica. Address: c/o BBC,
London. Starsign: Capricorn.
Hobbies: painting,
water-skiing.

DUNSTAN, Paul
Reporter/producer
b. 29.1.38 Birmingham.
Trained as newspaper

reporter, Birmingham,
Manchester, Middle East. TV:
reporter, newsreader,
producer Birmingham,
Leeds; YTV Calendar
reporter, newsreader,
producer; documentaries:
The Bradford Godfather; A
Crisis in the Family; It's a Bit
Frightening; Once in a
Lifetime; Sunley's Daughter;
Nine Miles High In A Hot Air
Balloon; Don't Ask me; Don't
Just Sit There; Discovery;
Stay Alive with Eddie McGee.
Education: Solihull School,
Warwicks. m. Shirley,
1 d. Joanna, 1 s. Jonathan.
Address: Goldsborough,
North Yorks. Starsign:
Aquarius. Hobby: arguing
with the tax man. Unfulfilled
ambition: to play for Leeds
United.

DURDEN-SMITH, Neil
Commentator/presenter
b. 18.8.33 Richmond, Surrey.
Served in the Royal Navy
1952-62, and BBC producer
1963-66. Films incl: The
Games. Radio: Test Match;
World Cup; County
Championship and Gillette
Cup. Resident panellist
Treble Chance; Forces
Chance and Sporting

Chance. Presenter: Champion's Choice; Sports Special; Review of the Sporting Press. Reporter for Today; World at One; Outlook; Movie-Go-Round; The World Today; Rugby Union; Badminton, hockey, etc. TV incl: cricket; hockey; Rugby Union; International polo; sailing; bowls; rowing and county shows; Mexico and Munich Olympics. Reporter for ITN; World of Sport and Grandstand; chairman Tournament and Money Matters. Education: Aldenham and Royal Naval College. m. TV presenter Judith Chalmers, 1 d. Emma, 1 s. Mark. Address: Durden-Smith Communications, London SW3. Starsign: Leo. Hobbies: theatre and films, playing all forms of sport, reading newspapers. Unfulfilled ambition: to sing and dance like Fred Astaire.

DUTTINE, John
Actor b. 15.3.49 Barnsley, Yorks. After training at the Drama Centre, London, rep at Glasgow Citizen's Theatre, Watford and Nottingham. TV incl: Armchair Theatre; Pin to See the Peepshow; Z Cars; Holding On; Warship; Lord Peter Wimsey; Rooms; Coronation Street; Spend, Spend, Spend; Jesus of Nazareth; Beryl's Lot; Angels; Law Centre; Saturday, Sunday, Monday; Devil's Crown; People Like Us; Wuthering Heights; Strangers; The Mallens. Address: c/o Peter Browne

Management, London SW9. Starsign: Pisces. Hobbies: making wine/beer and drinking it, gardening, walking. Unfulfilled ambitions: to have a cottage in the country, and to play Hamlet.

DYSON, Noël
Actress b. 23.12.16 Newton Heath, Manchester. Trained at RADA followed by rep at Oxford, Birmingham and Windsor. Other stage work incl: musicals; Dear Miss Phoebe; A Girl Called Jo; Watergate Theatre Club revue; Book of the Month; Playbill; Restoration of Arnold Middleton; Sisters (Royal Exchange Theatre, Manchester). First TV appearance in The Guinea Pig for the BBC 1948. Has since become one of TV's most in demand actresses. TV incl: Joan and Leslie; Coronation Street (Ida Barlow); Emergency–Ward 10; Z Cars; Potter; The Secret Orchards and Nanny in Father, Dear Father. Education: Roedean and finishing school, Paris. m. Kenneth Edwards (dec), 1 step-d. Jennifer. Address: c/o Jimmy Garrod, London SE21. Starsign: Capricorn. Hobbies: gardening, my poodles and helping to promote the Roller Disco, the Roxy Rollers Dance Group. Unfulfilled ambitions: to speak French fluently, and to be able to spell.

E

EBSEN, Buddy
Actor b. 2.4.08 Belleville,
Illinois, USA. Started as a
dancer, his first Broadway
role being as a dancer in
Ziegfeld's 1928 production of
Whoopee with Eddie Cantor.
Teamed up with his sister as
a dancing partner for many
years. His dancing was seen
in such films as Lucky Star;
Captain January (with Shirley
Temple); The Girl of the
Golden West and Broadway
Melody of 1938 (with Judy
Garland). Other films incl:
Attack; Between Heaven and
Hell; The House; Night
People; Breakfast at Tiffany's
and The Interns. Best known
for his parts in Davy Crockett;
The Beverly Hillbillies and
more recently, Barnaby
Jones. Education: University
of Florida. m. (1st) (dis),
(2nd) Nancy, 6 d. Susannah,
Cathy, Bonnie, Kiersten (from
2nd m), Libby, Alix (from
1st m), 1 s. Dusty (from
2nd m). Address: Newport
Beach, Calif. Starsign: Aries.
Hobbies: sailing, fishing,
politics, good books, music,
art, US and Civil War history.

ECCLES, Donald
Actor b. 26.4.08 Nafferton,
Yorks. Was originally in an
insurance office. Worked with
St Pancras People's Theatre,
London (amateur) before first
professional stage
appearance in New York
1930; first London
appearance 1934. Wide
experience in West End, on
tour and in rep at
Birmingham, Malvern
Festival, Royal Shakespeare
Company, Oxford and
Mermaid, London. Recent
stage work incl: Hadrian the
Seventh; Forty Years On; A
Family and A Fortune;
Sorrows of Frederick. Much
radio and TV incl: Emma;
Chain of Straw; Nine Tailors;
Dr Who; Shadow of the
Tower; Softly, Softly; The
Pallisers; Platanov;
I Claudius; Everyman – Trial
for Blasphemy; Legend of
Arthur; Crown Court;
Coronation Street; The
Avenue; Quatermass;
Rumpole of the Bailey; St
Vitus' Dance; Brideshead
Revisited. Education:
Bridlington and Highgate
Schools. Address:
Ovingdean, Sussex.
Starsign: Taurus. Hobbies:
painting, gardening.

EDDINGTON, Paul
Actor b. 18.6.27 London.
First stage appearance with
ENSA in Colchester Garrison
Theatre 1944. Rep at
Birmingham and Sheffield
before training at RADA
1951. Then rep at Ipswich
and TV (including The
Adventures of Robin Hood);

London stage debut 1961.
Joined Bristol Old Vic
following year, leaving in
1963 to appear in A Severed
Head in America. Returned to
Bristol Old Vic 1965 and has
since appeared in many
plays there and in London's
West End, incl: Absurd
Person Singular; Donkey's
Years; Ten Times Table;
Middle-aged Spread. Wide
TV experience incl: Special
Branch; The Good Life; Yes,
Minister. A governor of the
Old Vic Theatre Trust since
1975. Education: The
Friends' School, Sibford
Ferris, Oxon. m. actress
Patricia Scott, 1 d. Gemma,
3 s. Toby, Hugo, Dominic.
Address: c/o ICM, London
W1. Starsign: Gemini.
Hobbies: music, reading, art.

EDEN, Mark
Actor b. 14.2.28 London.
Fairground worker at
Margate and Ramsgate
before joining Swansea rep
as assistant stage manager
1958. Further rep experience
at Llandudno, Richmond,
Windsor, Royal Court and
Royal Shakespeare
Company. Films incl: Dr
Zhivago; The L-Shaped

Room; The Password is Courage; Attack on the Iron Coast; Seance on a Wet Afternoon. TV incl: many plays; The Saint; The Avengers; Catchhand; Crime Buster; Lord Peter Wimsey; The Top Secret Life of Edgar Briggs; Jesus of Nazareth; Wilde Alliance; General Hospital; Crown Court; London Belongs to Me; Sam; Law Centre. Education: London state schools. m. Diana, 1 d. Polly, 2 s. David, Saul. Address: c/o Brian Wheeler, London W4. Starsign: Aquarius. Hobbies: playing piano, doing crosswords, writing, decorating and talking to the kids. Unfulfilled ambition: to see clean streets in the London borough of Wandsworth.

EDMONDS, Noel
Disc jockey b. 22.12.49 Ilford, Essex. While a student teacher chose to become a Radio Luxembourg DJ (1968) rather than take up a place at Surrey University. Went to BBC 1969 and a year later took over Kenny Everett's daily slot Radio One Breakfast show 1973-78. TV: introduced Top of the Pops; Come Dancing; Multi-Coloured Swap Shop; Hobby Horse; a panellist on New Faces; host of Juke Box Jury. Education: Brentwood School. m. Gill. Address: Weston Turville, Bucks. Starsign: Capricorn.

EDWARDS, Adrian
Announcer b. 3.4.48 Windsor, Berks. Formerly a maths master. Actor/writer with Cambridge Footlights. Now with Southern TV. Education: St John's College Cambridge. Address: Southampton. Starsign: Aries. Hobbies: music, theatre and making whoopee. Unfulfilled ambitions: to read the clock correctly at closedown; to write a musical/comedy based on Das Kapital; to stage Wagner's Ring of the Nibelung on ice.

EDWARDS, Ian
Sports correspondent b. 23.5.42 Barmouth, Wales. Editor of university newpaper 1963-64. Newspaper training as general reporter specialising in arts and music with Western Mail 1966-69. News assistant, BBC Wales in Cardiff 1969-71; sports correspondent, Tyne Tees TV 1971-75 when he became ITN's sports correspondent. Education: Friars Grammar, Bangor and University College of Wales, Cardiff (BA Hons modern languages). m. Mari, 1 d. Catrin,

1 s. Steffan. Address: Teddington, Middx. Starsign: Gemini. Hobbies: music, tennis, squash. Unfulfilled ambition: to conduct the London Symphony Orchestra at the Royal Festival Hall.

EDWARDS, Jimmy
Actor/comedian b. 23.3.20 Barnes, Surrey. Served in the RAF (decorated DFC) during the war and made his stage debut at London's Windmill Theatre 1946 and radio debut the same year. Starred in such long-running radio series as Take It From Here; My Wildest Dream; Does the Team Think? Many stage shows incl: pantomimes; Maid of the Mountains revival; Big Bad Mouse; Doctor in the House; Oh! Sir James! (which he wrote). TV incl: Whack-O!; Seven Faces of Jim; Bold as Brass; I Object; John Jorrocks Esq; The Auction Game; The Fossett Saga; Jokers Wild; Sir Yellow; Charley's Aunt; The Glums. Education: St Paul's Cathedral Choir School; St John's College, Cambridge (MA). m. Valerie (dis). Address: Fletching, Sussex. Starsign: Aries. Hobbies: hunting, shooting, polo.

EGAN, Peter
Actor b. 28.9.46 London. Wanted to be an artist, but studied for the stage at RADA and while still a student there was invited by Sir John Clements to join the Chichester Festival Theatre company. This was followed

by work with the Royal Shakespeare Company and the National Theatre. Other stage incl: Journey's End; What Every Woman Knows; Engaged; Rolls Hyphen Royce; You Never Can Tell (to re-open the Lyric Theatre, Hammersmith). Films incl: One Brief Summer; The Hireling (BAFTA Award for Most Promising Newcomer 1974); Callan; Hennessy. TV break came with Big Breadwinner Hog. Other TV incl: Mother Love; The Inheritors; The Organisation; The Love School; The Deep Blue Sea; Lillie; The Kitchen; Prince Regent. Education: St George's Secondary Modern School, Maida Vale, London. m. actress Myra Frances, 1 d. Rebecca. Address: c/o Fraser and Dunlop Ltd, London W1. Starsign: Libra. Hobbies: travel, swimming, poker, working, good wine. Unfulfilled ambitions: to play in the men's singles at Wimbledon and win!; to write a best-selling novel.

Revolution and came to England. Trained at Bristol Old Vic Theatre School and has since appeared in more than 90 productions on stage, film, radio and TV. Stage incl: Pitlochry Festival; Hyppolytus; A Patriot for Me; La Musica; Fiddler on the Roof; Lies, etc. Films incl: And Soon the Darkness; Countess Dracula; Fun and Games; The Rebel; San Ferry Anne; The Naked Edge; Kremlin Letter; Scorpio, Greek Tycoon. Radio plays incl: Semmelweiss; Daphne Laureola; Cousin Bette. Numerous plays and series on TV incl: Supernatural; The Saint; The Baron; The Avengers; The Foundation; Why Can't We Go Home?; Biggles; Fall of Eagles; Vienna 1900; The Wyngate Trilogy; Tussy; Timeslip; Marked Personal; Upstairs, Downstairs; Crimes of Passion; New Scotland Yard; Blood Wedding; The End of the Equation; Foreign Affairs; Conrad; The Jean Rhys Woman; Bartok; The Assassination Run. Education: High School education in Hungary. Address: c/o Trafalgar Perry Ltd, London WC2. Starsign: Gemini. Hobbies: painting, writing, making things. Unfulfilled ambitions: to direct a film, however small; to write a book or two.

Drama spent a year with the Old Vic Company 1958-59. since 1964 has been in succession as an announcer with Tyne Tees TV, Southern TV, and ABC TV. Joined Thames TV 1968. Has done a number of radio commercials. TV incl: Rainbow; Whodunnit?; Pauline's People; Armchair Thriller. Education: Pitman's College, Birmingham. m. actress Joan Scott. Address: c/o Thames TV, London. Starsign: Scorpio. Hobbies: golf and wasting time. Unfulfilled ambition: scratch handicap at golf.

EMERY, Dick
Comedian/singer b. 19.2.17 London. Started in amateur shows, then chorus work and pantomime; Gang Shows in RAF, Windmill 1948. Radio incl: Happy Holiday; Educating Archie; Emery at Large. Films. TV incl: Two's Company; It's a Square World; The Army Game; Ooh, You Are Awful; Find The Lady (with Mickey Rooney); The Dick Emery Show. Pantomimes. Extensive tours of Australia and New Zealand. 1973 BBC Personality of the Year Award. Royal Command Performance. m. dancer Josephine Blake. Address: c/o Elliott Young Productions, London W1. Starsign: Pisces. Hobbies: motor bikes, flying, sailing.

ELES, Sandor
Actor b. 15.6.36 Hungary. Left Hungary as a student at the time of the 1956

ELSMORE, Philip
Actor/announcer b. 16.11.37 Stourport- on- Severn, Worcs. After training at Webber Douglas School of

ENGLISH, Arthur
Actor b. 9.5.19 Aldershot.
Ex-sergeant instructor in the
RAC and former painter and
decorator who was 30 before
he went into show business.
Became famous by
parodying the Spiv, but went
'straight' 20 years later. Stage
incl: London's Windmill
Theatre; Royal Variety;
revues; pantomimes;
summer season. TV incl:
Follyfoot; Copper's End;
How's Your Father; Dixon of
Dock Green; Crown Court;
Not in Front of the Children;
Doctor in the House; The
Ghosts of Motley Hall; Are
You Being Served?; Funny
Man and many plays.
Education: 'Very little', he
claims. m. (1st) Ivy (dec);
(2nd) dancer Teresa Mann,
1 d. Ann, 1 s. Anthony (both
from 1st m). Address: c/o
Patrick Freeman
Management, London W6.
Starsign: Taurus. Unfulfilled
ambition: 'to stay as happy as
I am now.'

ENSIGN, Michael
Actor b. 13.2.44 Safford,
Arizona, USA. Trained at
London Academy of Music
and Drama. Stage

appearances incl: Irene;
Royal Shakespeare Co. Films
incl: Midnight Express;
Assassin. TV incl: Colditz;
Life at Stake; Everyman.
Education: University of Utah
(BA degree). Address:
Battersea, London. Starsign:
Aquarius. Hobbies: music
(organ and harpsichord),
reading, jogging. Unfulfilled
ambition: to write a novel.

ESHLEY, Norman
Actor b. 30.5.45 Bristol.
Started work in a bank but left
to join Bristol Old Vic School.
First professional
appearance was in Orson
Welles' film The Immortal
Story. Other films incl: Blind
Terror; The Disappearance;
Yanks. Stage incl: Romeo
and Juliet; Measure for
Measure; Hamlet;
Midsummer Night's Dream;
Vivat Vivat Regina; Twelfth
Night; Arms and the Man.
Has appeared in many TV
plays and series incl: Randall
and Hopkirk; Parkin's Patch;
Bouncing Boy; Vienna 1900;
The Onedin Line; The Skin
Game; Wingate; Warship;
The Duchess of Duke Street; I
Claudius; Supernatural;
Secret Army; 1990; Justice;
Thriller; The Strength of
Gemini; Man About the
House; Mother Makes Five;
Return of the Saint; The
Sweeney; George and
Mildred. Education: Bristol
Grammar. m. actress/singer
Millicent Martin (dis).
Address: Kensington,
London. Starsign: Gemini.
Hobbies: football, cricket,

archaeology, horse-racing.
Unfulfilled ambitions: lots.

ESLER, Gavin
TV reporter b. 27.2.53
Glasgow. Newspaper
background as Thomson
Newspapers graduate
trainee and two years with
Belfast Telegraph. Reporter/
presenter Spotlight, BBC's
weekly Northern Ireland
current affairs programme.
Education: George Heriot's
School, Edinburgh;
University of Kent,
Canterbury (BA); Leeds
University (MA in Anglo-Irish
literature). Address: c/o BBC,
Belfast. Starsign: Pisces.
Hobbies: reading,
swimming, all sports,
Northern Ireland, music,
travel. Unfulfilled ambition: to
spend a year working in
America.

EVANS, Barry
Actor/director b. 18.6.43
Guildford, Surrey. Trained at
Central School of Speech
and Drama. TV incl: Doctor in
the House; Crossroads;
Armchair Theatre; Love
Story; Mind Your Language.
Address: c/o Hazel Malone
Management, London SW13.

Starsign: Gemini. Hobbies: photography, gardening, animals, ecology. Unfulfilled ambition: to be a gentleman farmer with 600,000 acres or a hobo with a smallholding.

F

EVERETT, Kenny
Disc jockey/presenter
b. 25.12.44 Liverpool.
Wanted to become a priest.
Jobs in a bakery, advertising
agency and newspaper
office before making a name
as a DJ with Radio
Luxembourg. Subsequently
with Capital Radio and on TV
for BBC and ITV. TV incl: Nice
Time; The Kenny Everett
Explosion; Making Whoopee;
Ev; The Kenny Everett Video
Show. Created the fabulous
Capt Kremmen. Education:
Peter Clavier School for junior
African missionaries.
m. ex-singer Audrey
Middleton. Address: London
W11. Starsign: Capricorn.
Hobby: squash. Unfulfilled
ambition: to have the world's
biggest collection of
doobries.

FAIRFAX, Diana
Actress b. Melbourne,
Australia. Came to England
1956. RADA followed by rep
at Crewe, Bristol and
Nottingham. Radio
experience as a child in
Australia. West End stage
incl: Hay Fever; Month of
Sundays. TV plays and series
incl: Seven Faces of Woman;
Just William. Education:
Sydney Church of England
Girls' Grammar. m. actor
Derek Godfrey, 2 d. Julia,
Pippa. Address: c/o LWT,
London SE1. Hobbies:
needlework; reading; walks
in the country; home
decorating.

FAIRLEY, Peter
Science journalist b. 2.11.30
Kuala Lumpur, Malaya.
Started as a newspaper
reporter, then London
Evening Standard 1954 for
14 years. Numerous radio
and TV broadcasts covering
all the Apollo Missions to the
moon and travelled to every
continent in the world. ITN
Science Editor and TVTimes
Science Editor since 1968.
Author of several books.
Science Editor, Capital Radio
since 1975. Education:
Sutton Valence School and
Sidney Sussex College,
Cambridge (BA Hons).
m. Vivienne, 1 d. Josephine,
3 s. Alastair, Duncan, Simon.
Address: London W1.
Starsign: Scorpio. Hobbies:
writing, gardening and
woodwork. Unfulfilled
ambition: could be fulfilled on
a circular bed.

FALK, Peter
Actor b. 16.9.27 New York.
Probably the highest paid
actor in TV history – gets two
million dollars for four
90-minute episodes of
Columbo. Got the acting bug
when he was 16, but it was 10
years before he became a

professional actor. In the
interim he attended Hamilton
College; enlisted in the
Merchant Marine, making
two trips to Europe and a
six-months tour of South
America, working as a cook;
returned to Hamilton and
enrolled in the New School fo
Social Research (BA in
political science) and
Syracuse University (MA in
public administration); took a
post as efficiency expert to
the Budget Director of
Connecticut, Hartford. While
taking an acting course, his
tutor advised him to try his
luck on Broadway and within
a month had landed a
number of off-Broadway
parts; Broadway debut was
in Shaw's St Joan with
Siobhan McKenna. Started in
Columbo 1972 (second
Emmy award). His mascot/
trademark raincoat is his
own, having bought it in New
York while on his way to
England in 1967. His right
eye was removed at the age
of three because of a tumour.
Films incl: Murder Inc.; A
Pocketful of Miracles (Oscar
nominations for both);
Husbands; Anzio; Micky and
Nickey; Women Under the
Influence; The Cheap
Detective; Today is Forever.
TV incl: The Trials of O'Brien;
guest appearances in nearly
every major programme; The
Price of Tomatoes (first
Emmy). m. (1st) designer
Alyce Mayo (dis);
(2nd) actress Shera Danese,
2d. Kackie, Cath. Address:
Beverly Hills, Calif. Starsign:
Virgo. Hobbies: golf, pool,
painting.

FARLEIGH, Lynn
Actress b. 3.5.42 Bristol.
Studied at London Guildhall
School of Music and Drama,
then rep at Salisbury,
Canterbury and Richmond
before joining Royal
Shakespeare Company
1966. Stage productions incl:

All's Well That Ends Well (also
on TV); Revengers Tragedy;
The Homecoming; The
Doctor's Dilemma; A Room
With a View; Brand; Friends;
Exiles; Ashes; Suzanna
Andler; Sovereignty under
Elizabeth; Brand; Shout
Across The River; Hang of the
Gaol; Close of Play. Films
incl: Three Into Two Won't Go;
A Phoenix Too Frequent;
Voices; The Word. TV incl:
Z Cars; Hallelujah
Handshake; Eyeless in Gaza;
The Guardians; New
Scotland Yard; Public Eye;
The Strauss Family; Bill
Brand; Scenes from Family
Life; Fall of Angels; Steptoe
and Son; Cakes and Ale;
Cottage to Let; The Velvet
Glove; Murder Most English;
Scorpion Tales; The Three
Kisses; Harry. Education:
Bristol High School. m. actor
Michael Jayston (dis),
2 s. Joe, Matthew. Address:
c/o Boyack and Conway,
London W1. Starsign:
Taurus. Hobbies: gardening,
canal pottering. Unfulfilled
ambition: to act in a Chekhov
play at the Theatre Royal
Bristol.

FARRELL, Mike
Actor b. 6th February, St
Paul, Minn. Always wanted to
be an actor, but it was only
after two years in the Marine
Corps that he began to study
drama seriously at Los
Angeles City College and
University College of Los
Angeles. It was there he met
the girl who was to become
his wife. Appeared in many
plays at local theatres. Films

incl: Capt Newman MD; The Graduate; The Americanisation of Emily; Targets; The Longest Night; The Questor Tapes; Battered. In addition to M*A*S*H (he claims to have watched every episode), his TV work incl: The Interns; The Man and The City; Mannix; The Bold Ones; Marcus Welby MD; Owen Marshall; Harry O. Education: Hollywood High School. m. actress Judy Hayden, 1 d. Erin, 1 s. Michael. Address: San Fernando Valley. Starsign: Aquarius. Hobby: reading, mainly psychology and politics.

FARRINGTON, Kenneth
Actor b. 18.4.36 Peckham, London. Originally wanted to study languages but after acting at school became a founder member of the National Youth Theatre and later went to RADA. TV incl: The Splendid Spur; An Age of Kings; The Prime Minister's Daughter; The Expert; Love Story; Kipling; Z Cars; Softly, Softly; The Tomorrow People; Coronation Street (in which he appears intermittently as Annie Walker's son in order to do stage work); Danger UXB; New Girl In Town; General Hospital; Crown Court; Tycoon. Stage incl: The Outcry; Edward II; Nil Carborundum; The Little Hut; Saturday, Sunday, Monday; The Lion In Winter; Da; Getting On; A Man For All Seasons; This Story of Yours; Blythe Spirit; The Odd Couple; The Taming of the Shrew; The Norman Conquests. Films incl: One Way Pendulum; Submarine XI; The Knack. Education: Alleyn's. m. actress Patricia Heneghan, 1 d. Theresa, 2 s. James, Mark. Address: Clapham, London. Starsign: Aries. Hobbies: home-made wine and beer, photography, playing soccer, squash. Unfulfilled ambition: 'to have own theatre and company to act and direct.'

FEARN, Shelia
Actress b. 3.10.40 Leicester. Trained at RADA. Rep at Nottingham then joined a touring company. Films incl: Billy Liar; A Hard Day's Night; The Likely Lads. TV incl: Gazette; The Likely Lads; Whatever Happened to the Likely Lads; The Flockton Flyer; George and Mildred; episodes of Love Story; Thriller; and numerous TV plays. Education: grammar school. Address: c/o Peter Browne Management, London SW9. Starsign: Libra. Hobbies: reading, gardening. Unfulfilled ambition: to work with Morecambe and Wise, Ronnie Barker and The Muppets (not necessarily in that order!).

FEAST, Fred
Actor/dramatist/ playwright b. 5.10.29 Scarborough. Originally a variety artist. Has appeared in 70 TV plays incl: award-winning Soldier and Me; Another Sunday and Sweet F A; Ready When You Are Mr McGill. TV also incl: Days of Hope; Bill Brand; Country Matters and Fred Gee in Coronation Street. Education: Graham Sea Training School, Scarborough. m. Kathleen, 3 d. Julia, Andrea, Helen. Address: c/o Granada TV, Manchester. Starsign: Libra. Hobbies: gardening, fishing. Unfulfilled ambitions: to play in London's West End, Broadway and Hollywood; to have a play he has written for TV, Skyhook's Ticket to San Fernando Valley, produced.

FERGUSON, Clive
Reporter/presenter b. 30.12.51 Lurgan, N Ireland. Freelance on current affairs on radio and reporter and TV presenter of BBC's Northern Ireland regional programmes, incl:

Scene Around Six.
Education: Lurgan College
and Trinity College, Dublin.
m. Irene. Address: c/o BBC,
Belfast. Starsign: Capricorn.
Hobbies: cricket; music; TV;
cinema; reading. Unfulfilled
ambitions: to further my
career in television
journalism and to fly
Concorde.

FERRIGNO, Lou
Muscleman b. 9.11.51
Brooklyn, New York. The Hulk
in The Incredible Hulk, which
is also his favourite cartoon
character. Former sheet
metal worker. Began
body-building when he was
16 and won Mr Teenage
America contest 1971 and Mr
America title 1973. Following
year won Mr World and Mr
Universe titles. Appeared in
the body-building
documentary film Pumping
Iron, followed by TV
documentaries Superstars
and The World's Strongest
Men. Then came overnight
stardom in The Incredible
Hulk. m. former psychology
student Sue. Starsign:
Scorpio. Hobby: carpentry.
Unfulfilled ambition: to open
a keep-fit business.

FIELD, Mike
Reporter/presenter b. 8.3.39
Enfield, Middlesex. Junior
reporter with Kent
Messenger before National
Service. Then BBC
(producer, reporter, editor),
London Broadcasting
Company (editor) and
presenter/ reporter for
Southern TV. Education: Sir

Roger Manwood's School,
Sandwich. m. Rosalind,
1 s. Jonathan. Address:
Ashford, Kent. Starsign:
Pisces. Hobbies: cricket,
racing, reading and
bird-watching. Unfulfilled
ambition: to be commentator
for the Derby.

FIELDING, Douglas
Actor b. 6.6.46 London.
Trained at LAMDA then 10
years as Sgt Quilley in
Z Cars. Other TV incl: Softly,
Softly; Callan; Tales of
Mystery and Imagination;
Crackerjack; Jackanory.
Education: Tulse Hill School,
London. m. (1st dis),
(2nd) Norreen, 2 d. Nicola,
Sereina. Address: c/o CCA,
London SW6. Starsign:
Gemini. Hobbies: scuba
diving; football; cricket;
cooking; gardening.
Ambition: to keep working.

FINCH, Jon
Actor b. 2.3.42 Caterham,
Surrey. Seven years in rep
before films and TV. Films
incl: Sunday, Bloody Sunday;
Macbeth; Lady Caroline
Lamb; Frenzy; The Man with
the Green Cross; The Final
Programme; Diagnosis

Murder; A Faithful Woman;
Battle Flag; Death on the Nile;
La Sabina. TV incl: Z Cars;
Crossroads; Coronation
Street; Counterstrike; Plays of
the Month; Steve; Ben Hall;
The Avengers; Richard II;
Henry IV Parts I and II.
Address: c/o CCA, London
SW6. Starsign: Pisces.
Hobby: motor racing.
Unfulfilled ambitions: to
napalm the House of Lords;
to back Richard Morgan to
world motor racing
champion.

FINLAY, Frank
Actor b. 6.8.26 Farnworth,
Lancs. Former butcher's
assistant who, at the age of
25, decided he wanted to
become an actor. Trained at
RADA and went into rep at
Guildford and at Coventry
where he appeared in
Chicken Soup and Barley
and moved with the play to
London's Royal Court
Theatre. Many productions at
that theatre incl: Roots;
Sergeant Musgrave's Dance;
Chips With Everything
(Clarence Derwent Award for
Best Actor). Joined the
National Theatre 1963 where
his roles included Iago to

Olivier's Othello (Oscar nomination and elected to Hollywood's Famous Five 1966). Other stage incl: Chichester Festival; Son of Man; After Haggerty; Saturday, Sunday, Monday (and on TV); Plunder; Watch it Come Down; Kings and Clowns; Filumena. Films incl: The Molly Maguires; The Three Musketeers; The Four Musketeers; The Wild Geese; The Thief of Baghdad; Sherlock Holmes – Murder by Decree. On TV he has portrayed Casanova; Shylock; Sancho Panza; Hitler; Voltaire; Napoleon; other TV incl: Count Dracula; Bouquet of Barbed Wire. Education: St Gregory's, Farnworth. m. Doreen, 1 d. Cathy, 2 s. Stephen, Daniel. Address: c/o Al Parker Ltd, London W1. Starsign: Leo. Hobbies: keep-fit; swimming; reading biographies and historical novels; music (Mozart to pop); gardening.

FISH, Michael
Weatherman b. 27.4.44 Eastbourne, Sussex. Has been with the Meteorological Office for 17 years and has made appearances as a TV weatherman for six years. Also appeared on various BBC TV programmes where a 'scientific expert' was needed, and written and narrated several schools radio programmes. Education: Eastbourne College and The City University. m. Susan, 2 d. Alison, Nicola. Address:

c/o BBC, London. Starsign: Taurus. Hobbies: philately, travel, gardening. Unfulfilled ambitions: to travel the world, to present Tomorrow's World.

FITZALAN, Marsha
Actress b. 10.3.53 Bonn, Germany. Daughter of the Duke of Norfolk. Trained at Webber Douglas Academy of Dramatic Art. Rep at Windsor, Canterbury, Hornchurch, Ipswich, York and Crewe. TV incl: Angels; Duchess of Duke Street; Upstairs, Downstairs; Armchair Thriller; Dick Barton; Thundercloud; Shelley; Pride and Prejudice. Films incl: International Velvet. Stage: New Shakespeare Company. Education: Convent of the Sacred Heart, Woldingham, Surrey. m. actor Patrick Ryecart. Address: c/o CCA, London SW6. Starsign: Pisces. Hobbies: riding, skiing, knitting, reading. Unfulfilled ambitions: to win Badminton Horse Trials or to have own situation comedy series.

FLACKES, William D
Political correspondent

b. 14.4.21 Newtown Cunningham, Co Donegal. Extensive experience in Northern Ireland journalism and Press Association parliamentary reporter at Westminster 1947-57. Joined BBC 1964. Education: a variety of Northern Ireland schools. m. Mary, 1 d. Sandra. Address: c/o BBC, Belfast. Starsign: Aries. Hobbies: none worth mentioning.

FLANAGAN, John
Actor b. 30.4.47 Ripley, Derbyshire. Got the taste for acting while in college shows. Trained at Central School of Speech and Drama, then into rep at Bristol Old Vic. Came to the fore on TV through Parkin's Patch. TV incl: Callan; Freewheelers; Z Cars; The Sweeney; Thriller; Public Eye; The Naked Civil Servant; The Soft Touch; Crown Court; Kids. Wrote Bricks Without Straw but did not appear in it. Education: Ripley Technical School. Address: c/o William Morris Agency, London W1. Starsign: Taurus. Hobbies: football (playing, watching and talking), reading and learning. Unfulfilled ambition: 'None – Ambition is the last refuge of the failure (Oscar Wilde).'

FLEMYNG, Robert   OBE
Actor/director b. 3.1.12 Liverpool. Formerly a medical student, he first appeared on the stage in Truro in 1931 and was in his

first London part in 1935 after three seasons at Liverpool Playhouse. Was appearing on Broadway when the Second World War was declared and he returned to England to join the RAMSC. Rose to the rank of lieutenant-colonel, was awarded the Military Cross and other decorations. Returned to the stage in 1945. Wide theatre experience in London, on tour and abroad. Stage incl: French Without Tears; The Cocktail Party; The Guinea Pig (also the film) and many others. Films incl: The Blue Lamp; The Man Who Never Was; The Young Soldiers; Medusa Trap; Four Feathers. Has been in TV since 1949 and between 1961 and 1964 had leading parts in two long-running series, Family Solicitor and Compact. Other TV incl: Probation Officer; Spy Trap; Enemy at the Door. Education: Haileybury College. m. Carmen, 1 d. Caroline. Address: c/o ICM, London W1. Starsign: Capricorn. Hobby: work.

FLETCHER, Cyril
Comedian b. 25.6.13

Watford. Formerly an insurance clerk. Famous for his odd odes which he began writing about his schoolmasters and his first boss. Became a comedian in 1936, studied at the Guildhall School of Music and Drama and soon had his own radio programme, Dreaming of Thee. Has been on radio, TV, in cabaret, summer season and pantomime ever since. First televised in 1936. Many series on TV include: What's My Line?; That's Life; Gardening Today. m. actress partner Betty Astell, 1 d. actress Jill. Address: Sussex. Starsign: Cancer. Hobbies: gardening and the countryside. Unfulfilled ambition: 'I have fulfilled them all!'

FLETCHER-COOK, Graham
Actor/announcer b. 3.11.63 Edmonton, London. Trained at Anna Scher Children's Theatre. Member of Screen Actors Guild (of America). Stage incl: Happy Birthday Wanda June. Films incl: Bugsy Malone; A Little Romance. TV incl: Survivors; Horizon; Our Show – presenter; Saturday Banana; You Must Be Joking; Rebecca of Sunnybrook Farm; Orphan Train (Bestsellers, USA, 1979). Education: Bowes Road and Creighton Schools, London. Address: c/o Anna Scher Children's Theatre. Starsign: Scorpio. Hobbies: collecting film magazines and Marvel comics, making films,

skate-boarding. Unfulfilled ambition: to be a film director.

FLINT, Berni
Singer b. 26.5.52 Southport, Lancs. His training, he claims, was 'annoying people from the age of 10 by singing over somebody else's recordings'. But he started singing while in the Royal Navy. That was before he was 'discovered' on Opportunity Knocks which he won for a record 13 weeks. He soon gave up his job as a laundry van driver and has been cleaning up in show business ever since. His credits ('My teeth are my own!' he says) are mainly on TV as guest on many shows as well As Berni and Stu and Pop Gospel. Also summer show and cabaret. His first single, I Don't Want to Put a Hold on You, which he wrote with his brother Mike, was a Top Ten Hit. Other singles incl: Southern Comfort; If I Had Someone Like You; Beautiful Loser; Albums: I Don't Want to Put a Hold on You; Early Morning Rain; Just Live a Movie. Education: he calls it 'comprehensive'; in fact, it was Our Lady of Lourdes School, Southport. m. Jane. Address: Birkdale, Southport. Starsign: Gemini. Hobbies: golf, badminton, tennis, football.

FORD, Anna
Newscaster b. 2.10.43 Tewkesbury, but brought up in Wigton, Cumbria. Taught for Open University in Belfast for two years before

Granada's Reports Action. Has also been a researcher and presented schools programmes. Reporter with Man Alive 1977; and later same year presented Tomorrow's World. Joined ITN as newscaster 1978. Voted Most Popular TV Personality (Female) by TVTimes readers 1978-79. Education: Manchester University (economics graduate). m. Dr Alan Brittles (dis). Address: c/o ITN, London. Starsign: Libra. Hobby: gardening.

FORD, Petronella
Actress b. 4.2.46 Leeds. TV incl: The Sad Decline of Arthur Maybury; Softly, Softly; Barlow; Shoulder to Shoulder; Clouds of Witness. Films incl: Dr Faustus; Agamemnon. Stage incl: The Mousetrap. Education: Oxford University (hons degree in English). Address: Balham, London. Starsign: Aquarius. Hobbies: writing, tennis. Unfulfilled ambition: to finish writing a play.

FORDE, Peter
Farming editor b. 28.7.32 Manchester. Journalistic

experience on provincial newspapers in Manchester and West Country. TV series incl: Farm and Country News; Acres For Profit; The Happiness Business for Westward TV. Education: St Bede's College, Manchester. m. Josephine, 2 d. Amanda, Emma, 1 s. Simon. Address: Saltash, Cornwall. Starsign: Leo. Hobbies: all sports; swimming; wandering through rural Europe; good food; good wine. Unfulfilled ambitions: to visit cities which were glamorised in old films – New Orleans, Rio de Janeiro, Buenos Aires, Shanghai, Bangkok, and to return to Hong Kong.

FORDYCE, Keith
Commentator/presenter b. 15.10.28 Lincoln. Began with British Forces Network and has since done many shows and series of wide variety both for BBC and ITV. Radio incl: Housewives Choice and World-Wide Family Favourites. TV incl: Thank Your Lucky Stars; Juke Box Jury; Ready, Steady, Go; Come Dancing; Treasure Hunt; Miss Westward; Miss England; Miss UK; Miss

World; Picture Parade; The Groucho Marx Show; Kitchen Garden. Education: Lincoln School and Emmanuel College, Cambridge (hons degree (MA) in Law). m. Anne, 4 d. Rebecca, Kim, Julie, Samantha. Address: Torbay Aircraft Museum, High Blagdon, Paignton, Devon (of which he is curator). Hobbies: gardening, aviation, food and drink, staying in the Isles of Scilly. Unfulfilled ambition: to visit every aircraft museum in the world.

FORSYTH, Bruce
Entertainer/comedian/ singer/actor b. 22.2.28 Edmonton, London. Left school at 14 and started his working life as Boy Bruce, The Mighty Atom. But not 'discovered' until 1958 when, while in summer season at Babbacombe, he was asked to compere Sunday Night at the London Palladium. Since then he hasn't looked back. Stage incl: Windmill Theatre 1945-51 with a two-year break in the RAF; Little Me; Birds on the Wing; The Bruce Forsyth Show; one-man show at London Palladium; The Travelling Music Show; Bruce Forsyth on Broadway. Films incl: Star; Heironymous Merkin; Bedknobs and Broomsticks; Seven Deadly Sins. TV incl: Music Hall; The Bruce Forsyth Show; The Canterville Ghost; The Mating Game; The Generation Game; Bring on the Girls; Bruce and More Girls; The Entertainers;

Bruce's Big Night. Education: Latimer School, Edmonton. m. (1st) former partner Penny Calvert (dis); (2nd) Anthea Redfern, 5 d. Deborah, Julie, Laura (from 1st m), Charlotte, Louisa (from 2nd m). Address: c/o London Management, London W1. Starsign: Pisces. Hobby: golf. Unfulfilled ambitions: to play better golf and to work more internationally both on stage and in films.

FOSTER, Barry
Actor b. 21st August, Beeston, Notts. After training at Central School of Speech and Drama joined Anew McMaster's company touring Eire in classical repertoire. London debut in Fairy Tales of New York at the Comedy Theatre where he has also appeared in My Place; Let's Get a Divorce; Getting Away With Murder. Stage also incl: Next Time I'll Sing to You; The Private Ear and the Public Eye (New York); Nottingham Playhouse; The Basement; Tea Party; After Haggerty; Scribes; Rear Column; Master Builder. Films incl: King and Country; The Family Way; Twisted Nerve; Battle of Britain; Ryan's Daughter; Frenzy; Sweeney; Wild Geese. TV incl: Hamlet; Mogul; Taste of Honey; Van Der Valk; Divorce His, Divorce Hers; Fall of Eagles; Old Times; Wingate; Three Hostages; A Family Affair. Education: Southall County Grammar. m. singer Judith Shergold, 2 d. Joanna,

Miranda, 1 s. Jason. Address: c/o Al Parker Ltd, London W1. Starsign: Leo. Hobbies: music, golf. Unfulfilled ambition: to win a gold watch.

FOSTER, Julia
Actress b. 2.8.43 Lewes, Sussex. First job at Eastbourne, then with Brighton rep as an assistant stage manager. Also rep in Harrogate, Worthing and Richmond. Became a regular in Emergency–Ward 10 which led to other TV parts and such films as Term of Trial; The Loneliness of the Long Distance Runner. Other films incl: Two Left Feet; The System; The Bargee; Alfie; Half a Sixpence. Made her West End debut in Travelling Light, followed by What the Butler Saw; Flint; Lulu; Notes on a Love Affair; The Day After the Fair; St Joan (Oxford); The Singular Life of Alfred Nobbs. Nominated Best Actress on London Stage 1970-73. TV incl: The Planemakers; Love Story; Crime and Punishment; A Fly on the Wall; Mr Axelford's Angel; Good Girl; The Adventures of Moll Flanders; Wilde Alliance. Education: Lourdes Convent, Brighton. m. (1st) singer Lionel Morton (dis), (2nd) vet Bruce Fogle, 2 d. Emily (from 1st m), Tamara (from 2nd m), 1 s. Benjamin (from 2nd m). Address: c/o ICM, London W1. Starsign: Leo.

FOSTER, Marian
Journalist/broadcaster b. 19.3.48 Newcastle upon Tyne. Wide experience of radio and TV on various talk programmes, news, etc. Own music programme, Songbook on BBC's Radio 4 in 1978. TV incl: Newsview; Today at 6; Newsquest; Late Look (Tyne Tees); Swedish TV and Norddeutsche Rundfunk; About Women (Anglia); Pebble Mill at One; South East Journey; The Other Side of Ulster; Sunday Worship at Pebble Mill; Young Musician of the Year; NHK (Japan) Summit Conference Special. Education: grammar school and Newcastle University (BA Hons and Dip Ed). Address: c/o BBC, Birmingham. Starsign: Pisces. Hobbies: music – piano playing and choral singing (with London Symphony Chorus), gardening, cycling. Unfulfilled ambition: to have a heated swimming pool in the back garden.

FOX, Edward
Actor. National Service in the Coldstream Guards and a job

in a Kingston store, before going to RADA followed by several years mainly in rep. Films incl: The Battle of Britain; The Jokers; The Go-Between; A Doll's House; The Day of the Jackal; I'll Never Forget What's His Name; The Duellists; The Squeeze; A Bridge Too Far; The Big Sleep. TV incl: Portrait of A Lady; Loyalties; Shooting the Chandelier; Edward and Mrs Simpson. Voted Best Actor on TV by TVTimes readers 1978-79. (Edward Fox has requested that no details of his private life be included in his entry).

FRANCIS, Derek
Actor b. 7.11.23 Brighton. Went into acting when he came out of the Army in 1947. TV incl: Oh, Brother!; Justice; Dickens of London; The New Avengers; Sexton Blake; Nicholas Nickleby; The Provincial Lady; The Strange Affair of Adelaide Harris. Films incl: several Carry On films; Say Hello To Yesterday; To The Devil A Daughter. Stage incl: with Old Vic 1955-59; Laughter (Royal Court); Charley's Aunt (Adelphi). Education: Varndean School, Brighton; Brighton School of Art. m. Penny, 2 d. Tessa, Julia. Address: c/o Marina Martin Ltd, London W1. Starsign: Scorpio. Hobbies: puppetry, period costume research. Unfulfilled ambition: to play Falstaff.

FRANCIS, Jan
Actress b. 5.8.51 London. Trained as a dancer and worked with Royal Ballet before deciding to become an actress. First stage part was in The Farmer's Wife at Cheltenham. Films incl: Dracula. Most experience in TV which incl: Hawkeye the Pathfinder; Ann of Green Gables; Lonely Man's Lover; Sutherland's Law; Village Hall; Looking for Clancy; The Launderette; Love's Labours Lost; Rooms; London Assurance; The Duchess of Duke Street; Raffles; Secret Army; The Party of the First Part; The Racing Game; Ripping Yarns; Target; Casting the Runes; Good Companions. m. Martin C Thurley. Address: c/o Peter Browne Management, London SW9. Starsign: Leo.

FRANCIS, Nina
see Zuckerman, Nina

FRANCIS, Tony
Reporter b. 17.11.46 Leicester. Journalistic experience on Leicester Mercury and BBC Radio Leicester. Then TV with BBC Midlands. Education:

Gateway Grammar School, Leicester; St John's College, Cambridge (MA Modern Languages). Widower, 2 s. Benjamin, Barnaby. Address: Solihull, West Mids. Starsign: Scorpio. Hobbies: football, cricket, tennis, squash, painting, travel, learning more languages. Unfulfilled ambition: to write a best-selling novel.

FRANKLYN, William
Actor b. 22.9.26 Kensington, London. Spent 10 years in Australia where his father, actor Leo Franklyn, was working. On returning to England appeared in My Sister Eileen when he was 15. Wartime service with Paratroops until 1946. Post-war career started in Arsenic and Old Lace on Southsea Pier followed by rep at Ryde and Margate (with Brian Rix). First West End break in The Love of Four Colonels. One of the first stars of ITV, appearing in the first ITV play, Mid-Level. Other TV incl: The Makepeace Story; The Last Flight; many early ITV series; Top Secret; No Cloak, No Dagger; Paradise Island; What's On Next?; Masterspy. Did Schweppes commercials for nine years and has been in more than 50 films. Education: Haileybury, Melbourne. m. (1st) actress Margot Johns (dis), (2nd) actress Suzanna Carroll, 3 d. Sabina (from 1st m), Francesca, Melissa (from 2nd m). Address: c/o Fraser and Dunlop, London

W1. Starsign: Virgo/Libra cusp. Hobby: cricket.

FRASER, Bill

Actor b. 5.6.08 Perth, Scotland. Began his working life in a bank, but the theatre lights beckoned and he joined a touring rep company. Since then he has played everything from Dame in pantomime to Shakespeare, including performances with the National Theatre Company. Now one of our best character actors, his training, he says, has been '55 years in the business'. Before the war, in which he served in the RAF, he ran the Connaught Theatre, Worthing. Made his name on TV as Snudge in The Army Game and Bootsie and Snudge. Other TV incl: Foreign Affairs; That's Your Funeral; The Corn is Green. Films incl: Doctor at Large; All The Way Up; Up Pompeii; Up the Chastity Belt; Up the Front; Last Tribute; The Corn is Green. Education: Strathallan School. m. Pamela Cundell. Address: c/o Peter Crouch Associates Ltd, London W1. Starsign: Gemini. Hobby: working.

FRASER, John

Actor b. 18.3.32 Glasgow. Started on stage when he was 16 with the Citizens' Theatre and while there was introduced to TV in a serial version of Kidnapped. He did two seasons with the Old Vic in London and made many West End appearances, incl: Sleuth

and Crown Matrimonial. Films incl: The Dam Busters; The Good Companions; El Cid; The Trials of Oscar Wilde. TV also incl: The Rivals of Sherlock Holmes; A Legacy; The Doll; Thundercloud. Books incl: novels, Clap Hands if You Believe in Fairies; The Bird in the Bush. Has also written a play, Cannibal Crackers. Education: Glasgow High School. Address: c/o Fraser and Dunlop, London W1. Starsign: Pisces. Hobby: writing. Unfulfilled ambition: to write a best seller.

FRASER, Ronald

Actor b. 11.4.30 Bonnybridge, Stirlingshire. After National Service in the Army, trained at RADA and went to Glasgow Citizen's Theatre before making his London debut in The Good Sailor. Joined the Old Vic 1954. Stage incl: The Long and the Short and the Tall (and film); The Ginger Man (and TV); Entertaining Mr Sloane. Has appeared in many films and TV. Films incl: The Sundowners; The Best of Enemies; The Castaways; The Pot Carriers; The Punch

and Judy Man; Rentadick; Swallows and Amazons; Paper Tiger; Come Play With Me; The Wild Geese. TV incl: The Lonesome Road; Sword of Honour; the Misfit; Conceptions of Murder; A Man in the Zoo; Mr Big; The Bass Player and the Blonde; Do You Come Here Often?; The Sweeney; Spooner's Patch. m. former actress Elizabeth Howe (dis), 2 d. Fiona, Alison. Address: c/o Crouch Associates, London W1. Starsign: Aries.

FROST, David OBE

Author/interviewer/ presenter/tycoon b. 7.4.39 Tenterden, Kent. First TV as reporter for This Week, but achieved overnight success when picked to host That Was the Week That Was. This was followed by A Degree of Frost; Not So Much a Programme, More a Way of Life; The Frost Report; The Frost Programme; Frost Over England; Frost Over America; We British; The Wilson Interviews; The Nixon Interviews. Books: I Gave Them a Sword, (Frost on Nixon). Vast business interests. Founder and shareholder in London Weekend Television. Education: grammar schools; Caius College, Cambridge (hons degree in English) where he edited university magazine, and ran Footlights. Address: Kensington, London. Starsign: Aries. Hobbies: football, cricket.

FULLERTON, John
Sports presenter b. 22.5.43
Ballymena, Co Antrim.
Started in accountancy.
Full-time journalist since
1976 with Ulster TV.
Education: Ballymena
Secondary Intermediate.
m. Linda, 3 s. Darren,
Nicolas, Gareth. Address:
Ballymena, Co Antrim, N
Ireland. Starsign: Gemini.
Hobbies: 'my work in sport,
plus watching sporting
occasions – particularly
soccer'. Unfulfilled
ambitions: to meet Perry
Como and former England
skipper Bobby Moore.

G

GABLE, Christopher
Actor b. 13.3.40 London.
Ended a 10-year career as an
international ballet dancer
(he was one of The Royal
Ballet's highest paid stars) to
become an actor. First
'straight' appearance was at
Watford Rep in The Picture of
Dorian Gray. Has since
appeared at Oxford,
Manchester, London fringe
theatres and a year with the
Royal Shakespeare
Company. His break came
with appearances in Ken
Russell films incl: The Music
Lovers; The Dance of the
Seven Veils; A Song of
Summer; The Boy Friend.
Other films incl: The Slipper
and the Rose. TV incl: Willy;
The Devil's Crown; Tycoon;
The Jack Buchanan Story.
Education: Royal Ballet
Schools. m. former soloist
with Royal Ballet Carole
Needham, 1 d. Emma,
1 s. Tomas. Address: c/o
Leading Artists, London
SW1. Starsign: Pisces.
Hobbies: cooking,
gardening.

GALL, Sandy
Newscaster/reporter
b. 1.10.27 Penang, Malaya.
Started career on Aberdeen
Press and Journal. As
reporter for Reuter's for 10
years and since 1963 for ITN
has travelled virtually all over
the world. Speaks fluent
French and German. Book:
Gold Scoop, a novel about
Africa, 1977. Education:
Glenalmond and Aberdeen,
Bonn and Mainz Universities.
m. Eleanor, 3 d. Fiona,
Carlotta, Michaela,
1 s. Alexander. Address:
Penhurst, Kent. Starsign:
Libra. Hobbies: golf, writing
thrillers. Unfulfilled
ambitions: to be a bestseller
and into single figures at golf.

GAMBON, Michael
Actor. Started dancing at
Dublin's Gate Theatre. Then
went on to the National
Theatre, Chichester Festival,
Royal Shakespeare
Company and rep at
Birmingham, Coventry,
Liverpool and Regent's Park
Open Air Theatre. Stage incl:
Mother Courage; The
Recruiting Officer; Juno and
the Paycock; Major Barbara;
When Thou Art King; Not
Drowning but Waving;
Otherwise Engaged; The

Norman Conquests; Just
Between Ourselves; Zoo
Story; Alice's Boys; Betrayal;
Close of Play. TV incl: The
Challengers; The Borderers;
The Other One. 1 s. Address:
c/o Larry Dalzell Associates
Ltd, London WC2. Hobby:
collecting Victorian
machinery.

GARDEN, Graeme
Actor/scriptwriter b. 18.2.43
Aberdeen. Son of a doctor,
he studied medicine at King's
College Hospital in London.
Chose to become involved in
show business after writing
for radio, incl: I'm Sorry, I'll
Read That Again. With Bill
Oddie also wrote some of the
Doctor TV series. Other TV
incl: Twice a Fortnight;
Broaden Your Mind; The
Goodies; Charlie's Climbing
Tree. Records incl: Funky
Gibbon; The In-Betweenies.
Education: Cambridge
University, where he was a
member of the Footlights
Club. m. Liz, 1 d. Sally.
Address: Cricklewood,
London. Starsign: Aquarius.

GARDNER, Andrew
Presenter b. 25.8.32
Beaconsfield, Bucks. 6ft 5in

tall, first newscaster of News
at Ten with Alastair Burnet in
July 1967. Started in radio
journalism in Central African
Fedn, reporting extensively in
Africa. Returned UK 1961;
freelanced as reporter/
scriptwriter for BBC; joined
ITN later that year as reporter/
newscaster for Roving
Report and Dateline, then
News at Ten. Newscaster on
first Transatlantic Telstar
programme 1962;
commentator for Queen's
Silver Wedding service and
Princess Anne's wedding.
Presenter of Thames at 6
since 1977. Education:
Dauntsey's School, Wilts.
m. Margaret, 4 s. Mark,
Adrian, Maxwell, Adam.
Address: c/o Thames TV,
London. Starsign: Virgo.
Hobby: Victorian
microscopy. Unfulfilled
ambition: to retire!

GARDNER, Llew
Journalist b. 9.12.29
Scotland. Newspaper
background on Northampton
Chronicle; Daily Worker; The
People; Tribune and Sunday
Express before TV on Three
After Six. Other TV incl: This
Week; Take Two; Thames At
Six; Personal Choice; People
and Politics; Thames Debate;
TV Eye. Education: he claims
it to be negligible.
m. journalist Merry Archard,
2 s. Patrick, Daniel (twins).
Address: c/o Thames TV,
London NW1. Starsign:
Sagittarius. Hobby: watching
football. Unfulfilled ambition:
to play in goal for Scotland at
Hampden Park.

GARNER, James
Actor b. 7.4.28 Oklahoma.
Had 50 jobs before he turned
to acting; he called to see a
producer friend who offered
him a job in the stage
production of The Caine
Mutiny Court Martial, and
he's been an actor ever
since. A part in Cheyenne
followed and then Maverick
and The Rockford Files. Films
incl: Darby's Rangers;
Marlowe; Support Your Local
Sheriff; Grand Prix. Served in
Korea with the US Army and
was awarded the Purple
Heart. m. actress Lois
Clarke, 2 d. Greta, Kimberly
(step-d). Address: Los
Angeles. Starsign: Aries.

GASCOIGNE, Bamber
Much travelled
question-master b. 24.1.35
London. National Service in
Grenadier Guards.
Scholarship to Yale School of
Drama. Wrote Share My
Lettuce, 1957. Later dramatic
critic, The Spectator and the
Observer. Chairman of
University Challenge since
1962. Presenter of Cinema
1964. Devised The Auction
Game and scripted The Four
Freedoms; The Trouble With

Women; wrote and
presented The Christians.
Books: World of Theatre; The
Great Moghuls; Treasures
and Dynasties of China;
Murgatreud's Empire; The
Heyday; The Christians.
Education: Eton; Cambridge.
m. Christina Ditchburn.
Address: Richmond, Surrey.
Starsign: Aquarius.

GASCOINE, Jill
Actress b. 11th April,
Lambeth. Trained at the Italia
Conti Stage School, then rep
at Nottingham, Dundee,
Glasgow, Worthing,
Hornchurch and Leicester.
TV incl: Rooms; Plays for
Britain; General Hospital; The
Norman Wisdom Show;
Three Kisses; Balzac;
Z Cars; Softly, Softly; Dixon of
Dock Green; Within These
Walls; Holding On; Six Days
of Justice; Justice; Raffles;
Beryl's Lot; Peter Pan;
Oranges and Lemons; The
Onedin Line. Education:
Kingston Grammar School.
2 s. Sean, Adam. Address:
c/o Marina Martin
Management, London W1.
Starsign: Aries. Hobbies:
gardening, writing bad
scripts, cooking and dieting.

GAUNT, William
Actor/director b. 3.4.37
Pudsey, Yorks. Trained at
RADA then rep at Worthing,
Bath, Salisbury and
Cheltenham. Spent a year in
America and returned to
direct productions at
Birmingham, Coventry and
Cheltenham, interrupted by a
spell in the army. TV incl: 54

Minute Theatre; Waiting For
Wanda; Climate of Fear;
Probation Officer; Harper's
West One; Sergeant Cork;
Softly, Softly; The
Champions; Holly; The Saint;
Cottage to Let; Nobody's
House; The Foundation.
Appointed artistic director of
Liverpool Playhouse July
1979. Education:
Giggleswick School; Waco
University, Texas. m. actress
Carolyn Lyster. 1 d. Matilda,
1 s. Albie. Address:
Liverpool. Starsign: Aries.
Hobbies: walking, music,
gardening. Unfulfilled
ambition: to own and retire to
a working farm.

GEESON, Judy
Actress b. 10.9.48 Arundel,
Sussex. Trained as a dancer,
but turned to acting while
attending the Corona Stage
School. Though well-known
on films and TV, her first
London appearance was as
Desdemona in An Othello at
the Open Space Theatre.
Has also appeared with
Young Vic and the Royal
Shakespeare Company and
toured in An Ideal Husband
and The Sleeping Prince.
Films incl: To Sir, With Love;

Here We Go Round the Mulberry Bush; Prudence and the Pill; Hammerhead; Doomwatch; The Executioner; Good-bye Gemini; Two Gentlemen Sharing; Three Into Two Won't Go; Ten Rillington Place; Branigan; The Eagles Landed; Domonique. A couple of her first parts on TV were in Dixon of Dock Green and Emergency–Ward 10. Other TV incl: The Fifty-first State; The Newcomers; Dance of Death; Lady Windermere's Fan; The Skin Game; A Room With a View; Poldark; Danger UXB; She. Address: c/o Hazel Malone Management, London SW3. Starsign: Virgo. Hobbies: photography, travelling.

GEORGE, Beti
Radio and TV journalist b. 19.1.39 Coedybryn, Dyfed, S Wales. Started in radio by preparing contributions to a daily current affairs programme Bore Da. Producer/ presenter of fortnightly lunch-time radio programme Ar Ben y Ffordd and co-presenter of Heddiw, daily TV magazine/ current affairs programme. Also presenter of various radio and TV documentaries incl: Welsh National Opera Co; George Guest at Cambridge; A Nun's Story; Gypsies; Women in Rugby. Education: Llandysul Grammar and University College of Wales. 1 s. Iestyn. Address: c/o BBC, Cardiff. Starsign: Capricorn. Hobby: needling. Unfulfilled ambition: 'to be the

first female Director General of the BBC by the time I'm 150 years old'.

GERRIE, Malcolm
Presenter/producer b. 9.5.50 Newcastle upon Tyne. Presenter of Lyn's Look In and Saturday Shake Up for Tyne Tees TV and producer of rock magazine programme Alright Now! Also produced first dramatised version of the Who's rock opera Tommy at Ryhope School, Sunderland. Education: 14 different schools (incl: three secondary moderns, one comprehensive and one grammar); Durham University; Sunderland Polytechnic (B Ed). m. Linda Anne. Address: Peterlee, Co Durham. Starsign: Taurus. Hobbies: music; cinema; reading; filling in forms; eating. Unfulfilled ambition: to be a great rock guitarist.

GIANT HAYSTACKS
Wrestler b. 10.10.47 London. Weighs 35st. m. Rita, 3 s. Martin, Steven, Noel. Address: c/o Joint Promotions Ltd, London SW9. Starsign: Libra.

Hobbies: walking, swimming, boxing. Unfulfilled ambition: to be knighted.

GIELGUD, Sir John CH
Actor/director b. 14.4.04 London. A great-nephew of Dame Ellen Terry, he studied for the stage at Lady Benson's school and RADA, winning scholarships at both. First appearance on the stage was at the Old Vic in 1921 as the Herald in Henry V. Since then, during a distinguished career spanning more than 50 years as an actor, director and manager, he has established himself as one of the world's greatest actors, notably in Shakespearian roles; he has played Hamlet more than 500 times. During and since the Second World War he has further distinguished himself in his one-man show, Ages of Man, and in such plays as The Importance of Being Earnest; The Lady's Not For Burning; Nude With Violin; Home; 40 Years On; No Man's Land (also on TV). Has done a great deal of radio work and his films incl: The Good Companions (1932) and more recently Gold; Galileo; Murder on the Orient Express. TV debut was in A Day By The Sea (in the part he had played on stage) in 1959. Other TV incl: The Cherry Orchard; Ivanov; The Mayfly and the Frog; Deliver Us From Evil; Edward the Seventh; Roald Dahl's Tales of the Unexpected (Neck); Why Didn't They Ask Evans?; English Gardens. Books:

Early Stages
(autobiography); Stage
Directions; Distinguished
Company. Chevalier of the
Legion of Honour; hon
degree of Doctor of Law (St
Andrews University), hon
degree DLitt (Oxford
University); knighted in
Coronation Birthday honours,
1953; Companion of Honour,
1977. Education:
Westminster School.
Address: c/o International
Creative Management,
London W1. Starsign: Aries.

GILBERT, Philip
Actor b. 29.3.31 Vancouver
BC, Canada. Appeared in
college plays before coming
to England where he has
widened his experience in
rep, London's West End and
on TV. TV incl: The Tomorrow
People; Till Death Us Do Part;
Mr Big; Citizen Smith.
Education: Vancouver
College. Address: c/o Eric
Glass Associates, London
W1. Starsign: Aries. Hobbies:
gardening and antiques.
Unfulfilled ambition: to
discover an 'Old Master' in
the attic.

GILFEATHER, Frank
Sports presenter and editor
b. 30.12.45 Dundee.
Journalistic training as news
reporter on morning and
evening papers; former
deputy sports editor,
Aberdeen Evening Express
before joining Grampian TV.
Editor/ presenter of
Grampian TV's Sportscall
programme. Editor/ reporter
for 1976 documentary We

Won The Cup. Education: St
John's High School, Dundee.
m. Sharron, 1 d. Lucy,
2 s. Paul, Steven. Address:
Aberdeen. Starsign:
Capricorn. Hobbies: reading,
cinema, watching sport.
Unfulfilled ambition: to cover
a major international sports
event.

GILLESPIE, Gary
Reporter/presenter
b. 30.3.50 Bangor, Co Down.
Seven years in newspapers
and independent radio.
Political correspondent for
Downtown Radio 1976. Then
joined Ulster TV in 1977.
Motoring editor, Ulster TV
1978. Education: Bangor
Grammar; Belfast College of
Business Studies. Address:
c/o Ulster TV, Belfast.
Starsign: Aries. Hobbies:
squash; water-skiing; music;
Manchester United; rugby;
amateur drama. Unfulfilled
ambition: to fly on the space
shuttle.

GILLIES, Anne Lorne
Singer/presenter b. 21.10.44
Stirling, Scotland. Began as
folk singer (especially
Gaelic) before training
privately in Edinburgh, Italy

and London as a classical
singer. Made debut on stage,
radio and TV during four
years at Edinburgh
University. TV incl: Mainly
Magnus; There Was a Girl;
Anne Lorne Gillies; Rhythm 2;
World of Music; Sounds of
Britain; Something to Sing
About; About Gaelic; Scottish
Radio Industries Award as
best TV newcomer 1975.
Appeared in Royal Jubilee
salute concert in presence of
the Queen in Edinburgh
1977. American debut New
Jersey Arts Centre 1978.
Education: Edinburgh
University (MA); LRAM
(singing, teaching); London
University (post graduate
cert in education). m. Neil
Fraser, 1 d. Marsaili,
1 s. Robbie. Address:
Glasgow. Starsign: Libra.
Hobbies: writing for children
– especially in Gaelic;
dress-making and
embroidery; toy-making;
drawing and illustrating (incl
an award-winning book);
public speaking. Unfulfilled
ambitions: to invent
(a) a 25-hour day and/or
(b) a self-cleaning house of
gracious proportions.

GILMORE, Dennis
Actor b. 14.8.49 Hillingdon,
Middx. Began as a child
model, then into films incl:
Cops and Robbers; Cup
Fever; Fahrenheit 451. TV
incl: Just William;
Crossroads; Search and
Rescue; Nicholas Nickleby;
The Flockton Flyer; Lord
Tramp; Z Cars; Bedtime
Stories; Dead of Night;

Doctor in Charge; The Edwardians; Please Sir!; Worzel Gummidge. Education: Aida Foster Stage School. m. Lynda, 2 d. Debby, Sarah, 1 s. Denis. Address: c/o Aida Foster Ltd, London NW8. Starsign: Leo. Hobbies: stamps, go-karting, football, golf, riding, playing the drums, repairing cars.

GILMORE, Peter
Actor b. 25.8.31 Leipzig. Came to England when six years old and was brought up by relatives in Nunthorpe, Yorks. Left school at 14 to come to London to work in a factory. Went to RADA before doing National Service in the Army. Discovered he had a voice and for years was in musical groups, cabaret and musical shows. Stage shows incl: Grab Me a Gondola; Lady at the Wheel; Valmouth; Love Doctor; Hooray for Daisy (Bristol Old Vic); Follow That Girl; Lock Up Your Daughters. Films incl: The Dress Factory; Seven Cities To Atlantis and many Carry On films. Best known as Capt Onedin in The Onedin Line on TV. Other TV incl: The

Beggar's Opera; Hugh and I; The Doctors. Education: Quaker school.
m. (1st) actress Una Stubbs (dis), (2nd) actress Jan Waters (dis), 1 s. Jason (adop). Address: c/o William Morris Agency, London W1. Starsign: Virgo. Hobby: gazing at architecture. Unfulfilled ambition: to write one good script.

GLASER, Paul Michael
Actor b. 25.3.44 Cambridge, near Boston, Mass. Attended several colleges and universities incl Harvard where he gained a Master's degree in acting and directing. While at Harvard did five seasons of rep. Came to England to study at RADA and Stratford 1964. Stage debut in rock version of Hamlet. Established himself on Broadway and later appeared in various TV series (Kojak; Cannon; The Rockford Files; The Streets of San Francisco; The Waltons) before overnight success of Starsky and Hutch. Films incl: The Great Houdini (TV); Fiddler on the Roof; Butterflies Are Free.

GODDARD, Linda Joy
Actress b. 19.10.47 Ramsgate, Kent. Trained in ballet, modern dancing; amateur dramatics while at Edinburgh University. Joined Traverse Theatre Workshop Co in Edinburgh, then Lindsay Kempe Mime Troupe, Stomu Yamash'tas' Japanese company touring Europe, dancing

engagements abroad and pantomime, rep and Joint Stock Theatre Company. TV incl: People Like Us; The Professionals; Within These Walls and several plays. Education: Newington Junior; Clarendon House Grammar; Edinburgh University. Address: London NW2. Starsign: Libra/Scorpio. Hobbies: painting, drawing, dancing. Unfulfilled ambitions: to read stories on the radio; to make films; to be involved with a children's programme.

GODDARD, Liza
Actress b. 20.1.50 Winchester. Started acting with Farnham Rep. Went to Australia with family 1965, acted on Australian TV, returned this country 1969 and has worked on stage, radio and TV. Stage incl: Sign of the Times; No Sex Please – We're British. Radio: The Victoria Line. TV incl: Take Three Girls; Yes, Honestly; The Brothers; The Upchat Line; The Greatest; Blankety Blank; Pig in the Middle; Murder At The Wedding. Education: Farnham Girls' Grammar; Arts Educational

Trust. m. actor Colin Baker,
1 s. Tom. Address: Muswell
Hill, London. Starsign:
Aquarius. Hobbies: tapestry,
horse-riding, health foods.
Unfulfilled ambitions: to ride
across Afghanistan on a
horse; to make a western film.

GODFREY, Derek

Actor b. 3.6.24 London. Was
studying to be an architect
when he got caught up in the
war and was an RAF radio
operator flying in Liberators
and Warwicks for three years.
Turned to the stage on
demob and after training at
the Old Vic Theatre School,
went into rep including
Nottingham (where he met
his wife-to-be) and Bristol Old
Vic. Stage incl: many
classical roles, especially
with the Old Vic and Royal
Shakespeare Companies. TV
incl: Anthony Trollope; The
Pallisers; Churchill's People;
Electra; Under Western Eyes;
John MacNab; Warship;
Nicholas Nickleby.
Education: Emmanuel
School, London. m. actress
Diana Fairfax, 2 d. Julia,
Philippa. Address: c/o Fraser
and Dunlop Ltd, London W1.
Starsign: Gemini. Hobby:
pottering.

GOODYEAR, Julie

Actress b. 29th March, Bury,
Lancs. Started in rep at
Oldham. Bet Lynch in
Coronation Street. Other TV
incl: Family at War; Nearest
and Dearest; War of Darkie
Pilbeam; City '68; The
Dustbinmen. Education: Bury
Grammar. m. (dis). 1 s. Gary.

Address: c/o Granada TV,
Manchester. Starsign: Aries.
Hobbies: cooking,
gardening, music.

GORDON, Hannah

Actress b. 9.4.41 Edinburgh.
Trained at Glasgow College
of Dramatic Art then rep at
Dundee, Glasgow, Coventry,
Windsor and Leatherhead.
Wide radio and TV
experience incl: What Every
Woman Knows; David
Copperfield; Middlemarch;
Love Story; The Rat
Catchers; Dr Finlay's
Casebook; The Exiles;
Hadleigh; Brett; Victims;
Heloise and Abelard; Great
Expectations; Scobie in
September; Allergy; My Wife
Next Door; Dear Octopus;
Upstairs, Downstairs;
Telford's Change. Film:
Spring and Port Wine. Book:
Woman at the Wheel. Stage
incl: What Every Woman
Knows; Othello; Baggage;
Can You Hear Me At The
Back?. Education: Trinity
Academy; Michael St Denis
School, Edinburgh.
m. lighting cameraman
Norman Warwick, 1 s. Ben.
Address: Weybridge, Surrey.
Starsign: Aries.

GORDON, Noele

Actress b. 25th December,
East Ham, London. Trained
at RADA, then rep in
Edinburgh, Birmingham and
London before such stage
successes as Black Velvet;
Let's Face It; The Lisbon
Story (also the film); Big Ben;
Diamond Lil (with Mae West);
Brigadoon; pantomimes; Call
Me Madam; Grayson's
Scandals; Royal Variety
Performance. Went to
America to study TV and
returned to join ATV 1955 as
advisor on women's
programmes. TV incl:
Week-End; Fancy That; Tea
with Noele Gordon; Lunch
Box; Midland Profile; Hi-T!;
Crossroads; Noele Gordon
Takes The Air. Chosen by
John Logie Baird for his early
experiments in colour TV.
Eight times Top Female TV
Personality in TVTimes Top
Ten Awards poll and first
member of the TV Hall of
Fame. Four times winner of
Female TV Personality of The
Year Sun Award. Education:
Ilford Convent. Address: c/o
ATV, Birmingham. Starsign:
Capricorn. Hobbies:
gardening, theatre.
Unfulfilled ambition: to fly on
Concorde – anywhere!

GORING, Marius

Actor b. 23.5.12 Newport,
Isle of Wight. Studied for the
stage under Harcourt
Williams before joining the
Old Vic School in 1921. Has
since become one of our
most outstanding character
actors. Speaks French and
German and has made

frequent visits to the continent acting in French and German. Entered films in 1936, specialising in Grand Guignol roles. Films incl: Spy in Black; A Matter of Life and Death; Odette; Circle of Danger; The Barefoot Contessa; Quentin Durward; Ill Met by Moonlight; The Moonraker (1958). TV incl: The Adventures of the Scarlet Pimpernel; The Expert; Edward and Mrs Simpson. Education: Perse School, Cambridge and Universities of Frankfurt, Munich, Vienna and Paris. m. (1st) Mary Westward Steel (dis), (2nd) actress Lucie Mannheim (dec), 1 d. Phyllida (by 1st m). Address: c/o Film Rights Ltd, London W1. Starsign: Gemini.

GRAND, Elaine
Interviewer b. 8.6.28 Canada (of British parents). Worked for BBC in Canada before making her home in Britain in 1958. Joined Associated Rediffusion and subsequently worked for BBC, and Granada, TWW and Southern TV companies. Also produced programmes for Granada and ATV. Joined Thames TV 1973 and is now a regular interviewer on After Noon Plus. Education: Winnipeg, Canada; Richmond, Surrey. widow, 3 step-d. Rebecca, Trudi, Jessica, 1 s. David. Address: c/o Thames TV, London NW1. Starsign: Gemini. Unfulfilled ambition: to be able to get up early.

GRANGE, Robert
Actor b. 6.9.38 Gravesend. Trained at the Central School of Speech and Drama and won Elsie Fogerty and Sir John Gielgud scholarships. While still a student took part in BBC TV Monitor film The Class. Rep at Worthing and Birmingham followed by two years with the Royal Shakespeare Company. Plays in London incl: Roots; The Trojan Wars; Nathan the Wise; Hamlet; Three Months Gone. Actor/ narrator with Ballet for All led to the part of The Narrator in A Wedding Bouquet with the Royal Ballet at Sadler's Wells, on tour and on radio. Has toured in September Tide; The Sacred Flame; The Fourposter; Game of Kins and Ten Times Table. TV incl: Softly, Softly; The Expert; The Friendly Persuaders; The Cedar Tree. Flaxton Boys; Ace of Wands; Callan; Man at the Top; Robin's Nest; Miss Jones and Son; The House of Caradus. His education, he says, was 'unremarkable'. Address: c/o NEMS Management, London SW3. Starsign: Virgo. Hobbies: reading (especially history), chess, travel, a little gardening, jogging. Unfulfilled ambitions: to tackle the classical roles and to work with my personal idol, Olivier.

GRAY, Charles
Actor b. 29.8.28 Bournemouth. First professional appearance was at Regent's Park Open Air Theatre. Subsequently joined the Royal Shakespeare Company at Stratford-upon-Avon Memorial Theatre and, later, The Old Vic Company. Stage also incl: Expresso Bongo; Everything in the Garden (London West End debut); Kean (New York); Poor Bitos (Clarence Derwent Award for Best Supporting Performance, 1964); The Right Honourable Gentleman (New York); Ardele; Cause Célèbre; The Philanthropist (also on TV). Films incl: The Night of the Generals; You Only Live Twice; The Man Outside; The Secret War of Private Frigg; The Devil Rides Out; Mosquito Squadron; The File of the Golden Goose; The Lord High Executioner; Oliver Cromwell; The Rocky Horror Picture Show. Wide TV experience dating back to 1966 when he appeared in an American colour production of Anastasia. Other TV incl: The Moon and Sixpence; Hay Fever; Ross; Menance; The Cherry Orchard; The Merchant of Venice; Lady Windermere's Fan; The Millionairess; Upstairs, Downstairs; Song of Songs;

The Upper Crusts; Twelfth Night; Fall of Eagles; The Ventures; Churchill's People. London Assurance; Cheers; Richard II; Hazell; Julius Caesar; Heartland. Address: c/o London Management, London W1. Starsign: Virgo.

GRAY, Michael
Reporter/interviewer/ presenter b. 25.6.47 Potters Bar, Herts. Farm worker before joining the Diss Express 1964, Worthing Gazette 1965-68, BBC Radio Brighton 1968-70 when joined Southern TV's Day By Day. Lectures extensively to public services and armed forces. TV: The Day the Sea Caught Fire 1970, documentaries incl: Men in the Middle and Afloat sailing series since 1976. Education: Eye Grammar School; Ipswich Civic College. m. Angela, 2 d. Tanya, Sara. Address: c/o Southern TV. Starsign: Cancer. Hobbies: rugby, sailing, member of Lions International (charity organisation). Unfulfilled ambition: to sail around the world.

GRAYSON, Larry
Comedian b. 31.8.30 Banbury. Never anything else but an entertainer, he learned his trade in summer shows and touring revues. Unknown till a spot on Saturday Variety 1972. Shut That Door!! series followed and subsequently The Good Old Days; Celebrity Squares; his own shows; The Generation Game.

Education: Nuneaton. Address: c/o BBC, London. Starsign: Virgo.

GREAVES, Bob
Presenter b. 28.11.34 Sale, Cheshire. Journalist on Sale and Stretford Guardian, Nottingham Evening News and Daily Mail, Manchester, first as reporter, then assistant news editor and news editor 1963-71. TV: Granada TV presenter; Granada Reports (since 1968); Reports Action and miscellaneous regional programmes. Education: Sale Grammar School. m. (1st) Maureen Ashbrooke (dis), (2nd) Susan Woodford (dis), 1 d. Cathy, 2 s. Mark, Chris (by 1st m). Address: Hale, Cheshire. Starsign: Sagittarius. Hobbies: films, football-writing, putting up bookshelves that don't fall down. Unfulfilled ambition: to have unfulfilled ambitions at all stages of my life.

GREEN, Alan
Sports journalist b. 25.6.52 Belfast. Local newspaper experience before becoming a BBC news trainee. Presenter Good Morning

Ulster and work as regional journalist, then sports reporter, presenter, producer for BBC in Northern Ireland. TV incl: Scoreboard; Sportsweek; Sportsound; Scene Around Six. Education: Methodist College, Belfast and Queen's University, Belfast (BA Hons, modern history). Address: Co Down, Northern Ireland. Starsign: Cancer. Hobbies: all sports, cinema, criticising TV (mostly my own work!). Unfulfilled ambition: too many to list, but the most immediate aim is to become a TV sports producer, 'as it pays better'.

GREEN, Hughie
Entertainer/compere b. 2.2.20 London. Brought up in Canada. Discovery of Bryan Michie who gave him his own radio show at 14. War service with the Royal Canadian Air Force. TV incl: Double Your Money (1955); Opportunity Knocks (1963); The Sky's the Limit; Hughie's Full House. Education: 'lacking'. m. childhood sweetheart Claire (dis), 1 d. Linda, 1 s. Christopher. Address: Baker Street,

London W1. Starsign:
Aquarius. Hobbies: flying,
golf, model railways.

GREEN, Michael
Industrial journalist
b. 8.10.43 York. Newspaper
training, beginning on
Somerset County Gazette
and taking in Bristol Evening
Post, Daily Mail and Daily
Telegraph before joining ITN
August 1973. Fronted much
of ITN coverage of the 1974
miners' strike, and the fall of
the Heath government; the
Court Line collapse; the state
rescues of Chrysler and
British Leyland; The
Callaghan Govt's attempts to
persuade trade unions to limit
pay rises voluntarily.
Education: Wellington
School, Somerset. m. Judy,
1 d. Xanthe, 1 s. Oliver.
Address: c/o ITN, London
W1. Starsign: Libra. Hobbies:
would-be guitarist and
pianist; squash (occasional),
cricket (rare), enjoyer of
theatre and concerts,
collector of books (of which
too few are read), lover of
countryside and outdoor
pursuits. Unfulfilled ambition:
to retain youthful
inquisitiveness whilst
acquiring understanding and
tolerance essential for the
job.

GREENAWAY, Jeremy
Reporter b. 14.9.42 London.
Reporter on weekly papers in
West and North of England.
Daily Express 1964-70. The
Sun 1970-73. Freelance
radio broadcaster 1974-77
(BBC, LBC, IRN, ILR

Plymouth Sound). Joined
Westward TV 1977. Radio
incl: reports on BBC on cod
war from Iceland;
investigative programme on
Concorde; mackerel fishery
boom. TV incl: reporter/
researcher/ scriptwriter
Westward Report; reporter/
researcher Save The
Conqueror!; reporter No
Place To Go, a documentary
on fishing industry; reporter
Disaster, a programme on
storms in West; reporter/
co-presenter Welcome
Home Naomi! on return of
Naomi James. Education:
Norfolk House prep school,
North London; Ashburton
College, Devon, Newton
Abbot College of Art.
m. Margaret (dis),
2 d. Louise, Isobel,
1 s. James. Address: c/o
Westward TV, Plymouth.
Starsign: Virgo. Hobbies:
sailing, sound recording,
riding, good food and wine.
Unfulfilled ambition: to have
late night/ early morning
radio chat/ record
programme.

GREENE, Richard
Actor/producer b. 25.8.18
Plymouth. Left school at 18

and joined the Jevan
Brandon Thomas rep
company. Toured in French
Without Tears and had several
big parts in films. Hollywood
contract in 1938 and
appeared in Four Men and a
Prayer; My Lucky Star;
Kentucky; before returning to
England to join the Royal
Armoured Corps. Served
three months in the ranks,
went to Sandhurst and was
commissioned in the 27th
Lancers in May 1944. Stage
appearances incl: Desert
Rats; I Capture the Castle.
Recently in plays at Yvonne
Arnaud Theatre, Guildford,
Chichester Festival and on
tour. Has appeared in more
than 40 films in England and
America incl: Forever Amber;
Lorna Doone; Desert Hawk;
Captain Scarlett. Famous for
his title role in the TV series
The Adventures of Robin
Hood (143 programmes).
Then bred thoroughbreds in
Ireland. Recent TV incl: A
Man For Loving; The Doctors;
The Morecambe and Wise
Show; Dixon of Dock Green;
Mrs Bixby and the Colonel's
Coat. Education: Cardinal
Vaughan School. m. Beatriz
Robledo. Address: c/o
Vincent Shaw Associates,
London W14. Starsign:
cusp of Leo and Virgo.
Hobbies: sailing; fishing;
riding; tennis; golf; reading;
writing. Unfulfilled ambition:
to ride in the Grand National.

GREENWOOD, Paul
Actor b. 2.8.43
Stockton-on-Tees. Trained at
Guildhall School of Music

and Drama then rep at Chesterfield, Harrogate and Birmingham and TV parts in Coronation Street and Z Cars. Big TV break came when he played Lulu's boy-friend in It's Lulu. Other TV incl: musical version of No Trams to Lime Street; The Growing Pains of P.C Penrose; Rosie; Heartland. Wrote and sang the Rosie signature tune. Education: Stockton and in any part of the world where his father was serving in the RAF. Address: c/o Peter Charlesworth Ltd, London SW7. Starsign: Leo. Hobbies: rambling, reading, music from Mozart to Bowie. Unfulfilled ambition: to write.

GREENWOOD, Roger
Journalist b. 29.5.48 Manchester. Journalistic training, Bolton Evening News. TV: Channel TV, Jersey, presenter/reporter Calendar, Calendar Sport, producer/reporter sports features, documentaries. m. Susan Linda, 1 s. Andrew. Address: Otley, West Yorks. Starsign: Gemini. Hobbies: playing most sports, the clarinet, painting, wining and dining. Unfulfilled ambitions: to remain ambitious in spite of the vast wealth through autonomy achieved by mid-40's; to figure out a way of accumulating vast wealth.

GRIEVE, John
Character actor b. 14.6.24 Glasgow. Trained at Royal Scottish Academy of Music

and Drama, Glasgow. Five seasons with Citizen's Theatre, Glasgow. TV incl: numerous New Year shows; Oh, Brother; The Vital Spark; Doctor at Sea. Education: North Kelvinside, Glasgow. Address: c/o David White Associates, London W1. Starsign: Gemini. Hobbies: football (favourite team: Partick Thistle), collecting gramophone records and concert-going (when possible). Unfulfilled ambition: to have been involved in opera.

GRIVES, Steven
Actor b. 16.3.51 Lordswood, Warwicks. Stage debut at the age of 14 in Camelot at London's Drury Lane Theatre. Trained at the London Drama Centre before appearing in The Old Ones at the Royal Court. Stage also incl: Northcott Theatre, Exeter (Hamlet; West Side Story; Arms and the Man; Sleuth; The Rivals). Regent's Park Open Air Theatre (Love's Labours Lost and Othello). Films incl: The Virgin Soldiers and Two-a-Penny. TV incl: Chips With Everything; Frankenstein;

The Stars Look Down; The Nearly Man; The Ravelled Thread; The Brylcreem Boys; The Light That Shines; Breakaway Girls; Flambards; Danger UXB. Education: Chiswick County Grammar, London. m. dress designer Margitta Lang. Address: c/o Marina Martin Management, London W1. Starsign: Pisces. Hobbies: horse-riding, reading, driving, chess. Unfulfilled ambition: to win the Grand National.

GROUT, James
Actor b. 22.10.27 London. Trained for the stage at RADA and made his first professional appearance at the Old Vic 1950 in Twelfth Night. Wide stage experience since incl: three seasons at Stratford Memorial Theatre. Other stage incl: The Mousetrap; Ross; Half a Sixpence (and on Broadway); Flint; Straight Up; Lloyd George Knew My Father; 13 Rue de l'Amour. Has also directed for reps incl: Coventry, Hornchurch, Leatherhead, Leeds and Oxford. Many TV appearances incl: The First Lady; Turtle's Progress; Diary of a Nobody; Born and Bred; All Creatures Great and Small; Z Cars; Sister Dora; The Marriage Counsellor; Hymn for Jim; Jenny Can't Work Any Faster; Microbes and Men. Education: Trinity Grammar School. m. Noreen. Address: c/o Crouch Associates, London W1. Starsign: Libra. Hobbies: music, friends and falling off

horses. Unfulfilled ambition: to have an unfulfilled ambition.

GUARD, Pippa
Actress b. 13.10.52 Edinburgh. Trained at RADA where she won the Academy's Most Promising Actress award. Two years with the Royal Shakespeare Company. Also been in pantomime at Birmingham. TV debut was in The Mill on the Floss. Other TV incl: The Mallens; The Tempest. Educated in Canada where her father is an engineer. Address: c/o Richard Stone, London WC2. Starsign: Libra. Hobbies: walking, gardening, cooking, dancing. Unfulfilled ambition: to go round the world.

GUINNESS, Sir Alec CBE D/Litt (Oxon)
Actor b. 2.4.14 London. Formerly a copy-writer in an advertising agency until winning a scholarship to the Fay Compton School of Dramatic Art. First appeared walking on in Libel in 1934. Joined John Gielgud's company the same year and later the Old Vic where he played Hamlet in modern dress in its entirety. In 1941 joined the Royal Navy and was commissioned a year later. Returned to the stage in 1946 in his own adaptation of The Brothers Karamazov. Other stage incl: The Prisoner; Hotel Paradiso; Ross; Wise Child; Habeas Corpus; A Voyage Round My Father; A Family and a Fortune; Yahoo; The Old Country. Entered films in 1947 in Great Expectations. Other films incl: Oliver Twist; Kind Hearts and Coronets; The Lavender Hill Mob (Academy Oscar nomination); The Man in the White Suit; The Captain's Paradise; The Lady Killers; the Horse's Mouth (Venice Award as actor and Academy Oscar nomination for his script); The Bridge on the River Kwai (British Film Academy and Academy Oscar awards); Our Man in Havana; Tunes of Glory; A Majority of One; Lawrence of Arabia; Doctor Zhivago; The Quiller Memorandum; The Comedians; Scrooge; Brother Sun, Sister Moon; Murder by Death; Star Wars (Academy Oscar nomination). TV incl: The Wicked Scheme of Jebel Jacks (USA); Conversation at Night; Caesar and Cleopatra; Gift of Friendship; Tinker, Tailor, Soldier, Spy. Education: Pembroke Lodge, Southbourne; Roborough, Eastbourne. m. Merula Salaman, 1 s. actor Matthew Guinness. Address: c/o London Management, London W1. Starsign: Aries. Unfulfilled ambition: to write a decent, even if unsuccessful, play.

GUTTERIDGE, Lucy
Actress b. 28.11.56 London. Trained at the Central School of Speech and Drama. Theatre incl: rep at Norwich. Films incl: The Greek Tycoon. TV incl: The Devil's Crown;

The Marrying Kind; End of Season; Betzy; Renoir My Father; Skin (Tales of the Unexpected); Sweet Wine of Youth; Love in a Cold Climate. Education: Garden House (private school); Holland Park Comprehensive; The Marist Convent; Walbrook College for Further Education. m. Andrew Hawkins, 1 d. Isabella. Address: c/o Boyack and Conway, London W1. Starsign: Sagittarius. Hobbies: reading, physical activity – dancing, movement, interest in people, drawing. Unfulfilled ambitions: to become a serious dramatic actress, playing classical roles in the theatre; to experience more film work.

GUYLER, Deryck
Actor b. 29.4.14 Wallasey, Cheshire. Started acting with Liverpool Rep Company, but it was his creation of Frisby Dyke (the first time an actor had used the Liverpool accent on the air) in Tommy Handley's wartime show ITMA, that brought him recognition. Has since appeared in numerous

productions in all entertainment media, but notably on TV in Please Sir! and the Eric Sykes shows. Other TV incl: Three Live Wires; That's My Boy!; Best of Enemies. Has been a fanatical devotee of washboard playing since his schooldays. Education: Liverpool College. m. former singer Paddy Lennox, 2 s. Peter, Christopher. Address: c/o Felix de Wolfe, London WC2. Starsign: Taurus. Hobbies: toy soldiers (he has a collection running into thousands), traditional jazz records and his washboard.

GWYTHER, Geraldine
Actress b. 15.11.32 London. Trained at Guildhall School of Music and Drama. Rep, tours, TV, incl: General Hospital. Education: Tollington Girls High, Muswell Hill, London. m. actor George Waring, 1 d. Georgina, 1 s. Geoffrey. Address: c/o Bernard Gillman Ltd, Tolworth, Surrey. Starsign: Scorpio. Hobbies: gardening, cooking. Unfulfilled ambition: to be in another successful TV series.

H

HAGMAN, Larry
Actor b. 21st September, Texas, where he was also brought up. No formal training for the theatre but his apprenticeship was served under distinguished direction of Margaret Webster at the Woodstock Rep Theatre, the Margo Jones Company in Dallas and musical productions of St John Terrell. Came to London to appear in South Pacific with his mother, Mary Martin. While here was called up and met and married his wife. Maj. By the time he was 20 had appeared in more than 50 plays and some 100 TV shows. Best known on TV for his part in I Dream of Jeannie and more recently as J R in Dallas. m. Swedish designer Maj, 1 d. Heidi, 1 s. Preston. Starsign: Virgo

HAIGH, David
Reporter/interviewer
b. 11.8.36 Liverpool.
Newspaper, radio and TV
journalist 1954. Joined
Southern TV 1970.
Education:
Newton-le-Willows Grammar
School and others.
m. Wendy. Address:
Canterbury, Kent. Starsign:
Leo. Hobbies: cricket,
refereeing rugby football,
writing. Unfulfilled ambition:
to write a novel to outsell
Harold Robbins.

HAIGH, Kenneth
Actor b. 25.3.31
Mexborough, Yorks. After
National Service and work as
a builder's labourer, he
studied for the stage at the
Central School of Speech
Training and Dramatic Art.
First stage part in Drogheda,
Eire 1952 in Othello. Since
appeared in many plays in
this country and America.
Founder member of the
English Stage Company at
London's Royal Court
Theatre and created the part
of Jimmy Porter in Look Back
in Anger. Other stage incl:
The Zoo Story; Royal
Shakespeare Company;

Maggie May; The Hotel in
Amsterdam; Marching Song;
Chichester Festival;
American Shakespeare
Theatre, Stratford,
Connecticut. Lectures on
drama at Yale University,
where he is an honorary
professor. Films incl:
Cleopatra; Eagle in a Cage; A
Hard Day's Night; Saint Joan;
A Lovely Way to Die; The
Bitch. TV incl: Man at the Top;
Search for the Nile; Moll
Flanders; Dad; Hazlitt in
Love; Come the Revolution; A
Good Human Story.
Education: Gunnersbury
Grammar, London. m. model
Myrna Stephens. Address:
c/o John Redway and
Associates Ltd, London W1.
Starsign: Aries.

HALL, Bob
Presenter/reporter/
newscaster b. 29th October
Ilkley, Yorks. Local and
national newspaper and
radio experience before
joining BBC TV as presenter/
reporter. Border TV chat
show, current affairs,
parliamentary programme
chairman; World of Sport film
and match reporter; ATV
Today, Right Now presenter
and film reporter for Left,
Right and Centre, political
magazine. Education: Prince
Henry's School, Otley, Yorks.
m. Janet, 1 d. Sara,
1 s. Mathew. Address:
Halesowen, West Mids.
Starsign: Scorpio. Hobbies:
sport, photography, driving,
being with family. Unfulfilled
ambition: none – but
ambitious.

HALL, Stuart
Presenter b. 25.12.34
Ashton-under-Lyne, Lancs.
Trained as a caterer and
motor engineer to help his
father run the family
business. Wanted to be a
professional footballer and
played for Crystal Palace in
1953. Also raced cars at
Oulton Park and Silverstone.
Got into radio when he
complained about the
commentaries and BBC
invited him to join their
commentating team.
Succeeded David Vine as
anchorman of It's A Knockout
1972. More usually seen as
regular presenter of BBC's
northern magazine
programme Look North/
Nationwide North West. Also
radio commentator on
soccer, motor racing and
current affairs. Book: Stuart
Hall's Look North Cook Book.
Education: Glossop
Grammar and Manchester
College of Technology.
m. Hazel, 1 d. Francesca,
1 s. Daniel. Address: c/o
BBC, Manchester. Starsign:
Capricorn. Hobby: collecting
antique clocks (he claims to
have the largest collection in
the UK). Unfulfilled ambition:
'I never had any'.

HALLAM, John
Actor. b. 28.10.42 Lisburn,
N Ireland. Trained at RADA,
he has appeared at the
National Theatre and with the
Royal Shakespeare
Company and been in more
than 20 films incl: Hennessy;
Love and Bullitts; Murphy's
War; A Last Valley; Villain;

Antony and Cleopatra;
Burden of Proof; Nicholas
and Alexandra. TV incl:
Devil's Crown; The Regiment;
Wings; Arnhem, The Story of
an Escape; Cicero; The
Pallisers; The Mallens.
Education: St Albans School.
m. Vicky, 3 d. Kate, Nancy,
Molly, 1 s. Luke. Address:
c/o ICM, London W1.
Starsign: Scorpio. Hobbies:
horse-riding, gardening,
reading, the countryside.
Unfulfilled ambitions: to have
an ambition; to be as good as
George C Scott, Marlon
Brando, Montgomery Clift.

HAMILL, Desmond
TV reporter b. 2.11.36
Dublin. After service in the
army (the Devonshire
Regiment) and the 5th Battn
the King's African Rifles in
Kenya 1955-59, joined the
Kenya Broadcasting Service
1960-64 and Rhodesian TV
1964-66. Was with the BBC
1966-67 when he joined ITN.
ITN political correspondent,
European/Common Market
correspondent, and crime
correspondent. Education:
English School, Heliolopolis,
Egypt, and Exeter School,
Devon. m. Brigid, 1 d. Sara.

1 s. Sean. Address: c/o ITN,
London. Starsign: Scorpio.
Hobbies: gardening, squash.

HAMILTON, David
TV compere/disc jockey
b. 10.9.39 Manchester.
Entered TV as script-writer
with ATV. Became TV
announcer with Tyne Tees in
1961. TV incl: Compere of
Top of the Pops; Seaside
Special; World Disco Dance
Championships. Beauty
contests incl: Miss TVTimes;
Miss Thames. Ringmaster for
Chipperfields Circus.
Panellist on Celebrity
Squares and Blankety Blank.
Straight man in TV series with
Ken Dodd and Tommy
Cooper. Radio: David
Hamilton Show for BBC since
1973. Appeared in three
major pantomimes and two
feature films. Education:
Glastonbury Grammar.
m. Sheila (dis), 1 d. Jane,
1 s. David. Address: c/o
BBC, London. Starsign:
Virgo. Hobbies: tennis,
squash, football. Unfulfilled
ambition: to host own national
TV series.

HAMPSHIRE, Susan
Actress b. 12.5.42 London.

Trained as a ballet
dancer and spent a year with
the Festival Ballet when she
was 15. Grew too tall for ballet
and went into rep, first at
Bognor Regis, then Oxford
and the London Arts Theatre.
From there she went into
Expresso Bongo. Other
stage incl: Follow That Girl;
Fairy Tales of New York; The
Ginger Man; Past Imperfect;
The Sleeping Prince; Peter
Pan; The Taming of the
Shrew; Chichester Festival;
The Crucifer of Blood. Films
incl: Monte Carlo or Bust;
Violent Enemy; David
Copperfield; A Time for
Loving; Living Free; Neither
the Sea nor the Sand; Dr
Jekyll and Mr Hyde; Bang.
Probably best known on TV;
has won an American Emmy
as Best Actress on three
occasions – The Forsyte
Saga (1970); The First
Churchills (1971); Vanity Fair
(1973). Other TV incl: The
Pallisers; Words on War.
Education: Hampshire
School, London. m. French
film director Pierre
Granier-Deferre (dis),
1 d. Victoria (dec),
1 s. Christopher. Address:
c/o Chatto and Linnit, London
W1. Starsign: Taurus. Hobby:
music.

HANCOCK, Sheila
Actress b. 22.2.33
Blackgang, Isle of Wight.
Trained at RADA, started her
career in rep (Dartford,
Oldham, York, Guildford and
Bromley) and had a spell with
Cyril Fletcher's concert party

at Sandown, where she met her first husband-to-be. First break came when she took over from Joan Sims in Breath of Spring in London, and was with Kenneth Williams in One Over the Eight. Stage also incl: The Anniversary (also film); Fill the Stage With Happy Hours; Rattle of a Simple Man (Actress of the Year Award, 1962); Entertaining Mr Sloane (New York and TV); Royal Shakespeare Company; So What About Love?; Absurd Person Singular; The Deja Revue; The Bed Before Yesterday; Annie. Films incl: Light Up The Sky; Doctor in Love; Carry on Cleo; Take a Girl Like You. TV incl: The Rag Trade; The Bed Sit Girl; Mr Digby Darling; Horizontal Hold; The Mating Machine; Now Take My Wife; But Seriously – It's Sheila Hancock; God Our Help. m. (1st) actor Alec Ross (dec), (2nd) actor John Thaw, 2 d. Melanie Jane (from 1st m), Joanne (from 2nd m), 1 step-d. Abigail. Address: c/o Barry Burnett Organisation Ltd, London W1. Starsign: Pisces.

HANDL, Irene
Actress/author b. 26.12.02 London. Trained at Embassy School of Acting and went straight into West End play, George and Margaret. Many other plays, films and radio and TV appearances incl: Hancock's Half-Hour; Educating Archie; Mum's Boys; For the Love of Ada; Goodnight Mrs Puffin;

Two-way Stretch; Heavens Above; Last Remake of Beau Geste; Hound of the Baskervilles; Maggie and Her. Education: Maida Vale High School for Girls. Address: c/o London Management, London W1. Starsign: Capricorn. Hobbies: cooking, gardening, going to films, art, dogs, having fun. Unfulfilled ambition: 'to have my novels made into films'.

HANLEY, Jenny
Actress b. 15.8.47 Gerrards Cross. Trained as a nanny and children's nurse, but became a model and had been in most branches of show business before becoming presenter of Magpie in 1974. Stage incl: Sabrina Fair; How To Ruin Your Health; Not Now Darling (on tour). Films incl: The Private Life of Sherlock Holmes; On Her Majesty's Secret Service; Tam-Lin; Joanna; Scars of Dracula; A Victory for Danny Jones. Radio: Capital Radio drama. TV incl: The Persuaders; Shirley's World; The Golden Shot; Softly, Softly; Task Force (for five years); And Mother Makes Five; Robert's Robots; Man About the House; Warship; Emmerdale Farm; And Maisy Too (which she also wrote); The Return of the Saint. Educated all over the Southern Counties and in Switzerland. Address: c/o John Mahoney Management, London NW1. Starsign: Leo. Hobbies: driving, cooking, fishing and tapestry.

Unfulfilled ambition: to find an ambition of an extraordinary and dangerous nature that she has not already done on Magpie.

HANDS, Jeremy
Reporter/presenter b. 4.4.51 Torquay, Devon. Journalistic apprenticeship with Hendon and Finchley Times group, then reporter for Herald Express, Torquay. Researcher with Westward TV, reporter with Border TV. Education: St Marylebone Grammar, London. m. Julia, 1 s. Thomas. Address: Tring, Herts. Starsign: Aries. Hobbies: sailing, writing, football, cricket, maritime history. Unfulfilled ambition: 'to beat my father at darts'.

HANN, Judith
Reporter/presenter b. 8.9.42 Littleover, Derby. Journalistic training with Westminster Press. Freelance for BBC. TV incl: Tomorrow's World. Books: What About the Children?; The Family Scientist. Twice won the Glaxo Award for science writers. Education: Parkfield Cedars, Derby, and Durham University (BSc in zoology)

where she edited the university paper. m. TV news editor John Exelby, 2 s. Jake, Daniel. Address: Ealing, London W5. Starsign: Virgo. Hobby: cooking. Unfulfilled ambition: to live in the remotest of country areas.

HANSON, Susan
Actress b. 2.2.43 Preston, Lancs. Worked as a singer/dancer before going into rep at Edinburgh, Bristol Old Vic, The Mermaid in London and Newcastle. Also worked in films (incl: Catch Us If You Can) before joining Crossroads in 1965. Other TV incl: Nearest and Dearest; Going For a Song. m. singer Carl Wayne. Address: c/o ATV, Birmingham. Starsign: Aquarius. Hobbies: collecting Victorian dolls, travel.

HARCOURT, Reg
Political editor b. 6.3.33 London. Newspaper experience in the provinces and Fleet Street before joining ATV 18 years ago as a reporter. Editor of Left, Right and Centre; presenter ATV Today; Platform for Today; Midland Member. Education:

grammar school. m. (2nd) Anne, 1 s. Nicholas. Address: Edgbaston, Birmingham. Starsign: Pisces. Hobby: listening to all kinds of music. Unfulfilled ambition: dinner at Maxim's.

HARDWICK, Alan
Reporter/presenter b. 20.8.49 Staveley, Derbyshire. On leaving school he trained in journalism with local newspapers. Gained wide journalistic experience as general reporter, sports reporter, sub-editor, news editor and editor, on daily and weekly newspapers throughout Britain. Joined the Calendar team at Yorkshire TV 1973. Education: Secondary school and since then as a journalist. m. Julie, 1 d. Clare. Address: c/o Yorkshire TV, Lincoln. Starsign: Leo. Hobbies: reading, trying to renovate old houses, cycling, driving 'hairy' cars and trying to get into the national sunbathing team. Unfulfilled ambitions: to abolish queueing, to retire rich at 45 and to travel widely abroad.

HARDY, Robert
Actor b. 29.10.25 Cheltenham. Began his career with Royal Shakespeare Company at Stratford-upon-Avon. First caught the viewer's eye as David Copperfield, Prince Hal and in The Troubleshooters. Other TV incl: Age of Kings; Henry V;

Coriolanus; Mogul; Manhunt; Elizabeth R; Daniel Deronda; Edward the Seventh; Mussolini in Caesar and Claretta; Upstairs, Downstairs; Hannah; The Duchess of Duke Street; Picardy Affair; Chronicle– History of the Longbow; Horses In Our Blood; All Creatures Great and Small. Films incl: The Spy Who Came In From the Cold; How I Won The War; Ten Rillington Place; Young Winston; Blood Will Have Blood; Yellow Dog; Frog; Le Silencieux; Le Gifle. A Liveryman of the Worshipful Company of Bowyers, he claims to be the only one who makes bows. Book: Longbow: A Social and Military History. Education: Rugby and Oxford (degree in English). m.(1st) (dis), (2nd) actress Sally Cooper, 2 d. Emma, Justine, 1 s. Paul. Address: Henley-on-Thames. Starsign: Scorpio. Hobbies: horses, archery. Unfulfilled ambition: 'To play Falstaff, Lear, etc, etc'.

HARGREAVES, Allan
Presenter/reporter/inter-viewer b. 2.5.35 Hong Kong.

Joined the army 1952 and was posted to Cyprus as 2nd Lieut in The Royal Berkshire Regiment. After leaving the army joined the Cyprus Mail and was a regular broadcaster on Cyprus Radio 1959-60. Until 1968, when he and his family returned to Britain, he was attached to the British Forces Broadcasting Service in Tripoli, Tobruk and Malta where he was Station Controller. From 1968-77 he was reporter/presenter on Thames TV's Today. Also presented many documentaries and outside broadcasts. When Capital Radio started in 1973 he presented their first 90-minute Open Line phone-in and for a year continued to do so five nights a week. Also devised and presented other programmes. Deputy Editor Thames at 6, 1978-79 when he joined the reporting team of Thames Report. Education: King's School, Parramatta, Australia; Junior King's School, Canterbury, Kent; St Martin's School of Art (graphic design), London. m. Rosemary, 2 d. Philippa, Joanna. Address: c/o Isobel Davie Ltd, London W1. Starsign: Taurus. Hobbies: painting and reading. Unfulfilled ambition: 'still working on it'.

HARGREAVES, Jack OBE
Presenter b. 31.12.11 Yorkshire. Born into farming, started career as a vet's assistant. Also journalist/ editor Lilliput, managing editor Picture Post and radio writer and producer in London, and chief of information for the National Farmers' Union. First appeared on Southern TV 1959 for short series Gone Fishing; still there with Out of Town; How and other TV incl: The Young Tigers; The Explorers; Three After Six; Country Boy. Deputy Programme Controller, Southern TV 1964-76. Education: Merchant Taylors; London University. m. Isobel. Address: c/o Southern TV, Southampton. Starsign: Capricorn. Hobby: all country pursuits.

HARPER, Gerald
Actor b. 15.2.31 London. Wanted to be a doctor but became interested in acting at school. After National Service trained at RADA. Then to London Arts Theatre, followed by Liverpool Playhouse before returning to London for Charley's Aunt (with Frankie Howerd); Free As Air; Ross. Tours in America (with Old Vic and Boeing-Boeing). Films: Tunes of Glory; The Admirable Crichton; League of Gentlemen; The Lady Vanishes. Radio: Sunday Affair (Capital Radio). TV incl: The Sleeper; The Corsican Brothers; Adam Adamant; Gazette; Hadleigh. Education: Haileybury. m. (1st) Jane Downs (dis), (2nd) Carla, 1 d. Sarah Jane (from 1st m); 1 s. Jamie (from 2nd m). Address: London.

Starsign: Aquarius. Hobbies: horse-riding, skiing, chess. Unfulfilled ambition: to eat a decent meal every day.

HARRIS, Anita
Singer/actress b. 3.6.42 Midsomer Norton, Somerset. Won talent contest when three years old at Chippenham. Moved with her family to Bournemouth when she was seven; then ice-skating, learning the piano and dancing lessons. Charley Ballet in Italy, sang in Las Vegas 1959 then joined the Granadiers and later the Cliff Adams Singers. London shows incl: Way Out in Piccadilly; Talk of the Town; pantomime, Peter Pan. Films incl: Follow That Camel; Carry on Doctor. TV incl: series with Lance Percival; Bernard Braden; Tommy Cooper; Benny Hill; Arthur Haynes; Des O'Connor; The Saturday Crowd; Funny You Should Ask; Anita in Jumbleland. Numerous records. Education: Hampshire School of Drama, Boscombe. m. manager Mike Margolis. Address: Kensington, London and a cottage near Bournemouth. Starsign: Gemini. Hobbies: ice-skating, golf.

HARRIS, Keith
Ventriloquist b. 21.9.47 Chester. Self-taught, he made debut at 14 and began designing and making own 'characters'; now has a family of more than 100. TV debut in Let's Laugh and five days later was on Opportunity

Knocks. First appeared in summer season at Rhyl in 1964 and has since appeared in numerous summer shows, pantomimes, as well as radio, cabaret and overseas tours. TV incl: Cuddles and Co, guest spots on major variety shows and host of Black and White Minstrel Show 1977 and 1978. Education: St John's Junior and Chester Secondary Modern. Address: c/o Peter Dulay, London. Starsign: Virgo. Hobbies: do-it-yourself, dancing, eating good food. Unfulfilled ambition: to star in own TV show in England.

HARRIS, Rolf OBE
Entertainer/singer/ songwriter/ musician/ artist/ cartoonist b. 30.3.30 Perth, Western Australia. Parents Cardiff-born but emigrated to Australia. Expert swimmer at 10 and junior backstroke champion of Australia at 15. Started career by winning Australian radio talent contest 1949. Came to Britain as art student 1952. First break on stage was One Under the Eight, followed by TV programmes Showcase

(with Benny Hill) and It's a Great Life. Exhibited at Royal Academy 1954, 1955. Returned to Australia 1959 to produce and star in children's series and own show. Came back to Britain via Canada and US as a success. Talk of the Town; Royal Variety Performance. TV incl: own series; many progs for children; Hey Presto; It's Rolf; The Rolf Harris Show; Rolf On Saturday, OK?. Records incl: Tie Me Kangaroo Down, Sport; Sun Arise; Two Little Boys; Jake the Peg. Education: Perth Modern; Perth University and Teachers' Training College. m. sculptress Alwen Hughes, 1 d. Bindi. Address: c/o International Artistes, London WC2. Starsign: Aries. Hobbies: painting, making jewellery, collecting rocks, fixing old chairs, anything to do with working wood, photography.

HARRIS, Sandra
Interviewer/presenter b. 1942 Australia. Came to England when she was 21. After working for BBC radio programme World at One, joined Thames Today team; introduced Take Two with Llew Gardner. Now presents People In The News nightly on Thames At 6. Education: Methodist Ladies College, Perth, Australia. m. businessman Jafar Ramini, 2 s. Nidal, Tarek. Address: c/o Thames TV, London NW1. Starsign: Aquarius. Hobbies: tennis,

collecting teapots. Unfulfilled ambition: to fly across the New Victoria on a Peter Pan wire.

HARRISON, Cathryn
Actress b. 25.5.59 London. No formal acting training. Films incl: Images; The Pied Piper; Black Moon; Blue Fire Lady. TV incl: The Intruders; The Witches of Pendle; Romance (Moths); Joe and Mary; Lisa; The Return of the Saint; Wuthering Heights. Currently with Royal Shakespeare Company, Stratford-upon-Avon. Education: private, comprehensive and secondary modern schools in England and America. Address: c/o William Morris Agency, London W1. Starsign: Gemini. Hobbies: cooking, painting, riding, reading, writing, swimming. Unfulfilled ambition: to walk through the Himalayas to Ladakh.

HART, Tony
Artist b. 15.10.25 Maidstone, Kent. Joined the 1st Gurkha Rifles in India 1940 and, discovering his talent for art, spent his off-duty time at art

school in Madras. Eventually he returned to London and took a job as a window designer. Has been doing freelance art work and graphics for TV since 1952. Resident artist on Vision On since 1955. Other TV incl: Take Hart. Education: All Saints Margaret Street (choir school); Clayesmore and Indian Military Academy. m. Jean, 1 d. Carolyn. Address: c/o BBC, London. Starsign: Libra. Hobbies: cooking, building walls. Unfulfilled ambition: to find a blue Himalayan poppy – in the Himalayas!

HARTY, Russell
TV journalist b. 5.9.34 Blackburn, Lancs. Came to TV through lecturing in America and Britain, being a housemaster at Giggleswick and answering an advertisement for an arts producer which led to his work on Aquarius and his own chat show Eleven Plus. Has been a talk show host for seven years, incl: Russell Harty Plus and Saturday Night People. Winner of International Emmy for his Dali programme, Hello Dali, and a Golden Harp award for another documentary, Finnian Games. Education: Queen Elizabeth School, Blackburn; Exeter College, Oxford. Address: c/o London Weekend TV, London SE1. Starsign: Virgo. Hobby: sitting down and looking at the wall. Unfulfilled ambition: 'imitating Mike Yarwood doing me'.

HARVEY, Andrew
Reporter/presenter b. 3.3.44 Buckinghamshire. Trained in journalism with the Middlesbrough Evening Gazette under the Thomson Organisation Graduate Training Scheme before news reporting on BBC radio and TV and Nationwide. Presenter/ reporter BBC TV regional magazines incl: South Today and Points West in Bristol which he also produces. Also a reporter on BBC2's Sport Two and sports reporter and commentator on Radio Bristol. Education: Bishop Wordsworth School, Salisbury; Oriel College; Oxford (hons degree in modern history). m. Philippa, 1 d. Lucy, 1 s. Daniel. Address: c/o BBC, Bristol. Starsign: Pisces. Hobbies: almost all sports except horse-racing. Unfulfilled ambition: to own a golf course (preferably in Spain).

HATCH, Richard
Actor b. 21.5.45 Santa Monica, Calif. The new inspector in The Streets of San Francisco after Keller (Michael Douglas) left to become a professor of criminology. Both parents were musicians and their son was studying to become a classical pianist when he was eight. But he got interested in acting while at school and when he left he joined a Los Angeles rep company which moved to New York. First break was a part in a serial All My Children which lasted two and a half years. Other TV incl: Cannon; Barnaby Jones; The Waltons; Hawaii Five-O; Kung Fu. Films incl: The Last of the Belles; Battlestar Galactica. Education: Washington High School, Santa Monica; Harbor College, San Pedro. Address: Los Angeles. Starsign: Taurus. Hobbies: jogging, gymnastics, pole-vaulting, playing his folk guitar.

HAVERS, Nigel
Actor b. 6.11.49 London. Broke the family tradition of going into Law (his father is Solicitor-General) by becoming an actor. Trained at the Arts Educational Schools. Spent a couple of years as Billy Owen in the radio serial, The Dales, and chief researcher for the Jimmy Young Show before his first TV part in Comet Among the Stars. His acting career really took off when he played the title role in Nicholas Nickleby. Other TV incl: A Raging Calm; Glittering Prizes; A Horseman Riding By; An Englishman's Castle; Coming Out. Education: Newton Court and Leicester University.

m. Carolyn, 1 d. Katharine. Address: c/o Leading Artists, London SW1. Starsign: Scorpio. Hobbies: golf, sport in general, reading, acting.

HAVILAND, Julian
Reporter b. 8.6.30 Iver Heath, Bucks. Trained as reporter on Surrey Advertiser; crossed Sahara to work as reporter on Johannesburg Star. Returned 1959; sub-editor Daily Telegraph, reporter London Evening Standard. Joined ITN in 1961 as reporter/ newscaster; political correspondent 1965, political editor. Education: Eton College, Windsor; Magdalene College, Cambridge. m. Caroline, 3. s. Peter, Charles, Richard. Address: Sydenham, London. Starsign: Gemini. Hobbies: exploring mountains and deserts, listening to music. Unfulfilled ambition: to climb Kilimanjaro.

HAWDON, Robin
Actor b. 28.3.39 Newcastle upon Tyne. Trained at RADA and rep at Chesterfield and York before his London debut in 1961 with Sir John Gielgud

and Sir Ralph Richardson in The Last Joke. Other stage incl: One Over the Eight; Misalliance; The Easter Man; George and Margaret. Films incl: Bedazzled. TV incl: Compact (for a year); The Flying Swan; The Main Chance; The Liver Birds; Chalk and Cheese. Is also a stage director and a playwright. His plays incl: the comedy hit, The Mating Game and There's a Small Hotel. Education: Uppingham School. m. Sheila Davies, 2 d. Lindsay, Gemma. Address: c/o Richard Stone, London WC1. Starsign: Aries. Hobbies: squash, moving house, dreaming of other careers. Unfulfilled ambition: to have no ambition.

HAYCOCK, Gerald
Reporter b. 13.1.51 London. Trainee on BBC journalists training scheme. Local radio (Solent) and national TV news (BBC) before joining Westward TV. Education: Wellington College, Berks; Stirling University, Scotland and Macalester College, Minnesota. Address: Kingswear, Devon. Starsign: Capricorn. Hobbies: sailing, hill walking. Unfulfilled ambition: to crew on an enormous ocean-going yacht through the Greek Islands.

HAYES, Geoffrey
Actor/presenter b. 13.3.42 Stockport, Cheshire. Left school at 15 and tried a variety of jobs (testing dyes in

a cotton mill, British Rail booking clerk, etc) before joining Oldham Rep, first as a scene shifter, then as an actor. Student at Royal Northern School of Music and Drama, Manchester. Reps incl: Liverpool, Dundee and Manchester. Became presenter of Rainbow in 1973. Other TV incl: Z Cars; Softly, Softly; Dixon of Dock Green. Education: Cheadle, Cheshire. Address: c/o Felix de Wolfe, London WC2. Starsign: Pisces. Hobby: listening to all kinds of music. Unfulfilled ambition: to win £600,000 on the pools.

HAYES, Patricia
Actress b. 22nd December, London. Stage training at RADA (where she won the gold medal). Went to Stratford to appear in Shakespeare and returned there in 1974 to play Maria in Twelfth Night. In between she has done a great deal of rep and other stage work, radio and TV. Made her name as the maid in Priestley's When We Are Married and first became known on radio in Ted Ray's Ray's a Laugh. Probably has since worked

with more comics than any
other actress, incl: Benny Hill;
Ken Dodd; Arthur Askey;
Spike Milligan; Terry Scott;
Bruce Forsyth; Hugh Lloyd;
Norman Vaughan; Arthur
Haynes; Tony Hancock.
Recent stage incl: Habeas
Corpus; Liza of Lambeth;
Filumena. TV gave her her
first tragic role in Edna, The
Inebriate Woman, for which
she won BAFTA's and the
Sun's Best TV Actress
Awards in 1971. Other TV
incl: Last of the Baskets; The
Trouble With You, Lilian; Till
Death Us Do Part; On the
Move; The Portland Millions;
Love Thy Neighbour; Cider
With Rosie; London Belongs
to Me; Tea Ladies. Films incl:
Goodbye Mr Chips; Carry On
Again Doctor; Fragment of
Fear. Education: Sacred
Heart Convent, London
SW18. m. actor Valentine
Brooke (dis), 2 d. Teresa,
Gemma, 1 s. actor Richard
O'Callaghan. Address: c/o
Herbert de Leon, London W1.
Starsign: Sagittarius.
Hobbies: housework,
gardening, any sort of work.

HAYMAN, Cyd
Actress b. 1.5.44 Bristol.
Wanted to become a
journalist, but turned to
acting through LAMDA (she
took various jobs to pay for
her fees), then rep at
Liverpool, Ipswich,
Folkestone and Mermaid,
London. Big chance came on
TV with her part as Nina in
Manhunt. Before that she had
been in Armchair Theatre; the
BBC's Wednesday Play;

Love Story. Other TV incl:
Clochmerle; The Lotus
Eaters; The Persuaders;
Crime of Passion; The Rivals
of Sherlock Holmes;
Casanova '73; The Rough
With the Smooth;
Forget-Me-Not; The Two
Ronnies; Rogue Male; The
Mourning Brooch. Films incl:
Percy; Guns Before Butter.
Address: c/o Nems
Enterprises, London SW3.
Starsign: Taurus.

HAYNES, Barri
TV presenter/ commentator
b. 6.10.32 Ventor, Isle of
Wight. Trained as journalist
with Kemsley newspapers
before starting in TV with
Teledu Cymru in 1960
presenting a weekly sports
programme and
documentaries. TV and radio
incl: Sportslight; Round
About 7; ATV Today; Miss
World; Come Dancing; adult
education; military tattoos;
Nightride; The Early Show;
etc. m. Mo, 2 d. Emma, Anna
Carys (step-d), 1 s. Nicholas.
Address: Thame, Oxon.
Starsign: Libra. Hobby: golf –
once a year.

**HAYWARD, Ronnie
('Squire')**
Comedian b. 27.7.42 Oxford.
Began as semi-pro comic
and progressed to
ventriloquism. Returned to
comedy as professional in
summer shows, pantomimes
and cabaret. TV incl: Sunday
Night at the London
Palladium; The Val Doonican
Show; Dean Martin's
Laugh-in; Candid Camera;

The Knockers; The Grass is
Greener. Writer of comedy
material. Education: City of
Oxford School; Oxford
Polytechnic. m. Susan,
1 d. Sally-Anne, 1 s. Justin.
Address: c/o Iris Mitchell,
Leytonstone, London E11.
Starsign: Leo. Hobbies: most
sports, including rugby
(ex-county player), bird
watching, fishing and country
walking. As a member of the
Council for Preservation of
Rural England, is in charge of
country walks, rights of way
and bridle paths in his home
town parish of Cumnor,
Oxon. Unfulfilled ambitions:
'to establish myself as a
country character on TV and
radio; to host a networked
countryside series'.

HEFFER, Richard
Actor b. 28.7.46 Cambridge.
Joined Bristol Old Vic from
Oxford University Dramatic
Society. Films: Faustus;
Women in Love; Waterloo;
Penny Gold. Stage incl: leads
in Poor Horace; Child's Play;
Ambassador. TV incl: The
Way We Live Now; Survivors;
Life and Death of Penelope;
Eustace and Hilda; Colditz;
Marriage and Love; Enemy at

the Door. Education: Oxford (MA Hons in English Lit and Language). 1 s. Toby. Address: c/o John Redway Association, London W1. Starsign: Leo. Hobbies: painting and drawing, target shooting, swimming, sailing, riding. Unfulfilled ambitions: to visit China, to fly a plane/balloon, to drive a steam engine.

HEINEY, Paul
Presenter b. 20.4.49 Sheffield. Training at Birmingham Rep and the Mermaid Theatre, London, before becoming an assistant film recordist with BBC TV. Also worked for BBC Radio Humberside, Radio 1 and Radio 4. Latest TV: That's Life. Education: High Storrs Grammar, Sheffield. Address: c/o Bagenal Harvey Organisation, London W1. Starsign: Aries. Hobby: yachting. Unfulfilled ambition: a single-handed transatlantic crossing.

HENDERSON, Dickie
Comedian/actor b. 30.10.22 London. Played in Hollywood version of Cavalcade when 10. Toured music-halls with famous father, Dick Henderson. Served in the army during the war. London revues and pantomimes after demob; first TV 1953, Face the Music followed by Arthur Askey series, Before Your Very Eyes; compered Sunday Night at the London Palladium. Then 120 Dickie Henderson Shows; a series, A Present for Dickie; BBC spectaculars; I'm Bob, He's Dickie and I'm Dickie – That's Show Business. Also many stage appearances: a year in Wish You Were Here; 20 months in Teahouse of the August Moon; also When in Rome; Stand by Your Bedouin; Come Live With Me; And the Bridge Makes Three. Now makes many working trips abroad, incl: USA, Australia, Canada, South Africa, Hong Kong, Holland. Seven Royal Command Performances. Education: privately in Hollywood; St Joseph's College, Beulah Hill, London. m. (1st) Dixie Ross (dec), (2nd) Gwynneth, 1 d. Linda (from 1st m), 1 s. Matthew (from 1st m). Address: c/o London Management, London W1. Starsign: Scorpio. Hobbies: golf and most sports. Unfulfilled ambition: to be a tax exile.

HENDERSON, Don
Actor/author b. 10.11.32 London. Auditioned for Royal Shakespeare Company for a 'dare', was accepted and has since had wide experience in the theatre, films and TV. Films incl: A Midsummer Night's Dream; Callan; The Ghoul; Brannigan; Escape from the Dark; The Voyage; The Prince and the Pauper; Star Wars. TV incl: The Sweeney; The Protectors; Frost Over England; Crown Court; Warship; Poldark; New Scotland Yard; Softly, Softly; Task Force; Dixon of Dock Green; The XYY Man; Van Der Valk; Crossroads; Get Some In; Angels; Strangers. m. Hilary (dec), 1 d. Louise, 1 s. Ian. Address: c/o Essanay Ltd, London W14. Starsign: Scorpio. Hobbies: writing, painting, drinking, lazing, sleeping late and thinking hard. Unfulfilled ambitions: 'to get income tax paid up to date and to become rich'.

HENDERSON, Maggie
Actress b. 17.6.47 Barking, Essex. Member Cambridge Footlights 1968-70. Stage incl: The Philanthropist; Dirty Linen; Mother Goose (Cambridge); Don't Just Lie There; The English Show (Second City Company, Toronto). Radio incl: Black Cinderella Two Goes East. TV incl: No Honestly; Oneupmanship; Doctor On The Go; Hazell; Wodehouse Playhouse; Cannon and Ball; Ragtime; Bod; All Star Record Breakers. Education: Barking Abbey School; Homerton College, Cambridge; London University (B Ed Hons). m. Robert McBain. Address: c/o Bernard Gillman Ltd, Tolworth, Surrey. Starsign: Gemini. Hobby: crossword puzzles.

HENDRY, Ian

Actor b. 13.1.31 Ipswich, Suffolk. Started as stooge to circus clown Coco, but after his army service decided to train for the stage at the Central School of Speech and Drama rather than become a clown. Rep at Hornchurch, Worthing, Edinburgh Festival and Oxford, where his appearance in Dinner with the Family took him to London and success. Has since appeared in nearly 500 TV productions and more than 50 films. Films incl: Simon and Laura; The Secret Place; Room at the Top; Sink the Bismarck; In the Nick; Children of the Damned; Live Now – Pay Later; This is My Secret; The Hill; Casino Royale; Get Carter; The McKenzie Break; Captain Kronos; Tales From the Crypt. TV incl: Police Surgeon; Emergency – Ward 10; Probation Officer; The Avengers (he was one of the original trio with Ingrid Hafner and Patrick Macnee); Afternoon of a Nymph; The Informer; The Lotus Eaters; Village Hall; the New Avengers; Crown Court. Education: Culford College, Suffolk. m. (1st) make-up artist Joanna (dis), (2nd) actress Janet Munro (dec), (3rd) former nanny Sandy, 3 d. Sally Fiona, Corrie Alexandra (from 2nd m), Emma Claire (from 3rd m). Address: c/o Roger Carey, London WC2. Starsign: Capricorn. Hobbies: woodwork, golf,

watching sport, writing poetry.

HENRY, Lenny

Comedy impressionist b. 29.8.58 Dudley, Worcs. Schoolboy winner of talent contests. TV debut in New Faces 1975 when 16. Summer seasons, pantomimes, cabaret and records. TV incl: The Fosters; Celebrity Squares; The Summer Show. First coloured entertainer to appear in stage version of Black and White Minstrel Show (also on TV). Education: Blue Coat Secondary Modern, Dudley. Address: c/o Mike Hollis, Bridgnorth, Salop. Starsign: Virgo. Hobbies: football, pop music (particularly Soul), reading, dancing. Unfulfilled ambition: 'to be good at my trade, to gain respect in my own particular field, especially in making people laugh'.

HENRY, Paul

Actor b. 1947 Birmingham. Trained at the Birmingham School of Speech and Drama and took the part of Benny in Crossroads in 1975 after eight years at Birmingham Rep. For a time he was also

Peter Stevens in the Archers. Stage work incl: Funny Peculiar (Westcliff-on-Sea); 1979 pantomime at Norwich. Record: Benny's Theme. TV also incl: Roads to Freedom; A Midsummer Night's Dream; The Recruiting Officer; Ten Torry Canyons; Romeo and Juliet; The Sweeney. m. Sheila, 1 d. Justine, 1 s. Anthony. Address: c/o John Cadell Ltd, London N6. Unfulfilled ambition: to keep on working.

HERSEE, Carol

'The Most Seen Girl on TV' b. 25.11.58 Redhill, Surrey. Achieved fame when she was eight as the girl on the TV Test Card. She was suggested by her father, a BBC engineer, when professional models proved unacceptable. It was decided to have a child because she would appear more natural and her clothes were less likely to date. On leaving school she became a seamstress at Berman's, the theatrical costumiers, and among the costumes she helped make were those for Danny La Rue's Aladdin pantomime at the London Palladium, the play A Little Night Music, and the films Julia and The Lady Vanishes. Since May 1979 she has been in the wardrobe department at Shepperton Studios working on costumes for the Flash Gordon film. Special award 1971 by Pye TV as the most seen girl on TV. Education: Farnham Comprehensive. Address:

c/o BBC, London W12.
Starsign: Sagittarius.
Hobbies: snooker, pool,
sewing. Unfulfilled ambition:
to have her own dress shop.

HILARY, Jennifer
Actress b. 14.12.42 Hants.
Stage-struck since the age of
four while in Cairo where her
father worked for BOAC.
Attended Elmhurst Ballet
School on return to England
and then to RADA at 16,
followed by rep at Liverpool
and Birmingham. Appeared
on Broadway before
London's West End in
Anouilh's The Rehearsal.
Other stage work incl: Wings
of a Dove; A Scent of Flowers;
A Month in the Country; The
Vortex; Dear Daddy; Sisters;
Relatively Speaking; Half
Life; Ivanov; Avanti. Films
incl: Becket; Heroes of
Telemark; The Idol; One Brief
Summer; Esther; Ruth and
Jennifer. TV incl: The Woman
in White; Deadline Midnight;
Sam; Second House;
Alphabetical Order;
Dr Aitkinson's Daughter; Pig
in a Poke; Charades.
Education: Elmhurst Ballet
School. Address: Chelsea,
London. Starsign:
Sagittarius. Hobbies:
collecting antiques,
travelling.

HILL, Benny
Comedian b. 21.1.25
Southampton. Various jobs –
weighbridge operator,
milkman, Army driver,
drummer – before stage
debut in Stars in Battledress
1941. Stage shows: Paris By
Night; Fine Fettle. Films: The
Italian Job; Chitty, Chitty,
Bang, Bang; Those
Magnificent Men in Their
Flying Machines. TV: own
shows for which he writes all
his own scripts and music.
Elected to TV Hall of Fame,
TVTimes 1978-79.
Education: Shirley School;
Western School; Taunton
Secondary, Southampton.
Address: Kensington,
London. Starsign: Aquarius.
Hobbies: work, travel.
Unfulfilled ambition: more
writing, less performing.

HILL, Jimmy
Presenter b. 22.7.28 Balham,
London. Began career in
football, first as an amateur
for Reading 1949. Turned
professional and joined
Brentford the same year.
Went to Fulham 1952;
chairman of the Professional
Footballers Assn 1957;
worked as TV commentator
and interviewer; manager of
Coventry City 1961; became
head of London Weekend's
sports unit 1967; deputy
controller of programmes
1971; wide business
interests. TV: World of Sport;
The Big Match; Grandstand;
Match of the Day. Education:
grammar school.
m. (1st) Gloria (dis),
(2nd) Heather, 2 d. (one from
each m), 3 s. (2 from 1st m,
1 from 2nd m). Address: c/o
Jimmy Hill Ltd, London W2.
Starsign: Leo/Cancer.
Hobbies: golf, riding, tennis,
bridge.

HILL, Vince
Singer b. 16.4.32 Coventry.
Started entertaining in local
pubs and clubs. Became
vocalist for Band of the Royal
Signals, then Teddy Foster
Band. Helped form vocal
groups Four Others and The
Raindrops before going solo
with recording The River's
Run Dry. First big record hit
Eidelweiss; others incl:
Roses of Picardy; Look
Around. Many singles and
albums. Long association
with Parade of the Pops
(radio) and Stars and Garters
(ITV). Appeared in almost
every top TV variety show;
starred in Roy Castle TV
series and They Sold a
Million; The Musical Time
Machine. Hosted 26-week TV
series in Canada. Also
international tours; Talk of the
Town and wrote score for TV
musical Tolpuddle.
Education: Whitemoor
School, Coventry. m. Anne,
1 s. Athol. Address: c/o Rod

Taylor, London. Starsign: Aries. Hobbies: photography, gardening, travelling, cooking, painting. Unfulfilled ambition: to be a successful writer.

HINDLE, Madge
Actress b. 19.5.38 Blackburn. Local amateurs, then Edinburgh Festival Fringe. TV: Nearest and Dearest; The Two Ronnies; Renee Bradshaw, now Renee Roberts, in Coronation Street since 1976. Education: local schools, Blackburn. m. Michael, 2 d. Charlotte, Frances. Address: c/o Fraser and Dunlop, London W1. Starsign: Taurus. Hobbies: humming and rocking. Unfulfilled ambition: 'I would like to be Judi Dench.'

HINES, Frazer
Actor b. 22.9.44 Horsforth, Yorks. Been in the 'business' since he was eight. By the time he was 15 he had appeared in half-a-dozen films and served apprenticeship in the theatre. Stage incl: Norman; Good Woman of Setzuan; Heirs and Graces; No Trams. Films incl: Zeppelin; Last Valley; The

Weapon. Has played Joe Sugden in Emmerdale Farm since its start 1972. Other TV incl: Dr Who. Also has a request programme on Pennine Radio. Education: Norwood College, Harrogate; Corona Stage School. Address: c/o Al Mitchell Associates, London WC2. Starsign: Virgo/Libra cusp. Hobbies: all sport, amateur jockey. Unfulfilled ambitions: to make a western film and to own a Derby winner.

HINES, Ronald
Actor b. 20.6.29 London. Drama school followed by rep, then signed up for films incl: Robin Hood; The Buccaneers; Tell It to the Marines. Other films incl: Whistle Down the Wind; The Angry Silence; Two-headed Spy; Sink the Bismarck; Rough Cut. TV incl: The Long Wait; Strictly for the Sparrows; The Boy Next Door; Parole; Elizabeth R; Not in Front of the Children; The Square on the Hypotenuse; The Dreaming Bandsman; The Rivals of Sherlock Holmes; Jackanory; Sutherland's Law; This Year, Next Year; Gossip from the Forest; Deep Concern; Shadows; The Professionals. Married with 3 children. Address: c/o Leading Artists, London SW1. Starsign: Gemini.

HIRD, Thora
Actress b. 28.5.13 Morecambe, Lancs. Classic start to show business: born of theatrical parents and carried on stage when a few weeks old. At 16 she was making her mark in rep and was 'discovered' and given a film contract. She was an overnight success with her first London appearance in Flowers For the Living in 1944. Has since appeared in hundreds of plays, films and radio and TV programmes. Stage roles range from the Nurse in Romeo and Juliet to the comedy maid in No, No, Nanette. Films incl: The Entertainer; Over the Odds; A Kind of Loving; Term of Trial; Rattle of a Simple Man; Some Will, Some Won't; The Nightcomers. Perhaps best known on TV for her series Meet the Wife; The First Lady; Ours is a Nice House and more recently, In Loving Memory and One Flesh and Blood. Other TV incl: The Hard Case; Albert Hope; The Bed; She Stoops to Conquer; Your Songs of Praise Choice; Thomas and Sarah and two Alan Bennett plays, Me, I'm Afraid of Virginia Wolf, and Afternoon Off. Education: private school. m. James Scott, 1 d. actress Janette Scott. Address: c/o Felix de Wolfe, London WC2. Starsign: Gemini. Hobbies: travel, reading. Unfulfilled ambitions: several!

HOCKIN, Bruce
Reporter/interviewer/ current affairs editor b. 23.5.36 Exmouth, Devon. Trainee journalist on Bideford and North Devon Gazette; reporter, feature writer, assistant news editor on Western Mail. Since 1968 regular presenter of HTV's Report West; Now It's Your Say; Press Call; Focus; Report Extra. Film documentaries: Longest River; Sweetest Salmon; Serenade in the City; Next Patient, Please. Education: Bideford Grammar.
m. Caroline, 1 d. Georgiana, 1 s. Giles. Address: c/o HTV, Bristol. Starsign: Gemini. Hobbies: cricket, walking, golf. Unfulfilled ambition: 'to revisit Suez Canal Zone of Egypt, my posting for National Service in mid-50's'.

HODGSON, Godfrey
Reporter/presenter b. 1.2.34 Horsham, Sussex. Journalistic experience with The Times (reporter); Observer (Washington correspondent); Sunday Times (editor of Insight) before reporting in more than 20 This Week programmes

for ITN 1965-7. Also presented more than a dozen What The Papers Say; Granada's documentary When In Rome on Italian oil bribery scandal 1976; two Weekend World specials on US presidential election 1976. Reporter/ scriptwriter for Granada documentary on 1972 presidential election How to Steal a Party. Education: Winchester College (scholar); Magdalen College, Oxford (Open Scholar and 1st Class hons); University of Pennsylvania. m (1st) Alice, (2nd) Hilary, 2 d. Jessica, Laura (from 2nd m), 2 s. Pierre, Francis (from 1st m). Address: London WC1. Starsign: Aquarius. Hobbies: talking, walking, reading, drinking. Unfulfilled ambition: 'la paix du coeur, les pastilles de menthes et l'ocean pour tombeau'.

HOLDEN, Jan
Actress b. 9.5.31 Southport. Trained at the Old Vic Theatre School and later joined the company. Toured in rep for two years. London stage incl: Speaking of Murder; Tunnel of Love and, more recently, Banana Ridge; Shut Your Eyes and Think of England. Her many TV appearances incl: The Odd Man; Emergency – Ward 10; Knight Errant; Harper's West One; Agony; The Saint; Casanova; Are You Being Served?; Rt Hon Mrs. Education: Lowther College, N Wales. twin d. Belinda and Arabella. 1 s. Simon.

Address: c/o Richard Stone, London WC2. Starsign: Taurus. Hobbies: gardening, interior decoration.

HOLLOWAY, Alison
Actress/presenter b. 2.2.61 London. Drama trained at Italia Conti Stage School to teacher's diploma. Stage incl: I and Albert (musical); Pandora's Box (Young Vic); pantomimes at Watford and Golders Green. TV incl: Phyllis Dixie; Last Summer (Play for Today); Clayhanger; Bunch of Fives; You Can't Be Serious; You Must Be Joking; presenter for Westward TV's Just the Job. Has also made language records for Sweden called Hands Up. Address: c/o Westward TV, Plymouth. Starsign: Aquarius. Hobbies: cooking, horse-riding, piano. Unfulfilled ambition: to operate on someone in hospital.

HOLLOWAY, Julian
Actor b. 1944 Penn, Bucks. Stage-struck while at prep school, got into TV by accident: while at RADA visited his father, Stanley Holloway, then making the

series Our Man Higgins; Julian was written into the series. Stayed to make another US series, Fair Exchange. Returning to England, went into revue and such films as The Knack; A Hard Day's Night; Hostile Witness; and parts in seven Carry On films. TV incl: Man From Haven; The Incredible Robert Baldick; The Edwardians; Bowler; Sprout; The Sweeney; The Reverent Wooing of Archibald; Helen – A Woman of Today; She; Secrets; Rebecca. Education: Harrow. m. actress Zena Walker (dis). Address: c/o Peter Crouch Ltd, London W1.

HOLOWAY, Mike
Actor/musician b. 28.1.61 Mile End, London. Been interested in music since he was two and was taught drumming by his grandfather. At nine he joined a group called The Young Revival and later formed Flintlock. Was 'discovered' while playing with them at a charity show. Method Acting school. Extensive stage tours; two films (both for America); numerous radio station features throughout Britain and the Continent. Made 360 programmes with the group and 80 independent appearances. TV incl: as actor– The Tomorrow People; as actor/musician with Flintlock– You Must Be Joking; The Magic Circle; Fanfare; Pauline's Quirkes. Education: Erkenwald Comprehensive;

Essex Music College (studying drums, percussion, music theory, trumpet, vibes and xylophone); Anna Scher Drama School. Address: Chelmsford, Essex. Starsign: Aquarius. Hobbies: model glider making, custom car mechanics, sports and music. Unfulfilled ambition: to play a drum duet with Buddy Rich.

HONEYCOMBE, Gordon
Presenter/writer b. 27.9.36 Karachi, British India. Is 6ft 5ins tall. Started as a radio announcer 1956, acted with the Royal Shakespeare Company for a couple of years and joined ITN as scriptwriter and newscaster 1965. Left to freelance 1977. Is also a writer of some accomplishment, having written several plays and dramatisations for the stage and TV and is the author of a number of novels. Stage incl: The Redemption; Paradise Lost (also radio); God Save The Queen; A King Shall Have a Kingdom (also radio). Radio: Lancelot and Guinevere. TV incl: The Golden Vision; Time and Time Again (Silver Medal, New York Film and TV Festival, 1975); Something Special (series); The Late, Late Show; Family History (series about how he traced his ancestry back to 1318). Novels incl: Neither the Sea Nor the Sand (also the screenplay); Dragon Under the Hill; Adam's Tale; Red Watch. Education: Edinburgh Academy and

University College, Oxford (MA in English Language and Literature). Address: c/o Isobel Davie Ltd, London W1. Starsign: Libra. Hobbies: brass-rubbing, genealogy, bridge, crosswords, curry, pigs. Unfulfilled ambition: to star in a London West End musical.

HOOKS, Linda
Actress b. 1952 Liverpool. Trained as chiropodist, then became a model, was Miss Britain and Miss International 1972 and Miss Cinema. Films incl: Carry On Dick; Carry On Behind; Carry On England. TV incl: The Jimmy Tarbuck Show; The Rough With the Smooth; Carry On Laughing; Space 1999; The Little and Large TV Show; Sale of the Century; Celebrity Squares; The Sweeney. Education: Childwall Valley High, Liverpool, and Bournemouth School for Girls. Address: c/o Aida Foster Ltd, London NW8. Starsign: Libra. Hobbies: cooking, cycling, table tennis, going to jumble sales. Unfulfilled ambition: 'to have my own TV series.'

HORDERN, Michael CBE
Actor b. 3.10.11
Berkhamsted, Herts. Grew
up on Dartmoor. Was once a
schoolmaster, then sold
school textbooks and
dabbled in amateur
dramatics which gave him a
taste for the stage. No
professional training before
becoming assistant stage
manager and understudy
and making his professional
debut in London in Othello in
1937. Two years in rep at
Bristol's Little Theatre where
he met the girl who was to
become his wife. Served in
the Royal Navy 1940-45 and
rose to the rank of
lieut-commander. Returned
to the stage 1946, the year in
which he made his TV debut
in the title role of Noah. Now
one of Britain's leading
character actors, he has
appeared in many plays,
films and TV productions.
Stage incl: King Lear (also on
TV); Flint; Richard II and
Jumpers (National Theatre);
The Tempest (RSC and on
TV); The Ordeal of Gilbert
Pinfold. Many films incl:
Alexander the Great;
Cleopatra; The VIP's; The
Spy Who Came in from the
Cold; The Taming of the
Shrew; Where Eagles Dare;
Anne of the Thousand Days;
El Cid; Khartoum; Theatre of
Blood; Alice's Adventures in
Wonderland; Quilp; Royal
Flush; The Slipper and the
Rose. TV incl: The Dock Brief;
What Shall We Tell Caroline?;
The Browning Version; The
Magistrate; Edward the
Seventh; Chester Mystery

Plays; Romeo and Juliet;
Roald Dahl's Tales of the
Unexpected. Education:
Brighton College. m. former
actress Eve Mortimer,
1 d. Joanna. Address: c/o
ICM, London W1. Starsign:
Libra. Hobbies: fishing (he
has devised a trout fly named
Hordern's Nymph) and
gardening.

HORSFALL, Bernard
Actor b. Bishops Stortford,
Herts, but raised in Sussex.
Became interested in drama
while at school but spent a
year in Canada supposedly
studying agriculture. On his
return he taught at a prep
school in Surrey and in 1950
enrolled at the Webber
Douglas Academy of
Dramatic Art to train to
become an actor. Left to join
a tour with Dundee Rep
Company and the Old Vic.
Recent stage incl: Who's
Afraid of Virginia Woolf? Films
incl: Shout at the Devil; Gold;
On Her Majesty's Secret
Service. TV incl: Dancers in
Mourning; Death of a Ghost;
Family Solicitor; Suspicion;
Beasts; General Hospital; Big
Boy Now; This Year, Next
Year; Enemy at the Door.
Education: Rugby School.
m. Jane, 2. d. Hannah,
Rebecca, 1 s. Christian.
Address: c/o Brian Wheeler
Personal Management,
London W4.

HOUNSELL, Margaret
Reporter/presenter
b. 19.6.47 Journalistic
experience on magazines,
newspapers and local radio

(Radio City) before joining
ATV. Education: grammar
school; London University.
Address: Birmingham.
Starsign: Gemini. Hobbies:
cinema, music.

HOWARD, Trevor
Actor b. 29.9.16 Cliftonville,
Kent. Taken to Sri Lanka at an
early age by his parents, then
to America and Canada
before returning to Britain.
Trained at RADA and after a
spell with RSC at Stratford,
went into the army, taking
part in the invasions of
Norway and Sicily and
returned to civvie street with a
Military Cross. Old Vic
1947-48. First big lead was in
Brief Encounter. Films since
incl: Odette; The Clouded
Yellow; Outcast of the
Islands; Gift Horse; The Third
Man; The Heart of the Matter;
Cockleshell Heroes; The Key;
Sons and Lovers; Mutiny on
the Bounty; Von Ryan's
Express; The Charge of the
Light Brigade; Ryan's
Daughter; Mary Queen of
Scots; Conduct
Unbecoming; The Count of
Monte Cristo; The Last
Remake of Beau Geste. Plays
incl: The Devil's General; The

Cherry Orchard; The Father; Two Stars for Comfort; Waltz of the Toreadors; Scenario; The Invincible Mr Disraeli; Napoleon at St Helena. Most recent TV: Catholics; Stars on Sunday; Scorpion Tales. Education: schools in Sri Lanka, Los Angeles, Canada, and Clifton College, Bristol. m. actress Helen Cherry. Address: Arkley, North London. Starsign: Libra. Hobbies: cricket, travel.

HOWARTH, Jack
Actor b. 19.2.1886 Rochdale. More than 60 years in the theatrical profession, starting at the age of 12 playing children's parts with Churchill's Minstrels in The Happy Valley, Llandudno. Stage director for the original productions of Dracula and Frankenstein in this country. Many years with Leslie Henson's company and was in 18 films and 100 TV programmes (incl the first play from Granada), before becoming Albert Tatlock in Coronation Street. Education: Board School in Rochdale. m. Betty, 1 s. John. Address: c/o International Artistes Representation, London W1 Starsign: Pisces. Hobbies: watching cricket, circuses.

HOWELL, Lisbeth
TV journalist b. 23.3.51 Liverpool. Joined Border TV after experience as BBC Radio Leeds producer

1974-77. Joined Granada TV June 1979. Education: Blackburn House High, Liverpool; Altrincham Grammar; Bristol University; Trinity and All Saints' College of Education, Leeds. Address: c/o Border TV, Carlisle. Starsign: Aries. Hobbies: reading, music, swimming.

HOWELL, St John
Reporter/presenter/actor/film director b. 22.6.41 King's Pyon, Herefordshire. After a spell at Birmingham Rep became producer of radio programmes. Later became presenter, interviewer and director in TV. Radio credits incl: Today; Woman's Hour; World at One; Pick of the Week; Living World; In Touch; Regional Extra. Also radio reporter for COI. TV: Nationwide; Pebble Mill; Dig This; Day and Night; The Sky at Night; Farming; St John on Fashion – Food (own series); Midlands Today. TV drama: Blue Peter; Tiswas; Magpie; Spy Catcher; The Net; also Captain Freddie of Captain Freddie's Pig Trotters (the band which does not have musical instruments).

Education: Bridgnorth Grammar; Birmingham College of Drama. Address: c/o BBC, Pebble Mill, Birmingham. Starsign: Cancer. Hobbies: flying, writing.

HOWERD, Frankie OBE
Comedian b. 6.3.22 York. Stage debut at 13. Camp concerts during the war. Revue and stage shows: Out of This World; Pardon My French; Way Out in Piccadilly; Charley's Aunt; Hotel Paradise; A Midsummer Night's Dream; Alice in Wonderland; A Funny Thing Happened on the Way to the Forum; Palladium pantomime 1968 and 1973. Films incl: The Ladykillers; Runaway Bus; Touch of the Sun; Jumping For Joy; Further Up The Creek; Carry On Doctor; Carry On Up the Jungle; Up Pompeii; Up The Chastity Belt; Up The Front; The House In Nightmare Park; Sgt Pepper's Lonely Hearts Club Band. TV incl: Fine Goings On; Up Pompeii; The Frankie Howerd Show. Many Royal Variety performances. Education: Shooters Hill School, Woolwich. Address: c/o RSO Management Ltd, London W1. Starsign: Pisces. Hobbies: tennis, swimming, music, reading. Unfulfilled ambition: to be king.

HOWMAN, Karl
Actor b. 13.12.53 Crayford,
Kent. Trained in the
National Youth Theatre, then
stage appearances in Teeth
'n' Smiles; Only a Game.
Films incl: That'll Be the Day;
Stardust; SOS Titanic;
Porridge. TV incl: Thirty
Minute Theatre; Armchair
Theatre; Play for Today;
Prodigal Daughter; The
Sweeney; Van Der Valk;
Warship; Life At Stake;
Jensen Code; Fortunes of
Nigel; Get Some In; People
Like Us; Angels; Blake's
Seven; Fox. Education: St
Augustine's, Belvedere;
Picardy Boys', Erith.
m. Clare, 1 d. Chloe.
Address: c/o Boyack and
Conway, London W1.
Starsign: Sagittarius.
Hobbies: snooker; cards;
football; reading; films;
moderate drinking; cricket;
tennis. Unfulfilled ambition: to
be able to play a musical
instrument.

HUDD, Roy
Comedian b. 16.5.36
Croydon, Surrey. Claims he
'trained in the University of
Life, variety, concert party
and pantomime'. But he
began in boys' clubs 1957
followed by holiday camp
and summer shows. TV
debut 1964 as a regular in
Not So Much a Programme,
More a Way of Life. Other TV
incl: Hudd; The Illustrated
Weekly Hudd; Up Sunday;
The Roy Hudd Show; Pebble
Mill at One; The 607080
Show; Sunday Night at the
London Palladium; London
Night Out; Tell Me Another;
Looks Familiar; Quick on the
Draw; Blankety Blank;
Celebrity Squares; Seaside
Special; Hold the Front Page;
The Good Old Days; Look
Who's Talking; The Eamonn
Andrews Show; Sooty, and
various chat and variety
shows. Radio incl: The News
Huddlines. On stage recently
appeared as Fagin in the
revival of Oliver! An expert on
old music-hall, especially
Max Miller, he has devised a
one-man show based on
golden oldies from the halls.
Education: School of Hard
Knocks (he says). m. Ann,
1 s. Max. Address: London
NW11. Starsign: Taurus.
Hobbies: walking, sleeping,
talking, and music-hall
(history and songs).
Unfulfilled ambition:
retirement at 42.

HUDSON, Rock
Actor b. 17.11.25 Winnetka,
Illinois. Childhood ambition
was to be a bus driver but
decided he would be an
actor after being in school
plays. After two years in US
Navy he moved to Los
Angeles hoping to break into
films. Movie debut was one
line in Fighter Squadron in
1949, but it got him a
contract. Made his name in
Magnificent Obsession in
1954 and made over 50 films
between 1955 and 1959 incl:
Never Say Goodbye; Giant;
Written on the Wind; Battle
Hymn; Something of Value;
Tarnished Angels; A Farewell
to Arms; This Earth is Mine;
Pillow Talk. Other films incl:
Darling Lili; Seconds; Pretty
Maids All in a Row; Embryo.
Theatre: I Do, I Do. Best
known to TV audiences for
McMillan and Wife and
McMillan. Other TV incl:
Wheels; The Martian
Chronicles. Record: Rock
Gently. Education: New Trier
School, Winnetka.
m. secretary Phyllis Gates
(dis). Starsign: Scorpio.

HUGHES, Geoffrey
Actor b. 2.2.44 Liverpool.
Training at Stoke-on-Trent
Rep, films and TV for the past
17 years. London stage incl:
Maggie May; Say Good-night
to Grandma. Films incl: Virgin
Soldiers; Adolf Hitler, My
Part in His Downfall; The
Bofors Gun. TV: many plays
and series; currently Eddie
Yeats in Coronation Street.
Education: Abbotsford
School, Yorks. m. Susan.
Address: c/o Richard Stone,
London WC2. Starsign:
Aquarius. Hobbies: natural
history, music. Unfulfilled
ambition: 'to be acting when
I'm 98'.

HUNNIFORD, Gloria
TV presenter/interviewer
b. 10.4.40 Portadown, Co
Armagh. Had her own radio

programme in Canada 1959. In Northern Ireland for the BBC she was involved in another radio series, Up Country and a two-and-a-half hour daily programme, A Taste of Hunni. TV incl: Here's How; Songs of Praise; Jubilee bonfire celebrations; Big Band series. For BBC World Service: A Taste of Hunni – Irish Style. Records incl: LP Good Evening . . . Gloria. Education: Portadown College. m. Don Keating, 1 d. Caron, 2 s. Paul, Michael. Address: Hillsborough, Co Down. Starsign: Aries. Hobby: antique collecting.

HUNT, Gareth
Actor b. 7.2.43 London. Served in the Merchant Navy for six years after which he had a variety of jobs before training at Webber Douglas Academy of Dramatic Art. Rep at Ipswich, Bristol Old Vic, Coventry, Royal Court in London, and Watford before the Royal Shakespeare Company and the National Theatre. Stage incl: Conduct Unbecoming; Alpha Beta; Deathtrap. Films incl: Licensed to Love and Kill;

The House on Garibaldi Street; The World is Full of Married Men. Made impact on TV as the handsome footman in Upstairs, Downstairs and as Gambit in The New Avengers. Education: Singlegate School for Boys. m. Carol (dis), 1 s. Gareth. Address: c/o ICM, London W1. Starsign: Aquarius. Hobbies: golf, keep-fit, cricket, squash. Unfulfilled ambition: to play the piano under water.

HURNDALL, Richard
Actor b. 3.11.10 Darlington, Co Durham. Studied music in Paris before switching to acting. Trained at RADA and made stage debut 1930. First broadcast in 1933, since when he has been in many reps, including Stratford-upon-Avon Memorial Theatre, and toured in plays. West End shows incl: The Affair; The New Men; The Masters; Hostile Witness; Justice is a Woman; Highly Confidential. Former member of BBC drama rep company, has also appeared frequently on TV since 1946 incl: Z Cars; Softly, Softly; Dr Finlay's Casebook; Callan; Codename; The Avengers; The Power Game; It's Murder, But Is It Art?; The Inheritors; The Regiment; The Onedin Line; Van Der Valk; War and Peace; Public Eye; Hadleigh; The Protectors; Enemy At The Door; Philby, Burgess and Maclean. Education: Clarement; Darlington; Scarborough

College. m. (1st) Mona Berridge (dis), (2nd) Ivy Carlton (dec), (3rd) Margaret Ward, 1 d. (dec). Address: c/o Essanay, London W14. Starsign: Scorpio. Hobbies: genealogy, bridge, walking. Unfulfilled ambition: 'too late!'

HURT, John
Actor b. 22.1.40 Chesterfield. Studied at Grimsby Art School and St Martin's School of Art in London before going to RADA to study for the stage. Professional debut in TV programme, The Wild and the Willing. Most of his early work was on the stage incl: Little Malcolm and His Struggle Against the Eunuchs. Films incl: A Man For All Seasons; Sinful Davey; Before Winter Comes; In Search of Gregory; Forbush and the Penguins; Ten Rillington Place; Pied Piper; Midnight Express (BAFTA Award for Best Supporting Actor 1979); Alien. TV incl: The Naked Civil Servant (BAFTA Award for Best Actor 1975); I Claudius; Crime and Punishment; Tinker, Tailor, Soldier, Spy. Education: The Lincoln School, Lincoln. Address: c/o Plunket Greene Ltd, London SW1. Starsign: Aquarius.

I

INGLE, Su
Presenter/researcher
b. 23.4.55, London.
Experience of publicity
photography in film and TV
studios in London and
Hollywood before presenting
and researching radio and
TV programmes in this
country. Radio incl: Nature
Notebook; Living World. TV
incl: Wildtrack; Don't Ask Me;
Schools programme,
Science All Round; Ten on
Saturday, Wyatt's Place;
Help Yourself. Education: St
Paul's Girls' School, London;
Collingwood College,
Durham University (Botany
degree). Address: Clifton,
Bristol. Starsign: Taurus.
Hobbies: sailing and boating,
surfing, gliding, squash,
great interest in natural
history. Unfulfilled ambitions:
directing and producing.

IMRAY, June
Broadcaster/entertainer
b. 23.1.37 Peterculter,
Aberdeenshire. Primary
school teacher, announcer,
interviewer and presenter.
Tea Break (Thames TV); Pete
Murray's Open House; Junior
Points of View. Many
programmes for ITV, BBC
radio, STV, and now
Grampian TV (June Plus Two;
Sound of Britain). Records:
The Torry Quine; The Torry
Quine Again. Education:
Aberdeen Academy;
University of Aberdeen (MA);
Aberdeen College of
Education. m. Gerry Davis,
1 d. Emma, 1 s. Paul.
Address: Aberdeen.
Starsign: Aquarius. Hobbies:
reading, Scottish history,
work. Unfulfilled ambition: to
make a documentary on the
'herring quines' who followed
the fishing fleets at the turn of
the century.

INMAN, John
Actor b. 28.6.36 Preston.
One of his first jobs was a
window dresser in a London
store. When 21 became an
actor at Crew Rep. London
West End debut was in Anne
Veronica; stage work since
has incl: Salad Days; Let's
Get Laid; summer shows;

pantomime at Wimbledon, Bristol, Nottingham, Charley's Aunt. Achieved overnight success in TV series Are You Being Served?. Other TV incl: Odd Man Out; Celebrity Squares; The Good Old Days. Education: Claremont School, Blackpool. Address: c/o London Management, London W1. Starsign: Cancer. Hobby: work. Ambition: to keep working!

JACKSON, Gordon
Actor b. 19.12.23 Glasgow. Trained as a draughtsman but playing parts in radio plays on Children's Hour brought him to the notice of Ealing Studios. The Foreman Went to France was the first of more than 50 films, incl: Whisky Galore; Mutiny on the Bounty; Those Magnificent Men in Their Flying Machines; The Prime of Miss Jean Brodie; Night of the Generals and stage appearances in Macbeth; Hamlet; Hedda Gabler; What Every Woman Knows; Noah; Twelfth Night. TV incl: Ghost Squad; Dr Finlay's Casebook; The Soldier's Tale; The Professionals; but best known for the part of Hudson in Upstairs, Downstairs. Education: Hillhead High School, Glasgow. m. actress Rona Anderson, 2 s. Graham, Roddy. Address: Hampstead, London. Starsign: Sagittarius. Hobbies: music, gardening. Unfulfilled ambition: 'to be an actor – not acting, the real thing!'

JACKSON, Kate
Actress b. 29.10.49
Birmingham, Alabama. First
thought of becoming a
professional tennis player,
but turned to acting after
drama course at university.
While there worked as a
model and NBC tour guide.
After summer stock broke
into TV through Dark
Shadows. For four years was
in The Rookies, then Charlie's
Angels, the idea for the series
being hers. Other TV incl:
Killer Bees. Films incl: Limbo;
Thunder and Lightning.
Education: high school at
Birmingham; University of
Mississippi; Birmingham
Southern University.
m. Andrew Stevens, actor
son of actress Stella Stevens.
Starsign: Scorpio.

JACKSON, Michael
Actor b. 19.1.48 Liverpool.
Studied drama at University
of London and from there
went into rep at Sheffield.
Other rep experience at
Coventry, Birmingham and
Edinburgh. TV incl: Marked
Personal; Man About the
House; Hazell; Churchill's
People; Robin Hood; Anna
Karenina; A Woman's Place;

Crown Court; was also in the
Sweeney 2 film, for which he
won the London Evening
News Most Promising
Newcomer Award (Male)
1978. Education: Holt High
School, Liverpool; London
University. m. Peta Lunberg.
Address: c/o Peter Browne
Management, London SW9.
Starsign: Capricorn.
Hobbies: squash, tennis,
music, eating and cooking
wholefoods. Unfulfilled
ambitions: 'to form my own
production company for
theatre and films, and to work
for 11 months a year'.

JACOBS, David
Compere/interviewer
b. 19.5.26 London. First
broadcast as an
impressionist in Navy Mixture
while still in the Royal Navy.
Later became an announcer
with the Forces Broadcasting
Service in London. Chief
announcer, Radio Seal,
Ceylon 1945-47. Joined BBC
in 1947 as radio newscaster
but shortly after went
freelance and became one of
the busiest men on the air as
compere, disc-jockey and
actor (he played 23 parts in
the Journey Into Space radio
serial). Other radio incl: Pick
of the Pops; The David
Jacobs Show; Any
Questions?; Any Answers?;
Melodies For You. TV incl:
Juke Box Jury; The David
Jacobs Show; Miss World;
Eurovision Song Contest;
Frank Sinatra Show;
Wednesday Magazine; Tell
The Truth; Make Up Your
Mind; David Jacobs' Words

and Music; It's Sunday Night
With David Jacobs; Now Who
Do You Do?; Where Are They
Now? Many business
interests. Books: Jacobs
Ladder (autobiography);
Caroline. Education: Belmont
College; Strand School.
m. (1st) actress Patricia
Bradlaw (dis), (2nd) Caroline
(dec), (3rd) model Lindsay
Stuart-Hutcheson,
3 d. Carol, Joanna, Emma,
1 s. Jeremy (dec) (all by
1st m). Address: c/o Lewis
Joelle, London SW1.
Starsign: Taurus. Hobbies:
talking, listening and hotels.

JACQUES, Hattie
Actress/comedienne
b. 7.2.24 Sandgate, Kent. A
Red Cross nurse and a
welder during the war; in
1944 auditioned and
subsequently joined the
Players' Theatre, London.
After appearing in
pantomimes, plays and
revues, joined the Old Vic
company 1947-48. Stage
incl: Bells of St Martins; The
Two Mrs Carrols; Please
Teacher; Large as Life. Films
incl: Nicholas Nickleby;
Pickwick Papers; Make Mine
Mink; and many Carry On
films. Radio experience
dates back to Tommy
Handley's ITMA; Educating
Archie; Hancock's Half-hour;
Eric Sykes shows. TV incl:
Our House; Pantomania;
Happy Holidays; Celebrity
Squares; Eric Sykes shows
(coming up for the 20th year).
Education: Godolphin and
Latymer Schools. m. actor
John Le Mesurier (dis),

2 s. Robin, Kim. Address: c/o Felix de Wolfe, London WC2. Starsign: Aquarius. Hobbies: collecting records, old theatre postcards and Victoriana. Unfulfilled ambition: to fill in for Dame Margot Fonteyn.

JAEGER, Frederick

Actor/director b. 1928 Berlin. Came to England 1939 and took up acting at the suggestion of his English headmaster. Guildhall School of Music and Drama 1946-48 and started stage career at Preston Rep 1949. Many rep seasons in provinces before West End appearances such as The Comedy of Errors; Lock Up Your Daughters. Went into films 1956 which incl: The Black Tents; The War Lovers; The Iron Petticoat; Song of Norway; Ice Cold in Alex; Farewell Performance; The One That Got Away; Scorpio; One of Those Things; The Situation; 7% Solution; The Voyage; Nijinsky. Started TV 1955 in The Grove Family; appearances since incl: The Inside Man; The Pretenders; Special Branch; Warship; Z Cars; Department S; Ryan International; Little Women; Man at the Top; Persuaders; Paul Temple; Dr Who; Dixon of Dock Green; Jason King; Me Mammy; The Sweeney; Hadleigh; The Main Chance; Protectors; Oneupmanship; Nuts; The Dick Emery Show; Shelley; Home Movies; Doombolt Chase; New Avengers; The Professionals; Some Mothers Do 'Ave 'Em;

Omega Factor; The Fall and Rise of Reginald Perrin. Education: Germany, France, England.
m. (1st) painter Hazel Penwarden (dis); (2nd) Elizabeth, 2 step-d. Caroline, Sarah. Address: Petersham, Surrey. Starsign: Taurus. Hobbies: squash, gardening.

JAMES, Keith

Actor b. 10.12.37 Southend-on-Sea, Essex. Trained at the Guildhall School of Music and Drama, then rep at Dundee and York before London's West End, Royal Shakespeare Company and Edinburgh Festival. Many films, documentaries, TV programmes and more than 100 commercials. Films incl: Operation Snatch; Dutchman; A Challenge for Robin Hood; The Ruins Within. TV incl: Softly, Softly; Hugh and I; The Mind of Mr J G Reeder; Champion House; Coronation Street; Gazette; Dr Who; Counter Strike; Castle Haven; Target; Public Eye; Keep It in the Family. For many years was a 'regular' in the Dick Emery Shows; has also been in Bernie Winters, Frankie Howerd and Mike Yarwood shows. Education: Wentworth High School for Boys, Southend. m. health visitor Betty, 2 d. Natalie, Alison, 1 s. Jonathan. Address: c/o Beryl Seton Agency, London WC2. Starsign: Sagittarius. Hobby: photography. Unfulfilled ambition: to keep busy.

JARVIS, Martin

Actor b. 4th August Cheltenham. Started in Manchester after training at RADA (silver medal and Vanburgh Award). Soon came to London where his stage work incl: Cockade; Poor Bitos; Man and Superman; The Spoils of Poynton; The Bandwagon; The Prodigal Daughter; The Rivals (and in America). Played Edward VIII in The Woman I Love at Bromley and scored personal success in She Stoops to Conquer in Canada and at Hong Kong Arts Festival. His films incl: The Last Escape; Ike (in which he played George VI). Many radio performances incl: War and Peace; Great Expectations; also readings and the author of several short stories for radio. TV incl: The Forsyte Saga; Nicholas Nickleby; The Pallisers; Ross; After Liverpool; The Samaritan; Zigger Zagger; True Patriot; David Copperfield; Killers; Charades; Enemy at the Door. Education: Whitgift School, Croydon; London University. m. actress Rosalind Ayres, 2 s. Toby, Oliver. Address: c/o London Management, London W1. Starsign: Leo. Hobbies: music, Indian food, movies, work, interior design.

JASON, David

Actor b. 2.2.40 Edmonton, London. Became an electrician on leaving school, but all his spare time was devoted to amateur

theatricals. His actor brother, Arthur, helped to get him his first professional part in South Sea Bubble at Bromley. More rep then Peter Pan. A Dick Emery season at Bournemouth led to the part of Captain Fantastic in Do Not Adjust Your Set, which established him on TV including: Hark at Barker; Six Dates With Barker; Doctor in the House; Doctor at Large; Doctor at Sea. Other major TV series incl: The Top Secret Life of Edgar Briggs; Lucky Fella; A Sharp Intake of Breath. Films incl: The Odd Job. Recent radio: Week Ending; Jason Explanation. Education: 'Some education', he says. Address: c/o Richard Stone, London WC2. Starsign: Aquarius. Hobbies: gliding and skin diving. Unfulfilled ambitions: to work in America and fly to Mars.

JAYSTON, Michael
Actor b. 29.10.35 Nottingham. Studied at Guildhall School of Music and Drama, then rep at Salisbury, Bristol Old Vic, Royal Shakespeare Company and National Theatre. Films incl: Cromwell;

Nicholas and Alexandra; Follow Me; Bequest to the Nation; Tales That Witness Madness; Craze; The Internecine Project. TV incl: The Power Game; Mad Jack; Charles Dickens; Beethoven; Mr Rolls and Mr Royce; Jane Eyre; Merchant of Venice; Quiller; King Lear; She Fell Among Thieves; Last Romantic; Gossip From the Forest; Tinker, Tailor, Soldier, Spy. Education: Becket School, Nottingham. m. Ann. Address: c/o Leading Artists, London SW1. Starsign: Scorpio. Hobbies: cricket, reading, darts, sport on TV, going racing, etymology, rolling up trouser legs, listening to humorous anecdotes from Freddie Jones, Nigel Stock, Thora Hird and Stuart Pedlar.

JEFFREY, Peter
Actor b. 18.4.29 Bristol. No training for the stage but had 12 years of varied theatrical work, mainly with Bristol Old Vic and the Royal Shakespeare Company, before working in TV. Recent stage incl: Donkey's Years and (for the National Theatre) For Services Rendered. Films incl: Becket; The Fixer; If . . .; Ring of Bright Water; Anne of the Thousand Days; The Horsemen; The Odessa File; Midnight Express. TV incl: The Planemakers; Triangle; Villette; Elizabeth R; Boys and Girls Come Out to Play; Cakes and Ale; The Common; Destiny; London Belongs to Me; Porridge; Mr and Ms Bureaucrat; The Old

Crowd; The Atom Spies. Education: Harrow; Pembroke College, Cambridge. Address: c/o London Management, London W1. Starsign: Aries. Hobbies: golf, squash.

JENSEN, Kid
Disc jockey b. 4th July Victoria, Canada. Became a disc jockey at 16 and worked for radio stations in Canada before joining Radio Luxembourg in 1968. After six years moved to Radio Trent and in 1975 switched to the BBC where he has been ever since. Has his own show Mon-Fri on Radio 1 and presents Quiz Kid. TV also incl: Top of the Pops; Pop Quest; Pop 45; Nationwide; hosted British Rock and Pop Awards. Travels thousands of miles a year to present his live disco shows. Education: Canada. m. former Icelandic air hostess Gudrun, 1 d. Anna-Lisa. Address: c/o John Miles Organisation, Bristol. Starsign: Cancer. Hobbies: cooking, most sports, including football (he is a QPR supporter). Unfulfilled ambition: to have his own TV show.

JEWEL, Jimmy
Actor/comedian b. 4.12.12 Sheffield. First appeared on stage in Huddersfield when he was 10; in London when he was 16. Worked as a solo act until teamed up with cousin Ben Warriss 1934, partnership that continued until 1966. Radio series Up the Pole 1947 shot them to

fame; TV debut 1948 followed by The Jewel and Warriss Show; Sunday Night at the London Palladium; It's a Living. Stage incl: The Sunshine Boys; Comedians; Clown Jewels. TV since 1966: Nearest and Dearest; Thicker Than Water; Spring and Autumn; Funny Man; A Spanner in the Works. Education: Left school at 14 to work with father (comedian, same name). First went in to scenic studio with father, making scenery, props. Worked in father's sketches and revues as, stage manager, feed to father, juvenile lead, acrobat, dancer, etc. m. Belle, 1 adopted d., 1 s. Kerry. Address: London W8. Starsign: Sagittarius. Hobby: golf.

Crystal Palace National Sports Centre from 1962. After war service in the RAF he taught for a while before joining the Central Council of Physical Education in 1947. TV incl: Wimbledon (1956-69); Seeing Sport linkman (1956-65); Commonwealth Games athletics 1958; Olympic Games 1972; World and European Gymnastic Championships (1978-79); Winter Sports, World Cup and World Championship Skiing and Bobsleigh (1966 onwards); All-England Badminton Champ. Education: Bangor Normal College, N Wales (Teachers' Cert); Loughborough College of Physical Education (Dip Physical Education). m. Inez, 1 d. Madeleine. Address: Dulwich Common, London SE2. Starsign: Sagittarius. Hobbies: golf, skiing, reading, conversation. Unfulfilled ambition: to make a continuing and worthwhile contribution to the development of sport and physical recreation in this country for the benefit of the community as a whole.

Sade (and film); Mister. Films incl: Deadfall; The Bliss of Mrs Blossom; Far from the Madding Crowd; Otley; Goodbye Gemini; The Man Who Haunted Himself. TV incl: Sword of Honour; Treasure Island; Cold Comfort Farm; Uncle Vanya; The Caesars; Germinal; Nana; Secret Orchards; Sweeney Todd; The Ghosts of Motley Hall; In Loving Memory. Named world's best TV actor at Monte Carlo International TV Festival 1969 for his performance in The Caesars. Education: Grammar School, Longton. m. actress Jennifer Heslewood, 3 s. Toby, Rupert, Casper. Address: Charlbury, Oxfordshire. Starsign: Virgo. Hobbies: cooking, pottering around dreaming in the garden, watching seeds grow that he has planted, talking to locals in the pub. Unfulfilled ambition: to go mountaineering.

JONES, Gemma
Actress b. 4.12.42 London. Wanted to be a nurse, but after learning French in France went to RADA where, like her father Griffith Jones before her, she was a gold medallist. After 'resting', a period of rep and TV parts, stage roles incl: There'll Be Some Changes Made; Baal; The Marriage of Figaro; Alfie; Ashes; Getting On; Cabaret (Sheffield); The Homecoming. Films incl: Ken Russell's The Devils. TV incl: The Typewriter; The Spoils of

JONES, Emlyn
Commentator b. 9.12.20 Buckley, Clwyd. Specialising in gymnastics and winter sports, he has been Sports commentator since 1955 and is now one of the most powerful men in British sport as Director General of the Sports Council (since 1978). Before that he was Director,

JONES, Freddie
Actor b. 12.9.27 Stoke-on-Trent. Started as a laboratory assistant but a drama course at Tamworth and a scholarship to the Rose Bruford College of Speech and Drama set him on an acting career. Rep and Royal Shakespeare Company. London stage incl: Marat

Poyntum; The Lie; Forget-Me-Not Lane; The Duchess of Duke Street. 1 s. Luke. Address: c/o Larry Dalzell Associates Ltd, London WC2. Starsign: Sagittarius.

JONES, Ken
Actor b. 20.2.30 Liverpool. Sign writer and amateur actor before training at RADA and joining Joan Littlewood's Theatre Workshop in London in The Hostage. Considerable stage and TV work since. TV incl: Z Cars (first episode); Hunter's Walk; Go For Gold; Germinal; Her Majesty's Pleasure; Last of the Baskets; The Wackers; The Squirrels; First Class Friend; Films incl: SWALK; File of the Golden Goose; Sherlock Holmes. Education: secondary modern. m. actress/writer Sheila Fay. Address: c/o David White Associates, London W1. Starsign: Pisces. Unfulfilled ambition: to direct another film.

JONES, Lewis
Actor b. 21.3.24 Tredegar, Mon. Trained at RADA and toured in rep incl: Edinburgh, London, Leatherhead. Left acting for nearly a decade and became a salesman. Made comeback at National Theatre and a variety of TV work culminating in General Hospital. Also rep at Bromley and Coventry. Stage incl: Almost Free; Who Killed Agatha Christie? Education: Hereford Cathedral School. m. (1st) actress Mary Thornton (dec), (2nd) actress Paddy Frost, 2 d. Elizabeth, Catherine (from 1st m), 1 s. Robert (from 1st m). Address: c/o John Penrose, London W8. Starsign: Aries.

JONES, Maggie
Actress b. 21st June London. After training at RADA played with rep companies all over the country. London stage incl: Kean. TV incl: The Forsyte Saga; Nearest and Dearest; Sam; Coronation Street; Lovely Couple; Rosie. m. lawyer J O Stansfield. Address: c/o NEMS Management Ltd, London SW3. Starsign: Gemini. Hobbies: history, decorating.

JONES, Paul
Singer/actor b. 24.2.42

Portsmouth. Started a skiffle group while still at school and then a blues band while at Oxford. Had a number of jobs before joining Manfred Mann in 1963. Went solo 1966. Has since branched into acting and started another band, The Blues Band in 1979. Stage incl: Fun-War; Muzeeka; Conduct Unbecoming; Pippin; The Banana Box; Pilgrim; Hamlet; Othello; Mrs Warren's Profession; Drake's Dream; Measure for Measure; Joseph and the Amazing Technicolour Dream Coat. Films incl: Privilege; The Committee. TV incl: A Bit of Discretion; As You Like It; Square One; Z Cars; The Sweeney; Great Big Groovy Horse; The Songwriters; The Protectors; Traces of Love. Education: Portsmouth Grammar, then via an Edinburgh school to Jesus College, Oxford University. m. writer Sheila Macleod, 2 s. Matthew, Jacob. Address: c/o Chatto and Linnit Ltd, London WC2. Starsign: Pisces. Hobbies: collecting old 'blues' records and old theatre postcards.

JONES, Peter
Actor/author b. 12.6.20 Wem, Salop. Rep experience and many plays and revues in London's West End and films. Radio incl: In All Directions; Just a Minute; Hitch-hiker's Guide to the Galaxy. TV incl: Oneupmanship; Mr Big; Mr Digby Darling; The Rag Trade; M'lords, Ladies and

Gentlemen (chairman);
Cabbages and Kings;
Blankety Blank; Celebrity
Squares; Give Us a Clue.
Education: Wem Grammar
School; Ellesmere College.
m. American actress Jeri
Sauvinet, 1 d. Selena
Carey-Jones, 2 s. Charlie,
Willie. Address: London
NW8. Starsign: Gemini.
Hobbies: drawing, cooking,
reading, making plans.
Unfulfilled ambitions: to
speak perfect French, play
the piano, ski, appear in What
The Papers Say.

JONES, Steve
TV/radio presenter b. 7.6.45
Crewe, Cheshire. Musician,
teacher, ice-cream salesman
before becoming a radio DJ
in 1972. DJ on Radio Clyde
1973-78 and voted Scottish
radio personality of the year
1977. TV incl: Battle of the
Comics; The Jones Boy; It's
Friday; I'm Steve Jones;
Sneak Preview; Steve Jones
Illustrated; Watch This
Space; Edinburgh Festival
Show; Bruce's Big Night;
Saturday Morning Show;
Steve Jones Game Show.
Education: Crewe Grammar;
College of St Mark and St
John, Chelsea. m. Lolita, 3 s.
Marc, Jason, Oliver.
Address: c/o Tony Meehan
and Associates, Glasgow.
Starsign: Gemini. Hobbies:
golf, swimming, tennis,
current affairs.

JONES, Wendy
Presenter/producer b. 8.6.46
Rugby, Warwicks. Started
career as cub reporter at 16.
Weekly and evening paper
experience, Cheshire,
Derby, Birmingham, before
joining BBC as radio reporter
on World at One.
Documentary: A Life Worth
Living? ATV reporter 1970,
launched Ladies Night,
regional all female audience
show 1975; became its
presenter and producer
1975. Education: Rugby High
School. m. Warwickshire
County golfer Richard
Anthony Squires. Address:
Solihull, Warwicks. Starsign:
Gemini. Hobbies: addicted to
dresses – spending too
much on clothes; renovating
ancient country house;
buying antiques and looking
in junk shops; work.
Unfulfilled ambition: to
present fully networked
audience shows.

JOYCE, Yootha
Actress b. 20.8.27 London.
Trained at RADA then rep
and radio before joining Joan
Littlewood's Theatre
Workshop. Stage incl: Fings
Ain't Wot They Used t' Be;
Man in the Glass Booth;

Palladium pantomime,
Cinderella. Films incl: the
Pumpkin Eaters; A Man For
All Seasons; Fragments of
Fear. TV incl: Brothers in Law;
Me Mammy; The Victoria
Line; Man About the House;
Nobody Does It Like Marti;
George and Mildred.
m. actor Glyn Edwards (dis).
Address: c/o Joy Jameson
Ltd, London SW1. Starsign:
Leo. Hobbies: clothes, two
terriers, a cat and a
racehorse.

JUDD, Edward
Actor b. 4.10.32 Shanghai,
China. Started acting when
16 and supported himself
doing various jobs between
parts. First acted at Bolton's
Theatre, London, followed by
rep at Windsor and
Nottingham. Stage incl: The
Long and the Short and the
Tall; The Tinker. Films incl:
The Criminal; The Day the
Earth Caught Fire; The First
Men in the Moon; Strange
Bedfellows; The Longships.
TV appearances started with
Sixpenny Corner which led to
many other roles incl: The
Human Jungle; Invasion;
Island of Terror; The Trouble
Shooters; Intrigue; Z Cars;
General Hospital;
Flambards. Educated in the
Far East. m. (1st) actress
Gene Anderson (dec), (2nd)
actress Norma Ronald, 2 d.
Deborah (from 1st m),
Fenella. Address: c/o Crouch
Associates, London W1.
Starsign: Libra. Hobbies:
watching football, cricket and
tennis, painting, reading
modern American literature,
listening to music.

JUNKIN, John
Actor/writer b. 29.1.30
Ealing, Middx. Started as a
schoolmaster, but turned to
script-writing after various
jobs, including liftman and
labourer. Joined Joan
Littlewood's Theatre
Workshop in 1960. Stage
incl: Sparrers Can't Sing;
Maggie May; The Four
Musketeers. Films incl: Hard
Day's Night; Kaleidoscope;
The Brass Target. Radio incl:
five series of Hello Cheeky.
Has written, co-written and
appeared in hundreds of TV
shows incl: Sam and Janet;
Junkin (four series); Marty;
Looking For Clancy; Out; The
Ravelled Thread; Dick
Turpin; Penmarric. Has also
written many songs with
Denis King. Education:
council and grammar
schools. m. Jennie,
1 d. Annabel. Address: c/o
Richard Stone, London WC2.
Starsign: Aquarius. Hobbies:
crosswords, reading,
quizzes, Scrabble, plotting to
overthrow Willy Rushton.
Unfulfilled ambition: to
become a successful pop
group and live in Antigua.

K

KALIPHA, Stephan
Actor b. 1940 Trinidad.
Came to England 1959 after a
year on a Norwegian
merchant ship as an engine
room cleaner. Variety of jobs
(wine porter, restaurant cook
and club barman) before E15
Acting School for two years.
Plays at Canterbury, Oxford,
Royal Court, Mermaid and
Ambiance Theatres. West
End: Play Maas. TV incl:
Callan; World in a Room;
Black Christmas; The
Professionals; Mixed
Blessings. Address: c/o LWT,
London SE1.

KAREN, Anna
Actress b. 19.9.36 South Africa. Trained at the South African National Theatre before coming to England when she was 17 to join LAMDA. Lived in Italy for four years where her then husband was training to be an opera singer. Returned to England when marriage broke up. Rode elephants in Christmas circus, toured with Lilac Time, rep and small TV parts before the part of Olive in On the Buses. Also in the three Buses films. Other TV: The Rag Trade. m. (1st) (dis), (2nd) Terry Duggan, 1 d. Gloria. Address: c/o LWT, London SE1. Starsign: Virgo. Hobbies: listening to music, fortune tellers, tennis, football.

KARLIN, Miriam OBE
Actress b. 23.6.25 London. Trained at RADA and first appeared on professional stage for ENSA. Many stage (Diary of Anne Frank; The Bad Seed; The Egg; Fiddler on the Roof; Bus Stop) and cabaret appearances, as well as films (Mahler; A Clockwork Orange), radio and TV incl: The Rag Trade.

Education: South Hampstead High for Girls. Address: c/o ICM, London W1. Starsign: Cancer. Hobbies: interior decorating and collecting paintings – when not involved in numerous campaigns (eg fighting the National Front, working for Soviety Jewry, Equity). Unfulfilled ambitions: to give my Mother Courage to a large audience (in town, on TV or both); to do my one-woman piece Lisolette on TV; to be asked to join either or both the RSC and National Theatre.

KAY, Bernard
Actor b. 23.2.38 Bolton, Lancs. Trained at Old Vic School, nine years' rep and Shakespeare Memorial Theatre. Films inc: Spy Story; Dr Zhivago; Darling Lili; Sweeney; Hunting Party; Voyage of the Damned. TV incl: Venturers; Clayhanger; Main Chance; Sweeney; Softly, Softly; Prince and the Pauper; Space 1999; Emmerdale Farm; Warship; Colditz; Rosie; Sutherland's Law; Target. Education: various schools during wartime. Address: c/o CCA Ltd, London SW6. Starsign: Pisces. Hobbies: music, reading, horses. Unfulfilled ambition: fame and riches.

KAY, Sylvia
Actress b. 1936 Altrincham, Cheshire. Studied psychology at Manchester University before becoming an actress. Some years in rep before first West End chance

– understudying Vivien Leigh in Duel of Angels. Since then, films and many TV plays and series incl: Rooms; After the Funeral; Time Factor; Mr Representative; False Witness; Seven Faces of Woman; Mixed Blessings. m. director Ted Kotcheff. 1 d., 2 s. Address: c/o LWT, London SE1.

KAYE, Tally Ho (Peter)
Sportsman/wrestler b. 24.8.40 Burnley. Was show-jumping from an early age and wrestling at the age of 10. Show-jumping wins at all major shows in Great Britain, incl: Dublin's International Horse Show. Education: university. m. international show-jumper Gillian, 1 d. Deborah, 1 s. Tony. Address: Burnley, Lancs. Starsign: Virgo. Hobbies: training and brass rubbings. Unfulfilled ambition: to have lunch with the Queen.

KEE, Robert
Journalist/presenter b. 5.10.19 Calcutta, India. Started as journalist on Picture Post, 1948-51; was Observer correspondent on Suez Crisis; contributor to

Sunday Times. Bomber pilot during the war; three years prisoner of war. Entered TV as a reporter for Panorama 1958-62; Television Reporters International 1963-64, and made Rebellion; This Year in Jerusalem, etc; This Week 1964-70; Looking For an Answer 1967; Robert Kee Reports 1968; Kee Interview 1971. First presenter of ITN's one o'clock news, First Report 1972-76; General Election and Referendum programmes 1974; General Strike Report; documentaries – France; E Germany; Jubilee; Spain 1976-77; Faces of Communism 1977-78. BBC general features 1979. Books incl; A Crowd is Not Company; The Impossible Shore; A Sign of the Times; Broadstrop in Season; Refugee World; The Green Flag; A History of Irish Nationalism. Education: Stowe and Magdalen College, Oxford (History Exhibition). m. (1st) Janetta (dis), (2nd) Cynthia, 2 d. Georgiana, Sarah, 2 s. Alexander, Benjamin (dec). Address: Kew Green, Surrey. Starsign: Libra. Hobbies: Irish history, swimming, cycling, listening to music, writing.

KEEGAN, Kevin
Footballer/TV personality b. 14.2.51 Armthorpe, Yorks. Started football career with Scunthorpe United in 1967 at the age of 16 and transferred to Liverpool FC 1971. Played for Liverpool for six years

before joining SV Hamburg. European Footballer of the Year 1978 and captain of England 41 times. Member of the ITV panel for 1978 World Cup; has since joined BBC. Other TV incl: Focus on Football (coaching series on ITV); Brian Moore Meets Kevin Keegan. Autobiography: Kevin Keegan. m. Jean, 1 d. Laura Jean. Address: Hamburg, W Germany. Starsign: Aquarius.

KEEN, Diane
Actress b. 29.7.46 London. Brought up in Kenya, didn't settle in England until she was 19. Unknown until chosen for The Cuckoo Waltz. Other TV incl: Crossroads; The Fall of the Eagles; Softly, Softly; Public Eye; The Legend of Robin Hood; The Sweeney; The Feathered Serpent; Country Matters; Crown Court; The Sandbaggers. Education: several schools in Kenya and privately tutored. m. (dis), 1 d. Melissa. Address: c/o Barry Burnett, London W1. Starsign: Leo. Hobbies: Egyptology, antiques. Unfulfilled ambitions: to drive a Formula 1 racing car competing in a big race; to go down the Amazon; to own a large farm.

KEEN, Geoffrey
Actor b. 21.8.18 London. Joined Bristol Old Vic Theatre School when 15. Left to work in a paint factory, then won a scholarship to RADA and has scarcely stopped working since. In the army during the war, then Stars in Battledress. Numerous plays (Alice's Boys), films (more than 100 incl: The Angry Silence; Cromwell; Dr Zhivago; Born Free; Living Free; Moonraker) and TV. Best known for the Troubleshooters. Other TV incl: The Venturers; Justice; Mr Rolls and Mr Royce; The Atom Spies; Purple Twilight; Churchill and the Generals; Crown Court. m. (1st) actress Hazel Terry, (2nd) actress Doris Groves, 1 d. Mary (from 2nd m). Address: c/o London Management, London W1. Starsign: Leo. Hobby: gardening.

KEITH, Penelope
b. 2nd April Sutton, Surrey. Trained at Webber Douglas

Academy of Dramatic Art, then rep at Chesterfield, Lincoln and Manchester. After a time with the Royal Shakespeare Company ('carrying a spear', she says), she returned to rep in Cheltenham. Stage incl: Plaza Suite; How the Other Half Loves; Fallen Angels; The Norman Conquests; Donkey's Years (and TV); The Apple Cart; The Millionairess. Most recent film: The Hound of the Baskervilles. Early TV was in Six Shades of Black. Other TV incl: Kate; The Pallisers; Two's Company; Jackanory; Saving It For Albie; Private Lives; The Good Life; Morecambe and Wise Christmas Show 1977; To the Manor Born; The Norman Conquests. Awards incl: Variety Club Show Business Personality of the Year, Society of West End Managers Award for Best Comedy Performance (Donkey's Years), BAFTA Award for Best Light Entertainment Performance (The Good Life), all in 1977; BAFTA Award for Best TV Actress (Saving It For Albie and The Norman Conquests) and Radio Industries Club Celebrity Award as BBC TV Personality of the Year, both 1978. Education: private school. m. Rodney Timson. Address: c/o Howes and Prior Ltd, London W1. Starsign: Aries.

KEITH, Sheila
Actress b. 9th June, Aberdeen. Trained for the stage at Webber Douglas Academy of Dramatic Art Stage work has included Present Laughter; Mame (with Ginger Rogers); appearances at Liverpool Rep, Coventry, Bristol Old Vic and Leatherhead. Films incl: Ooh You Are Awful; House of Whipcord; Frightmare; The Comeback. TV incl: David Copperfield; Moody and Peg; Ballet Shoes; Within These Walls; Angels; The Cedar Tree; Jubilee; Roof Over My Head; Working Arrangements; Heartland; Racing Game; Rings on Their Fingers; Swing, Swing Together; Agony; Bless Me Father. Education: Aberdeen High School. Address: c/o Peter Campbell, NEMS Management Ltd, London SW3. Starsign: Gemini. Hobbies: fresh air, browsing in book shops, nature study. Unfulfilled ambition: to keep working.

KELLY, Chris
Producer/writer/presenter b. 24.4.40 Cuddington, Cheshire. Taught French and Spanish for nearly two years before joining Anglia TV as announcer and newsreader in 1963. Other TV incl: quiz-master of Sixth Form Challenge; Zoo Time; Junior Criss Cross Quiz; Anything You Can Do; Clapperboard; Wish You Were Here; Friday Live; World in Action; The Royal Film Performance. Education: Downside School and Clare College, Cambridge, where he was drama critic of Varsity, the university newspaper.

m. Vivien, 1 d. Rebecca, 1 s. Nicholas. Address: c/o Granada TV, London W1. Starsign: Taurus. Hobbies: films, books, plays, Abbot ale, darts. Unfulfilled ambition: to get an early night.

KELLY, David
Actor b. 1930 Dublin. Based in Ireland. Wide experience on stage but better known on TV incl: Public Eye; Never Mind the Quality, Feel the Width; many Armchair Theatre plays and the one-armed washer-up in Robin's Nest. m. actress Laurie, 1 d. Miriam, 1 s. David. Address: c/o International Artistes, London W1.

KEMP, David
Producer/political correspondent b. 19.5.37 Manchester. Reporter/feature writer/leader writer on newspapers incl: The Scotsman, Glasgow Herald, Minneapolis Star (USA) and Winnepeg Tribune (Canada), before joining Granada TV. Credits incl: Reports Politics; World in Action; The State of

the Nation; Opinion; Party conference outside broadcasts and election specials; The Nuts and Bolts of the Economy; City at Risk. Education: Edinburgh Academy; Edinburgh University. Address: London, SW6. Starsign: Taurus. Hobbies: Shakespeare, Wagner, travelling by train. Unfulfilled ambition: to pass my driving test.

KEMPSON, Rachel
Actress b. 28.5.10 Dartmouth, Devon. Trained for the stage at RADA and made her first stage appearance at Stratford-upon-Avon 1933. Appeared in rep at Oxford, Liverpool and with the Royal Shakespeare Company, the English Stage Company and the National Theatre Company at the Old Vic. Many distinguished roles, her most recent incl: A Family and a Fortune; The Old Country. Films incl: The Captive Heart; Georgy Girl; The Jokers; Tom Jones; Charge of the Light Brigade; The Virgin Soldiers; Jane Eyre. TV incl: Jane; Jennie; Elizabeth R; Love For Lydia; Winter Ladies; Sweet Wine of Youth; Kate the Good Neighbour. Education: St Agnes School, East Grinstead; Oaklea, Buckhurst Hill. m. actor Sir Michael Redgrave CBE, 2 d. actresses Vanessa and Lynn, 1 s. actor Corin. Address: c/o Hutton Management, London SW5. Starsign: Gemini. Hobby:

gardening. Unfulfilled ambition: to be a writer.

KENDAL, Felicity
Actress b. 25.9.46 Birmingham. Taken to India when three months old by her parents who were travelling actors. Grew up learning her art as a strolling player, eventually playing leading roles. Returned to Birmingham to live with an aunt. Her break came with a TV play with John Gielgud, The Mayfly and the Frog. Stage work incl: Regent's Park Open Air Theatre; Kean; The Norman Conquests. TV incl: Crime of Passion; The Woodlanders; The Dolly Dialogues; Love Story; Edward the Seventh; The Good Life. Films incl: Shakespeare Wallah (about her parents' life in India); Valentino. Education: various convents while on tour. m. actor Drew Henley, 1 s. Charley. Address: Putney, London. Starsign: Libra.

KENDALL, Kenneth
BBC TV newsreader b. 7.8.24 South India but brought up in Cornwall.

Former schoolmaster and wartime captain in the Coldstream Guards. Joined BBC in 1948, was a newsreader 1955-61 when he left to freelance, but returned to BBC in 1969. Voted best dressed newsreader by Style International and No 1 newscaster by Daily Mirror readers 1979. Other TV incl: Songs of Praise; Dr Who; Adam Adamant. Education: Felsted School, Essex; Oxford University (MA). Address: c/o Lewis Joelle, London SW1. Starsign: Leo. Hobbies: racing, theatre, gardening, dogs.

KENNEDY, Ludovic
Writer/broadcaster b. 3.11.19 Edinburgh. War service in Royal Navy (midshipman to lieutenant RNVR) 1939-46. Started writing as freelance journalist. Widely experienced TV broadcaster. Introduced Profile 1955-56; ITN newscaster 1956-58; introduced This Week 1958-60; commentator Panorama 1960-63; producer/reporter Television Reporters International 1963-64. Other TV incl: Time Out; World at One; The Middle Years; The Nature of Prejudice; Face the Press; 24 Hours; Ad Lib; Midweek; Newsday; Tonight. Films incl: The Singers and the Songs; Scapa Flow; The Sleeping Ballerina; Battleship Bismarck; Life and Death of the Scharnhorst; U-Boat War; The Rise of the Red Navy;

Lord Haw-Haw. Books incl: Sub-Lieutenant; Nelson's Band of Brothers; One Man's Meat; Murder Story; Ten Rillington Place; The Trial of Stephen Ward; Pursuit: The Chase and Sinking of the Bismarck; A Presumption of Innocence: The Amazing Case of Patrick Meehan; The Portland Spy Case; The British at War (general editor); Menace: The Life and Death of the Tirpitz. Education: Eton and Christ Church, Oxford (MA). m. former ballerina Moira Shearer, 3 d. Ailsa, Rachel, Fiona, 1 s. Alastair. Address: c/o AD Peters, London WC2. Starsign: Scorpio. Hobbies: shooting, golf.

KENNEDY, Sarah
Announcer b. 8.7.50 East Grinstead, Surrey. Worked in radio in Singapore and Germany before joining BBC Radio in London. Joined Southern TV 1978. Education: Notre Dame Convent, Lingfield. Address: c/o Southern TV, Southampton. Starsign: Cancer. Hobbies: squash, walking, theatre, cooking. Unfulfilled ambition: to read the nine o'clock news on BBC TV.

KENNEDY, Sheila
Announcer b. 1936 London. Originally a dancer, dancing in several shows and pantomimes before her first success as a dancer in the Drury Lane production of The King and I. Stayed with the show for 18 months, then

went to Northampton as Principal Girl in pantomime. In rep for two years. Two year stint in Salad Days then auditioned as singer for Westward TV, but instead became their regular announcer. Later moved to Manchester, then Birmingham, before going to London to join Thames TV. m. Tom Singleton. Address: c/o Thames TV, London NW1.

KENSIT, Patsy
Actress b. 4.3.68 London. No drama school training. Has appeared in TV commercials, films and TV programmes. Films incl: The Great Gatsby; Alfie Darling; The Bluebird; Hanover Street. TV incl: Churchill's People; Quiet as a Nun; Dickens of London; The Foundation; Prince Regent; King Arthur; Penmarric. Education: St Catherine's Convent.
Address: c/o William Morris Agency, London W1. Starsign: Pisces. Hobbies: riding, singing and dancing.

KERNAN, David
Actor/singer b. 23.6.38 London. Made his first stage appearance with Sadler's Wells Opera when he was 11. Decided to go into show business when he was 19 and joined Huddersfield Rep. Learnt his craft 'in the chorus and repertory'. Has since made many stage appearances outside London and in the West End, incl: Where's Charley?; On the Brighter Side; For Amusement Only (world tour); Our Man Crichton; A Little Night Music; Side By Side With Sondheim. Films incl: Zulu; Otley; Mix Me a Person; Carry On Abroad; The Day of the Jackal. Has made hundreds of TV appearances incl: That Was the Week That Was; Not So Much a Programme; Churchill's People; Upstairs, Downstairs; Omnibus; Song By Song. Education: Bournemouth Technical College. Address: c/o Barry Burnett, London W1. Starsign: Cancer. Hobbies: tennis, swimming, trying to be a writer. Unfulfilled ambitions: to be a good writer, a better performer and to be rich.

KEY, Janet
Actress b. 10.7.45 Bath, Somerset. Trained at Bristol Old Vic School, then rep at Bristol Old Vic, Royal Shakespeare Co and National Theatre. TV incl: Cousin Bette; Tenant of Wildfell Hall; State of Emergency; Trial; Donati

Conspiracy; Man at the Top; The Crezz; The Marriage Vow; The Catherine Wheel; Telford's Change; Kiss and Tell; The Square Leopard. Education: St Nicholas, Bath; Bath High. m. actor/writer Gawn Grainger. 1 s. Charles. Address: c/o Peter Browne Management, London SW9. Starsign: Cancer. Hobbies: yoga, reading, Arsenal F C. Unfulfilled ambitions: 'to keep my bank account in the black for a whole year; to finish converting our house. (Could the two be connected?)'.

KING, Dave
Actor/comedian/singer b. 23.6.29 Twickenham, Middx. Left school at 12 and after several jobs joined Morton Fraser Harmonica Gang when he was 15. National Service in the RAF and was in unit's rep company. Returned to variety on leaving RAF and later went solo. An appearance in Television Music Hall led to compering Show Case, and since 1955, his own show, recordings (Memories Are Made of This), stage shows, pantomime and visits to America for TV appearances.

Now going 'straight' with appearances in The Sweeney; Coronation Street; Pennies From Heaven; Hazell. m. dancer Jean Hart, 2 d. Cheyenne, Kiowa. Address: South Cerney, Glos. Starsign: Cancer. Hobbies: model railways, American folklore.

KING, Nigel
Sports commentator/music presenter b. 24.11.38 Welwyn Garden City, Herts. Ballroom and pop concert DJ and not only a sports commentator but also a competitor. Radio incl: Night Ride; After Seven. TV incl: World of Sport (rallycross and hot rod/stock car racing commentating); Star Soccer; Southern Soccer; also various radio and TV commercials and motor sport commentator at various circuits. Education: Alleyne's Grammar School, Stevenage, Herts. m. Evelyn, 1 d. Lindsay, 1 s. Gary (twins). Address: c/o Bagenal Harvey Organisation Ltd, London W1. Starsign: Sagittarius. Hobbies: football referee, motoring, gardening, photography. Unfulfilled ambition: to try anything– at least once!

KINNEAR, Roy
Actor b. 8.1.34 Wigan. Trained for the theatre at RADA. After rep at Nottingham, Glasgow, Edinburgh and Perth joined Joan Littlewood's theatre group in London.

Subsequently in Palladium pantomime and with Royal Shakespeare Company. First came to the fore through That Was The Week That Was. Followed by A World of His Own; A Slight Case Of . . .; Inside George Webley; and appearances in many plays and series. Many films incl: Juggernaut; The Last Remake of Beau Geste. Education: Heriots, Edinburgh; National Service, which he claims is the University of Life. m. actress Carmel Cryan, 2 d. Kirsty, Karina, 1 s. Rory. Address: Roehampton. Starsign: Capricorn. Hobby: answering questionnaires sent by Who's Who On Television.

KIRKBRIDE, Anne
Actress b. 21.6.54 Oldham, Lancs. Trained at Oldham Rep. TV: Another Sunday; Sweet F A; Deirdre in Coronation Street since 1972. Education: Counthill Grammar School, Oldham. Address: Scouthead, Oldham. Starsign: Cancer. Hobby: embroidery. Unfulfilled ambition: to play a good comedy part.

139

KOSSOFF, David
Actor/writer/ furniture
designer b. 24.11.19
London. Trained as a
furniture draughtsman and
studied art and architecture.
Joined Unity Theatre in 1942
and stayed there until he
joined the BBC Rep
Company in 1945. Stage incl:
Yellow Star; The Love of Four
Colonels; Make Me an Offer;
It Shouldn't Happen to a Dog;
Enter Sally Gold; A Funny
Kind of Evening; According
to Kossoff. Films incl: The
Young Lovers; Svengali; A
Kid for Two Farthings; The
Iron Petticoat; Woman For
Joe; House of Secrets. TV
incl: The Bespoke Overcoat;
The Outsider; The Larkins;
Kossoff and Company; A
Little Big Business.
Education: elementary
school and Northern
Polytechnic. m. Margaret
(Jennie), 2 s. Simon, Paul
(dec). Address: Hatfield,
Herts. Starsign: Sagittarius.
Hobbies: conversation,
watching other actors work,
tending his 1930 Baby
Austin.

after the war though he had
started acting while in Polish
prisoner of war camp
1940-45. More than 100 films
and about 1000
performances on TV, some
notable ones (his choice)
being in Pickwick Papers;
Antigone; Shadow Squad;
Crane; Curry and Chips;
Mess Mates; Orlando; Sally
Ann; The Shillingbury
Blowers. Education:
Dunstable Grammar School.
m. former table tennis
international Pinkie Barnes,
1 s. actor Jonathan Kydd.
Address: Kensington,
London. Starsign: Aquarius.
Hobbies: cricket, soccer,
racing, watching TV, reading,
writing. Unfulfilled ambition:
to make enough money to
publish my own Who's Who
on TV.

KYDD, Sam
Actor b. 15.2.15 Belfast.
Came into show business

L

LACK, Simon
Actor b. 19.12.17 Cleland,
Scotland. Started with
Brandon-Thomas Rep Co in
Glasgow and Edinburgh
1935-37 before moving to
London. Wide experience in
radio and theatre. Served
with Lancs Fusiliers and The
Buffs during the war. TV incl:
Ah, Wilderness; Troilus and
Cressida; R3; The Fortunes of
Nigel; The Little Minister; The
Apple Cart; The Linden Tree;
Within These Walls; 1990;
The Borderers; Dr Who;
Special Branch; Ross; South
Riding; Paul Temple;
Doomwatch; Weir of
Hermiston; Enemy at the
Door; Telford's Change; The
Case of Cruelty to Prawns;
The Killers. Education:
Eastbank Academy,
Scotland. Address: c/o
Essanay Ltd, London W6.
Starsign: Sagittarius.
Hobbies: skiing, reading.

LACEY, Ronald
Actor/drama teacher
b. 28.9.35 Harrow, Middx.
After National Service went to
drama school. Acting debut
in TV play The Secret Agent.
Then rep. Stage incl: St Joan.
Films incl: How I Won the
War; The Likely Lads;
Charleston. Other TV incl:
Harsh World; Search Party;
Pigs Ear with Flowers; My
Flesh, My Blood; Blackmail;
Hands with a Magic Touch;
The Adventures of Don
Quixote; Dylan; Colditz;
Churchill's People; Porridge;
Mayor of Casterbridge;
Tropic. Education: Harrow
Weald Grammar School.
m. Mela, 1 d. Rebecca (by
1st m), 2 s. David (by 1st m),
Matthew (by 2nd m).
Address: c/o Joyce Edwards
Representation, London SE1.
Starsign: Libra. Hobby:
collecting Victoriana.

LADD, Cheryl
Actress b. 12.7.51 Huron,
South Dakota, USA. Always
wanted to be an actress;
singing and dancing lessons
from the age of eight; sang
with a jazz group when 16;
moved to Hollywood late
1970. After modelling and
more than 100 TV
commercials got a small part
in film, Jamaica Reef, in
which she met her future
husband, son of film actor
Alan Ladd. Succeeded Farah
Fawcett-Majors in Charlie's
Angels 1977. Other TV incl:
The Rookies; Ironside; The
Partridge Family; Happy
Days; Police Woman;
Fantastic Story; The
Muppets. Films incl:
Marriage of a Young
Stockbroker. Record: Cheryl
Ladd, Think It Over. m. David
Ladd, 1 d. Jordan. Address:
Beverly Hills, Calif. Starsign:
Cancer. Hobbies: tennis,
gymnastics, scuba diving.

LAINE, Cleo OBE
Singer/actress b. 28.10.27
Southall, Middx. Started as
hairdresser's apprentice,
then librarian, salesgirl, and
pawnbroker's valuer, before
being introduced to John
Dankworth after singing at
Southall British Legion Hall in
1951. Signed up to sing with
the Dankworth band. Has
appeared solo in cabaret,
jazz and other festivals in
Britain and abroad and sung
with London Philharmonic,
Royal Philharmonic, Halle,
Scottish National Orchestras.
Stage incl: Flesh to a Tiger;
Under the Sun; The Trojan
Women; A Midsummer
Night's Dream; her own one
woman show, Talk of the
Town; Showboat. Many TV
appearances incl: Cleo and
John. Education: state
schools. m. (1st) George
(dis), (2nd) John Dankworth,

1 d. Jacqueline (from 1st m), 2 s. Stuart (from 1st m), Alec (from 2nd m). Address: Wavendon, Milton Keynes. Starsign: Scorpio. Hobby: cooking.

LAMBERT, Angela
Journalist b. 14.4.40 London. Started in journalism but after three years joined the Treasury and worked as PPS to Lord Longford, as Colonial Secretary and then Lord Privy Seal and Leader of the House of Lords, 1965-68. Resumed journalism; joined The Sun 1969; became reporter with ITN 1972-76; reporter on The London Programme 1976-77 when became reporter on Inside Business. Education: St Hilda 's College, Oxford (philosophy, politics, economics). m. (dis), 2 d. Marianne, Binkie, 1 s. Johnny. Address: c/o Thames TV, London NW1. Starsign: Aries. Hobbies: politics, books, cats, Oriental rugs. Unfulfilled ambition: 'to be sent on a long assignment to the Middle or Far East to make my own documentary'.

LANDEN, Dinsdale
Actor b. 4.9.32 Margate, Kent. Spent a time at the Florence Moore Drama School before National Service in the RAF and while in the RAF formed a drama group. Joined Worthing Rep when he returned to civilian life. Stage incl: The Housemaster; Play on Love; The Philanthropist; Alphabetical Order; Plunder; The Merchant of Venice; Bodies. Films incl: The Valiant; We Joined the Navy; Mosquito Squadron; Every Home Should Have One. Radio incl: The Family Film; The Joke About Hilary Spite. TV incl: Great Expectations; Canterbury Tales; The Mask of Janus; The Spies; Mickey Dunne; London Assurance; Devenish; Fathers and Families; Glittering Prizes; Pig in the Middle. Education: King's School, Rochester. m. actress Jennifer Daniel. Address: Putney, London. Starsign: Virgo. Hobbies: golf, walking.

LANDON, Michael
Actor b. 31.10.36 Forest Hills, New York. Trained at Warner Bros acting school after career as athlete cut short by an arm injury. First big part in I Was a Teenage Werewolf; other roles in films and TV series. Part in Western series, Restless Gun, got him the part of Little Joe in Bonanza. Now stars in his own show, Little House on the Prairie. Education: University of Southern California. m. (1st) Dodie, (2nd) actress Lynn Noe, 3 d. Shawna Leigh, Cheryl and Leslie Ann (step-ds.)

(from 2nd m), 3 s. Mark, Josh (from 1st m), Michael (from 2nd m). Address: Beverly Hills, Calif. Starsign: Scorpio. Hobbies: golf, swimming.

LANDRY, John
Actor b. 14th February, Nairobi, Kenya. Came into show business 1960, since when he has trained at RADA and has played a variety of supporting roles. TV success came with his part in Turtle's Progress, a spin-off from The Hanged Man, a series in which he played the same part. Other TV incl: Dick Emery shows; Dickens of London. Stage incl: Shut Your Eyes and Think of England. Education: Alleyn's School, Dulwich, London. Address: c/o French's, London W1. Starsign: Aquarius. Hobbies: reading, cars.

LANGFORD, Bonnie
Child actress b. July 1964 London. First stage appearance at four months; first public appearance at 15 months when she danced in specially made ballet shoes. Since been in Gone With the Wind 1972; Gypsy in London, South Africa and America,

was in Australian Ballet's Don Quixote with Nureyev. One of the stars of Bugsy Malone film. TV incl: Opportunity Knocks; Just William. Education: Italia Conti Stage School. Address: c/o LWT, London SE1.

LANGLEY, Bob
Writer/broadcaster
b. 28.8.39 Newcastle upon Tyne. Scriptwriter and programme presenter at Tyne Tees TV for five years before joining BBC as newsreader. Worked as reporter, presenter and interviewer on sundry programmes incl: 24 Hours; Panorama; Nationwide; Pebble Mill; Saturday Night at the Mill. Also wrote and appeared in BBC film series, The Pennine Way; The Border Line; Lakeland Summer. Education: 'very little', he claims. m. Patricia. Address: c/o BBC, Pebble Mill, Birmingham. Starsign: Virgo. Hobbies: writing; mountaineering; Americana; playing the guitar (badly); swimming; squash; history and the cinema. Unfulfilled ambition: to be a tax exile.

LANGTON, Diane
Actress b. 31st May Somerset, but brought up in Fulham, London. Wanted to be a ballet dancer but studied at the Corona Stage School after a summer season at Yarmouth made her realise she was not dedicated enough for ballet. After touring, musicals, summer shows and

pantomimes, her big break came when she joined the cast of Hair. Straight acting career started with Joan Littlewood's company in London where her stage credits incl: the musicals Pippin; Jesus Christ Superstar; A Little Night Music; A Chorus Line; Songbook. TV incl: The Rag Trade; Let There Be Langton or a Whole Lot of Loving. Education: Holy Cross, Fulham. m. (1st) (dis), (2nd) actor Derek James, 1 s. Jaymie (from 1st m). Address: c/o Leading Artists Ltd, London SW1. Starsign: Gemini. Hobbies: ballet, sewing, reading philosophy. Unfulfilled ambitions: to have a good recording career; to give concerts and perhaps to do a musical in America.

LANNING, David
Writer/sports commentator
b. 24.3.38 Parkstone, Dorset. Journalism: Evening Echo Bournemouth, Poole & Dorset Herald, Romford Recorder, Daily Sketch, TVTimes. Sports commentary: with ITV since 1970, specialising in speedway racing, darts. Every major networked transmission on speedway and darts since 1970 on ITV. Six series of The Indoor League (Yorkshire TV). Two series of Golden Darts (Thames TV) as compere/commentator. Two series Match of the Week (Anglia). Soccer commentaries for Southern Television. Two series Butlins Grand Masters (ATV). Now on exclusivity contract with London Weekend Television. Sports specialist on TVTimes. Speedway and darts columnist on The Sun. Books on speedway and darts. Education: Poole Grammar School (1949-54). m. Leona Jacqueline Linford, 1 d. Alyson, 2 s. Russell, Phillip. Address: Hornchurch, Essex. Starsign: Aries. Hobbies: West Ham Utd, archive digging for sporting statistics, maintaining swimming pool, drinking, travel. Unfulfilled ambitions: to become established as soccer commentator and the world's foremost authority on the upkeep of swimming pools.

LARGE, Eddie
Impressionist/comedian
b. 25.6.42 Glasgow. Moved to Manchester as a child. First ambition was to be a footballer and was associate schoolboy with Manchester City FC before accident ended that career. Met Syd Little in a Manchester pub and teamed up as singing duo. Turned to comedy in northern clubs before winning appearance on

Opportunity Knocks 1971. TV since incl: Crackerjack; Who Do You Do?; Now Who Do You Do?; David Nixon Show; Seaside Special; Wheeltappers and Shunters Social Club; Wednesday at Eight; Little and Large Tellyshow; Little and Large Show; Disneytime. Stage incl: seasons at London Palladium, pantomimes and summer seasons and cabaret. Education: grammar school. m. Sandra, 2 d. Alison, Samantha. Address: c/o Norman Murray, London Management, London W1. Starsign: Cancer. Hobbies: golf, keep-fit, supporting Manchester City FC. Unfulfilled ambition: to score three goals at Wembley helping Manchester City win the Cup.

LA RUE, Danny
Entertainer/comedian b. 23.7.27 Cork, Ireland. Started career in naval concert parties, then rep, cabaret, pantomime, spectacular stage shows. One of Britain's highest paid performers whose commitments limit his TV appearances to four a year, incl: Charley's Aunt; The Ladies I Love; Tonight with Danny La Rue; Come Spy With Me; many appearances in The Good Old Days; New Faces panellist. Address: c/o Sonny Zahl Associates, London W1. Starsign: Leo. Hobby: work.

LAVENDER, Ian
Actor b. 16.2.46 Birmingham. Trained at Bristol Old Vic School, followed by rep at Canterbury. While there he joined Dad's Army team and continued throughout series. Other TV incl: Mr Big; Come Back, Mrs Noah; The Glums. m. actress Suzanne Kerchiss (dis), 2 s. Daniel, Sam. Address: c/o Richard Stone, London WC2. Starsign: Aquarius.

LAWLEY, Sue
Broadcaster/journalist b. 14.7.46 Dudley, Worcs. Journalistic training with Thomson Regional Newspapers before joining BBC in Plymouth. Associated with Nationwide 1972-75 and since 1977 and Tonight 1975-76. Also involved with General Election and Budget programmes and presenter of British Academy of Film and Television Arts programme. Education: Dudley Girls High and Bristol University. m. David Ashby, 1 s. Tom. Address: c/o BBC, London W12. Starsign: Cancer. Hobbies: family, cooking, bridge, golf.

Unfulfilled ambition: to have a record in the charts.

LAWSON, Sarah
Actress b. 6.8.28 London. Decided to become an actress when she was 12. Webber Douglas Drama School, then rep at Perth, Ipswich, Felixstowe. Films, radio and TV. First TV role in live play The Odd Man for BBC and first ITV science-fiction serial, The Trollenburg Terror. Latest: Within These Walls. Many guest appearances. m. actor Patrick Allen, 2 s. Stephen, Stuart. Address: c/o London Management, London W1. Starsign: Leo. Hobby: tapestry.

LAYTON, George
Actor/writer b. 2.3.43 Bradford, Yorks. Trained at RADA (where he won the Emile Littler Award). Leading parts at Coventry and Nottingham; appeared on Broadway in Chips With Everything and starred in an Australian production of Funny Peculiar. His films incl: Stand Up Virgin Soldiers for which he was nominated most promising newcomer in the 1977 Evening News Film

Awards. Has starred in many TV series incl: the Doctor series; It Ain't Half Hot, Mum; My Brother's Keeper; The Sweeney; Murder; Robin's Nest. Has co-written (with Jonathan Lynn) more than 60 TV shows incl: the Doctor series; My Brother's Keeper; My Name is Harry Worth and half of the recent series of Robin's Nest. Books incl: The Balaclava Story; The Fib. Education: Belle Vue Grammar, Bradford. m. publicity executive, 1 d. Claudie, 1 s. Tristan. Address: c/o Barry Burnett Organisation, London W1. Starsign: Pisces. Hobbies: soccer, tennis, (no real hobbies). Unfulfilled ambition: 'to carry on doing work I enjoy and do more directing'. (He made his debut as a director in 1978).

LEACH, Rosemary
Actress b. 18.12.25 Much Wenlock, Shropshire. Trained at RADA and wide rep experience incl: Amersham, Coventry, Birmingham, Liverpool, Bristol Old Vic. First appeared on TV in 1960. Has since been in many Armchair Theatre plays; two series of The Power Game; three series with Ronnie Corbett (No That's Me Over Here); Sadie It's Cold Outside; Life Begins at Forty; Rumpole of the Bailey; Germinal; Roads to Freedom; On the Move (educational series); Jackanory; The Office Line; plays incl: Cider With Rosie; Birthday; Don Quixote;

Disraeli; Hindle Wakes; Just Between Ourselves; Tiptoe Through the Tulips; Hands; Tolstoy; also presenter of The English in Love. Films incl: That'll Be the Day; S O S Titanic. Education: grammar school. m. (dis). Address: c/o David White Associates, London W1. Starsign: Sagittarius. Hobbies: gardening, cooking.

LE BEAU, Bettine
Actress b. 23.3.36 Antwerp. Show business training in Belgium and Paris. Radio incl: The Likely Lads; Any Questions. Films incl: San Ferry Ann; Devil's Daffodil; My Last Duchess. TV incl: Benny Hill Show; The Prisoner; Norman; Mike and Bernie Show; Call My Bluff; Going for a Song; For Men Only; The Edwardians. Chairman of charity organisation Feminine Touch. Education: Belgium, France and England. m. Peter Lebow, 1 d. Candice, 1 s. Jeremy. Address: c/o Aida Foster Ltd, London NW8. Starsign: Aries. Hobbies: writing; speaking; reading; interior decorating; antiques; working for charity. Unfulfilled ambitions: to be an international celebrity, and 'to give something to this earth before I leave it'.

LEE, John
Actor b. 31st March Launceston, Tasmania. Theatre and radio work from an early age. Recent TV incl: The Wilde Alliance; Warship; Birds Fall Down; Nicest Man

in the World; Horseman Riding By; When The Boat Comes In; Our Kid. Education: Melbourne, Australia. m. Jocelyn, 1 d. Joanna, 3 s. Nicolas, Jonathon, Christopher. Address: c/o Roger Carey, London WC2. Starsign: Aries. Hobby: do-it-yourself. Unfulfilled ambition: to pilot an aircraft.

LEECH, Richard
Actor b. 24.11.22 Dublin. Though qualified as a doctor, he joined the Dublin Gate Theatre while still a medical student. Gave up medicine (he was a house surgeon at Neath Hospital, Glamorgan for a while) to be an actor. Has since made many appearances on London's West End stage incl: A Man For All Seasons; The Lady's Not For Burning (and in America); The Right Honourable Gentlemen; Relative Values and more recently, Whose Life Is It Anyway?. Many film and TV appearances in such series as Z Cars; The Avengers; Danger Man; Public Eye; No Hiding Place; Special Branch. Other TV incl:

Gazette; The Gold Robbers; The Doctors; Family at War; Crown Court; Edward the Seventh; Warship; Village Hall; Pope Pius XII; The Duchess of Duke Street; Rooms; Dickens of London; Dr Who. Education: Baymount Prep School; Haileybury College; Trinity College, Dublin.
m. (1st) Helen Hyslop Uttley (dec), (2nd) Diane Pearson, 2 d. theatre designer Sarah Jane McClelland, actress Eliza McClelland. Address: c/o Chatto and Linnit, London W1. Starsign: Sagittarius. Hobbies: gardening, bricklaying, home movies. Unfulfilled ambition: 'to act with my daughter and son-in-law in a play designed by my other daughter'.

LEEMING, Jan
Presenter/interviewer b. 5.1.42 Kent. Fifteen years experience in theatre, radio and TV in New Zealand, Australia and England; now with BBC Midlands. Education: St Joseph's Convent Grammar School, Abbey Wood, Kent; Ewell Technical College. Address: c/o BBC, Pebble Mill, Birmingham. Starsign: Capricorn. Hobbies: theatre, learning about music, fashion, travel. Unfulfilled ambitions: to have her own chat show; to research and produce documentary programmes about interesting people; to visit Peru and Japan; to be happy.

LEES, Michael
Actor b. 5.9.27 Bury, Lancs. Trained at RADA. TV incl: Sam, The Cedar Tree; Rooms; People Like Us; Plain Murder; Malice Aforethought; Thomas and Sarah; Tropic; Pride and Prejudice. Films incl: Cuba. Education: De La Salle College, Dalford. Address: c/o Roger Storey Ltd, London W1. Starsign: Virgo. Hobbies: walking, trees, Wagner, observing other people. Unfulfilled ambition: to play Macbeth.

LEGGATT, Alison
Actress b. 7th February London. Studied for the stage at the Central School of Dramatic Art, winning the Gold Medal and making her stage debut in 1924. Has since appeared in many distinguished plays incl: Cavalcade; This Happy Breed; Tonight at 8.30 (with Noël Coward and Gertrude Lawrence); One Way Pendulum (also film and TV) for which she won the Critic's Award for Actress of the Year. Films incl: Goodbye Again; A Funny Thing Happened on the Way to the Forum; Far From the Madding Crowd;

Goodbye Mr Chips. TV incl: A Tale of Two Cities; The Old Wives Tale; Home and Beauty; Jonathan Miller's Alice in Wonderland; Sanctuary; Edward the Seventh. Education: St Winifred's, Eastbourne. m. (dis), 1 s. restauranteur Nick Clarke. Address: c/o Fraser & Dunlop Ltd, London W1. Starsign: Aquarius.

LEIGH, Alison
Reporter b. 18.5.49 Kidderminster, Worcs. Started in BBC local radio, researcher for Nationwide (responsible for campaign which led to Mobile Home Act of Parliament), then reporting, Westward TV 1974-77 (four network series which she produced and co-presented, and half-hour weekly current affairs programme, Westward Report). Anglia TV, appearing on Probe and About Anglia. Now reporter on Radio 4 programme, Today in addition to freelance TV work. Education: Manchester University (BA Hons in Hispanic studies). m. Hugh Allan Sinclair Brown. Address: Cottenham, Cambs. Starsign: Taurus. Hobbies: learning guitar, yoga and keep fit, home-made wine, cooking. Unfulfilled ambitions: to play guitar; to travel in South America and Asia; to be employed full-time making documentaries.

LEIGH-HUNT, Ronald

Actor b. 5th October London. Theatrical family background. Trained at the Italia Conti Stage School after leaving the army. Played many parts but is probably still best remembered for first starring role on TV in 1956 as King Arthur in The Adventures of Sir Lancelot. First show in London's West End was first production of The King and I in 1953. Stage also incl: Funny Girl (with Barbra Streisand) in London 1966; most recent – touring with Sleuth. Played in more than 30 films incl: Le Mans (with Steve McQueen). TV incl: Rogue Herries; The Freewheelers; Crossroads; countless plays, serials and comedy shows (with Dick Emery, Norman Wisdom and many others); Crime of Passion; Dr Who; On the Green. Education: Tiffins. widower, 1 d. Laura. Address: c/o NEMS Management Ltd, London SW3. Starsign: Libra. Hobbies: motor-racing, tennis, golf. Unfulfilled ambition: 'to produce the series I have written and created for television.'

LE MESURIER, John

Actor b. 5.4.12 Bedford, but brought up in Bury St Edmunds and London. Studied for the stage at Fay Compton's Drama School, followed by rep, pantomime, cabaret, variety and London's West End. Served in the army during the war. Many films and much TV.

Films incl: Those Dangerous Years; Private's Progress; I'm All Right, Jack; Punch and Judy Man; We Joined the Navy; Mouse on the Moon; Pink Panther; Never Take No For an Answer; Casino Royale; Salt and Pepper; Magic Christian; Brief Encounter; Confessions of a Window Cleaner; Jabberwocky; Stand Up Virgin Soldiers; Spaceman and King Arthur; The Fiendish Plot of Dr Fu Manchu. On TV he has been in Dad's Army (and the film) since 1969; other TV incl: The Traitor (Best TV Actor 1971 Award); The Goodies; Doctor at Large; Anywhere But England; A Class By Himself; Rust; Mr Loveday's; Little Outing; Silver Wedding; High Ground; Flint; A Christmas Carol; 3.2.1; The Dick Emery Show; Worzel Gummidge. Records incl: What is Going to Become of Us All? Education: Sherborne. m. (1st) actress Hattie Jacques (dis), (2nd) Joan, 2 s. Robin, Kim. Address: c/o Peter Campbell, London SW3. Starsign: Aries.

LEWIS, Peter

Broadcaster/actor/producer b. 13.9.46 Welsh, but born just outside the land of his fathers. At one time was probably the youngest full-time professional broadcaster in the country. In addition to news and sport and current affairs commentating, presented network film programme, Movie Magazine, when he

was 17. Fourteen years of daily newscasting, fronting news and magazine programmes, children's programmes, sport, adult education, quiz shows, plays, commercials and interviews. Other TV incl: presenting Home and Design; London Weekend TV's Friday night programmes; co-presenting HTV West's news magazine, Report West. Has worked for most of the ITV companies as well as BBC radio and TV. Is on the Boards of several companies. Education: Cardiff Arms Park and agricultural college. m. Rita, 3 s. Benjamin, Toby, Daniel. Address: c/o Pamela Juvenile, New Management Ltd, London W1. Starsign: Virgo. Hobbies: rugby, karate, motorsport and any physical activity for which he isn't too old. Unfulfilled ambition: to run his own farm.

LEWIS, Tony

Compere b. 6.7.38 Swansea. Former captain, Glamorgan County Cricket Club and England captain in eight Tests 1972-73: Presenter HTV Wales Sports Arena since 1973, HTV Wales

Image, also Sport on 4 (BBC Radio) and Saturday Night at the Mill. Education: Neath Grammar School; Christ's College, Cambridge (History). m. Joan, 2 d. Joanna, Anabel. Address: c/o Bagenal Harvey Organisation, London W1. Starsign: Cancer. Hobbies: cricket, golf, music. Unfulfilled ambition: to win the British Open Golf title off a handicap of 16½.

Sutherland's Law; The Case of Eliza Armstrong; Madame Bovary; Survivors; Lillie (playing Bertie). Education: Hamilton Boys' High School. m. Joan, 1 d. Charlotte, 1 s. Edward. Address: c/o St James's Management, London SW1. Starsign: Aries/Taurus cusp. Hobby: model aeroplanes. Unfulfilled ambition: to play in a spectacular, star-studded Western.

LIJERTWOOD, Lucita
Actress b. 1921 Trinidad. Trained as an accountant, came to England 1956 to educate her children. After working in a wages dept of a large company, ran her own hairdressing business 1960-65. Took up acting seriously 1970 and TV appearances incl: Honey Lane; Doomwatch; Within These Walls; The Fosters; Red Letter Day; The Angels; The Rag Trade.
3 d., 1 s. Rory. Address: c/o LWT, London SE1. Hobby: helping crippled children in Herne Hill district where she lives.

LILL, Denis
Actor b. 22.4.42 Hamilton, Waikato, New Zealand. Royal New Zealand Air Force 1958-65, trained as an airframe mechanic. Toured NZ with NZ Players and came to UK 1967. In rep and with the National Theatre before TV: The Regiment; Fall of Eagles; plays and series incl: Love Story; Main Chance; Warship; Spytrap;

LINDEN, Jennie
Actress b. 8.12.40 Worthing, Sussex. Went from her private school to train as a teacher of drama at the Central School of Speech and Drama and has a Central School Diploma and is an International Phonetic Associate. Stage incl: Never Too Late; Thark; My Fat Friend; On Approval; Hedda Gabler; also her own show of verse, prose and song, I Say, I Play. Films incl: Dr Who and the Daleks; Women in Love; A Severed Head. TV incl: The Trouble With England; You Can't Win; For King and Country; Present Laughter; Return of Favours; Seasons of the Year; Lady

Windermere's Fan; The Persuaders; Sister Mary; Little Lord Fauntleroy; Lillie; Charlie Muffins; Dick Turpin. Several radio plays. Education: private school, West Preston Manor, Sussex. m. antique dealer Christopher Mann, 1 s. Rupert. Address: c/o Roger Carey, London WC2. Starsign: Sagittarius. Hobbies: endless, but include music (piano); gardening; restoring antique furniture; collecting antiques, building on to cottages; reading; philosophy; UFO research; spiritualism, etc. Unfulfilled ambition: to sing light opera.

LINDLEY, Richard
TV reporter b. 25.4.36 Winchester, Hants. Made commercials for advertising agency before joining ITN as current affairs reporter 1964. Covered Biafra, Vietnam, Cambodia and Bangladesh wars. Joined BBC for current affairs coverage and Panorama 1972. Education: Bedford School; Cambridge University (BA Eng Lit) where he ran the university film society. m. with two children. Address: c/o BBC TV, London W12. Starsign: Taurus. Hobby: constantly propping up a decrepit old London house. Unfulfilled ambition: 'to find a better programme than Panorama – if there is one'.

LIPMAN, Maureen
Actress b. 10.5.46 Hull.
Always wanted to act and
trained at LAMDA. Much
stage experience incl:
London's Royal Court
Theatre; Old Vic (The Front
Page; The Good Natured
Man); Candida; The Ball
Game; Tira Tells Everything
There is to Know About Her;
Royal Shakespeare
Company (As You Like It); the
Stables Theatre. Films incl:
Up the Junction; Gumshoe.
Radio incl: Delivery; Special
Co-respondent; Mother
Figure. Now well known for
her role in Agony, but other
TV incl: Couples; Doctor at
Large; The Soft Touch; Don't
Ask Us; The Lovers; The
Evacuees; File It Under Fear
(Thriller); Codename; The
Knowledge; The Sporting
Club Dinner; Rogue Male;
Which is Which?; Give Us a
Clue; Cabbages and Kings;
Crown Court. Education:
Newland High School, Hull.
m. playwright Jack
Rosenthal, 1 d. Amy,
1 s. Adam. Address: c/o
Saraband Associates,
London W1. Starsign:
Taurus. Hobby: finding time
to think of one. Unfulfilled
ambitions: to write; to direct;
to do more filming; to be
better looking; to cook better.

LITTLE, Syd
Comedian b. 19.12.42
Blackpool. Solo guitarist and
singer in Manchester pubs
before teaming up with Eddie
Large as singing duo. Turned
to comedy in northern clubs
before winning appearance

on Opportunity Knocks 1971.
TV since incl: Crackerjack;
Who Do You Do?; Now Who
Do You Do?; David Nixon
Show; Seaside Special;
Wheeltappers and Shunters
Social Club; Wednesday at
Eight; Little and Large
Tellyshow; Little and Large
Show; Disneytime. Stage
incl: seasons at London
Palladium, pantomimes,
summer shows and cabaret.
Education: secondary
school. m. Sheree,
1 d. Donna, 1 s. Paul.
Address: c/o London
Management, London W1.
Starsign: Sagittarius.
Hobbies: making model
boats, keep-fit. Unfulfilled
ambition: to help Nelson fight
the battle of Trafalgar.

LLOYD-ROBERTS, Sue
TV reporter b. 27.10.51
London. Joined ITN as
general news reporter 1976
straight from university. Has
since covered many foreign
assignments in France,
Spain, Switzerland, Hong
Kong and Singapore.
Education: Cheltenham
Ladies' College; St Hilda's
College, Oxford (BA Hons,
history and modern

languages). Address: c/o
ITN, London W1. Starsign:
Scorpio. Hobbies: theatre,
opera, skiing. Unfulfilled
ambition: to make money.

LODGE, David
Actor b. 19.8.21 Rochester,
Kent. Began in Gang Shows
and music hall where he
perfected his art. Has
appeared in over 120 films
(from Cockleshell Heroes to
The Pink Panther). Also many
series and appearances on
television, incl: Lovely
Couple; Spike Milligan's Q8;
Murder at the Wedding.
Education: St Nicholas
Church School; City Day
Continuation School. m. Lyn.
Address: c/o Joan Gray,
Personal Management,
Sunbury-on-Thames, Middx.
Starsign: Leo. Hobbies.
Grand Order of Water Rats
and the Variety Club of Great
Britain. Unfulfilled ambition:
to front a big band for a
concert.

LOE, Judy
Actress b. 6.3.47
Manchester. Worked in rep at
Chester and Crewe after
university. Stage incl: Hair; A
Game Called Arthur; No Sex
Please – We're British;

Middle-Age Spread. TV incl: Ace of Wands; General Hospital; Edward the Seventh; Woodstock; Man of Straw; Z Cars; Miss Jones and Son; The Upchat Line; Couples; Crown Court; Robin's Nest; Ripping Yarns; Heartland; Visitors for Andersons. Education: Urmston Grammar and University of Birmingham (BA in Drama and English). m. actor Richard Beckinsale (dec), 1 d. Kate. Address: c/o Fraser and Dunlop Ltd, London W1. Starsign: Pisces. Hobby: writing poetry. Unfulfilled ambitions: to do good work, maintain one's integrity and add a little magic to people's lives.

LORD, Jack
Actor b. 30.12.30 New York City, USA. Came into acting through making training films for the navy. Before that he had been third mate in the Merchant Navy, studied fine art at New York University, organised his own art school in Greenwich Village (some of his work has been acquired by the Metropolitan Museum of Art), took flying lessons and got a private pilot's licence. First acting break in TV series, Man Against Crime. Many roles in dozens of series, incl: Stoney Burke, but best known as Steve McGarrett in Hawaii Five-O. Films incl: God's Little Acre; Man of the West; Doctor No. Education: New York University. m. (1st) (dis), (2nd) fashion designer Marie de Narde. Address: Oahu,

Hawaii. Starsign: Capricorn. Hobbies: painting, writing, collecting art.

LOVE, Geoff
Bandleader/composer/arranger b. 4th September, Todmorden, Yorks. Started as a motor mechanic but interested in music since 11 when he joined a local amateur orchestra. Turned professional at 17 when he joined a stage band with which he tap-danced and sang. Spent six years in the army (King's Royal Rifle Corps) and learnt orchestration while in the band. After the war joined Harry Gold and His Pieces of Eight. Made first recordings 26 years ago; has since received about 12 gold and numerous silver discs for the sale of his records. Also a platinum for his Western Movie Themes. Also records as Manuel and the Music of the Mountains and in 1980 celebrates 21 years under this title. Frequent radio and TV appearances, but probably best-known for his work with Max Bygraves on the Max Bygraves TV programmes. Education: Roomfield Boys' School, Todmorden. m. Joy, 2 s. Capital Radio DJ Adrian Love and computer lecturer Nigel Love. Address: c/o Noel Gay Organisation, London WC2. Starsign: Virgo. Hobbies: music, water skiing. Unfulfilled ambition: 'to stay as lucky as I am'.

LOVE, Walter H
Presenter b. 22.6.35 Belfast. Joined BBC in London as a studio manager in 1958. Subsequently worked in Edinburgh and Belfast in the same capacity. Appointed staff announcer 1962, working on both radio and TV on a wide range of programmes. Presenter of Radio Ulster's morning magazine programme, Day by Day since November 1978. Freelance since September 1st, 1979. Education: Regent House School, Newtownards, Co Down. Address: c/o BBC, Belfast. Starsign: Gemini. Hobbies: sailing, wine-making, jazz. Unfulfilled ambition: to win the pools while young enough to enjoy it.

LOWE, Arthur
Actor b. 22.9.15 Hayfield, Derbyshire. Wanted to join the Merchant Navy but failed the eyesight test and joined the cavalry. Also took a RADA course and after the war joined a rep company at Hulme, Manchester. Guest appearances elsewhere, then leading parts in Call Me Madam; Pal Joey and the

Pyjama Game in London. TV career took off, after many appearances, as Mr Swinley in Coronation Street. Other TV incl: Pardon the Expression; Turn Out the Lights; Dad's Army (and on stage); Let's Get Away From It All; Bless Me, Father. m. actress Joan Cooper, 1 s. Stephen, 1 step-s. David. Address: c/o Peter Campbell, London W1. Starsign: Virgo.

LUCAS, Michael
Reporter b. 2.12.51 Jersey, Channel Islands. Trained with Channel TV as reporter 1975-78; anchorman for Channel's Report at Six; writer and commentator of networked film report, Jersey Battle of Flowers, 1978. Currently presenter/interviewer Border TV's Look Around and reporter for Border's Dog Show. Education: Victoria University of Manchester (BA Hons in French studies). Address: c/o Border TV, Carlisle. Starsign: Sagittarius. Hobbies: tennis, horse-riding, swimming, squash. Unfulfilled ambition: to compete in the Badminton Three Day Event Horse Trials.

LUCAS, William
Actor b. 14.4.25 Manchester. Trained at Bradford Theatre School after serving in the Royal Navy during the war. Rep at Liverpool and other parts of the country. London stage incl: Amber for Anna; Ring of Jackals; Dual Marriageway. Films incl:

Sons and Lovers; The Professionals; Payroll; Bitter Harvest. TV incl: Portrait of Alison; The Paragon; The Infamous John Friend; Rigoletto; A Flea off Pepe; Champion Road; Flower of Evil; Mogul; Warship; Black Beauty; The Spoils of War. Education: Manchester. 2 s. Daniel, Thomas. Address: c/o Joy Jameson, London SW1. Starsign: Aries. Hobby: walking. Unfulfilled ambition: to retire.

LUCKHAM, Cyril
Character actor b. 25.7.07 Salisbury, Wilts. One of TV's most distinguished actors. Originally wanted a career in the Royal Navy, but was invalided out 1931 as a lieut. Trained for stage with Arthur Brough Players and Folkestone Dramatic School. First stage part was as footman in The Admirable Crichton at Folkestone. Since then has been in rep at Folkestone, Manchester, Bristol, Liverpool, Coventry, Southport, and was a member of the Royal Shakespeare Company for three seasons. Has been in more stage, TV plays and

series than he can remember. West End plays incl: The Family Reunion; Photo Finish; You Never Can Tell. Films incl: Anne of the Thousand Days; A Man For All Seasons; The Pumpkin Eater; The Naked Runner; Providence. TV incl: Vote, Vote, Vote for Nigel Barton; The Forsyte Saga; Company of Five; Scotch on the Rocks; The Guardians; Public Eye; The Venturers; Father Brown; Jennie; The Cedar Tree; Wodehouse Playhouse; What Every Woman Knows; The Camerons; The Omega Factor; Murder at the Wedding; Sweet Wine of Youth; My Son, My Son; North and South; Donkey's Years. Education: RN Colleges, Osborne and Dartmouth. m. actress Violet Lamb, 1 s. opera singer Robert. Address: c/o Larry Dalzell Associates Ltd, London WC2. Starsign: Leo. Hobbies: music, cricket, ornithology.

LULU
Singer/actress b. 3.11.48 Lennoxtown, Stirlingshire. Started singing in concert party when she was nine. First record, Shout, in 1963. Has been in many pop and variety shows since as well as twice playing the title role in Peter Pan. In addition to being chosen for a Royal Variety Performance and joint winner of the Eurovision Song Contest (1969), she has also been voted the World's and Britain's Top Girl Singer and Britain's Top TV Performer. Her films include To Sir With

Love and her numerous TV appearances include 10 TV series for the BBC. Education: Whitehall Senior Secondary, Dennistown, Glasgow. m. (1st) Maurice Gibb of the Bee Gees (dis), (2nd) hairdresser John Frieda, 1 s. Jordan (from 2nd m). Address: c/o Marion Massey, London W14. Starsign: Scorpio. Hobbies: water skiing, buying clothes.

LUMLEY, Joanna
Actress b. 1.5.46 Srinagar, India. A brief period in a craft and furniture shop was followed by a move to London and a modelling course. After appearing in Queen magazine, her modelling career took off. Subsequently concentrated on acting. Stage incl: Don't Just Lie There, Say Something; Othello; Me Old Cigar. Films incl: Some Girls Do; On Her Majesty's Secret Service; Tam Lin; The Breaking of Bimbo; Games Lovers Play. TV incl: The Mark II Wife; Release; Two Girls; It's Awfully Bad For Your Eyes, Darling; Coronation Street; The Protectors; General Hospital; The New Avengers; Steptoe and Son; Sapphire and Steel. Education: Micheldene Primary School; Army School, Kuala Lumpur; St Mary's Anglican Convent, Hastings. m. Jeremy Lloyd (dis), 1 s. James (born 1968). Address: c/o ICM, London W1. Starsign: Taurus. Hobbies: collecting junk, painting, drawing, reading.

Unfulfilled ambition: to build an enormous four-poster bed for herself.

LYNCH, Joe
Actor b. 16.7.25 Cork. Trained at Cork Opera House then Abbey Theatre, Dublin for five years. Radio Eireann Rep Co. Has sung in London's Albert Hall and America's Carnegie Hall. Many stage, cabaret, film and TV appearances. Films incl: The Girl With Green Eyes; Young Cassidy; Ulysses. TV incl: Eveline; The Gamblers; The Showing Up of Blanco Posnet; Never Mind the Quality, Feel the Width; Slattery's Mounted Foot; Great Big Blonde; The Out of Town Boys; Rule Britannia, and all the voices in children's cartoon series, Chorlton and the Wheelies; The Wotsit from Whizz-Bang. Education: Blackrock College; Skerries College; Cork School of Music. m. former concert singer Marie, 2 d. Linda, Emmy, 1 s. Mark. Address: Weybridge, Surrey. Starsign: Cancer. Hobbies: horse-riding, golf, playing the flageolet. Unfulfilled ambitions: to make a parachute jump; to sing jazz on British TV.

LYNN, Dame Vera DBE
Singer b. 20.3.17 London. First public appearance as singer when seven, joined juvenile group and ran her own dancing school. After broadcasting with Joe Loss and Charlie Kunz, sang with

Ambrose Orchestra 1937-40. Then went solo. Voted most popular singer in Daily Express poll 1939 and named Forces Sweetheart. Sang to troops in Burma 1944, also in Holland, Denmark, Sweden, Norway, Germany, Canada, New Zealand, Australia. Many radio shows: Sincerely Yours; Big Show (USA). Stage incl: Applesauce; London Laughs; Las Vegas. TV appearances in Britain and America, Royal Variety performances. Records incl: Auf Wiederseh'n; Yours; White Cliffs of Dover; We'll Meet Again. Book: Vocal Refrain (autobiography). Education: Brampton Road School, East Ham, London. m. musician Harry Lewis, 1 d. Virginia. Address: Ditchling, Sussex. Starsign: Pisces/Aries. Hobbies: gardening, sewing, painting, swimming.

M

MacCORMICK, Donald
TV journalist b. 16.4.39
Glasgow. Former
schoolmaster turned
broadcasting journalist in
1968. Presenter/reporter
Grampian TV (1968-70), BBC
Scotland (1970-75), BBC's
Tonight (1975-79).
Education: King's Park
School, Glasgow; Glasgow
University. m. Liz Elton,
1 d. Sarah, 2 s. Donald, Niall
(all by previous m.). Address:
Chiswick, London. Starsign:
Aries. Hobbies: against these
in principle – but quite likes
theatre and wine.
Compulsive newspaper
reader. Unfulfilled ambition:
to be able to smoke a good
cigar again without
becoming re-addicted.

MacARTHUR, James
Actor b. 8.12.37 Los
Angeles, Calif. Brought up in
showbiz environment as
adoptive parents were
actress Helen Hayes and
playwright Charles (Front
Page) MacArthur. Acting
debut at age of eight in The
Corn is Green in summer
theatre. Many plays (Life With
Father; Invitation to a March)
and films incl: Kidnapped;
Third Man on the Mountain;
Swiss Family Robinson; The
Light in the Forest; The
Interns; To Be a Man;
Spencer's Mountain: The
Truth About Spring; The
Battle of the Bulge; The
Love-Ins. Has played the part
of Danny Williams in Hawaii
Five-O since the series
started. Education: Allen
Stevenson School, New York;
Solebury School, New Hope,
Pennsylvania; Harvard
University. m. (1st) actress
Joyce Bulifant (dis),
(2nd) actress Melanie
Patterson, 1 d. Mary,
1 s. Charles (both from
1st m). Address: Honolulu,
Hawaii. Starsign: Sagittarius.
Hobbies: surfing, shooting.

MACHIN, Peter
Actor b. 4.12.46
Bexleyheath, Kent. Trained at
Guildhall School of Music
and Drama (gold medal)
1969-71. Then Royal
Shakespeare Co, Bristol Old
Vic and Shaw Theatre,
London. TV incl: Love for
Lydia; Blasphemy – Gay
News Trial; People Like Us.
Education: Bexley Technical
High. m. Ann, 1 s. Joseph.
Address: c/o Ken McReddie,

London W1. Starsign: Sagittarius. Hobby: renovating old furniture.

MacKAY, Fulton
Actor b. 12th August Paisley. Trained to become a quantity surveyor but after serving in the Black Watch during the war decided to be an actor and went to RADA. Much theatre work incl: The Royal Lyceum, Edinburgh; The Old Vic; The National Theatre; The RSC; Manchester Royal Exchange. TV incl: Strife; The Blind Man; Special Branch; Porridge; Willie Rough; The Foundation; Clay, Smeddum and Greenden; Three Tales of Orkney; Choices; Ghosts; The Master of Ballantrae. Films incl: The Brave Don't Cry; Laxdale Hall; Porridge; Gumshoe. Has written several plays for TV under a pseudonym. Education: Clydebank High School. m. Irish actress Sheila Manahan. Address: c/o NEMS Enterprises, London SW3. Starsign: Leo. Hobby: oil painting.

MacKENZIE, Bill
Political correspondent b. 14.6.37 Inverness. Ten years in full-time politics; chairman Points North, Grampian TV's political programme. Education: Inverness Royal Academy; Edinburgh College of Commerce. m. Anne Ross, 2 d. Alison, Fiona. 1 s. Ross. Address: Aberdeen. Starsign: Gemini. Hobbies: rugby, cricket, golf.

MACKLIN, Keith
Journalist/commentator b. 19.1.31 Newton-le-Willows, Lancs. Newspaper journalism and radio commentating. TV incl: Songs of Praise; A Spoonful of Sugar; Sunday Quiz. ITV's London-based report for 1972 Olympics and World Cup Commentator 1974. Linkman for Border's Lookaround. Education: Prescot Grammar School; Manchester Polytechnic. m. Shelia, 1 d. Heather. Address: Widnes, Cheshire. Starsign: Capricorn. Hobbies: watching, reporting and occasionally playing all sports; Chinese and Indian food. Unfulfilled ambition: to stop bothering about unachieved ambitions.

MacLAURIN, Brian
Journalist b. 7.12.49 Brookfield, Renfrewshire. Newspaper experience on Renfrewshire Gazette, Greenock Evening Telegraph, Scottish Daily Express, before joining Scottish Television in Glasgow, and then ATV in Birmingham as industrial correspondent. Moved to

Oxford to set up ATV News and Information Centre 1979. Education: Rannoch School, Perthshire; Edinburgh College of Technology. m. Wendy, 1 d. Katie, 1 s. Peter. Address: c/o ATV Centre, Oxford. Starsign: Sagittarius. Hobbies: do-it-yourself fanatic, squash.

MACLEAN, Don
Comedian b. 11.3.44 Birmingham. Began entertaining in clubs and pubs in Midlands area, then holiday camp entertainer. TV debut in Crossroads; also in Billy Cotton's Music Hall; Roy Castle Show; The Good Old Days; In All Directions; Jokers Wild; White Heather Club; Out For the Count; Crackerjack; The Black and White Minstrels; Celebrity Squares; The Cheapest Show On The TV. Radio incl: own series Maclean Up Britain; Wit's End. Also comedy records. Education: St Philip's Grammar School, Birmingham. m. Antoinette, 1 d. Rachel, 1 s. Rory. Address: c/o Morris Aza, London NW11. Starsign: Pisces. Hobbies: making

models of First World War aeroplanes, squash. Unfulfilled ambitions: to star in own named TV series and to beat Leonard Rossiter at squash – 'providing the Rising Damp doesn't get to his legs first.'

MacLEOD, Donny
Presenter b. 1.7.32 Stornoway, Isle of Lewis, Scotland. Former art student, sculptor, naval officer and town councillor, he started his TV career with Grampian TV and was former anchorman on Reporting Scotland. Worked with Nationwide and with Scottish Documentary Unit in Glasgow before joining Pebble Mill in 1973. Other TV incl: Macleod at Large; Saturday Night at the Mill; The Best of Scottish. Education: Royal College of Commerce, Glasgow; Gray's School of Art, Aberdeen. m. Shirley, 1 d. Catherine, 3 s. David, Iain, Kevin. Address: c/o BBC, Pebble Mill, Birmingham. Starsign: Cancer. Hobbies: fishing, photography.

MacLEOD, Kenneth
Presenter b. 6.1.28 Scotland. Started in rep in Harrogate and Folkestone. TV debut was as the Duke of Montano in Othello for the BBC, televised from Alexandra Palace in 1949. Joined Associated Rediffusion three months before the company opened and was the first person to be seen on ITV when transmission began in

the UK. Presented such programmes as Teatime at the Embassy and Late Extra. Has been anchorman of Westward TV's nightly news magazine, Westward Diary, since the station opened in 1961. Education: King's School, Canterbury. Address: c/o Westward TV, Plymouth. Starsign: Capricorn. Hobbies: music, carpentry (rough), restoring antique woodwind instruments. Unfulfilled ambition: to play flute in the Royal Philharmonic Orchestra (any rank!).

MacLEOD, Lesley
Announcer b. 5.7.33 Ceres, Fife, Scotland. Taught at Capshard Primary School, Kirkcaldy, Fife before joining Grampian TV. Presenter of Wings 'n' Things; Scene on Saturday. Education: Bell Baxter High School, Cupar, Fife; Aberdeen College of Education (B Ed). Address: c/o Grampian TV, Aberdeen. Starsign: Cancer. Hobbies: music, reading, occasional yoga, very occasional squash. Unfulfilled ambition: to learn to hang wallpaper.

MACNEE, Patrick
Actor b. 6.2.22 London. Always determined to be an actor; won a scholarship to Webber Douglas Academy of Dramatic Art; went into rep at Letchworth Garden City. Came to London in Little Women after touring. First film: Life and Death of Colonel Blimp. Served in the Royal Navy 1942-1946. Returned to the stage including two years at Windsor Rep. Toured America with Old Vic production of A Midsummer Night's Dream 1954 and until 1959 was commuting between Britain, America and Canada where he helped to pioneer TV. Starred in The Avengers 1961 and made such an impact that he will always be associated with his role of John Steed. Films incl: The Elusive Pimpernel; Small Back Room; Scrooge; Three Cases of Murder; Battle of the River Plate; Les Girls; Doctors Wear Scarlet; King Solomon's Treasure. Much TV in Canada and America as well as Britain incl: Thriller; The New Avengers. Education: Summerfields Prep School, Banbury, Oxfordshire; Eton. m. (1st) actress Barbara Douglas (dis), (2nd) Catherine Woodville (dis), 1 d. Cordon Bleu cook Jennie, 1 s. TV producer and director Rupert (both from 1st m). Address: c/o John Redway and Associates Ltd, London W1. Starsign: Aquarius. Hobby: living.

MacPHERSON, Archie
Sports broadcaster
b. 10.11.34 Glasgow. Was a teacher before making a second career in broadcasting 15 years ago. Former headmaster of a school in Lanarkshire until began working for BBC on a part-time basis, then, 10 years ago, he joined full time in Glasgow to cover sport. Education: Jordanhill College (BA in educational studies). m. Jess, 2 s. Douglas, Stewart. Address: Mount Vernon, Glasgow. Starsign: Scorpio. Hobbies: writing, golf. Unfulfilled ambition: to commentate on Scotland's World Cup final.

MacPHERSON, Rory
Newscaster b. 7.6.35. After National Service was in Diplomatic Service 1960-67 rising to be a First Secretary in the Foreign Office. With The Economist for two years before joining ITN as reporter and newscaster. Diplomatic correspondent 1973. Education: Glenalmond and Jesus College, Oxford. Address: c/o ITN, London W1. Starsign: Gemini.

Hobby: playing tennis with Ivor Mills and Reginald Bosanquet.

MADELEY, Richard
Reporter/presenter
b. 13.5.56 Romford, Essex. Started as a reporter on the Brentwood Argus 1972. News editor of East London Advertiser when 19; then reporter and news producer at Radio Carlisle before joining Border TV as reporter/presenter 1978. Education: Coopers' Company Grammar, Bow, London; Shenfield School, Brentwood, Essex. m. Lynda Ruth. Address: c/o Border TV, Carlisle. Starsign: Taurus. Hobbies: acoustic guitar; reading; sun-lover; studying social and military effects of Second World War; sports; travelling abroad; eating out. Unfulfilled ambition: to visit America.

MADOC, Philip
Actor b. 5.7.34 Merthyr Tydfil. First rate linguist (seven languages), his studies took him to the University of Vienna where he was first foreigner to win the diploma of Interpreters'

Institute. After two years as interpreter, intended lecturing at Gothenburg University. Instead he went to RADA. Well-known on TV for his 'baddie' roles, incl: Manhunt; The Last of the Mohicans; Barlow at Large; Rivals of Sherlock Holmes; Hawksmoor; Woodstock; less villainously in Another Bouquet; The Goodies; Dad's Army. Education: Universities of Wales and Vienna. m. actress Ruth Madoc, 1 d. Lowri, 1 s. Rhys. Address: c/o Duncan Heath Associates, London W8. Starsign: Cancer. Hobbies: wind-surfing, badminton, languages. Unfulfilled ambitions: to play Napoleon and become Foreign Secretary.

MAGILL, Ronald
Actor b. 1922. First opportunity to tread a real stage came during the war in which he served in the Royal Corps of Signals and toured with Stars in Battledress. On demob became a tyre salesman but after a year joined a travelling company, Arena, and has since played almost every theatre outside London. Also actor and director at Nottingham Playhouse for nine years. Some TV and a Charlton Heston film, Julius Caesar, before becoming licensee, Amos Brearly in Emmerdale Farm. Education: Sir Josiah Mason Orphanage, Birmingham. Address: Leeds.

MAGNUSSON, Magnus
Presenter b. 12.10.29
Reykjavik, Iceland. Family
moved to Scotland when he
was nine months old and he
has lived there ever since.
Started as a reporter on
Scottish Daily Express.
Occasional TV engagements
led to interviewing on
Tonight. Thereafter
Chronicle; Cause For
Concern; Unsolved
Mysteries; Mainly Magnus;
Mastermind; Living Legends;
Vikings. Books incl: BC:
Archaeology of the Bible
Lands; Introducing
Archaeology; Viking
Expansion Westwards.
Education: Edinburgh
Academy; Jesus College,
Oxford. m. journalist Mamie
Baird, 3 d. Sally, Margaret,
Anna, 1 s. Jon. Address:
Balmore, near Glasgow.
Starsign: Libra. Hobby:
translating Icelandic sagas
and novels into English.

MAJORS, Lee
Actor b. 23.4.40 Wyandotte,
Michigan. Grew up in
Kentucky being adopted by
relatives on the death of his
parents. A star athlete while
at school, he might have had

a football career, but a back
injury during a game ended
those hopes. He opted to
follow the example of his
teenage idol James Dean
and went to California to try
his hand at acting and
several jobs later he was
signed for The Big Valley,
which ran for four years. He
was already established as a
TV personality when offered
the role of Steve Austin in The
Six Million-Dollar Man. Other
TV incl: The Men from Shiloh;
The Ballad of Andy Crocker.
Films incl: Will Penny; The
Liberation of L B Jones; The
Gary Francis Paver Story;
The Norseman; The Naked
Sun; Piranha. Education:
Universities of Indiana and
Eastern Kentucky.
m. (1st) childhood
sweetheart Kathy (dis),
(2nd) actress Farrah
Fawcett-Majors, 1 s. Lee
(from 1st m). Address: Bel
Air, California. Starsign:
Taurus. Hobbies: avid
sportsman, fishing, hunting,
golf.

MAKEPEACE, Maggie
TV presenter of popular
scientific programmes
b. 31.1.44 Fulmer, Bucks.
She claims her training was
hours of watching TV and an
uncontrollable enthusiasm.
This led to Don't Ask Me
which she co-presented with
Dr Magnus Pyke and Dr
Buckman, and How to Stay
Alive. Education: Newcastle
University (BSc Hons
zoology); Aberdeen
University (MSc ecology).
Address: c/o Scottish Wildlife

Trust, Edinburgh. Starsign:
Aquarius. Hobbies:
photography, bird-watching,
changing jobs. Unfulfilled
ambition: to present her own
series.

MALCOLM, John
Actor b. 26.3.36 Stirling.
Trained at RADA, experience
in rep touring and West End.
Built Traverse Theatre,
Edinburgh 1962-63, then two
years with Royal
Shakespeare Company. Built
the Theatre Chipping Norton
1973-77. Since 1966 mainly
TV, incl many TV
documentaries such as
Watergate; This Week 1844.
Also Enemy At The Door.
Education: Archbishop
Holgate's School for Boys,
Barnsley. 1 d. Aimée-Louise,
1 s. Nathaniel. Address:
Oxford. Starsign: Aries.
Hobby: arguments.
Unfulfilled ambition: to win an
argument on a fair basis.

MALDEN, Karl
Actor b. 22.3.14 Chicago,
Illinois. Originally a
steelworker, but enrolled in
the Goodman Theatre
dramatic school of the
Chicago Art Institute with the

idea of becoming a stage hand. A small part in a play changed his mind and he paid his way at Goodman by playing professional basketball. From there he went to New York Actors' Studio and success on Broadway in the original stage production of A Streetcar Named Desire, which he repeated in film of the same name. Other films incl: Ruby Gentry; On the Waterfront; The Hanging Tree; Pollyanna; Birdman of Alcatraz; Hot Millions; Boomerang; Phantom of the Rue Morgue; Baby Doll; One-eyed Jacks; Parrish; How The West Was Won; Gypsy; The Cincinnati Kid; The Billion Dollar Brain; Patton. First TV was as Mike Stone in The Streets of San Francisco. Well-known for the thoroughness with which he prepares for a part, he now teaches his craft for a month each year at various American Universities. m. former actress Mona Graham, 2 d. Mila, Carla. Starsign: Aries. Hobbies: sports (particularly basketball), collecting antiques, card tricks (which he learnt doing his homework for The Cincinnati Kid).

MALONE, Roger
Sports compere/ commentator/ writer b. 31.5.33 Alexandria, Egypt. Started on newspapers (Daily Express, Daily Herald) and now Daily Telegraph sports man in the West. Launched Westward Sports

Desk 1960. HTV Sports West compere and soccer outside broadcast commentator since 1968. ITV World Cup commentator, Mexico 1970, West German 'guest' World Cup commentator 1974 and 1978. Education: grammar schools in Rugby, Hereford, Isle of Man and Bristol. m. (dis), 1 d. Kate, 2 s. Keith, Giles. Address: c/o HTV, Bristol. Starsign: Gemini. Hobbies: playing golf, watching TV (particularly all sports), reading (particularly sporting biographies and Dick Francis). Unfulfilled ambitions: a second hole-in-one; a first "perfect" commentary.

MALONEY, Michael
Actor b. 19.6.57 Bury St Edmunds. While doing a drama course at LAMDA was spotted in a college production of The Boy Friend for his first professional part as Mark Telford in the TV series, Telford's Change. Since then his work has been on stage as the back legs of a pantomime cow at Glasgow and playing the same character as in the TV programme in Can You Hear Me At the Back? in London's West End. Education: Ladycross, Seaford, Sussex; Ampleforth College, York. Address: c/o William Morris Agency, London W1. Starsign: Gemini. Hobby: cycling. Unfulfilled ambition: to be a writer/director.

MANGOLD, Tom
TV reporter b. 20.8.34 Hamburg, W Germany. Was a reporter on the Sunday Mirror and the Daily Express before joining BBC TV News. Has since covered current affairs and associated with 24 Hours and Panorama. Education: Dorking Grammar School. m. Valerie Ann Hare, 2 d.Sarah, Abigail. Address: c/o BBC TV, London W12. Starsign: Leo. Hobbies: trampolining, playing blues harp, talking shop.

MANNING, Hugh
Actor b. 19.8.20 Birmingham. Began working life as trainee accountant, but switched to acting and trained at Birmingham School of Speech Training and Dramatic Art. Birmingham Rep 1945, then Bristol Old Vic and London Old Vic. Probably best known for his part as Hunter in Kathleen Harrison's TV series Mrs Thursday. Other TV incl: Sergeant Cork; The Avengers; The Sullivan Brothers; The Venturers; Poldark; Emmerdale Farm. Many stage productions incl: Stalingrad; The Cherry Orchard; Paragraph for Mr

Blake. Education: Moseley Grammar. Address: c/o Plunket Greene Ltd, London W1. Starsign: Leo. Hobbies: gardening, tennis, bridge, travel. Unfulfilled ambition: to play Othello.

MANVILLE, Lesley
Actress b. 12.3.56 Brighton. Trained at Hove Academy of Music and Italia Conti Stage School. TV incl: Young Eyes; Village Hall; Softly, Softly; Barlow; Emmerdale Farm; The Emigrants; King Cinder; A Bunch of Fives; General Hospital; Wings. Stage incl: pantomime, National Theatre, Royal Shakespeare Company. Education: St Andrews Infant and Primary; Nevill Secondary Modern, Hove. Address: Chiswick, London. Starsign: Pisces. Hobbies: horse riding, cooking, tapestry, needlework. Unfulfilled ambitions: to do a musical; to have children.

MARKHAM, Petra
Actress b. 17th March, Prestbury, Cheshire. Trained at Webber Douglas Academy of Dramatic Art and Oldham Rep. Has since

appeared at Greenwich, York and Oxford and with the National Theatre (in Equus) and with the Joint Stock Company. Films incl: Get Carter; The Hireling. Extensive radio work incl: Vanity Fair. TV incl: The Regulars; Something for the Children; Albert and Victoria; A Killer in Every Corner; Ace of Wands; Public Eye; Z Cars; Softly, Softly; St Joan (for schools); Life at Stake; Michael Palin Show; After Julius. Address: c/o Al Parker Ltd, London W1. Starsign: Pisces. Hobbies: reading, walking, cinema, cooking.

MARRIATT, Andrew
Motor sports commentator b. 20.9.43 Wolverhampton. Motor sporting reporter with Derbyshire Advertiser, Motoring News, Autosport, Motor Sport and The Sun. Race reader for Raymond Baxter; since 1975 motor sports commentator for ITV World of Sport and ATV sport reporter Independent Radio News. Has commented on major Grand Prix for SABC TV (South Africa) and American Public Service TV. Education: Tettenhall College, Staffs; Derby and District College of Technology. m. Elizabeth. Address: London W1. Starsign: Virgo. Hobbies: travel, rock music, car rallying (won tour of South Africa, Mintex Internation, fifth on the RAC Rally). Unfulfilled ambition: to win a round the world car rally.

MARSH, Reginald
Actor b. 17.9.26 London. No formal training for the stage – 'just hard work', he says; in other words many years rep and touring. Has been in rep in all parts of the country as well as periods with the RSC and National Theatre. Recent stage incl: The Chairman. Has also written a number of plays incl: The Death is Announced, in which he appeared on the stage and in the TV version, The Man Who Came to Die. Since 1958 has largely concentrated on films and TV. Films incl: The Sicilians; Shadow of Fear; Jigsaw; The Young Winston; The Day the Earth Caught Fire; Sky Pirates. TV incl: Coronation Street; The Planemakers; Gazette; The Power Game; The Ratcatchers; Barlow; My Name is Harry Worth; Whodunnit?; Bless This House; The Sweeney; Crown Court; The Good Life; many plays. Book: Much More Than Murder. Education: 'sufficient', he says. m. former actress Rosemary Murray, twin d. Rebecca and Alison, 2 s. Adam, Alexander. Address: c/o NEMS Enterprises, London SW3. Starsign: Virgo. Hobby: writing. Unfulfilled ambition: to be fit, active and lively at 80.

MARSHALL, Bryan
Actor b. 19.5.38 London. Came to acting via an insurance office, service in the army, as a salesman, amateur dramatics and

training at RADA. Rep at Bristol Old Vic, Chester, Scottish National Theatre before London West End debut in The Golden Rivet. Films incl: Man in the Wilderness; Rasputin – the Mad Monk; Alfie; Quatermass and the Pit; Mosquito Squadron; Viking Queen; I Start Counting; Because of the Cat; The Tamarind Seed; The Tip Off; The Spy Who Loved Me; The Long Goodbye. First TV in 1963 and claims to have been in every type of production except a Western. TV incl: Persuasion; Vanity Fair; Villette; The Tenant of Wildfell Hall; A Family at War; Desert War; Special Branch; The Avengers; Strange Report; Softly, Softly; Z Cars; The Forsyte Saga; Country Matters; A Place to Die; Rooms; My Good Woman; Sam and the River; Warship; Spawn; Out; The Professionals; The Mourning Brooch; Murder at the Wedding. m. Vicki, 3 s. Sean, Paul, Joshua. Address: c/o Duncan Heath Associates Ltd, London W8. Starsign: Taurus. Hobby: football.

MARSHALL, Peter

Presenter/interviewer
b. 11.4.45 Londonderry. After studying drama at the Arts Educational Trust and the Guildhall School of Music and Drama, became announcer/presenter with Ulster TV 1967-69. Moved to Anglia TV 1970-73 to work on

About Anglia; About Women; Sports Desk; Police Call; newsreader and presenter of several special programmes, such as Christmas Concert in Brass. After a period of freelance work with various ITV companies, joined Southern TV 1974 and Thames TV as permanent announcer 1976. Also presenter/interviewer Reports West for HTV. Education: St Columb's College, Londonderry; St Joseph's Teachers' Training College, Belfast. Currently taking degree course with Open University. m. Brenda, 1 d. Ruth, 1 s. Richard. Address: c/o Thames TV, London NW1. Starsign: Aries. Hobbies: cycling, swimming, weight training, writing, guitar. Unfulfilled ambition: to survive on an island alone.

MARTELL, Lena

Singer b. 15th May Glasgow. Started singing with her brother's band when she was 12. Sang with another band in Glasgow before going to London and winning a talent contest at Hammersmith Palais which got her an engagement in a club. She was spotted by George Elrick

who has managed her ever since. That was about 12 years ago; has since appeared in all the best clubs in Britain, the London Palladium, London's Festival Hall, and in Hong Kong, South Africa, Australia and Canada. Has also made five TV series for BBC and appeared as guest on many programmes. Recorded 15 albums which have earned her one platinum, three gold and several silver discs. Latest LP is Lena's Music, the title of her last TV series. Has written more than 30 songs. Education: Glasgow School of Art. Address: c/o George Elrick, London W8. Starsign: Taurus. Hobbies: painting, golf, song-writing.

MARTIN, Phil

Reporter/announcer
b. 30.4.43 London. Started with pirate radio stations, Radio England and Britain Radio 1966. Then went into newspaper journalism as staff reporter with Daily Express 1967-78. Became a presenter with Radio Newcastle 1978 and joined Tyne Tees TV 1979 as Northern Life reporter and announcer. Education: University College School, Hampstead; Bristol University. m. Penny, 2 d. Jennifer, Susi, 1 s. Tom. Address: Gosforth, Newcastle upon Tyne. Starsign: Taurus. Hobbies: country strolls, admiring others' gardens, collecting bric-a-brac. Unfulfilled ambition: 'to be able to choose when I retire'.

MARTYN, Nicky
Comedian b. 14.11.40
Warrington, Lancs. Began as
a musician/singer in
Warrington, later establishing
himself as a comedy
entertainer. Breakthrough
came in the initial series of
ATV's New Faces. He was the
winner of his programme and
went on to host all the
Winners Shows including the
grand finale at the London
Palladium. Other TV incl:
guest appearances in many
other TV shows; The Summer
Show; It's a Grand Life if You
Don't Weaken. Education:
Redhill Junior, Birmingham;
Silver Street School,
Warrington; Bewsy
Secondary Modern,
Warrington; Warrington
Technical College.
m. Edwina, 1 d. Philippa,
1 s. David. Address: c/o The
Neil Johnson Theatrical
Agency, Warrington.
Starsign: Scorpio. Hobby:
do-it-yourself. Unfulfilled
ambition: to star in a film.

MASSEY, Anna
Actress b. 11.8.37
Thakeham, Surrey. Always
wanted to be an actress.
Became a star overnight

when 17 in her first part in The
Reluctant Debutante. Other
theatre incl.: Dear
Delinquent; The School for
Scandal; The Right
Honourable Gentleman; The
Flip Side; The Elder
Statesman; The Miracle
Worker; The Prime of Miss
Jean Brodie; Donkey's Years;
Heartbreak House; Jingo.
Films incl: Vault of Horror;
Frenzy. Many TV plays and
series incl: The Green of the
Year; The Pallisers; Couples;
Rebecca. Education: mainly
private school in London, but
also in America and
Switzerland and with private
families in Paris and Rome.
m. actor Jeremy Brett (dis),
1 s. David. Address: Fulham,
London. Starsign: Leo.

MATHIAS, Glyn
ITN Home Affairs
correspondent b. 19.2.45
South Wales. Started as a
reporter on South Wales
Echo before joining BBC at
Southampton. Political
correspondent for ITN 1973
and Home Affairs
correspondent since 1979.
Education: Llandovery
College; Jesus College,
Oxford; Southampton
University. m. Sian,
1 d. Megan, 1 s. Mathew.
Address: c/o ITN, London
W1. Starsign: Pisces.
Hobbies: squash, walking,
reading, talking.

MATTHEWS, Francis
Actor b. 2.9.31 York. Started
his career at Leeds Rep when
he was 17. Service in the
Royal Navy then more rep

including Oxford and
Bromley. From the latter he
was chosen for a leading role
in No Escape with Flora
Robson and subsequently in
Bhowani Junction with Ava
Gardner. Radio incl: Not in
Front of the Children; Local
Time; Stop the World; Double
Trouble. First TV of note was
in Francis Durbridge serial,
My Friend Charles; has since
been in many films and over
200 TV plays or series.
Probably best known as TV's
Paul Temple. Other TV incl: A
Little Big Business; My Man
Joe; Trinity Tales;
Middlemen; Roof Over My
Head; Don't Forget to Write;
Morecambe and Wise
Christmas Shows 1971 and
1978; Leslie Crowther
Scrapbook. Education: St
Michael's Jesuit College,
Leeds. m. actress Angela
Browne, 3 s. Paul, Dominic,
Damien. Address: c/o
Richard Stone, London WC2.
Starsign: Virgo. Hobbies:
writing, tennis, cricket.

MATTHEWS, Jessie OBE
Actress/singer b. 11.3.07
London. One of a family of 11,
she made her dancing debut
in Bluebell in Fairyland when

she was 10 and subsequently became the singing, dancing sweetheart of the Twenties and Thirties with such stage and film hits as Wild Rose; Evergreen; Charlot and Cochran revues in London and America; The Good Companions; It's Love Again; Climbing High. She was 16 when she made her American debut in New York in a Charlot revue. After the war she turned more to straight drama and had many successes in rep and on tour and a season at Bristol Old Vic until 1963 when she became radio's Mrs Dale in Mrs Dale's Diary until the serial ended in 1969. Has visited Australia twice to star in Larger Than Life and Janus. Films incl: The Hound of the Baskervilles. Recent TV appearances (also in Canada) incl: Nanny's Boy; The Good Old Days; The Nicest Man in the World; Edward and Mrs Simpson; Winter Ladies. Autobiography: Over My Shoulder. Education: Pulteney Girls School, Soho, London. m. (1st) actor Henry Lytton (dis), (2nd) actor Sonnie Hale (dis), (3rd) Brian Lewis (dis) 1 adopted d. Catherine (now Countess Grixoni). Address: c/o CCA, London SW6. Starsign: Pisces. Hobbies: sewing, reading, swimming, shooting, riding. Unfulfilled ambition: 'to appear in a Shakespearean production – definitely'.

MATTHEWS, Stephen
Political and current affairs journalist b. 1.2.46 Torquay. Trained on North Devon Journal-Herald and BBC radio before joining Westward TV to present Westward Report; editor Politics West, Westward Report and Summer of 79. Political interviewer. Education: Torquay Grammar. m. Diana,

1 d. Victoria, 1 s. Richard. Address: Wembury, Plymouth. Starsign: Aquarius. Hobbies: gliding, powered flying, sailing. Unfulfilled ambitions: to report an American election during the week and go gliding in Texas at the week-end.

MAYNARD, Bill
Actor b. 8.10.28 Farnham, Surrey. Always wanted to be an actor, but started in Variety. A season at Skegness Butlin's with Terry Scott led to the TV series Great Scott – It's Maynard for which they were teamed and made stars. But Bill wanted to act so was off TV for 10 years. First play was a thriller, You Too Can Have a Body, at Worthing. Also acted at Nottingham and with other reps and pantomime. First film: Till Death Us Do Part. Other films incl: Hitler: My Part in His Downfall; Confessions of a Pop Performer. Best known for his TV work which incl: Coronation Street; The Life of Riley; Paper Roses; Kisses at Fifty; Oh, No, It's Selwyn Frogitt; Paradise Island; Bill

Maynard in Person. Books incl: The Yo-Yo Man (autobiography). Education: Kibworth Beauchamps Grammar School. m. Muriel, 1 d. Jane, 1 s. Martin. Address: c/o Richard Stone, London WC2. Starsign: Libra. Hobbies: snooker, golf, watching other people (ie his friends) work! Unfulfilled ambition: 'I quote from Shaw: To have an unfulfilled ambition is the last refuge of a failure'.

MAYNARD, Patricia
Actress b. 16.2.42 Beighton, nr Sheffield. Trained at Guildhall School of Music and Drama. Films incl: Last Days of Hitler. TV incl: General Hospital; Within These Walls; The Sweeney; This Year, Next Year; Crown Court. Education: comprehensive. m. actor Dennis Waterman, 2 d. Hannah, Julia. Address: c/o Peter Browne Management, London SW9. Starsign: Aquarius.

MAXINE, Brian
Professional wrestler/ singer/ song-writer b. 13th August Liverpool. Former boxer. Trained to championship

standard by ex-British heavyweight champion Billy Robinson. Former undefeated welterweight champion of Great Britain; current British middleweight champion. Taught himself to play guitar; three LPs to date; one, I'm Your Man, with all words and music written by him. Recently had some of his songs accepted for recording by American country singer, Waylon Jennings. Education: Grange Secondary Modern, Ellesmere Port. m. Mary, 1 d. Clare, 2 s. Kevin, John. Address: c/o Showcase Music, London W2. Starsign: Leo. Hobbies: all indoor and outdoor sports, all types of music. Unfulfilled ambitions: to win a world wrestling title; to get into the Top 20 and go on Top of the Pops with Legs and Co and receive a gold disc to go with the wrestling gold belt and crown.

MAY, Julie
Actress b. 10.4.27 London. Experience with amateur Gilbert and Sullivan societies, the Tower and Unity Theatres, London. West End stage appearances incl: Lionel Bart's Blitz; old-time music hall. TV incl: many Ken Loach productions, incl Cathie Come Home; Up the Junction; Coming Out Party; In Two Minds. Also People Like Us; A Horseman Riding By; Crime and Punishment; The Fox; Family Affair; Saturday Party; The Country Party. Films incl: Work Is A Four-letter Word; Hot

Millions; No Hard Feelings; A Family Affair; The Stick-up; The Staircase. Education: City of London School for Girls; Willesden Art School; Central School of Art and Crafts (Pictorial Metal Engraving). m. actor Will Stampe. Address: c/o Sonny Zahl Associates, London W1. Starsign: Aries. Hobbies: antiques dealing and restoration, metal engraving, avidly watching TV. Unfulfilled ambition: 'to win sufficient money on the Pools or Premium Bonds, thus helping my husband realise his ambitions'.

McBRIDE, Hazel
Actress b. 24.3.49 Enfield, Middx. No formal training for the stage. Experience at Hull, Billingham, Bolton, Bristol Old Vic, Sheffield, Croydon and Windsor. Also Tarantara, Tarantara in London's West End. Films incl: Fear at Layton Cross; Van Der Valk; Space 1999. Radio incl: Dr Finlay's Casebook; Lord Peter Wimsey. TV incl: Edward the Seventh; Within These Walls; The Man Who Liked Elephants; Dickens of London; Sutherland's Law; General Hospital; Survivors; MacKinnons; The Big H; Secret Army. Education: Queen Elizabeth's Grammar School, Barnet; Bristol University (BA history). m. teacher James Mason. Address: c/o Carole James Management, Richmond, Surrey. Starsign: Aries. Hobbies: horse-riding, swimming, walking, painting.

McCALLUM, David
Actor b. 19.9.33 Glasgow. After training at RADA went into rep and, in 1957, was given a seven year film contract with the Rank Organisation. Films incl: Billy Budd; Freud; The Great Escape; The Greatest Story Ever Told; Mosquito Squadron; Frankenstein; King Solomon's Treasure. While making The Greatest Story Ever Told was picked for TV series, The Man From UNCLE, in which he appeared for four years and won international fame. Other TV incl: Colditz; The Adventures of the Invisible Man; Kidnapped; Sapphire and Steel. Also directed an episode of Explorers. Education: University College School, London. m. (1st) actress Jill Ireland (dis), (2nd) fashion model Katherine Carpenter, 1 d. Sophie, 4 s. Paul, Jason, Valentine, Peter. Address: Beverly Hills, California. Starsign: Virgo. Hobby: cosmology.

McDONALD, Trevor
Journalist/broadcaster b. 16.8.39 San Fernando, Trinidad. At the age of 20

started reporting for local radio stations in Trinidad. Went on to become announcer, sports commentator and assistant programme manager. Joined Trinidad TV in 1962. Came to London in 1969 to join BBC World Service. Joined ITN as a reporter in 1971 and since then has frequently been seen as a newscaster. Education: won a college scholarship. m. Beryl, 1 d. Joanne, 1 s. Timothy. Address: c/o ITN, London W1. Starsign: Leo. Hobbies: collecting books (especially interested in political biographies), international politics, philosophy.

McENERY, Peter
Actor/director b. 21.2.40 Walsall. Studied drama while at school and joined Brighton Pier Theatre at the age of 16. Played in rep at Brighton and Peterborough and then became a member of the Royal Shakespeare Company. Stage incl: Flowering Cherry; Romeo and Juliet; Merchant of Venice; The Jew of Malta; The Seagull; The Devils; Rosencrantz and Guildenstern Are Dead; Hamlet; Ashes; The Diary of Albie Sachs; Pericles. Films incl: The Fighting Prince of Donegal; The Moon Spinners; The Game is Over; Entertaining Mr Sloane; Negatives; The Adventures of Gerard; The Atlantic War. TV incl: Candida; Progress to the Park; Omnibus; Clayhanger; The Aphrodite

Inheritance. Education: Walsall and Hove schools. m. Julie. Address: c/o Fraser and Dunlop, London W1. Starsign: Pisces. Hobbies: squash, skiing (water and snow), war gaming.

McEWAN, Geraldine
Actress b. 9.5.32 Old Windsor. Always wanted to be an actress but started in an office and got a few walk-on parts at Windsor Rep. Was assistant stage manager at 16 and her first juvenile lead at 17. First success a year later in Who Goes There? Six years with the National Theatre and with the Royal Shakespeare Company at Stratford. Other stage work incl: For Better For Worse; The Member of the Wedding; The Entertainer; Dear Love; The Little Hut; Oh, Coward; On Approval; Look After Lulu. TV incl: The Witch; Candida; Separate Tables; Pandora; We're Strangers Here; Hopcraft Into Europe; The Statue and the Rose; The Prime of Miss Jean Brodie. Education: Windsor High School. m. Hugh Cruttwell, Principal of RADA, 1 d. Claudia, 1 s. Gregory. Address: Barnes, London. Starsign: Taurus.

McGEE, Henry
Actor b. 14.5.29 Kensington, London. Trained at Italia Conti School then Open Air Theatre, Regent's Park. Rep at Northampton, Leatherhead and tour of Australia. Appeared in many TV plays and series; No

Hiding Place; Emergency – Ward 10; Softly, Softly; Z Cars; The Avengers and Feydeau farces, before becoming one of the best straight men in the business for many comics incl: Tommy Cooper; Frankie Howerd; Dickie Henderson; Benny Hill. TV incl: Up the Workers; Rising Damp; No – That's Me Over Here! (Ronnie Corbett); The Worker (Charlie Drake). Education: Stonehurst. Address: c/o Margery Armstrong, London SW1. Starsign: Taurus. Hobbies: gliding, sailing, collecting old prints and engravings.

McGUGAN, Stuart
Actor b. 2.3.44 Stirling, Scotland. Three years as a journalist before going to Royal Scottish Academy of Dramatic Art, Glasgow. Then rep seasons at Canterbury, Newcastle, Leeds, Royal Shakespeare Company, American Conservancy Theatre, San Francisco. TV incl: Anne of Avonlea; Beasts; Oil Strike North; Six Days of Justice; Rob Roy; Man of Straw; The Mourning Brooch; It Ain't Half Hot, Mum; regular presenter

Playschool. Stage incl:
Bedroom Farce; The
Crucible. Education: Forfar
Academy, Angus. m. Annie.
Address: Worlingworth,
Suffolk. Starsign: Pisces.
Hobbies: growing flowers
and vegetables; running;
renovating cottages.
Unfulfilled ambitions: to
brillantly play the lead in the
most artistically and
commercially successful TV
series known to mankind; to
finish renovating the
above-mentioned cottage.

MacKAY, Colin
Political editor Scottish TV
b. 27.8.44 Glasgow.
Researcher/reporter with
Border TV 1967-70, politics
reporter Grampian TV
1970-73 and political editor
STV since 1973. Presents
weekly politics programme,
Ways and Means;
anchorman for General
Elections and other special
programmes and,
occasionally, non-political
in-depth interviews (incl:
Sophia Loren and Kingman
Brewster, the US
Ambassador) called From
the Top. Education:
Kelvinside Academy,
Glasgow; Glasgow
University (MA Hons
English). Address: c/o
Scottish TV, Glasgow.
Starsign: Virgo. Hobbies:
music (especially opera),
reading, talking.

McKELLAR, Kenneth
Singer/composer/ writer
b. 23.6.27 Paisley, Scotland.
Gave his first concert in a

local hall when 13. Continued
singing while at school,
university and during his first
two years working in forestry.
Eventually gave up forestry
as singing was taking up too
much time. Has made many
records of classical and
popular music, and has done
many tours, especially
Australia and New Zealand.
Has appeared a number of
times at the London
Palladium and made the
sound track for the film The
Great Waltz. Is a director of
Radio Clyde. TV incl: Night
Music; The Rolf Harris Show;
The Good Old Days; At Home
With Kenneth McKellar;
Kenneth McKellar at Home.
Education: John Neilson
Grammar School; Aberdeen
University (BSc Forestry).
m. Hedy, 1 d. Jane,
1 s. Kenneth. Address:
Lenzie, Scotland. Starsign:
Cancer. Hobbies: cooking,
reading.

McKENZIE, Julia
Actress b. 17.2.42 Enfield,
Middx. Trained at the
Guildhall School of Music
and Drama. Great deal of TV
experience incl: World of
Jerome Kern; Andre Previn
Talks to Stephen Sondheim;
The Two Ronnies; John Curry
Special; Song by Song by Ira
Gershwin; Frost's Weekly;
Stanley Baxter Big Picture
Show; Celebrity Squares;
Roy Hudd Show; Battle of the
Sexes; Mike Douglas Show
(coast to coast in America);
Russell Harty Show; Maggie
and Her. Education:
Tottenham County School.

m. actor/director Jerry Harte.
Address: c/o April Young,
London WC2. Starsign:
Aquarius. Hobbies: cooking,
the theatre. Unfulfilled
ambitions: to do a drama
series and play Annie Oakley
in Annie Get Your Gun.

McKERN, Leo
Actor b. 16.3.20 Sydney,
Australia. Trained as an
electrical engineer. Spent
two and a half years in the
army before coming to
England in 1946 to follow the
girl he eventually married.
Three years with the Old Vic,
two years with the Royal
Shakespeare Company.
Then sold his home and
possessions and returned
with his family to Australia
after filming Ryan's
Daughter. Came back to
work here. Theatre incl: Rollo;
Othello; A Man for All
Seasons; (London and New
York); Crime and
Punishment. TV incl: The
Prisoner; The Sun is God; On
the Eve of Publication; An
Afternoon at the Festival;
Rumpole of the Bailey.
Education: Sydney Technical
High. m. actress Jane
Holland, 2 d. Abigail, Harriet.

Address: Oxfordshire.
Starsign: Pisces. Hobbies:
sailing, swimming, ecology,
environment preservation.

McMANUS, Mark
Actor b. 1940 Hamilton,
Lanarkshire. After leaving
school had a number of jobs
before going to Australia,
1960, where he drifted into
acting and spent 10 years
there as an actor. Returned to
England and joined the Royal
Court Theatre and the
National Theatre. TV incl:
Colditz; Crown Court; The
Brothers; Sam; The
Foundation. m. Paulette,
1 d. Kate, 1 step-s.
Christopher. Address: c/o
ATV, Birmingham.

McMANUS, Mick
Professional wrestler b. 11th
January London. Trained at
John Ruskin Amateur
Wrestling Club, London, and
since then has literally fought
his way to the top. The man
viewers love to hate has been
British Welterweight
Champion twice and was
recently European
Middleweight Champion.
Collects antiques and, apart
from the wrestling ring,

recent TV has included
Celebrity Squares.
Education: Wilson's
Grammar School, London.
m. Barbara, 1 s. Tony.
Address: c/o Dale Martin Ltd,
London SW9. Starsign:
Capricorn. Hobby: golf.
Unfulfilled ambition: 'to be a
golf pro (no chance!)'.

McQUARRIE, Dermot
Reporter b. 21.11.48
Greenock, Renfrewshire.
Experience with Gibraltar
Broadcasting Corporation,
BBC and Grampian TV
before joining Scottish TV,
Glasgow. World TV exclusive
on the blow-out at the Bravo
platform in the Ekofisk oilfield,
North Sea. The documentary,
Blow-out At Bravo was
nominated for the Best
Actuality Filming Award by
British Academy. Education:
St Joseph's College,
Dumfries. m. Elizabeth,
3 d. Catherine, Louise,
Roseleen, 2 s. Jonathan,
Robert. Address: Rutherglen,
Glasgow. Starsign: Scorpio.
Hobbies: squash, golf,
gardening. Unfulfilled
ambition: to make
documentaries in Middle
East, Arctic and Antarctic.

MELFORD, Jill
Actress b. 23.11.34 London.
Theatrical family background
and an experienced interior
decorator. Evacuated to
America during the war.
Theatre debut in New York
1949 as dancer in Oklahoma!
First London appearance
1953 in The Seven Year Itch.
Other stage plays incl: Auntie

Mame; Ulysses in Night-time;
The Life of the Party; The
Right Honourable
Gentleman; There's a Girl in
My Soup; Not Now, Darling;
Best of Friends; A Touch of
Spring; The Chairman. Films
incl: The Servant; Father,
Dear Father. TV inc: The
Organisation; The Life of
Victor Hugo; A Pin to See the
Peepshow; Ring Round the
Moon; Crossroads.
Education: Gardner School,
New York; Ballet Arts School,
New York. m. actor John
Standing (dis),
1 s. Alexander. Address: c/o
CCA, London SW6. Starsign:
Sagittarius. Hobby: work.
Unfulfilled ambition: to be a
millionairess.

MELLOR, Frank
Journalist b. 24.7.27
Warrington. Newspaper
training on weeklies,
evenings, national dailies,
and news agency work
before radio and TV incl:
Country Concerns; Fells,
Becks and Seashores; The
Other Man's Shoes; Look
North/Nationwide; Home
Ground; Network. Education:
grammar school (and court
reporting). m. Edie,
1 d. Susan. Address: c/o

BBC, Manchester. Starsign: Leo. Hobbies: game fishing; fell walking; the countryside; wine making. Unfulfilled ambition: to find time to write a book.

MERCIER, Shelia
Actress b. 1.1.19 Hull. Started stage career with Sir Donald Wolfit's company as did her brother, Brian Rix. Was WAAF adjutant during the war. Joined Brian's Whitehall Theatre company 1955 and was with him 11 years. Has played Annie Sugden in Emmerdale Farm since the programme started 1972. Education: French Convent, Hull; Hunmanby Hall, Yorks. m. theatrical manager Peter Mercier. 1 s. Nigel. Address: c/o Yorkshire TV, Leeds. Starsign: Capricorn. Hobbies: reading, sewing, dancing, tennis. Unfulfilled ambition: to have had a large family.

METCALFE, Adrian
Producer/commentator b. 2.3.42 Bradford, Yorks. Former news reporter on the Sunday Express and a member of the World of Sport team since the programme started. In 1961 was the fastest runner in the world over 400 metres (45.7 secs), a record that stood for 10 years. Former member of the British 4 by 400 metres relay team that won silver medals at both the Commonwealth Games and European Championships in 1962 and at the Tokyo Olympics in 1964. In 1963 he won a double gold in the World Student Games. He was ITV athletics commentator at the 1968 and 1972 Olympics. Has produced over 100 documentaries and over 300 outside broadcasts. Education: Roundhay School, Leeds; Brunt's Grammar, Mansfield; Magdalen College, Oxford. m. TV production assistant Anne Summerton, 1 d. Hannah, 1 s.Daniel. Address: c/o World of Sport, London Weekend TV, London SE1. Starsign: Pisces. Hobbies: physical self-rehabilitation, food and drink. Unfulfilled ambition: total physical self-rehabilitation.

MICHAEL, Ralph
Actor b. 26.9.07 London. His training was performances in eight Shakespearean plays a week on tour in England and fortnightly modern rep for five years in various theatres. Also acted in America and most European countries. Has appeared in scores of stage, film and TV roles. Performed in live TV at Alexandra Palace and Lime Grove from 1945. Has been in productions on all three channels, incl: Pirandello's Henry IV; Six Characters in Search of an Author; The Cocktail Party; and the Lord Chief Justice in Henry IV, Part 2. Education: Bembridge School, Isle of Wight. m. (1st) Fay Compton (dis), (2nd) actress Joyce Heron (dis), (3rd) actress Jain Cameron, 2 d. Joanna (from 2nd m), Arabella (from 3rd m). Address: London SW6. Starsign: Libra. Hobbies: writing, painting, swimming, playing squash and golf. Unfulfilled ambition: to be famous.

MICHELLE, Ann
Actress b. 11.8.52 Chigwell, Essex. Trained at Aida Foster Stage School. Experience largely in films and TV. Films inc: The Virgin Witches; Psychomania; Mistress Pamela; House of Whipcord; The Glass Cage; Young Lady Chatterley; A Place Beyond. TV incl: Out; The Greatest Thinkers; Come Back, Mrs Noah; Tarbuck's Luck; The Liver Birds. Education: Knewnham College Primary; West Hatch Technical High. m. Eddie Reeves. 1 s. Eddie. Address: c/o Aida Foster Ltd, London NW8. Starsign: Leo. Hobbies: motor cycling, fishing, swimming, singing, dancing, jogging. Unfulfilled ambitions: to star in an epic film and to direct films.

MICHELLE, Vicki
Actress b. 14.12.50 Chigwell, Essex. Elder sister of Ann (see above entry).

Also trained at Aida Foster Stage School and considerable experience of films and TV. Films incl: The Virgin Witches; Poor Bill Render; Supervisor's Progress; Alfie Darling; On the Crest of a Wave; The Sentinel; Queen Kong. TV incl: The Professionals; Come Back, Mrs Noah; Surprise, Surprise; The Goodies; The Les Dawson Show; The Dick Emery Show; The Two Ronnies; Space 1999; The Ken Dodd Show; Softly, Softly; Whatever Happened to the Likely Lads?; Task Force; Sporting Scenes. Education: West Hatch Technical High. m. Graham Fowler. Address: c/o Aida Foster Ltd, London NW8. Starsign: Sagittarius. Hobbies: squash, yoga, swimming, running. Unfulfilled ambition: to be an accomplished actress.

MICHELMORE, Cliff CBE
Commentator/presenter
b. 11.12.19 Cowes, Isle of Wight. Service in RAF, then with British Forces Network in Germany 1947-49 when he joined BBC to produce, direct and write for children's TV. Sports commentaries from 1951 and a nightly interview programme 1955-57. Countless appearances on BBC and ITV programmes incl: Tonight (1957-64); 24 Hours (1964-68); Our World (first world linked satellite programme 1967); Holiday (since 1969); space programmes; general elections; Talkback; Wheelbase; Chance to Meet; Across the Great Divide; Opinions Unlimited; A Ripe Old Age; Let's Pretend; People's Choice; Fleet Air Arm. Still remembered as presenter of Family Favourites from Hamburg on radio through which he met his wife who introduced the London side of the programme. Education: Cowes High; Loughborough College; Leicester College of Technology. m. broadcaster Jean Metcalfe, 1 d. Jenny, 1 s. Guy. Address: Whitehouse, Reigate, Surrey. Starsign: Sagittarius. Hobbies: golf and sitting around. Unfulfilled ambition: to keep working.

MIDDLEMASS, Frank
Actor b. 28.5.19 Eaglescliffe, Co Durham. Always wanted to be an actor and after nine years in the army, and without acting training, joined a rep company in Penzance in 1948. Other rep with Harry Hanson companies and at Oldham, Sheffield and, for a number of years, with the Old Vic in Bristol and London, touring with them in Russia, Poland, North and South America, Australia and New Zealand. Recent London West End stage incl: Little Boxes; Spitting Image; King Lear; Widowers' Houses; Rosmersholm. Also a national tour of Great Expectations. Films incl: Otley; Barry Lyndon; The Island. Numerous TV appearances incl: War and Peace; Arturo Ui; Kean; Me! I'm Afraid of Virginia Woolf; Measure For Measure; The Oresteia; A Family Affair; Crime and Punishment; and such series as Poldark; Emmerdale Farm; Raffles; Crown Court. Education: St Cuthbert's, Middlesbrough. Address: c/o Vernon Conway Ltd, London SW11. Starsign: Gemini. Hobbies: crosswords, Scrabble, talking.

MILLER, Graham
Presenter/reporter
b. 22.11.51 London. Newspapers, BBC Radio and Anglia TV before joining HTV. Presenter/reporter of HTV's Report West. Education: 'still learning', he says. Address: c/o HTV West, Bristol. Starsign: Sagittarius. Hobbies: sport, driving, music, listening, reading, judging beauty competitions. Unfulfilled ambition: to score a century at Lords.

MILLER, Mick
Comedian b. 25.2.50 Liverpool. Former goalkeeper for Port Vale FC. Turned to comedy and established himself in clubs

and theatres. Big
breakthrough on TV in The
Comedians, 1979.
Specialises in fast one-line
gags. m. Diana. Address: c/o
Forrester George, London
W1. Starsign: Pisces.
Hobbies: football, collecting
clowns. Unfulfilled ambition:
to have own TV series.

MILLIGAN, Spike
Actor/comedian/author
b. 16.4.18 Ahmaddnagar,
India. Spent early life in India,
Burma and Ceylon where his
father was in the army. Came
to Britain 1933. Started as
singer and trumpeter
1936-39, later guitarist.
Professional debut in Naples
1945. Radio debut,
Opportunity Knocks 1949.
Since then radio incl: Crazy
People (which eventually
became the Goon Show and
brought him fame); The Last
Goon Show of All. TV incl:
Idiot's Weekly; A Show Called
Fred; Son of Fred; Milligan at
Large; Milligan's Wake;
Muses With Milligan; The
World of Beachcomber; Q5;
Curry And Chips; The Other
Spike; Comedy Machine; Q6;
The Muppets; Q7; The Best of
British; Q8; Q9. Theatre incl:

Treasure Island; The
Bed-Sitting Room (and film);
Son of Oblomov; For One
Week Only. Films incl: The
Running, Jumping and
Standing Still Film; Watch
Your Stern; Suspect;
Postman's Knock; The Magic
Christian; The Great
McGonagall. Records:
Russian Love Song; The Ying
Tong Song; I'm Walking
Backwards For Christmas;
The Goons; The Snow
Goose. Books incl: Puckoon;
Adolf Hitler: My Part in His
Downfall; The Goon Show
Scripts; Small Dream of a
Scorpion; Badjelly the Witch;
Rommel? Gunner Who?; The
Spike Milligan Letters; Monty
– His Part in my Victory;
Mussolini – His Part in my
Downfall. Education:
Christian Brothers de la Salle,
Rangoon; London
Polytechnic. m. (1st) June
(dis), (2nd) singer Patricia
Ridgway (dec), 3 d. Laura,
Sile (from 1st m), Jane (from
2nd m), 1 s. Sean (from
1st m). Address: c/o Spike
Milligan Productions, London
W2. Starsign: Aries. Hobbies:
painting, restoring antiques.

MILLS, Sir John CBE
Actor b. 22.2.08 Felixstowe,
Suffolk. A star for nearly 50
years, started his career in
musical comedy (Mr Cinders;
Jill Darling; etc), then
progressed to more serious
roles. Stage incl: Charley's
Aunt (twice); Cavalcade;
Ross (New York); and more
recently, Veterans; At the End
of the Day; The Good
Companions; Great

Expectations; Separate
Tables. First film The
Midshipmaid with Jessie
Matthews 1931, since when
he has been in about 100
films incl: We Dive at Dawn;
The Way to the Stars; Great
Expectations; Scott of the
Antarctic; The History of Mr
Polly; Oh What a Lovely War;
Hobson's Choice; The
Colditz Story; Above Us the
Waves; Dunkirk; Ice Cold in
Alex; I Was Monty's Double;
Tiger Bay; Tunes of Glory;
Ryan's Daughter (for which
he received an Oscar);
Young Winston; Oklahoma
Crude; The Human Factor;
Trial by Combat; The Devil's
Advocate; The Thirty-Nine
Steps; The Big Sleep; Zulu
Dawn. TV incl: The Zoo Gang;
Roald Dahl's Tales of the
Unexpected (Galloping
Foxley); Quatermass.
Education: Norwich. m. (1st)
Aileen Raymond (dis), (2nd)
playwright Mary Hayley Bell,
2 d. actresses Juliet and
Hayley, 1 s. Jonathan.
Address: c/o ICM, London
W1. Starsign: Pisces.
Hobbies: painting, reading,
writing, staying at home.
Unfulfilled ambition: to stay at
home.

MILNE, John
Reporter/presenter
b. 13.5.42 Dundee.
Journalistic background with
D C Thomson Press, Dundee
and The Scotsman,
Edinburgh. Worked for the
Swiss Broadcasting Corpn in
Berne, before joining BBC in
Glasgow. Radio and TV
experience. TV incl:

Reporting Scotland/
Nationwide; Current
Account; Tuesday/Thursday
Night. Education: Harris
Academy, Dundee.
m. Jennifer, 2 s. Grigor,
Jonathan. Address: c/o BBC,
Glasgow. Starsign: Taurus.
Hobbies: squash, reading,
watching football. Unfulfilled
ambition: to have time to
think.

MONKHOUSE, Bob
Entertainer b. 1.6.28
Beckenham, Kent. Freelance
cartoonist from age of 12,
drawing comic strips and
writing short stories. Sold first
jokes to Max Miller in 1944.
Trained as cartoon film
animator with
Gaumont-British when 17½.
Conscripted into RAF 1946.
First radio broadcast in
Works Wonders; first TV: New
To You, both in 1948.
Became BBC's first contract
comedian. With ex-Dulwich
schoolfriend Denis Goodwin
(d.1975) formed a
script-writing team and
together they scripted
thousands of radio and TV
comedy shows for Arthur
Askey, Bob Hope, Jack
Benny, Jack Buchanan and
themselves. For a year they
wrote up to seven weekly
shows simultaneously.
London West End debut as
compere of Sauce Piquante,
1950. Stage also incl: Bob
Monkhouse Startime
(Blackpool); pantomimes;
Boys from Syracuse; Come
Blow Your Horn. Films incl:
Carry On, Sergeant; Dentist
in the Chair; Dentist on the

Job; Weekend With Lulu;
She'll Have to Go. Recent
radio incl: Punchline. TV
series incl: What's My Line?;
Do You Trust Your Wife?; My
Pal Bob; The Big Noise;
Candid Camera; For Love or
Money; Sunday Night at the
London Palladium; Mad
Movies; The Golden Shot
(1967-74); Celebrity Squares
(1974-79); I'm Bob – He's
Dickie; Bonkers! Works
principally as TV host and
cabaret attraction. Describes
himself as 'a standup
comedian'. Education:
Grange School, Beckenham;
Goring Hall, Goring-by-Sea;
Dulwich College.
m. (1st) Elizabeth (dis);
(2nd) secretary Jacqueline,
1 adopted d. Abigail
2 s. Gary, Simon. Address:
c/o Peter Pritchard Ltd,
London SW1. Starsign:
Gemini. Hobbies: collecting
vintage films, esp. silent
comedies; collecting original
artwork by great cartoonists,
esp. historic characters
(Popeye, Krazy Kat, Pogo,
etc). Unfulfilled ambition: a
dramatic film role.

MONTGOMERY, James
Reporter b. 16.9.45
Wimbledon, London. TV
experience in Australia
before joining Southern TV.
Regular presenter/
interviewer Day By Day; 15
documentaries; The Other
Side of Yesterday, a
programme of songs and
music by Montgomery and
sung by Montgomery.
Education: Marlborough
House School; Wellington

College; Magdalen College,
Oxford; The Sorbonne, Paris.
Address: c/o Southern TV,
Southampton. Starsign:
Virgo. Hobbies: swimming,
sunbathing, listening to
music. Unfulfilled ambition: to
conduct Rachmaninov's
Piano Concerto No 2 with
Sviatislav Richter at the
piano.

MOORE, Brian
Commentator b. 28.2.32
Benenden, Kent. Journalistic
experience with World
Sports, Exchange Telegraph,
The Times before joining
BBC then LWT. Compere of
The Big Match, On the Ball
and various ITV football
programmes. Education:
local primary; Cranbrook.
m. Betty, 2 s. Christopher,
Simon. Address: c/o E
Sommerfield, London W1.
Starsign: Pisces. Hobbies:
family life, animals, all sport.
Unfulfilled ambitions: to lead
the life of a country squire; to
find total peace of mind and
security; to do a commentary
on Gillingham (where he is a
director) winning the FA Cup.

MOORE, Dudley
Actor/musician/comedian/

writer b. 19.4.35 London.
Began learning the piano
when eight, the violin at 12
and the organ at 17. After
studying at the Guildhall
School of Music he was at
Magdalen College, Oxford
(1954-58), where he
obtained Bachelor of Arts
and Bachelor of Music
degrees. Joined Vic Lewis
Band and toured America; on
his return wrote incidental
music for Royal Court Theatre
plays and after a spell with
Johnny Dankworth's Band,
went into Beyond the Fringe
in Edinburgh, London and
New York. Stage also incl:
Play It Again, Sam; Behind
the Fridge (Australia, New
Zealand, London); Good
Evening (London, New York
and on tour in USA). Films
incl: 30 is a Dangerous Age,
Cynthia; Bedazzled; Monte
Carlo or Bust; The Bed-Sitting
Room; The Hound of the
Baskervilles; 10; The Ferret;
Foul Play. TV incl: Not Only
. . . But Also; Goodbye Again;
Music from a Cathedral; The
Muppet Show. Records incl:
Once More With Cook; Derek
and Clive (Live); Derek and
Clive Come Again; Strictly for
the Birds; The Clean Tapes
(The Very Best of Peter Cook
and Dudley Moore); The
Music of Dudley Moore.
Education: Dagenham
County High; Magdalen
College, Oxford.
m. (1st) model Suzy Kendall
(dis), (2nd) actress Tuesday
Weld (dis), 1 s. Patrick (from
2nd m). Address: c/o Mrs M
Walker, London SW3.
Starsign: Aries.

MOORE, Patrick OBE
Author/astonomer/ TV
presenter and personality
b. 4.3.23 Pinner, Middx. Was
about to go to university when
Second World War started.
Rigged his RAF medical and
flew as a navigator.
Passionately interested in
astronomy since the age of
six. Elected to the British

Astronomical Association
when he was 11. Has written
many books, including boys'
novels, science fiction and
science fact, incl: the
best-selling Moon Flight Atlas
and Atlas of the Universe. Is a
regular contributor to
magazines and journals. TV
incl: BBC's longest-running
programme, The Sky at Night
(started 1957); One Pair of
Eyes; coverage of various
space shots and many guest
appearances on
programmes such as The
Morecambe and Wise Show;
Face the Music; It's a
Celebrity Knockout; Blankety
Blank. Educated largely by
home tutors because of
childhood illness. Address:
Selsey, Sussex. Starsign:
Pisces. Hobbies: astronomy,
cricket, music, tennis.
Unfulfilled ambition: to be
able to play complicated
pieces by Chopin without
making any mistakes.

MORE, Johnny
Impressionist b. 14.2.34
Hulme, Manchester. Began
as a singer after winning
several talent contests.
Formed guitar/vocal duo and
worked in clubs before

turning solo. Breakthrough
on Opportunity Knocks. TV
incl: guests spots; Who Do
You Do?; Now Who Do You
Do?; London Night Out.
m. Brenda, 1 d. Elizabeth.
Address: c/o Bob Holmes
Management, London W1.
Starsign: Aquarius. Hobbies:
supporting Manchester
United and running his own
waste re-cycling business.
Unfulfilled ambitions: to star
in own TV series; to have a hit
record; to achieve stardom in
America.

MORECAMBE, Eric OBE
b. 14.5.26 Morecambe,
Lancs. Child entertainer and
winner of talent contests at
Morecambe for three
successive years. Booked for
Bryan Michie's Youth Takes a
Bow and met Ernie Wise
1941. Formed a double act
but touring was interrupted
by National Service as a
Bevin Boy in the mines.
Partnership resumed after
the war when both booked for
Lord John Sanger's Variety
Circus. Radio breakthrough
on Workers' Playtime and
own radio series, You're Only
Young Once. TV incl:
Running Wild; variety;
Sunday Night at the London
Palladium; The Morecambe
and Wise Show (BBC and
ITV). Numerous variety,
pantomimes, summer and
royal shows, tours of
Australia and Canada and Ed
Sullivan Show in America.
Films: The Intelligence Men;
That Riviera Touch; The
Magnificent Two. Freeman
City of London 1976; Doctor

of Literature, Lancaster University 1977. Education: Lancaster Road and Euston Road schools, Morecambe. m. Joan, 1 d. Gail, 2 s. Gary, Steven. Address: c/o Billy Marsh, London Management, London W1. Starsign: Taurus. Hobbies: bird-watching, football, fishing, photography. Unfulfilled ambitions: to see Luton win the FA Cup; to have a stretch of his own trout fishing waters.

MORGAN, Cliff
Broadcaster/administrator b. 7.4.30 Trebanog, Wales. One of the greatest fly-halves ever seen, he won 29 caps for Wales in eight seasons and captained the British Lions. Retired from rugby in 1958 and joined BBC Wales as radio sports organiser. Has performed many roles in broadcasting including commentator, quiz leader, disc jockey and director of children's programmes. Editor of Grandstand and Sportsview 1961-65, then editor of This Week. Returned to BBC as freelance, became head of radio outside broadcasts in 1975 and head of TV outside broadcasts later the same year. Recently presented Celebration on TV in which he also interviewed Princes Charles. Has written for Punch and other journals; was made a Druid at the Welsh National Eisteddfod 1979. Education: Tonyrefail Grammar School. m. Nuala, 1 d. Katie, 1 s. Nicholas. Address: c/o BBC, London

W12. Starsign: Aries. Hobby: music.

MORGAN, Garfield
Actor b. 19.4.31 Birmingham. Apprenticed as a dental mechanic before going to a Birmingham drama school. Started acting career with Arena Theatre, Birmingham. Besides acting also directs and was Director of Productions, Marlowe Theatre, Canterbury 1957-58, and at Manchester's Library Theatre 1959-60. Associate Director, Northgate Theatre 1976-78. Associate Director, Nottingham Playhouse 1978. Many plays and films incl: The Pumpkin Eater; The Story of Private Pooley; Perfect Friday. Entered TV in 1955 and has since made hundreds of appearances in such programmes as Softly, Softly; Spindoe; Judge Dee; Randall and Hopkirk (Deceased); Department S; Hadleigh; Dear Mother . . . Love Albert; The Sweeney. Education: 'negligible', he claims. m. Dilys Laye (dis). Address: c/o NEMS Management, London SW3. Starsign: Aries. Hobbies: golf, photography, riding – showjumping and eventing.

MORRIS, Johnny
Journalist/presenter/ entertainer b. 20th June Newport, Mon. While still a farm manager in Wiltshire, auditioned for the BBC using a piece written by himself. Did both jobs then gave up

farming in 1951 to work full time in radio and TV in the West Region of the BBC. Numerous radio plays, news reports and roving reports incl: Pass the Salt; Journeyman Johnny. TV incl: The Chestnut Man; Animal Magic; Johnny's Jaunt. Education: secondary school, Newport. m. Eileen. Address: Shefford Woodlands, Berks. Starsign: Gemini. Hobbies: music, gardening, watching people. Unfulfilled ambition: to play cricket for Gloucestershire.

MORRISON, Fran
Reporter/presenter b. early '50's Glasgow. Former BBC news trainee. Considerable radio and TV experience (producer Radio 4's World at One, news scriptwriter, news reporter). Now freelance. Co-presenter BBC Scotland's current affairs programme, Tuesday Night/ Thursday Night; reporter on Tuesday Documentary on Westminster School; various current affairs films and interviewer for Miss Scotland finalists. Education: St Andrew's University (MA Hons). Address: c/o BBC,

Glasgow. Starsign: Aquarius.
Hobbies: theatre; disco
dancing; horses; films; eating
out; attractive men.
Unfulfilled ambitions: to do
more work for the network; to
make more films abroad; to
have more fun.

MORRISON, Peter
Singing lawyer b. 14.8.40
Greenock, Scotland. A
practising lawyer who has
made a name for himself on
television since 1971, incl:
Castles in the Air: Show of the
North; Songs of Scotland
(1973, 1974, 1976, 1978);
Something to Sing About;
This is Peter Morrison;
various specials for BBC and
STV since 1974. Education:
Greenock Academy;
Glasgow University (MA and
LLB). m. Irene,
1 d. Jacquelyn, 1 s. Richard.
Address: Glasgow. Starsign:
Leo. Hobbies: singing; golf.

MOSLEY, Bryan
Actor b. 25.8.31 Leeds.
Served in the RAF (Air Traffic
Control) before training with
Esme Church Northern
Theatre School 1951-53. Rep
St Andrews, Perth, Derby,
Harrogate, York. Toured with

New Pilgrim Players: York
Mystery Plays 1957. TV:
Armchair Theatre (ABC); Play
of the Week (Anglia); The
Villains; The Planemakers; Z
Cars; Dr Who; The Saint; The
Avengers; No Hiding Place.
Alf Roberts in Coronation
Street since 1961. Many films
inc: Get Carter; Charlie
Bubbles; Far From the
Madding Crowd; A Kind of
Loving; This Sporting Life;
Rattle of a Simple Man.
Expert swordsman and
arranges fights for stage, film
and TV; founder member of
Society of British Fight
Arrangers. Was first actor to
be given special citation as
performer by American TV
and Radio Commercials
Festival (1969). Education:
Leeds Central High; Leeds
College of Art. m. Norma,
3 d. Jacqueline, Simone,
Helen, 3 s. Jonathan,
Bernard, Leonard. Address:
c/o Granada TV, Manchester.
Starsign: Virgo. Hobbies:
painting; drawing; fencing;
swimming; model soldier
making; travel. Unfulfilled
ambitions: to be good in
films; to spend more time
painting; to travel extensively
(preferably working).

MOTSON, John
Sports journalist/TV and radio
commentator b. 10.7.45
Salford, Lancs. Newspaper
experience with Barnet Press
Weekly Newspaper 1963-67
and Morning Telegraph,
Sheffield 1967-68 before
joining BBC Radio 1969-71,
when he went to BBC TV for
whom he has covered two

World Cups (1974, 1978);
commentated on two FA Cup
Finals (1977, 1979) and
reported on two Olympics
(1972, 1976). Probably best
known for his weekly football
commentaries on Match of
the Day, having covered
around 400 matches in eight
seasons for the programme
by the end of 1979.
Wimbledon tennis
commentator for BBC radio
1976-79. While a junior
reporter won two awards
from National Council for the
Training of Journalists – first
all-round performance in first
year exams, and a national
prize in the Proficiency
Certificate exams. Books:
Second to None; The History
of the European Cup (with
John Rowlinson). Education:
Culford School, Bury St
Edmunds. m. Anne.
Address: c/o BBC, London
W14. Starsign: Cancer.
Hobbies: reading, playing
sport, cinema, pop music,
jogging. Unfulfilled ambition:
to host a radio show of old
pop records.

MOULT, Ted
Farmer/writer/broadcaster
b. 11.2.26 Derby. Primarily a
farmer, but equally well
known to viewers as a
broadcaster on panel
games, quiz shows and
schools programmes. TV
incl: Target; What's My Line?;
Playschool; Blankety Blank;
Celebrity Squares.
Education: Derby School.
m. Marie Rose, 3 d. Anne,
Amelia, Ellen, 3 s. William,
Thomas, Patrick. Address:

Ticknell, Derby. Starsign: Aquarius. Hobby: 'thinking about what I'm going to do tomorrow'.

MOUNT, Peggy
Actress b. 2.5.18 Southend-on-Sea. Started as a secretary, but always wanted to be an actress. Many amateur shows before turning professional with Harry Hanson rep company. Many years in rep at Preston, Colchester, Wolverhampton, Liverpool. Big chance came with Sailor, Beware 1955 (stage and film). Probably best known for her TV roles in The Larkins. Other TV incl: George and the Dragon; Lollipop Loves Mr Mole; You're Only Young Twice. Stage incl: Romeo and Juliet; She Stoops to Conquer (both at the Old Vic); The Bandwagon; When We Are Married; The Rivals; There Goes The Bride; Il Campiello and Plunder (National Theatre); Mother Courage. Films incl: The Naked Truth; Hotel Paradiso; Inn For Trouble; One Way Pendulum; Ladies Who Do. Address: c/o Richard Stone, London WC2. Starsign: Taurus.

MOWER, Patrick
Actor b. 12.9.40 Pontypridd. Formerly an apprentice engineering draughtsman, but decided to train as an actor and went to RADA. Stage appearances since incl: House of Cards; Alfie; John Gabriel Borkman; The Boston Story. Films: The Devil Rides Out; The Doctor Wears

Scarlet; The Smashing Bird I Used to Know; The Cry of the Banshee. Many plays and series on TV incl: Front Page Story; Riviera Police; Dixon of Dock Green; Z Cars; The Avengers; Haunted; Callan; Special Branch; Target; The Flockton Flyer. Education: Oxford Grammar. m. childhood sweetheart Audrey, 1 d. Claudia, 1 s. Sam. Address: Holland Park, London. Starsign: Virgo.

MOWLEM, Carole
Actress b. 20th December near Epsom, Surrey. Trained as a dancer at Elmhurst Ballet School and began her career as a dancer at the London Palladium. Went into rep at Leatherhead, Coventry and Worthing to concentrate on acting and stage incl: Celebration; Look Homeward Angel; The Philanthropist and the National Theatre. Best known on TV as the cool secretary in The Brothers, but other TV incl: Freewheelers; Budgie; The Goldfinch; The Child Wants a Home. m. TV producer Antony Rouse, 1 d. Chlöe, 1 s. Harry. Address: c/o Joseph and

Wagg, London W1. Starsign Sagittarius. Hobby: gardening. Unfulfilled ambition: to play some Shakespeare.

MUIR, Frank
Scriptwriter/performer b. 5.2.20 Broadstairs, Kent. In the RAF 1940-46. Started writing seriously 1946 and following year teamed up with Denis Norden in Navy Mixture. Together for 17 years during which they wrote Take It From Here; Bedtime with Braden and TV series And So To Bentley; Whack-O!; The Seven Faces of Jim; Brothers-in-Law. Regular broadcaster on radio: My Word!; My Music; and on TV: Sound of Laughter; Call My Bluff; How to be an Alien; We Have Ways of Making You Laugh. BBC's Head of Comedy 1963; London Weekend's Head of Light Entertainment 1966-69. Books: You Can't Have Your Kyak and Heat It (with Denis Norden); The Frank Muir Book. Education: Chatham House, Ramsgate; Leyton County High. m. Polly, 1 d. Sarah 1 s. James. Address: Egham, Surrey. Starsign: Aquarius. Hobby: collecting books.

MULLARD, Arthur
Actor b. 19.9.12 Islington, London. Been in show business 30 years but his parts in Romany Jones and Yus My Dear were his first starring roles in TV. On leaving school was butcher's boy, professional boxer,

dance hall bouncer, rag and bone merchant and labourer. Started in show business as extra and stuntman in films after the war in which he was a sgt major in the Royal Artillery. Appeared in countless TV series, variety shows and commercials. Appears regularly on Celebrity Squares. Films incl: Casino Royale; Morgan, a Suitable Case for Treatment; Lock Up Your Daughters; Crooks and Coronets; The Great St Trinian's Train Robbery; Vault of Horror. m. (dec), 4 grand-children. Address: London N5. Starsign: Virgo. Hobby: supporting Arsenal.

MULLIN, Lawrence
Actor b. 5.8.53 Liverpool. Drama school and Bristol Old Vic Theatre School 1972-75, then reps at Crewe, Cardiff, Manchester, National Theatre, Royal Shakespeare Company. TV incl: Rocky O'Rourke; Coronation Street. Education: Catholic and comprehensive. m. Lynne Pearson. Address: c/o Zena Sharpe Personal Management, Manchester. Starsign: Leo. Hobbies:

rugby, tennis, pool, snooker, chess. Unfulfilled ambitions: 'to be respected by my profession and to keep playing many and varied characters in television, film and theatre'.

MUNDY, John
Programme presenter b. 27.9.53 Manchester. After five years in rep joined Tyne Tees TV as an announcer, then moved to HTV as station announcer before becoming regional presenter for BBC TV in Manchester. Education: Chetham's Hospital School, Manchester. Address: c/o Pan Artists, Manchester Starsign: Libra. Hobbies: ice hockey, horse riding. Unfulfilled ambition: to pilot Concorde.

MUNRO, Carmen
Actress b. Guyana. Came to England 1951 and worked first as script typist and then in Master Control for Associated Rediffusion in London. Amateur acting experience at the Unity Theatre before turning professional 1962. First stage appearance at Royal Court Theatre, London; theatre

appearances since incl: Period of Adjustment; The Applecart; The Blacks; There'll Be Some Changes Made. TV incl: Love Story; The Troubleshooters; Man of Our Times; Fenn Street Gang; Ace of Wands; The Persuaders; Playschool; How Do You Do?; The Fosters; General Hospital; Black Christmas; Mixed Blessings. m. (dis), 1 s. actor Gregory. Address: c/o LWT, London SE1. Hobby: travel.

MUNROE, Gregory
Actor b. 1954 London. Member of the National Youth Theatre at 15. Rep at Watford and Manchester. West End debut in Mardi Gras 1976. Also been in Short Sleeves in the Summer. TV plays and series incl: The Fosters; Alternative 3; The Siege of Golden HIll; Mixed Blessings. Address: c/o Plant and Froggatt, London W1. Hobbies: riding, pony trekking, music, dancing.

MURDOCH, Richard
Actor b. 6.4.07 Keston, Kent. First professional appearance in chorus of The Blue Train 1927. Wide

experience of stage, touring, summer season and pantomime. Best known on radio for Band Waggon; Much Binding in the Marsh; Men From the Ministry. TV incl: New Avengers; In the Looking Glass; Hazell; Owner Occupied; Warrior Queen; The Three Kisses; Rumpole of the Bailey; This is Your Life. Education: Charterhouse and Pembroke College, Cambridge. m. actress Peggy Rawlings, 2 d.Belinda, Jane, 1 s. Timothy. Address: c/o Essanay Ltd, London W14. Starsign: Aries. Hobbies: golf, sailing. Unfulfilled ambition: to have his own, successful TV series.

MURPHY, Brian
Actor b. 1933 Ventnor, Isle of Wight. Always wanted to act and after National Service with the RAF trained at RADA. Became a stalwart of Joan Littlewood's Theatre Workshop, but fame only caught up with him after 20 years in the business with a Palladium pantomime 1976 and TV series, Man About the House and George and Mildred. m. Carole, 2 s. Trevor, Kevin. Address: Chalk Farm, London.

MURRAY, Cheryl
Actress b. 31.7.52 Liverpool. Trained at LAMDA. TV: Vienna 1900; Dixon of Dock Green; Microbes and Men; Z Cars; Within These Walls; Zigger Zagger; Billy Liar; Crown Court; Suzie Birchall in Coronation Street since

1977. Education: Belvedere Girls Public Day School Trust; Elliot-Clarke School of Dance and Drama, Liverpool. m. (dis). Address: c/o Barry Burnett Organisation Ltd, London W1. Starsign: Leo. Hobbies: reading, dancing, study into reincarnation. Unfulfilled ambition: to understand fully why we are here.

MURRAY, Derek
Editor, current affairs b. 21.9.37 Belfast. Executive journalistic positions on Belfast Telegraph, Ireland's Saturday Night and Belfast Sunday News before joining Ulster TV as political correspondent and current affairs editor. Chairman of independent inquiry into future of soccer in N Ireland; treasurer of Commonwealth Games Council, N Ireland; member of management N Ireland Commonwealth Games Committee 1970 and 1974. Education: Annadale Grammar, Belfast. m. Evelyn, 3 d. Donna, Lorna, Gillian. Address: c/o Ulster TV, Belfast. Starsign: Virgo. Hobbies: squash, following soccer, boxing, track/field athletics. Unfulfilled

ambition: to make news on behalf of ordinary people rather than report it.

MURRAY, Pete OBE
Actor/compere b. 19.9.25 London. Trained at RADA (bronze medallist) followed by rep at the Arts Theatre, Cambridge and appearances in London's West End and on Broadway. Disc jockey on Radio Luxembourg and BBC. TV incl: Six-Five Special; Thank Your Lucky Stars; Juke Box Jury; Top of the Pops; Open House; The Last Enemy (play); Happily Ever After (series); Mum's Boys (series); Husband of the Year; Pop at the Mill; Blankety Blank. Education: St Paul's School, London. m. (1st) Germaine (dis), (2nd) Tricia, 1 s. Michael (by 1st m). Address: c/o Tony Lewis Enterprises Ltd, London W1. Starsign: Virgo. Hobbies: watching Arsenal, tennis, riding, theatre.

MURRICANE, Paul
Reporter/presenter b. 23.11.50 Glasgow. On leaving university joined Radio Clyde and read the

station's first news bulletin on
31.12.73. Joined Border TV
two years later and Scottish
TV two years after that.
Presenter Saturday Special,
weekly afternoon show, on
Radio Clyde; presenter/
reporter STV's Scotland
Today; reporter Scotland
Today Reports. Education:
Dartington Hall, Totnes,
Devon; New University of
Ulster, Coleraine, N Ireland.
m. Rita. Address: Hillhead,
Glasgow. Starsign:
Sagittarius. Hobby:
collecting receipts.
Unfulfilled ambition: to watch
the Parkinson programme
without falling asleep.

N

NEDWELL, Robin
Actor b. 27.9.46
Birmingham. Moved to
Cardiff at an early age and
while at school was
encouraged to become an
actor. Joined Welsh Theatre
Company, then Central
School of Speech and Drama
in London. Rep in
Birmingham, Liverpool,
Cheltenham, Bristol and
Sheffield. Appeared in
Polanski's film Macbeth but
mainly worked on the fights, a
hobby which he has taught at
drama schools. Latest film:
starring part with Trevor
Howard in Shillingbury
Blowers. On TV well-known
for the Doctor series, but has
also appeared in The Lovers;
Wedding Bells; The Upchat
Connection; The Pretenders.
Education: Monkton and
Canton High Schools,
Cardiff. Address: c/o John
Mahoney Management,
London W1. Starsign: Libra.
Hobbies: collecting
Japanese swords and prints,
reading.

NELLIGAN, Kate
Actress b. 16.3.51 London,
Ontario, Canada. Trained at
Central School of Speech
and Drama. Joined Bristol
Old Vic 1972 and made
London West End debut in
Knuckle. Other stage incl:
National Theatre (Measure
For Measure; Tales From the
Vienna Woods; Plenty); RSC
(As You Like It). Films incl:
The Romantic
Englishwoman; Count of
Monte Cristo; Dracula. TV
incl: The Four Beauties
(Country Matters); Onedin
Line; Treats; The Lady of the
Camelias; The Arcata
Promise; Licking Hitler;
Dreams of Leaving; Thérèse
Raquin; Measure For
Measure; Call My Bluff.
Education: University of
Toronto, Canada. Address:
c/o Chatto and Linnit, London
WC1. Starsign: Pisces.
Hobbies: swimming,
cooking, gardening.
Unfulfilled ambitions: too
many to list.

NEWBON, Gary
Sports presenter/ Assistant
Head of Sport, ATV.
b. 15.3.45 Cambridge.
Trained with Jeacock's News
Agency, Cambridge
(1964-67), Hayter's Sports
Agency, London (1967-68)
and Sunday Mirror, before
joining Westward TV 1968.
Joined ATV Network 1971 for
ATV sports programmes –
Star Soccer, Extra Time, ITV
Munich Olympics 1972 and
ITV World Soccer Cup 1974.
Other TV incl: ATV Sport;
Butlins Grand Masters Darts;
State Express Grand Masters
Snooker; Midlands Soccer
Player of the Season; ATV
Summer Sport. Also
contributor to World of Sport;
Mid-week Sports Special;
Birmingham International
Show-Jumping; ITN.
Education: Culford School,
Bury St Edmunds. m. Katie,
1 d. Claire, 2 s. twins
Laurence and Neil. Address:
c/o New Management Ltd,
London W1; ATV Network
Ltd, Birmingham. Starsign:
Pisces. Hobbies: squash,
golf, jazz, wine, Variety Club
of Great Britain (Birmingham
Press Officer) and Midlands
Soccer Writers (founder
secretary). Unfulfilled
ambition: to present a regular
network programme.

NEWMAN, Barry
Actor b. 1939. Paid for his
college education by playing
in a dance band and
financed his acting lessons
by taking odd jobs about
town. Originally wanted to be
an anthropologist, but
changed his mind after a
chance visit to see a Lee
Strasburg acting class. First
break was the part of a jazz
singer and musician in stage
production, Nature's Way.
For two years was in TV series
The Edge of the Night.
Turned down several offers
before accepting the part of
the unconventional lawyer in
Petrocelli. Films: The Lawyer;
Vanishing Point; The
Salzburg Connection; Fear is
the Key. Hobbies: A keep-fit
fanatic, he enjoys running,
tennis, swimming, and when
on location stays only at
hotels with gym facilities.

NICOLS, Rosemary
Actress/writer/ astrologer
b. 28th October, Bradford.
Family theatrical
background, trained at the
Central School of Speech
and Drama and went into rep
including Harrogate,
Frinton-on-Sea and
Wimbledon. First London
lead in Something Nasty in
the Woodshed. Other stage
incl: Fiddler on the Roof with
Topol. Films incl: The Guns of
Navarone; The Pleasure
Girls; The Mini Affair. On TV
she played Anabelle Hurst
throughout the Department S
series. Other TV incl:
Badger's Bend (her TV
debut); A Way of Living; Ann
Veronica (title role); Menace;
musical version of No Trams
to Lime Street; The
Persuaders; Fathers and
Sons; The Cedar Tree;
General Hospital. Has also
had her own folk music
programme on TV. Books
incl: The Loving Adventures
of Jaby. Education:
Haberdashers' Aske's Girls
School. m. writer Frederic
Mullally (dis). Address: c/o
Jan Dutton Management,

Richmond, Surrey. Starsign: Scorpio with Libra rising. Hobbies: astronomy, stamp collecting. Unfulfilled ambition: 'If there is something I really want to do, I invariably try to go off and do it – like becoming an astrologer. So until the next attack hits me – I don't know.'

NICHOLSON, Mavis
TV interviewer b. 19.10.30 Briton Ferry. Was first an advertising copywriter and when at 27, the first of her three sons was born, she decided that bringing up her children was a full-time job. Eventually took up freelance journalism and a chance appearance on a Today programme led to her breaking into TV at the age of 40. Her TV programmes incl: Mavis; Happy Returns; Mavis – Wanting to Know; Other People's Children; Volunteers; Medical Express; Good Afternoon; After Noon Plus; and for radio, Start the Week. Education: Cwrt Sart Mixed; Neath County School for Girls; University College of Swansea. m. journalist Geoffrey Nicholson. 3 s. Steve, Lewis, Harry. Address: c/o Thames TV, London NW1. Starsign: Libra. Hobbies: photography, cooking, the telephone. Unfulfilled ambition: to play rugby for Wales.

NICHOLSON, Michael
Foreign correspondent b. 9.1.37 Romford, Essex. One of British TV's most widely travelled newsmen.

War correspondent since 1968 and in 11 years has covered as many wars – more than any other living newsman. Won American EMMY nominations for film reports from Vietnam, Biafra, Cambodia, Middle East. Major awards incl: Cannes Film Festival Silver Nymph Award for best newsfilm of 1975 with The Battle of Newport Bridge, the last battle in South Vietnam; British Newsfilm Award for filming of Turkish paratroopers landing during their invasion of Cyprus 1975; Royal Television Society's Reporter of the Year Award 1978 for his reports during a four-month trek with UNITA guerillas in Angola. Books incl: The Partridge Kite; Red Joker. Education: University of Leicester (BA Hons Politics). m. Diana, 2 s. Tom, William. Address: Kew Green, Surrey. Starsign: Capricorn. Hobbies: tennis, skiing, writing novels, collecting cars. Unfulfilled ambitions: to play tennis and ski superbly; to write better novels.

NIGHTINGALE, Anne
Presenter/disc jockey b. 1st April, Osterley, Middx. Newspaper background (Brighton Evening Argus, Daily Sketch, Daily Express, Cosmopolitan etc) and an expert on pop music. Introduced The Who to TV and was hostess of TV pop show That's For Me. Other TV incl: Sing a Song of Sixpence; Before the Event; London

Scene; Pop Quest; The Old Grey Whistle Test. Was Radio 1's first girl disc jockey on Workshop. Other radio incl: What's New (also BBC World Service); Mailbag; Anne Nightingale's Request Show; Rock Around the World (for America). Education: St Catherine's Convent, Twickenham; Lady Eleanor Holles School, Hampton; Central London Polytechnic. m. (1st) writer Gordon Thomas (dis), (2nd) pop musician Binky Baker, 1 d.Lucy, 1 s.Alexander (both from 1st m). Address: c/o BBC, London W12. Starsign: Aries. No time for hobbies. Unfulfilled ambition: to finish 'the book'.

NIMMO, Derek
Actor b. 19.9.33 Liverpool. Started with insurance company, but soon went into rep at Bolton, followed by Nottingham, Oldham, Worcester, Clacton-on-Sea, Rotherham and New Brighton. Toured in Belle of New York and Room for Two, did roller skating act with his wife, formed an agency and ran jazz concerts, verse play The Hidden Ring in Edinburgh. Many West End

plays followed incl: Waltz of the Toreadors; Duel of Angels; How Say You?; The Amorous Prawn (and film); See How They Run; Why Not Stay For Breakfast?; Charlie Girl; Same Time Next Year. TV incl: Oh Brother!; All Gas and Gaiters; The World of Wooster; My Honourable Mrs; Oh Father; The Bed-Sit Girl; Just a Nimmo; Life Begins at Forty. Radio: The Dales; Just a Minute. Films incl: The Millionairess; Mr Ten Per Cent; The Yellow Hat; A Talent For Loving; One of Our Dinosaurs is Missing. Education: Quarry School. m. Pat, 1 d. Amanda, 2 s. Timothy, Piers. Address: Kensington, London. Starsign: Virgo. Hobbies: sailing and lying in a deck-chair.

NIMOY, Leonard
Actor b. 26.3.31 Boston, Massachusetts. Decided to become an actor after playing Hansel in Hansel and Gretel when he was eight. Studied English and drama at Boston College; followed by further studies at Pasadena Playhouse. Built up a stage and TV reputation after serving in the army. Then came Star Trek and his career rocketted. Other TV incl: Rawhide; The Virginian; Dr Kildare; Outer Limits; Mission Impossible. Films incl: The Balcony; Seven Days in May; Catlow; Baffled; Invasion of The Body Snatchers. m. former actress Sandra, 1 d. Julie, 1 s. Adam. Starsign: Aries.

Hobbies: reading, music, carpentry.

NORDEN, Dennis
Scriptwriter/performer b. 6.2.22 Hackney, London. Originally a theatre manager 1939-42. Wrote for troop shows in RAF 1942-45 after which he was a scriptwriter for variety shows. Teamed up with Frank Muir 1947-64 during which they wrote: Take It From Here; Bedtime With Braden for radio; for TV: And So To Bentley; Whack-O!; The Seven Faces of Jim; Brothers-in-Law; The Glums. Solo writer since 1964. Film scripts incl: Bueno Sera, Mrs Campbell; The Statue; Every Home Should Have One; The Water Babies. Regular broadcaster My Word!; My Music and on TV: The Name's The Same; How To Be an Alien; Looks Familiar; It'll Be Alright on the Night. Education: Craven Park and City of London Schools. m. Avril, 1 d. TV producer Maggie, 1 s. Address: c/o April Young, London WC2. Starsign: Aquarius. Hobbies: reading, loitering.

NORMAN, Barry
Writer/presenter b. 21.8.33 London. Journalistic background, mostly with the Daily Mail, before being made redundant when he became a freelance TV reviewer and in 1972 was invited to join panel on BBC2's Late Night Line-Up. This led to the Film series 1972-79 and The Hollywood

Greats, 1977/8/9. Books incl: End Product; A Series of Defeats; To Nick a Good Body; The Hollywood Greats. Education: Highgate School, London. m. Diana, 2 d. Samantha, Emma. Address: c/o BBC, London W12. Starsign: Leo. Hobby: cricket. Unfulfilled ambition: to open both batting and bowling for England.

NORMINGTON, John
Actor b. 28.1.37 Dukinfield, Cheshire. Opera student before becoming stage manager for Frank Fortescue rep companies. Rep experience as an actor with Manchester Library Theatre, Royal Shakespeare Company and the National Theatre. Films incl: Inadmissible Evidence; Stardust; Rollerball; The Thirty-Nine Steps; Death Game. TV incl: Coronation Street; Red Letter Day; Enemy at the Door; Upstairs, Downstairs; Edward the Seventh; Will Shakespeare; Turtle's Progress; Afternoon Off (Alan Bennett play). Education: Crescent Rd School, Dukinfield; Northern School of Music,

Manchester. Address: c/o
Peter Browne Management,
London SW9. Starsign:
Aquarius. Hobbies: opera,
theatre. Unfulfilled ambition:
to play all the comic roles in
Gilbert and Sullivan operas.

NORTON, Jim
Actor b. 4.1.38 Dublin.
Started as a boy soprano and
child actor before becoming
a DJ on Irish radio. Joined the
Abbey Theatre, Dublin, and
the National Theatre (1976) to
appear in Hamlet (Laertes);
Tamburlaine (Calyphas);
Playboy of the Western
World; Bedroom Farce. Also
in London productions of The
Contractor; The Changing
Room. Films: Straw Dogs;
Alfred the Great. TV incl:
People Like Us; Hunter's
Walk; Colditz; Against The
Wind (Australian TV); Cry of
the Innocents (NBC TV);
Light. Education: Christian
Brothers, Dublin. m. (dis),
2 d. Carol, Sarah. Address:
c/o Joy Jameson Ltd, London
SW1. Starsign: Capricorn.
Hobbies: music, athletics,
reading, jogging. Unfulfilled
ambitions: to travel round the
world – slowly!; to work in
America.

**OCKENDEN, Cyril Victor
OBE**
Weathercaster b. 12th July
Wimbledon, London.
Meteorological Office, Air
Ministry (assistant director).
Fellow Royal Met Soc, Fellow
American Met Soc.
Weatherman for Southern TV.
Education: Sir Walter St
John's School; King's
College, London University
(BSc Hons). m. Winifred,
1 d. Margaret. Address:
Winchester, Hants. Starsign:
Cancer. Hobbies:
electronics, photography.
Unfulfilled ambition: to see
and explain a thunderbolt.

O'CONNOR, Des

Entertainer b. 12.1.32 Stepney, London. Started career in RAF where he was ordered to enter a talent contest and won first prize. Redcoat at Filey holiday camp before making professional show business debut in Newcastle in 1953, followed by numerous seasons in variety shows up and down the country and developing into one of Britain's premier entertainers. Has had four cabaret engagements at London's Talk of the Town and celebrated his 1000th performance in 1972 during one of his record-breaking seasons there. Has made many appearances in America, Australia and Canada. Summer shows at Coventry, Eastbourne, Jersey, Isle of Man and Paignton. Compered several Royal Variety shows. TV incl: compere of Spot the Tune and Sunday Night at the London Palladium; For Love Or Money; own shows since 1963. TVTimes Favourite Male TV Personality for three years in succession (1971/2/3). Books incl: Somebody Laughed (autobiography). m. (1st) Phyllis (dis), (2nd) actress Gillian Vaughan, 3 d. Karen (from 1st m), Tracey, Samantha. Address: c/o London Management, London W1. Starsign: Capricorn. Hobbies: show business, horses. Unfulfilled ambitions: to be accepted

internationally as a performer; to make a TV series in America.

O'CONNOR, Tom

Comedian b. 31.10.40 Bootle, Lancs. Originally a maths and music teacher at St Joan of Arc School, Bootle; also performed in working men's clubs while still a teacher. Appeared in the second series of The Comedians on TV and became a full-time entertainer 1974. Opportunity Knocks, a summer season at Blackpool, followed by The Tom O'Connor Show; Wednesday at Eight; Royal Variety Performance 1976; Tom O'Connor at the Casino; pantomimes at Southport and Coventry; summer seasons at Yarmouth, Blackpool and Eastbourne; three TV series of London Night Out. Education: St James Junior, Bootle; St Mary's Grammar, Crosby; St Mary's College, Twickenham. m. former teacher Pat, 3 d. Ann, Frances, Helen, 1 s. Stephen. Address: Southport. Starsign: Scorpio. Hobbies: golf, snooker, football. Unfulfilled ambition: to have freedom of the City of Liverpool.

ODUNTON, Muriel

Actress b. 14.2.53 Ghana. Came to England with her parents when she was eight. Always wanted to be an actress. First stage role in 1976 in Parcel Post, then

returned to Oxford to take her English degree. Has since been in rep at Crewe and Sheffield, commercials, radio, and has had small parts in Jubilee and Return of the Saint before leading role in Mixed Blessings. Education: St Paul's Girls School; Oxford University. Address: c/o LWT, London SE1. Starsign: Aquarius. Hobby: dancing. Unfulfilled ambition: to succeed in her chosen profession.

O'FLAHERTY, Paddy

Presenter/reporter b. 30.6.43 Newry, Co Down, N Ireland. Worked as newspaper reporter for 15 years. Then reporter/presenter for Downtown Radio, leaving to join BBC in same capacity. Presented Make Mine Country and Hello Sunshine for BBC. Education: grammar school. m. Brenda, 1 s. Roderick. Address: Belfast. Starsign: Cancer. Hobbies: music (particularly the fiddle), reading, auctions. Unfulfilled ambition: to visit Nashville.

OGILVY, Ian
Actor b. 30.9.43 Woking, Surrey. Started backstage at London's Royal Court Theatre before training at RADA. Then rep at Colchester, Canterbury and Northampton. Stage incl: The Waltz of the Toreadors; The Millionairess; Chichester Festival. Films incl: Stranger in the House; The Sorcerers; Witchfinder General; The Invincible Six; Waterloo; Wuthering Heights; Fengriffin; No Sex Please – We're British!. Extensive TV plays and series (including The Liars; Upstairs, Downstairs; Catherine (Affairs of the Heart); A Walk With Destiny) before succeeding Roger Moore as Simon Templar in The Return of the Saint. TVTimes Award as Most Compulsive Character 1978/79. Education: Eton. m. former model Diane, 1 step-d. Emma, 1 s. Titus. Address: c/o Leading Artists, London SW1. Starsign: Libra.

OLIVER, Michael
Reporter/barrister b. 7.3.46 London. Joined ITN as a trainee (together with colleague Derek Taylor) when they both left Oxford in 1968. Studied for the Bar in his spare time. Has since been involved in extensive coverage of Ulster; the cod war; the Portuguese revolution and stories with a legal flavour. Favourite was a piece on Lord Denning's 80th birthday. Education: Brentwood School; Keble College, Oxford (MA). Address: c/o ITN, London W1. Starsign: Pisces. Hobbies: squash, pubs (especially with jazz or folk music), music (especially choral and opera), theatre, playing Spoof. Unfulfilled ambitions: to be Master of the Rolls and write television plays under a nom de plume.

O'MARA, Kate
Actress b. 10.8.39 Leicester. Studied for the stage at the Aida Foster School and worked at a Sussex girls' school as a speech therapist. Subsequently wide experience of stage, film and TV. Stage incl: Merchant of Venice; Of Mice and Men; Blithe Spirit; Sherlock's Last Case. Films incl: The Nativity; An Unknown Friend; Whose Child Am I?; The Tamarind Seed; The Horror of Frankenstein; The Vampire Lovers; Cannon to Cordoba; The Desperados; Corruption; Promenade; The Limbo Line; Great Catherine. TV incl: many guest appearances (Blankety Blank; Call My Bluff; The Movie Quiz; Those Wonderful TV Times), series (No Hiding Place, Weaver's Green; Court Martial; Danger Man, etc) and more recently The Main Chance; Codename; Paul Temple; Jason King; Pathfinders; The Protectors; Spy Trap; The Brothers; Whodunnit?; The Plank; also Dick Emery Show; Morecambe and Wise Show; The Two Ronnies; The Bruce Forsyth Show. Educated privately. m. actor Jeremy Young (dis), 1 s. Dickon. Address: c/o Barry Burnett Organisation, London W1. Starsign: Leo. Hobbies: classical music, prehistory, 17th and 18th century furniture.

O'SULLEVAN, Peter OBE
TV commentator b. 3.3.18 Ireland. Joined Press Association as racing correspondent 1945 and Daily Express in similar capacity 1950. Has been race broadcasting since 1946, incl: Australia, South Africa, Italy, France, USA. Education: Hawtreys; Charterhouse; College Alpin, Switzerland. m. Patricia. Address: c/o BBC, London W12. Starsign: Pisces. Hobbies: horse racing, travel, reading, art, food and wine. Unfulfilled ambition: to achieve a perfect race commentary.

O'SULLIVAN, Richard
Actor b. 7.5.44 Chiswick, London. Child star in films, Stranger's Hand; Dangerous Exile; Cleopatra; Cliff Richard musicals. Stage incl: The Government Inspector; Boeing, Boeing; Palladium

pantomime. TV incl: Doctor at Large; Doctor in Charge; Father, Dear Father (and film); Alcock and Gander; Man About the House; Robin's Nest; Dick Turpin. Education: Corona Stage School. m. model Diana Terry (dis). Address: Sunninghill, Berks. Starsign: Taurus. Hobby: soccer (plays regularly for charity teams). Unfulfilled ambition: to win the football pools.

OULTON, Brian
Actor b. 11.2.08 Liverpool. After training at RADA began in rep at Liverpool Playhouse. Served in Army during the war. Wide experience in theatre, rep and West End, films, TV and radio. Stage incl: His House in Order; The Brontës; More Just William; Hostile Witness; The National Health; Forty Years On. Films incl: several Carry On films; Devil's Disciple; The Thirty-Nine Steps; I'm All Right, Jack; Very Important Person; The Iron Maiden; The Intelligence Men; On the Buses. TV incl: Hotel Imperial; The Avengers; Emergency – Ward 10; Softly, Softly; The

Troubleshooters; George and the Dragon; The Gamblers; Department S; The Expert; Mr Digby, Darling; The Main Chance; Randall and Hopkirk (Deceased); Codename; Jason King; Father, Dear Father; Adventures of Black Beauty; Justice; Six Days of Justice; Rule Britannia; Crown Court; The Squirrels; Emily; Headmaster; The XYY Man; The Many Wives of Patrick; Happy Ever After; Just William; The Old Curiosity Shop; Brideshead; Revisited. Education: Wantage School. m. actress Peggy Thorpe-Bates, 1 d. Jennifer, 1 s. Nicholas. Address: c/o Patrick Freeman, London W6. Starsign: Aquarius. Hobby: writing plays and novels. Unfulfilled ambition: to see acting become a real profession like medicine and the law.

OWEN, Bill
Actor b. 14.3.15 London. No academic training before going into rep at 19. Since then he has been actor, dancer, pop song writer, playwright; panellist (in Tell the Truth), and been in pantomime. Stage incl: The Threepenny Opera; more recently, Pygmalion revival; the National Theatre (The Long Voyage Home). Has been in countless films incl: Perfect Strangers; The Way to the Stars; Easy Money; My Brother's Keeper; Holiday Camp; Once a Jolly Swagman; The Girl Who

Couldn't Quite; Hotel Sahara; The Ship That Died of Shame; Davy; Carve Her Name With Pride; Carry On Cabby; Georgy Girl; Oh, Lucky Man; In Celebration; The Comeback. TV incl: Taxi; Treasure Island; Coppers End; Coronation Street; The Likely Lads; Last of the Summer Wine. m. Kathie, 1 d. Kathie, 1 s. Tom. Address: c/o Richard Stone, London WC2. Starsign: Pisces. Hobby: fishing.

OWENS, Hugh
Deputy news editor/industrial correspondent b. 7.9.44 Rhosllannerchrugog, N Wales. Journalistic training on Wrexham Leader; Shropshire Star; Express and Star, Wolverhampton; with ATV Birmingham before joining Ulster TV (deputy news editor). Education: Ruabon Grammar. m. Lorraine, 1 step-d. Wanda. Address: c/o Ulster TV, Belfast. Starsign: Virgo. Hobbies: reading, walking, watching Wales beat England at rugby, listening to classical music. Unfulfilled ambition: to be rich.

P

PAGE, Pippa
Actress b. 20.5.55 Epsom,
Surrey. Trained at Arts
Educational School and
Grandison College. Started
career as member of Vernons
pop group but left to
concentrate on acting, and
was signed to play Mary in
Upstairs, Downstairs. Other
TV incl: Kim and Co; The Eric
Sykes Show; Van Der Valk;
Scrabble; Happy Ever After;
Backs to the Land. Stage incl:
The Englishman Amused;
pantomime and The Eric
Sykes Show. Films incl: Take
Me High; Man in the Middle.
Address: c/o Aida Foster Ltd,
London NW8. Starsign:
Taurus. Hobbies: flying (she
holds a pilot's licence for
single-engined aircraft),
riding, swimming, water
skiing, dancing. Unfulfilled
ambition: to be nominated as
best actress of the year.

PADBURY, Wendy
Actress b. 7.12.47
Stratford-upon-Avon.
Experience in rep at Colwyn
Bay, Bromley, Chester and
Brian Rix farces after training
at Aida Foster Stage School.
Films incl: Charlie Bubbles;
The Devil's Touch. TV incl:
The Dickie Henderson Show;
Crackerjack; Crossroads; Dr
Who; The Freewheelers;
David and Goliath;
Breaktime; You and Me;
Merry-Go-Round; The Many
Wives of Patrick; Crown
Court; The Three Graces; The
Emperor's Nightingale.
Education: Alcester
Grammar. m. Melvyn Hayes,
2 d. Joanna, Charlotte.
Address: c/o Aida Foster Ltd,
London NW8. Starsign:
Sagittarius. Hobbies:
upholstering, dressmaking,
reading, painting.

PAGETT, Nicola
Actress b. 15.6.45 Cairo.
Brought up in Hong Kong
and Japan because of her
father's work. Returned to
England in her early teens.
Studied at RADA followed by
rep at Worthing, tours,
Regent's Park Open Air

Theatre, London's Royal Court Theatre (where she made her West End debut in Widower's Houses), Greenwich and the National. Other stage incl: Voyage Round My Father; The Ride Across Lake Constance; A Family and a Fortune; Gaslight; Yahoo. Films incl: The Viking Queen; Anne of The Thousand Days; There's a Girl in My Soup; Operation Daybreak; Oliver's Story. TV incl: Barlow at Large; The Persuaders; Upstairs, Downstairs; The Rivals of Sherlock Holmes; Napoleon; The Sweeney; French Without Tears; Anna Karenina; War and Peace; Aren't We All; Love Story. Educated at boarding school. m. writer Graham Swannell, 1 d. Eve. Address: c/o Fraser and Dunlop Ltd, London W1. Starsign: Gemini. Hobbies: gardening, sewing.

PALIN, Michael
Writer/actor b. 5.5.43 Sheffield. With the Monty Python team helped to bring a new dimension to TV comedy both on BBC and ITV. As writer/actor TV incl: Do Not Adjust Your Set (1967-69); Complete and Utter History of Britain (1969); Monty Python's Flying Circus; Ripping Yarns; films incl: And Now for Something Completely Different; Monty Python and the Holy Grail; Monty Python's Life of Brian. As actor TV: Three Men in a Boat; film: Jabberwocky. Education: Shrewsbury

School; Brazenose College, Oxford. m. Helen, 1 d. Rachel, 2 s. Thomas, William. Address: c/o Jill Foster, London SW3. Starsign: Taurus. Hobbies: weaving, viniculture, acupuncture, tennis, vibraphone construction, ballooning, brass-rubbing, meteorology, fish.

PALK, Anna
Actress b. 23rd October Looe, Cornwall. Trained at RADA. Rep at Bristol, Leatherhead and Leeds. Stage incl: Smith By Any Other Name; School for Scandal; Present Laughter; Butley (in Vienna); Sexual Perversities (Chicago); a number of national tours. Films incl: Play It Cool; Fahrenheit 451; Tower of Evil; The Frozen Dead; The Nightcomers. Probably best-known on TV for her leading part in three series of The Main Chance. Other TV, many plays and series, incl: Camille 68; Major Barbara; Pleasant Dreams Fernando; The Dolly Dialogues; The Couch; The Prince Regent and Mrs Fitzherbert; The Persuaders; The Protectors; Jason King; Witch Hunt; Spy Trap; The New Avengers; Affairs of the Heart; Now is Too Late. Education: Rise Hall Convent, Yorks. m. stockbroker Derek Brierley, 1 s. Jonathan. Address: c/o Rolf Kruger, London SW5. Starsign: Scorpio. Hobbies: skiing, water skiing, riding.

PALMER, Geoffrey
Actor b. 4.6.27 London. No acting training but went straight into the theatre as assistant stage manager at London's Q Theatre. Now one of the busiest actors on TV, incl: The Fall and Rise of Reginald Perrin; Butterflies; Fawlty Towers. Stage incl: St Joan (Old Vic). Films incl: Oh Lucky Man; Michael. Radio incl: Vegetating; Destiny. Education: Highgate School. m. Sally, 1 d. Harriet, 1 s. Charles. Address: Great Missenden, Bucks. Starsign: Gemini. Hobbies: squash, gardening.

PARKIN, Leonard
Newscaster b. 2.6.29 Thurnscoe, Yorks. Began as a reporter on Wakefield Express series of weekly papers, then Yorkshire Observer, Bradford Telegraph and Argus and Yorkshire Evening News. Joined BBC Radio Newsreel and TV news 1954; correspondent in Canada 1960, Washington 1963-65; Panorama and 24 Hours 1965-67. ITN roving reporter (covering more than 50 countries) and News at Ten

newscaster since 1967. Was first to report to Britain news of President Kennedy's death in 1963. Presenter of News at One 1977; News at 5.45 1978; political interviewer ITN election specials, the Nation Decides and Europe Decides 1979. Education: Hemsworth Grammar School, Yorks. m. Barbara, 1 s. Jeremy. Address: Potters Heath, Welwyn, Herts. Starsign: Gemini. Hobbies: fly fishing for trout, collecting antiques. Unfulfilled ambitions: to get thinner and more fluent in French.

PARKINSON, Mary
Interviewer/TV producer b. 16.7.39 Doncaster, Yorks. Teacher of English and sports until co-presenting Tea Break with her husband Michael 1972. Has since been one of the presenters of Good Afternoon; After Noon; After Noon Plus. Education: Notre Dame Collegiate, Leeds; Endsleigh Sports College, Hull. m. TV presenter Michael Parkinson, 3 s. Andrew, Nicholas, Michael. Address: c/o 58 Queen Anne St, London W1. Starsign: Cancer. Hobbies: golf, watching cricket, reading. Unfulfilled ambition: to win a golf championship or a gold medal in the Olympics.

PARKINSON, Michael
Interviewer/TV presenter b. 28.3.35 Cudworth, Yorks. Entered journalism on local paper, then The Guardian; Daily Express; columnist on

Sunday Times. Producer/ interviewer with Granada's Scene; Granada in the North; World in Action; What the Papers Say; reporter on 24 Hours; sport (London Weekend) and Cinema; presented Tea Break with his wife before joining BBC in 1972, where he has his own chat show. Also in Australia 1979 and in 1980. Much radio work and author of many books incl: Bats in the Pavilion; Football Daft; Cricket Mad; The Woofits. Education: Barnsley Grammar School. m. TV presenter Mary Parkinson, 3 s. Andrew, Nicholas, Michael. Address: c/o 58 Queen Anne St, London W1. Starsign: Aries. Hobbies: cricket, football, cinema. Unfulfilled ambition: to captain England in Australia.

PARRY-JONES, David
Presenter/commetator b. 25.9.33 Pontypridd. Journalistic experience with Western Mail and Sunday Times and TV director with BBC Wales before going freelance 1967. Sunday Mirror columnist; presenter Wales Today; match commentator for TV rugby with BBC Wales; presenter Sports Line-Up (BBC Wales); Let's Look at Wales and other schools programmes. Books incl: Number Eight (with Mervyn Davies). Education: Cardiff High School; Merton College, Oxford. m. Janet, 1 d. Sian, 1 s. John. Address: Llandaff, Cardiff. Starsign: Libra. Hobbies: reading, music, squash. (Still!) unfulfilled ambition: to win the Ernie jackpot.

PARSONS, Nicholas
Actor/compere b. 10.10.28 Grantham, Lincs. Five years' engineering apprenticeship on Clydebank before acting and variety experience in Glasgow. Rep, cabaret and revues in London, including six months resident comedian at Windmill Theatre. Stage incl: West End lead in Boeing Boeing (15 mths); Say Who You Are; Uproar in the House. Films incl: Don't Raise the Bridge, Lower the River; many British comedies in the 60's. Radio incl: BBC Drama Rep Company in 50's; Chairman Just A Minute (13 years); Radio Personality Award 1967 for Listen To This Space. TV incl: Eric Barker television series (50's); 10 years straightman to Arthur Haynes (60's); guest appearances in many comedy shows, including Benny Hill Show (70's); compere, Sale of the Century since 1971. Producer and director of short film Mad Dogs and Cricketers.

Education: Colet Court; St Paul's School; Glasgow University. m. actress Denise Bryer, 1 d. Suzy, 1 s. Justin. Address: c/o Richard Stone, London WC2. Starsign: Libra. Hobbies: photography, sport, gardening. Unfulfilled ambitions: 'to play rugger for Scotland; cricket for England; squash for Great Britain – now utterly impossible'.

PASCAL, Francoise
Actress b. 14.10.49 Vacoas, Mauritius. Trained at the Conservatoire, Academie Francaise, Cours de Dance, Drama, Classique. Stage incl: Cosette in Jean Louis Barrault's production of Les Miserables at the Theatre Nationale Populaire. Films incl: One + One; Veronique; Girl in My Soup; Soft Beds and Hard Battles. TV incl: The Brothers; Mind Your Language; guest appearances in The Bruce Forsyth Show; Celebrity Squares; Blankety Blank; Those Wonderful TV Times. Records incl: Woman is Free. Education: Les Convents des Oiseaux, Paris. 1 s. Nicholas. Address: c/o Hazel Malone, London SW13. Starsign: Libra. Hobbies: riding, swimming, singing, dancing. Unfulfilled ambition: to be a musical star. (Part fulfilled with first record Woman is Free).

PAYNE, Jeremy
Journalist/presenter b. 10.3.46 Brentwood, Essex. Newspaper

experience in Britain and radio and TV work in New Zealand and Australia, before becoming concerned with Report West for HTV in Bristol. Education: Brentwood School. m. Carole, 1 d. Lisa. Address: Backwell, Bristol. Starsign: Pisces. Hobbies: squash, tennis, reading, child rearing. Unfulfilled ambition: to settle down quietly.

PEMBERTON, Charles
Actor/magician b. 19.9.39 Leyland, Lancs. One time policeman, trained for the stage at Rose Bruford College and went to Bristol Old Vic for two years. Rep at Southport, Manchester and Harrogate before going to London in 1967. Stage incl: The Mousetrap; Poor Horace; The Constant Wife; Play Mas. Films incl: Brannigan; The Omen; Black Joy; Let's Get Laid; Porridge. TV incl: Coronation Street; the Doctor series; Softly, Softly; Dixon of Dock Green; Dr Who; The Naked Civil Servant; Dickens of London; Crossroads; Return of the Saint; The Professionals; Danger UXB;

Hazell; Sapphire and Steel; On Giant's Shoulders; Company and Co. Education: St Mary's, Leyland. Address: c/o James Viccars Management, London N12. Starsign: Virgo. Hobbies: magic (he is a member of the Magic Circle), music, reading. Unfulfilled ambition: to perform a magic routine on TV.

PENTELOW, Arthur
Actor b. 14.2.24 Rochdale. Originally a cadet clerk in the police, but amateur dramatics was a spare-time interest. Served in Royal Navy for four years during the war and returned to Rochdale to become a student teacher. Joined Bradford Civic Theatre School to train as an actor and went into rep at Bristol Old Vic, Northampton and Birmingham. Was also in Orson Welles' production of Othello in London. Best known on TV as Henry Wilkes in Emmerdale Farm since the series started in 1972. Other TV incl: Z Cars; Armchair Theatre; The Troubleshooters; Coronation Street; Play For Today. Films incl: Privilege; Charlie Bubbles; United! Education: Rochdale Grammar. m. pottery teacher Jacqueline, 2 s. Nicholas, Simon. Address: c/o Green and Underwood Ltd, London WC2. Starsign: Aquarius. Hobbies: the countryside, gardening, tennis, music. Unfulfilled ambition: to keep working.

PERCY, Margaret
Newsreader/reporter
b. 2.5.44 Belfast. Started with Belfast Telegraph then a year in economics research and three years in town planning. Began in TV as announcer and reporter for Ulster TV before joining BBC in Belfast as newsreader. Became a freelance reporter and presenter, contributing to various TV and radio series incl: BBC2 News; BBC Northern Ireland News; Network UK; Woman's Hour; Hello Sunshine; Countryman; Songs of Praise; Young Musician of the Year; Scene Around Six; Look Where You Live; Ad Lib; With You Until Midnight. Education: Richmond Lodge; Belfast College of Technology. m. Norman, 1 s. Conal. Starsign: Taurus. Hobbies: skiing, hill walking, local studies, book collecting, reading. Unfulfilled ambition: 'to have Humphrey Burton stand in for me, as I once stood in for him'.

PERRIE, Lynne
Actress b. 7.4.31 Rotherham. Trained in local rep. Films

incl: Kes. TV: Slatterly's Mounted Foot; Leeds United; Follyfoot; Mrs Petty; Queenie's Castle; The Intruders; It was a Good Story, Don't Knock It. Ivy Tilsley in Coronation Street. Education: Rotherham Grammar School for Girls. m. Derrick Barksby, 1 s. Stephen. Address: c/o Denman Variety Agency, Nottingham. Starsign: Aries. Hobbies: crochet, golf, billiards. Unfulfilled ambition: to be the first woman to pilot Concorde or the next supersonic plane.

PERRY, Morris
Actor b. 28.3.25 Penge. Turned down for the Foreign Office and worked in a bank before studying for the stage at the Old Vic Theatre School. Rep at Exmouth, Swansea, Rochdale, Ludlow and Edinburgh Festivals, London's Royal Court Theatre and the Royal Shakespeare Company 1977-78. Latest theatre King Lear at Lancaster Rep. A great deal of TV, starting with a small part in the original Avengers series. Since then TV has incl: City Beneath the Sea; Armchair Theatre; Count of Monte Christo; The Troubleshooters; Rosmersholm; Special Branch; The Sweeney; Helen – A Woman of Today; Crown Court; Warship; Van Der Valk; General Hospital; Act of Rape; Thomas and Sarah; Secret Army; The Professionals. Education: Penge Grammar School;

Cambridge University. m. actress Margaret Ashcroft, 4 s. Frank, Matthew, William, Edmund. Address: c/o CCA Personal Management, London SW6. Starsign: Aries. Hobbies: piano, chess, reading Russian, standing on his head.

PERTWEE, Jon
Actor/comedian b. 7.7.19 London. Born into a theatrical family, it was inevitable that he eventually went on the stage. Trained at RADA, followed by rep including Jersey and Brighton. War service in the Royal Navy after which he turned to radio in Waterlogged Spa; Up the Pole and The Navy Lark. Films incl: A Funny Thing Happened on the Way to the Forum; The Ugly Duckling; Nearly a Nasty Accident; The House that Dripped Blood; Mr Drake's Duck; One of Our Dinosaurs is Missing; There's a Girl in My Soup; Oh Clarence. TV incl: Three of a Kind; Dr Who; Whodunnit?; Worzel Gummidge. Noted for his range of accents and voices. Recent stage incl: Irene. Education: Wellington House, Sherborne and Frensham Heights. m. (1st) actress Jean Marsh (dis), (2nd) Ingeborg Rhoesa, 1 d. Dariel, 1 s. Sean (both from 2nd m). Address: c/o Richard Stone, London WC2. Starsign: Cancer. Hobby: skin-diving.

PETTIFER, Julian
Presenter/reporter b. 21.7.35 Malmesbury, Wilts. Started with Southern TV 1958; joined Tonight 1962; war correspondent for 24 Hours 1965 and moved to Panorama 1969. As reporter for BBC his travels have taken him to Vietnam, Aden, Hong Kong, the Suez Canal zone and Northern Ireland. Documentary programmes incl: 90 South; War Without End; Millionaire; Vietnam – the Other World; and more recently, The Regiment; The Country Game; World About Us; The China Programme; The History of Civil Aviation. Education: Marlborough; St John's College, Cambridge. Address: c/o BBC, London W12. Starsign: Cancer. Hobby: travel.

PHILLIPS, Leslie
Actor b. 20.4.24 Tottenham, N London. Trained at the Italia Conti School and played boy roles on the London stage (debut was as a wolf in Peter Pan at the London Palladium 1935). Following year made film appearance in The Citadel. War service as a lieutenant in the Durham Light Infantry. Stage since incl: Boeing Boeing; The Deadly Game; The Big Killing; Roger the Sixth; The Man Most Likely To; Sextet; Not Now, Darling. Many films incl: Brothers-in-Law; The Smallest Show on Earth; some of the Carry On films and more recently Doctor in Love; Doctor in Clover; Doctor in Trouble; The Magnificent Seven Deadly Sins; Not Now, Darling; Don't Just Lie There; Not Now Comrade. Best known on radio for The Navy Lark. Tremendous amount of TV; in plays, musicals, series, guest appearances and games incl: Mrs Moonlight; A Murder Has Been Arranged; The Reluctant Debutante; Father, Dear Father; Our Man at St Marks; Culture Vultures; Foreign Affairs; Casanova 73; What's My Line?; Call My Bluff; Movie Quiz; The Golden Shot; Juke Box Jury; Celebrity Squares; Clever Stupid Game. Education: Chingford School. m. (dis.), 2 d. Caroline, Claudia, 2 s. Andrew, Roger. Address: c/o BBC, London W1. Starsign: Aries. Hobbies: collecting, photography, racing, travelling, sport. Unfulfilled ambition: to work in the National Theatre.

PHILLIPS, Sian
Actress b. 14.5.34 Carmarthenshire. Always wanted to be an actress. Began broadcasting in Welsh, then joined BBC Repertory at Cardiff. Won an Arts Council bursary to RADA, more radio work and then bi-lingual announcer for Land of Song. Many classic roles like Hedda Gabler; St Joan; Katherine in The Taming of the Shrew and Masha in The Three Sisters and films like Becket; Laughter in the Dark and Goodbye Mr Chips. TV incl: The Quiet Man; Don Juan in Hell; Thief; Women Can Be Dangerous; The Vessel of Wrath; Platonov; Shoulder to Shoulder; Twelfth Night; How Green Was My Valley; I, Claudius; The Achurch Letters; The Warrior Queen. Education: grammar school; University of Wales (hons degree in English and philosophy); hon Bard for services to Welsh Drama. m. actor Peter O'Toole (dis), 2 d. Kate, Pat. Address: c/o NEMS Ltd, London W1. Starsign: Taurus. Hobby: gardening.

PHOENIX, Patricia
Actress b. 26.11.24 Portnum, County Galway, Ireland. Started career in radio play 1939, Children's Hour 1940. Stage: Manchester Arts Theatre Company, rep, variety shows. Stage incl: Suddenly Last Summer; The Miracle Worker; The L-Shaped Room. TV: Coronation Street (since first episode in 1960, apart from three year break). Education: Fallowfield Central School, Manchester.
m. (1st) advertising executive (dis), (2nd) actor Alan Browning (dec).

Address: c/o Saraband
Associates, Manchester.
Starsign: Sagittarius.
Hobbies: reading, dogs,
gardening. Unfulfilled
ambition: 'to obtain a
modicum of common sense
before I die'.

PICKERING, Ronald
TV commentator/ sports
journalist b. 4.5.30 London.
Physical education teacher
and lecturer and AAA's
National Coach. TV
commentator on track and
field athletics, gymnastics,
weight-lifting, Alpine skiing,
ski jumping. Other TV incl:
We Are the Champions;
Sports Town; The Superstars;
The World About Us (Kenya
Runner; Cuba Sport and
Revolution; The Long Wait of
the Dragon). Books incl:
Athletics Yearbook; Strength
Training; Sport in Cuba etc.
Education: Stratford
Grammar School; College of
St Mark and St John
(teaching certificate);
Carnegie College of Physical
Education (Diploma);
Leicester University (M Ed).
m. Jean Catherine
Desforges, 1 d. Kim,
1 s. Shaun. Address: c/o
BBC, London W12. Starsign:
Taurus. Hobbies: sport,
photography, travel.

PIDDOCK, Helen
Reporter b. 2.4.49
Birmingham. Two and a half
years with BBC; with Radio
Birmingham as station
assistant; freelance reporter
and newsreader; Radio 4
producer; script editor TV

drama; ATV for past ten years
as reporter, ATV Today;
newsreader; presenter of
Letterbox; Pick of the Week;
Citizens Rights; Something
Different. Researcher and
writer for Tiswas and
Kidsworld. Education:
Edgbaston High School;
Lowther College, Abergele,
North Wales; Birmingham
University Law Faculty (LLB
Hons). Address: Rednal,
Birmingham. Starsign: Aries.
Hobbies: all sports – golf
(Warwickshire County
player), tennis (Schools final,
Wimbledon and Varsity
Blue), hockey (Varsity Blue),
fencing, squash, jigsaw
puzzles, music, dancing,
skiing. Unfulfilled ambition: to
be able to work six months of
the year as a TV reporter/
presenter, the other six
months skiing and writing
plays.

PIRRIE, Alastair
TV journalist/presenter
b. 9.5.54 Stockton-on-Tees.
Started as journalist with BBC
Radio Cleveland, then
presenter with BBC TV and
radio and reporter on Radio
4. After a spell as a DJ with
Radio Tees joined Tyne Tees

TV as a reporter. Radio incl:
On the Move; Gospel Road;
Sunday; Pirrie PM; Trains and
Boats and Planes; Well – It's
Different. TV incl: Parents and
Children; See You Sunday;
Northern Life; Generation
Scene; Three's Company;
Saturday Shakeup.
Education: grammar school
to 'A' level. Address:
Hartburn, Stockton-on-Tees,
Cleveland. Starsign: Taurus.
Hobbies: collecting old
Hollywood movies, writing
(rock music and short
stories), Unfulfilled
ambitions: to visit Far East; to
be rich enough to buy fish
and chips every night and not
care a damn.

PITMAN, John
TV reporter b. 18.11.40
Whitecroft, Glos. Newspaper
training on Gloucestershire
Echo, Brighton Argus and
Daily Mail. TV incl: Hyde Park;
Braden's Week; Man Alive;
Tonight; The Big Time; Times
Remembered; Let's Go
Naked; Decision. Education:
Bexhill and Cirencester
Grammar Schools. Address:
c/o BBC, London W14.
Starsign: Scorpio. Hobbies:
theatre, cinema, tennis.
Unfulfilled ambition: to
complete writing a book or
play.

PLEASENCE, Donald
Actor b. 5.10.19 Worksop,
Notts. Started as a railway
clerk at Swinton, Yorks — a
stop-gap job until he
became an actor. This he did
at Jersey Rep in 1939. After

service in the RAF (two years as a prisoner of war), returned to the London theatre and went into rep at Birmingham and Perth. Regular film and TV parts led to his appearance in The Caretaker in London and New York and the film. His career really took off with his part as a Nazi fanatic in The Man in the Glass Booth both in London and New York in 1967. Other stage incl: Poor Bitos. Great amount of film and TV work. Films incl: Suspect; The Big Day; The Scar; No Love For Johnnie; Dr Crippen; The Great Escape; The Greatest Story Ever Told; The Hallelujah Trail; The Fantastic Voyage; Cul de Sac; The Eye of the Devil; Night of the Generals; Soldier Blue and more recently, Tales from Beyond the Grave; Trial by Combat; The Last Tycoon; Sgt Pepper's Lonely Hearts Club Band; Oh God; The Eagle Has Landed; Dracula. TV incl: Montserrat; Moment of Truth; Misalliance; Thou Good and Faithful Servant; Colombo; Orson Welles Great Mysteries; Occupations; The Cafeteria; Shades of Greene; Captain Kopenick; The Joke; Hindle Wakes; Mrs Colombo. Books incl: Scouse the Mouse. Education: Ecclesfield Grammar School. m. (1st) actress Miriam Raymond (dis), (2nd) actress/singer Josephine Crombie (dis), (3rd) Israeli singer Meira Shore, 5 d. actress Angela Pleasence, Jean (from 1st m), Lucy, Polly (from 2nd m), Miranda (from 3rd m). Address: c/o Joy Jameson Ltd, London SW1. Starsign: Libra. Hobby: writing.

PORTER, Eric
Actor b. 8.4.28 London. Started on the stage at Stratford-upon-Avon; subsequently worked with companies run by Lewis Casson, Donald Wolfit, Barry Jackson and John Gielgud before Bristol and London Old Vics. Has acted in nearly all Shakespeare's plays, played Captain Hook in Peter Pan in 1971 and been in many films incl: The Fall of the Roman Empire; The Pumpkin Eater; The Heroes of Telemark; Kaleidoscope; The Lost Continent; Hands of the Ripper; Antony and Cleopatra; Nicholas and Alexandra; The Day of the Jackal; Hitler – the Last 10 Days; The Belstone Fox; Hennessy; Callan; The Thirty-Nine Steps. Achieved fame at 40 as Soames Forsyte in the TV blockbuster The Forsyte Saga. Other TV incl: The Wars of the Roses; Cyrano de Bergerac; Man and Superman; Spilt Champagne; Separate Tables; Morecambe and Wise Show; Macbeth; When We Are Married; The Canal Children; The Winslow Boy; Anna Karenina; Harry Secombe Christmas Show; Why Didn't They Ask Evans?; Churchill's People. TV Guild of Producers and Directors Actor of the Year Award 1967. Education: Tweeddale Elementary School, Carshalton, Surrey; Wimbledon Technical College. Address: c/o London Management, London W1. Starsign: Aries. Hobbies: woodwork, gardening.

POWELL, Robert
Actor b. 1.6.44 Salford, Lancs. Started in rep at Stoke-on-Trent, went to London in a musical that flopped, had a part in the Michael Caine film The Italian Job and then the TV part that brought him stardom in Doomwatch. Stage incl: Hamlet (at Leeds); Glasstown; Travesties (with Royal Shakespeare Company). Films incl: Secrets; Running Scared; The Asphyx; Asylum; Mahler; Tommy; Beyond Good and Evil; The Four Feathers; The Thirty-Nine Steps; Harlequin. Other TV incl: Bam, Pow, Zap; Shelley; Sentimental Education; Jude the Obscure; Mrs Warren's Profession; Mr Rolls and Mr Royce; The Caucasian Chalk Circle; Looking For Clancy; Jesus of Nazareth (voted Best Actor by TVTimes readers 1978); You Never Can Tell. Education: Manchester Grammar School and Manchester University. m. dancer Barbara Lord, 1 d. Katherine, 1 s. Barnaby. Address: c/o Boyack and Conway Ltd, London W1. Starsign: Gemini. Hobby: football.

PRENDIVILLE, Kieran
Reporter b. 25.12.47
Rochdale, Lancs. Started as
copy boy in Oldham Press
Agency and progressed to
reporter (1968). Spent three
and a half years in Fleet
Street (1969-72) before
becoming researcher then a
reporter for BBC TV
(1972-79) incl: That's Life;
Nationwide; Man Alive;
Holiday Programme;
Tomorrow's World; Risk
Business; Summer Sunday.
Also radio, incl: Archive
series, Findings. Education:
Cassock Nostra – Irish
Jesuits. m. Jan. Address: c/o
BBC TV, London W14.
Starsign: Capricorn.
Hobbies: watching football,
racing, playing cricket, Irish
music. Unfulfilled ambition:
'to write proper'.

PRINCE, Michael
Newsreader b. 29.7.44
Sutton Coldfield, Warwicks.
Trained at Webber Douglas
Drama School in London.
First job was a programme
researcher for ATV in 1963.
Became announcer in 1965.
Freelance since 1971. Has
worked for seven of the ITV
companies, mostly for

Southern, Thames and HTV
West, as announcer,
newsreader and programme
presenter. Education: Wylde
Green Prep; Denstone
College, Uttoxeter, Staffs.
m. Jean. Address: Sutton
Coldfield, Warwicks.
Starsign: Leo. Hobbies:
squash, tennis, swimming,
collecting antiques.
Unfulfilled ambition: to swim
the English Channel.

PURVES, Peter
Presenter/ interviewer/ actor
b. 10.2.39 New Longton, Nr
Preston, Lancs. A couple of
years in rep, tours and chorus
tenor at London Palladium
before TV appearances in
Z Cars; Girl in the Picture;
The Villains; Court Martial;
Luther; Dr Who (28
episodes); Girl in the Black
Bikini. Presenter Blue Peter
1967-78 (more than 850
programmes); All Star
Record Breakers Christmas
Specials 1974-79; Guest
appearances in Record
Breakers and Star Turn and
many Blue Peter Special
Assignments 1977-79. Also
Driver of the Year; Summer
Sunday; Firework Fiesta;
Cruft's Dog Show;
Stopwatch; We're Going
Places; Bullseye; The Acting
Game. Stage incl: Cinderella
(Guildford and Wilmslow).
Education: Arnold School,
Blackpool; Barrow Grammar;
Alsager Teachers' Training
College. m. writer Gilly
Fraser, 1 adopted d. Lisa,
1 s. Matthew. Address: c/o
Arlington Enterprises,
London W1. Starsign:

Aquarius. Hobbies: darts,
music, movies, theatre, all
sports. Unfulfilled ambition:
to make feature films.

PURCHES, Graham
Journalist b. 5.3.44
Portsmouth. Started as cadet
journalist in Australia then TV
in Melbourne and Hong
Kong. Currently reporter/
presenter Points West for
BBC in Bristol. Education:
Seaford College, Sussex.
m. Charlotte, 1 s. Samuel.
Address: Westbury-on-Trym,
Bristol. Starsign: Pisces.
Hobbies: yoga, running,
work. Unfulfilled ambition: 'to
persuade my son to sleep at
night'.

PYKE, Dr Magnus OBE
Scientist and TV personality
b. 29.12.08 London. Expert
in nutrition and populariser of
science. Has held several
important scientific and
research appointments.
Scientific adviser to the
Ministry of Food 1941-45,
secretary and chairman
British Association for the
Advancement of Science
1955-57 and president of the
Institute of Food Science and
Technology of the UK

1969-71. Travels the world lecturing on nutrition and is the author of many books on the subject. Became a TV personality after his retirement on Don't Ask Me (1974). Other TV incl: guest appearances on many programmes; Enough Food on Our Plate; Multi-Coloured Swop Shop; Celebrity Squares. Holds a Doctor of Philosophy degree and Fellowships of the Royal Institute of Chemistry, Institute of Biology, Institute of Food and Technology, Royal Society of Edinburgh. Education: St Paul's; McGill University, Montreal; University College, London. m. chartered accountant Dorothea, 1 d. Elizabeth, 1 s. John. Address: Hammersmith, London. Starsign: Capricorn. Hobbies: 'living is for real, not hobbies'. Unfulfilled ambition: 'to be better'.

PYNE, Frederick
Actor b. 30.12.36 London. Spent some time farming in Cheshire and Cambridgeshire. Signed on with the RAF and it was there he caught the theatre bug. Trained at RADA, then rep, followed by four years at the National Theatre at the Old Vic 1966-70. TV incl: Justice; Emmerdale Farm. Education: Holloway Grammar School, London. Address: c/o Yorkshire TV, Leeds. Starsign: Capricorn. Hobbies: music, foreign travel. Unfulfilled ambitions: to play Uncle Vanya; to visit India and Peru.

QUAYLE, Anna
Actress/writer b. 6.10.37 Birmingham. Trained at RADA after touring for a number of years in her actor/producer father Douglas Quayle's Company, for whom she made her first stage appearance in East Lynn at the age of four. Accomplished performer on stage, film and TV. Stage incl: Stop the World I Want to Get Off; Full Circle (which she wrote); Out of Bounds (Bristol); Pal Joey; Kings and Clowns. Films incl: Chitty Chitty Bang Bang; SOS Titanic; The Seven Per Cent Solution. TV incl: The Georgian House; What's My Line?; Jackanory Playhouse; Aquarius; What a Performance; The Light Princess; Henry V; Brideshead Revisited. Education: Convent of Jesus and Mary, Harlesden. m. Donald Baker, 1 d. Katy Nova. Address: c/o Elspeth Cochrane Agency, London SW4. Starsign: Libra. Hobbies: collecting books, exploring old buildings, churches, castles, etc, Siamese cats (she has five). Unfulfilled ambition: to work on a Fellini film.

QUAYLE, Lawrie
Reporter b. 6.12.38 Douglas, Isle of Man. Legal practice in Manchester and Liverpool before becoming a DJ overnight with Manx Radio 1966. Transferred to Radio Caroline 1968 and later same year joined Border TV as a reporter. Now with Westward TV's Westward Diary. Education: Manchester University (MA and LLB). m. (1st) Barbara, (2nd) Aelish, 1 d. Sheron, 1 s. Gary (both from 1st m). Address: Plymouth, Devon. Starsign: Sagittarius. Hobbies: all intellectual pursuits (reading, classical music), motor-cycling. Unfulfilled ambitions: professionally always to give value for money; socially to pack as much into each and every 24 hours as is possible.

QUINTEN, Christopher
Actor b. 12.7.57 Middlesbrough. Trained at Billingham Theatre School. Brian Tilsley in Coronation Street since Dec 1978. Other TV incl: Warship; Target; The Pink Medicine Show; The Little Big Show; Quatermass. Films incl: International Velvet. Education: Easterside Junior School; Brookside Secondary Modern. Address: c/o Bill Horne Personal Management, London WC2. Starsign: Cancer. Hobbies: gymnastics, keep-fit, photography. Unfulfilled ambition: to play the lead in a very successful film.

QUIRKE, Pauline
Actress b. 8.7.59 London. While still at school was in Dixon of Dock Green; Kids About Town; Days of Hope and regular member of the teenage cast of You Must Be Joking. Turning point in her career was as the autistic child in Jenny Can't Work Any Faster. Other TV incl: Pauline's Quirkes; Pauline's People; Lovely Couple; The Country Party; Special Offer. Education: Islington Green School, London. Drama training at Anna Scher Children's Theatre. Address: c/o Anna Scher Theatre Management, London N1. Starsign: Cancer. Hobbies: reading autobiographies, watching plays, decorating, pubs, discos, going to new places, eating out. Unfulfilled ambitions: to be a guest on Michael Parkinson's show; to go to America; to make a parachute jump.

R

RAE, Douglas
TV reporter/producer
b. 22.6.47 Edinburgh. First
job on leaving school was
copy boy on the Scottish
Daily Express. Had
newspaper jobs in Angus,
Glasgow and Dundee before
joining Scottish TV as
reporter and interviewer for a
current affairs programme.
Joined the Magpie team
1972. Returned to Scottish TV
to present his own
programme 1977. TV incl:
World Worth Keeping;
Edinburgh Festival Arts
programme 1974-76;
Edinburgh Film Festival
1977-79; Sneak Preview; Two
Plus Two; Today; Thames at
Six. Education: Edinburgh
Academy. Address: c/o
Scottish TV, Glasgow.
Starsign: Cancer. Hobbies:
films, travel, sport.

RADLEY, Gordon
Announcer/presenter/
newsreader b. 26.3.53
Bromley, Kent. Studied TV
and speech and drama;
promotion scriptwriter and
trailer maker at HTV and
Anglia TV and programme
presenter Grampian TV. Also
freelance announcer,
interviewer and has done
production work in radio.
Education: Bromley
Grammar; Stockwell College
of Education. Address: c/o
Grampian TV, Aberdeen.
Starsign: Aries. Hobbies:
walking, natural history,
horticulture, painting, yoga,
badminton. Unfulfilled
ambitions: to have his own
chat show; to read the news
for ITN.

RAFFLES, Mark
Comedian/pickpocket/
magician b. 22.1.22
Manchester. One of Europe's
top pickpocket comedy
entertainers. First stage
appearance at age of nine.
Later toured music halls,
theatres and night clubs. TV
incl: Music Hall; Club Night;

Roy Hudd Show; Ken
Goodwin Show; Braden's
Week; Pebble Mill; Seaside
Special; Second Generation
Big Top; Ken Dodd
Christmas Show;
Wheeltappers and Shunters
Social Club; David Nixon
Show; The Big Send-up; The
Jones Boy; Crackerjack;
M'Lords, Ladies and
Gentlemen. Consultant on
films involving sleight of hand
or picking pockets.
Education: secondary
school. m. Joan (also Mark's
secretary and personal
assistant), 2 d. Jacqui,
Wendy, 1 s. Tim (in singing
trio Golden Brandy).
Address: Cliftonville, Kent.
Starsign: Aquarius. Hobbies:
magic and promoting
professional career of his
three children. Unfulfilled
ambitions: to present his own
TV series and to pick the
pocket of the Chancellor of
the Exchequer.

RANCE, Petrina
Journalist. b. 3.1.48 London.
Trained as reporter with
Surrey Daily Advertiser,
Guildford and Nottingham
Evening Post. Worked with
Piccadilly Radio, Manchester
and LBC, London, before
becoming a reporter on
BBC's Today programme
and joining Yorkshire TV.
Education: St Martin-in-the-
Fields High School, London;
University of East Anglia
(Upper 2nd Hons Sociology);
Post-Graduate Diploma in
Journalism Studies,
University College, Cardiff.
Address: c/o Yorkshire TV,

Leeds. Starsign: Capricorn.
Hobbies: country strolls,
theatre, travelling.

RANDALL, Alan

Musical entertainer/ singer
b. 10.6.39 Bedworth,
Warwicks. Started career as
vibraphone player in Sonny
Rose Band. Eventually went
solo introducing George
Formby songs and ukelele
playing. Radio incl: Tony
Brandon Show; John Dunne
Show; Charlie Chester Show;
Jimmy Young Show; I
Remember George. TV incl:
top variety shows such as
Roy Castle Beats Time;
Seaside Special;
Wheeltappers and Shunters
Social Club; The Good Old
Days; Parkinson. Owns
several George Formby
ukeleles, records and
personal possessions.
Education: secondary
school. m. Mary, 1 d. Susan,
1 s. Martyn. Address: c/o
Elliott and Young Productions
Ltd, London W1. Starsign:
Gemini. Hobbies: driving,
playing golf, collecting
records. Unfulfilled
ambitions: to have his own TV
series; to gain recognition in
America.

RANTZEN, Esther

TV journalist b. 22.6.40
Berkhamsted, Herts. After
gaining a history degree at
Oxford, joined the BBC as a
radio effects girl before going
into research. Became a
production assistant on Man
Alive and then Braden's
Week, eventually appearing
on the show, researching and

writing her own material. Has
been presenting That's Life,
which she also produces,
since 1973. Other TV incl:
The Big Time; Miss United
Kingdom, 1978. Education:
North London Collegiate,
Edgware, Middx; Somerville
College, Oxford. m. TV
producer and Head of
General Features, BBC,
Desmond Wilcox. 1 d. Emily.
Address: c/o Noel Gray
Artists, London WC2.
Starsign: Cancer.

RAWLE, Jeff

Actor/writer b. 20.7.51
Birmingham. Worked at
Sheffield Playhouse on
leaving school until he went
to LAMDA to train as an actor.
A few weeks after leaving he
was chosen to play the part of
Billy Liar in the TV series of
the same name. TV since incl:
The Water Maiden; Death of a
Young Young Man; Beryl's
Lot; A Cost of Loving; Van Der
Valk; Send in the Girls; Crown
Court; Wilde Alliance; Leave
it to Charlie. Stage (West
End) incl: So Who Needs
Men; Equus; Once a
Catholic; Bent. Films incl: Life
Story of a Man Called Baal;
Correction Please; A Hitch in

Time. Radio incl: Semi
Detached; Daphne du
Maurier Short Stories; Still
Life. Education: grammar
schools in Birmingham and
Sheffield. Address: c/o David
White Associates, London
W1. Starsign: Cancer.
Hobbies: playing various
musical instruments, filling in
VAT forms. Unfulfilled
ambition: to direct films.

REDFERN, Anthea

Actress b. 14.4.51 Torquay,
Devon. Trained at the Lucy
Clayton Modelling School.
After her modelling course
became a photographic
model with the famous
fashion house of Christian
Dior in Paris 1969-70.
Auditioned for The
Generation Game at the
suggestion of Bruce Forsyth
whom she had met
previously at a beauty
contest. Hostess on The
Generation Game 1971-77.
TV also incl: Bruce's Big
Night; Celebrity Squares.
Miss London 1971.
Education: convent school.
m. (1st) footballer Robin
Stubbs (dis), (2nd)
entertainer Bruce Forsyth,
2 d. Charlotte, Louisa.
Address: c/o Billy Marsh,
London Management,
London W1. Starsign: Aries.
Hobbies: riding, swimming,
squash. Unfulfilled ambition:
to play a wider variety of
roles.

REDHEAD, Brian
Journalist b. 28.12.29
Newcastle upon Tyne.
Journalistic background;
Northern Editor of The
Guardian 1965-69; Editor,
Manchester Evening News
1969-75. Presenter Today
and chairman A Word in
Edgeways, both on Radio 4;
presenter Home Ground,
BBC North West. Education:
Newcastle Royal Grammar;
Downing College,
Cambridge (MA). m. Jenni,
2 s. Stephen, James and
twins William and Annabel.
Address: Cheadle Hulme,
Cheshire. Starsign:
Capricorn. Hobby: playing
the bass clarinet. Unfulfilled
ambition: to retire.

REES, Ken
TV reporter b. 26.1.44
Cardiff. Regular contributor
to ITV's News at 5.45 and
News at Ten. TV career
began 1968 as newscaster
for HTV's news magazine,
Reports West. Joined ITN
1978. Outside TV has
produced documentaries for
industry and education
establishments. Education:
Howardian High School,
Cardiff. m. Lynne, 1 d.
Samantha, 1 s. Christian.

Address: c/o Derek James
Organisation, Frome,
Somerset. Starsign:
Aquarius. Hobbies: work,
photography, clocks.
Unfulfilled ambition: to write a
funny book about television.

REID, Beryl
Actress b. 17.6.20 Hereford.
First appeared on stage in
concert party Bridlington
1936. Made reputation as
Monica in Educating Archie
(radio). TV, radio, clubs,
variety and revues (including
Half-past Eight in Edinburgh,
in which she did 427
sketches in one season),
before her first serious stage
play, The Killing of Sister
George (1965), followed
some years later by
Entertaining Mr Sloane.
Appeared in film versions of
both plays. Other stage work
incl: Blithe Spirit; Romeo and
Juliet; Spring Awakening and
Il Campiello (for the National
Theatre); The Way of the
World (Royal Shakespeare
Co). Has since largely
concentrated on TV incl: The
Rivals; Father, Dear Father;
The Edward Woodward
Hour; Harry Secombe Show;
The Goodies; The Good Old
Days; Alcock and Gander;
Wink to Me Only; Smike; The
Apple Cart; When We Are
Married; Flint; Tinker, Tailor,
Soldier, Spy; and her own
programmes. Films incl: The
Belles of St Trinians; Star;
Inspector Clouseau; The
Beast in the Cellar; No Sex
Please – We're British; The
Dock Brief. Education:
Ladybarn House; Withington

High; Levenshulme High,
Manchester. m. (1st) Bill
Worsley (dis), (2nd) musician
Derek Franklin (dis).
Address: Wraysbury, Middx.
Starsign: Gemini. Hobbies:
gardening, cooking, driving.
Unfulfilled ambition: to go on
working in all media.

RHODES, Pam
Presenter b. 22.9.50
Gillingham, Kent. Trained as
a dancer. Entered TV in 1969
as programme secretary for
Thames TV's Today
programme hosted by
Eamonn Andrews. Left in
1970 to organise a national
project for handicapped
children. Joined George
Mitchell's Black and White
Minstrels as singer/ dancer at
Paignton 1973 before
returning to Thames where
she was programme
organiser for This Week
1975-76. Then she joined
Anglia TV as presenter/
reporter for About Anglia.
Other TV incl: presenter
British Forces Broadcasting
(for troops in Germany);
World Around Us and
Merry-go-Round (schools
series); Hurdy Gurdy.
Education: Gosport County
Grammar School. Address:
c/o Isobel Davie Ltd, London
W1. Starsign: cusp of
Virgo/Libra. Hobbies:
teaching dancing to East End
children, old folks shows,
singing with Thames TV Big
Band (amateur), old time
music hall, piano and
xylophone. Unfulfilled
ambition: to be able to play
the piano really well.

RICHARD, Cliff
Singer/actor b. 14.10.40
Lucknow, India. Came to
England when he was seven.
On leaving school worked as
a clerk. First TV, Oh Boy!
series in 1958 with The
Shadows. Many TV, radio
and stage appearances and
records, including 100 hits.
No 1 hit record, We Don't Talk
Any More, Summer 1979.
First record Move It in 1958.
Gold discs (for selling more
than a million copies) each
for Living Doll; The Young
Ones; The Next Time; Lucky
Lips; Congratulations; Power
To All Our Friends; Devil
Woman. Also has 25 silver
discs, each for sales of more
than 250,000. Films incl:
Serious Charge; Expresso
Bongo; The Young Ones;
Summer Holiday; Wonderful
Life; Finders Keepers; Two a
Penny; Take Me High; His
Land. Education:
Riversmead School,
Cheshunt. Address: c/o
Gormley Management,
London NW1. Starsign: Libra.
Hobbies: swimming,
badminton, photography.
Unfulfilled ambition: to star in
a London West End rock and
roll musical.

RICHARD, Emily
Actress b. 25th January,
London. Studied at Webber
Douglas Academy of
Dramatic Art before joining a
touring children's theatre.
Rep at Crewe and Worcester
and Charley's Aunt in London
before joining BBC Rep in
1974. Other theatre includes
Royal Shakespeare

Company tour (Twelfth Night;
Three Sisters) in 1978 and
RSC Stratford season
1979-80. On TV played
leading part in Glittering
Prizes; then title role in Lorna
Doone and more recently in
Enemy at the Door. Other TV
incl: Kate; Father Brown;
Emmerdale Farm; An Affinity
with Dr Still. Education:
Channing School for Girls,
Highgate, London. Address:
c/o NEMS Management,
London SW3. Starsign:
Aquarius. Hobbies:
lace-making, embroidery,
weaving, reading,
gardening. Unfulfilled
ambition: to keep working.

RICHARDS, Gwyn
Presenter/reporter b. 6.6.36
Burton-on-Trent, Staffs.
Trained in textile
manufacture and design.
Rhodesian mounted police
for four years before
becoming radio producer/
announcer and TV
newscaster in Zambia.
Returned to England as
reporter for BBC's Midlands
Today, then anchorman of
ATV Today, followed by
return to BBC to present
Points West in Bristol.

Regional reporter for
Nationwide; presenter of
BBC West feature
programmes, Movie Magic;
Sports Show and Day Out;
many documentary films;
presenter of BBC2's
Something in the Wind and In
the Post; contributor to Best
of Brass 1979. Education:
Burton Grammar; Derby
Polytechnic; Law, Police and
Equitation, British South
Africa Police, Salisbury,
Rhodesia. m. Helen,
1 d. Phyllida, 1 s. Simon.
Address: c/o BBC, Bristol.
Starsign: Gemini. Hobbies:
squash, tennis, writing.
Unfulfilled ambition: 'to live
until I'm 100'.

RICHARDS, Vikki
Actress b. 29.12.49 Trinidad.
Trained at the Guildhall
School of Music and Drama,
since when her films have
incl: Percy's Progress;
Slaves. TV incl: Home Sweet
India; Man With the Power;
Forsters; The Onedin Line;
Marty Feldman Show; Night
School; Return of the Saint;
Bruce Forsyth's Big Night.
Education: Hammersmith
and West London College.
Address: c/o Richard
Jackson Personal
Management Ltd, London
SW1. Starsign: Capricorn.
Hobbies: painting, travelling.
Unfulfilled ambition: to write
plays.

RIGG, Carl
Actor b. Eton, Bucks. Trained
at the Central School of
Speech and Drama and the
RSC Studio. TV incl: Dr Who;

Crossroads; The Sweeney; Marked Personal; General Hospital; Targets. Education: grammar school. m. actress Maggie Wells, 1 s. Christian. Address: c/o Julia MacDermot Ltd, London W6. Starsign: Taurus/Gemini. Hobbies: sailing, fishing, diving. Unfulfilled ambition: to sail round the world.

RINTOUL, David
Actor b. 29.11.48 Aberdeen. Trained at RADA after winning a scholarship. Then rep, including Worthing, Chester, Newcastle, Edinburgh, Guildford. Stage incl: The Speakers (Theatre des Nations, Belgrade); National Theatre (The World Turned Upside Down; The Putney Debates). Films incl: Legend of the Werewolf. TV incl: Weir of Hermiston; The Flight of the Heron; The Hunchback of Notre Dame; 1990; Crown Court; Warship; Lillie; Prince Regent; Henry VIII; The Mallens; One Chance in Four; Pride and Prejudice. Education: Robert Gordon's College, Aberdeen; Edinburgh University (MA). Address: c/o Richard Stone, London WC2.

Starsign: Sagittarius. Hobbies: languages, food, horse riding. Unfulfilled ambition: moderate wealth.

RIPPON, Angela
Journalist/newscaster b. 12.10.44 Plymouth, Devon. On leaving school at 17 joined local daily newspaper working in the photographic department and after two and a half years joined the local Sunday Newspaper, The Independent, as a junior reporter. During this time she was a member of a team covering the Torrey Canyon disaster. In 1966 joined BBC Plymouth to report for and present Spotlight Southwest and Points West (Bristol). Joined Westward TV to edit and introduce women's programme, Open House, 1969; also produced Westward Report and three documentaries. In 1974 rejoined BBC as a news reporter and in 1975 helped present News Extra. In 1976 introduced 'new look' Nine o'clock News. Appeared in the 1976 Morecambe and Wise Christmas show (in which she danced) and presented the Eurovision Song Contest 1977. Other TV incl: the Rippon Reports series; The Country Game; contributions to Newsday on BBC2 and Top Gear. Newsreader of the Year 1977 and 1978. Education: Plymouth secondary and grammar schools. m. Christopher Dare. Address: c/o IMG, London

W1. Starsign: Libra. Hobbies: riding, gardening, cooking.

RIX, Brian CBE
Actor/theatrical manager b. 27.1.24 Cottingham, East Yorks. Began acting career with Donald Wolfit in Cardiff when he was 17. After National Service, first as a Bevin Boy then in the RAF, he ran rep companies at Ilkley, Bridlington and Margate and at 26 was a highly successful actor/manager. Became famous through his staging of Reluctant Heroes, both on tour and at London's Whitehall Theatre where it ran for more than four years. Long-running stage successes kept him at the Whitehall for 16 years before going to the Garrick and more successes. Has appeared in 11 films and more than 70 farces on BBC TV. Also hosted the first TV series for the mentally handicapped, Let's Go. Director of the Cooney Marsh Theatre Group in charge of five London theatres within the group. Education: Bootham School, York. m. actress Elspet Gray, 2 d. Shelley, Louisa. 2 s. Jamie, Jonathan. Address: c/o William Morris Agency, London W1. Starsign: Aquarius. Hobbies: amateur radio, cricket. Unfulfilled ambition: to retire with enough money so that all unachieved ambitions can be achieved.

ROACHE, William

Actor b. 25.4.32 Ilkeston, Derbyshire. After five years in the army, in which he received a commission in the Royal Welsh Fusiliers, he went into rep at Nottingham and Oldham. Films incl: Behind the Mask; His and Hers; Queens Guards. Has appeared regularly as Ken Barlow in Coronation Street since 1960. He and his wife run their own production company presenting plays and chat shows, in which they frequently appear. Education: Rydal School. m. Sara, 1 d. Vanya, 1 s. Linus. Address: c/o Spotlight, London WC2. Starsign: Taurus. Hobbies: philosophy, astrology. Unfulfilled ambition: 'if ambition is the desire for power, fame and honour, my ambition is to be rid of it'

ROBERTSON, Mick

Presenter b. 14.2.41 Petworth, Sussex. Trained as a teacher and worked with a play parks scheme in London before joining Thames TV, first as a researcher and then, in 1972, as Magpie compere, a job which has since taken

him all over the world. Keenly interested in football, is president of the Portsmouth Young Supporters' Club. Records incl one LP and two singles, including The Tango is Over. Education: Midhurst Grammar School. Address: c/o Thames TV, London NW1. Starsign: Aquarius. Hobbies: football, the cinema, restoring his cottage in Dorset. Unfulfilled ambition: to see Portsmouth in the First Division.

ROBINSON, Cardew

Actor/comedian b. 14th August Goodmayes, Essex. Began in variety straight from school, then rep and tours. Nickname 'The Cad' arose from a character he created in an RAF wartime Gang Show. First TV 1947, but has appeared in all entertainment media. Most recent stage incl: Camelot; Don't Just Lie There, Say Something. Films: Sorry Nurse; Come Play With Me. Radio: You've Got to be Joking. TV: Whodunnit?; Tell Us Another. Runs a radio and TV scriptwriting service. Education: Harrow County Grammar. m. (dis), 2 d. Leanne, Lindy. Address: c/o Peter Pritchard Ltd, London SW1. Starsign: Leo. Hobbies: golf, football, studying North American Indians. Unfulfilled ambition: to abolish one-way streets.

ROBINSON, Robert

Commentator b. 17.12.27 Liverpool. Trained as a journalist after National

Service in the West African Army Service Corps. First broadcast 1955. Radio: Today (1971-74); Stop the Week. TV incl: Points of View; Ask the Family; All Our Yesterdays; Call My Bluff; Brain of Britain; Robinson's Travels; The Book Programme; Word for Word. Books: Conspiracy; Landscape of Dead Dons. Education: Raynes Park Grammar School; Exeter College, Oxford (English language and literature). m. Josephine, 2 d. Lucy, Suzy, 1 s. Nicholas. Address: c/o BBC, London W12. Starsign: Sagittarius.

ROBSON, Zuleika

Actress b. 29.5.53 Acaster Malbis, Yorks. Trained at Corona Stage School. Stage incl: Romeo and Juliet; Equus; Alfie; Spring at Marino. Films: Cromwell; Revenge; Isadora; Blood on Satan's Claw. TV incl: Drama 1967; Jackanory Playhouse; Heidi; Blackmail; The Lion, the Witch and the Wardrobe; The Growing Summer; Sexton Blake; A Man of Our Times; Melissa; Hunter's Walk; The Changes; Anne of

Green Gables; Anne of Avonlea; The Anarchist; Bouquet of Barbed Wire; Wind of Change; People Like Us; Crown Court. Education: Sutherland House, Cromer, Norfolk; The Old Hall, Hethersett, Norfolk. Address: c/o Jim Thompson, London WC1. Starsign: Gemini. Hobbies: cinema, theatre, reading, cooking, travelling, writing, getting to like horses better. Unfulfilled ambitions: 'for my father to do for me what Margaret Mitchell did for Vivien Leigh; to be able to fill out my tax return forms without getting chronic migraines!'.

ROCCO, Mark
Professional wrestler b. 11.5.51 Manchester. Five years as amateur before turning 'pro' in 1969. British heavy middleweight champion and contender for world light heavyweight championship. Education: grammar school. m. Ann. Address: Whitefield, Manchester. Starsign: Taurus. Hobbies: horse riding, yachting, squash. Unfulfilled ambition: to hold world light heavyweight championship.

RODD, Michael
Reporter/presenter b. 29.11.43 North Shields. Joined Border TV 1965 and BBC Newcastle 1967. TV incl: Border News and Lookaround; News at Ten; Look North; Nationwide; Screen Test; Science Session; 24 Hours;

Tomorrow's World; The Risk Business; Tuesday Documentary. Education: Trinity College, Glenalmond; University of Newcastle upon Tyne. m. Nita, 3 s. Benjamin, Jonathan, Owen. Address: c/o BBC, London W14. Starsign: Sagittarius. Hobbies: music, building. Unfulfilled ambitions: very few.

RODGERS, Anton
Actor b. 10.1.33 Wisbech, Cambs. Trained at Italia Conti, appearances as boy actor in Carmen, Great Expectations and The Winslow Boy and rep experience at Birmingham, Northampton and Hornchurch before going to LAMDA. Joined cast of The Boy Friend 1957, since when has played many parts and directed large number of plays. Stage also includes Songbook. Films incl: Rotten to the Core; The Man Who Haunted Himself; Scrooge. TV incl: Ukridge; The Elusive Pimpernel; The Organisation; Zodiac; Rumpole of the Bailey; Lillie. Education: Westminster. m. Morna, 1 d. Thalia, 1 s. Adam.

Address: c/o Leading Artists, London SW1. Starsign: Capricorn. Hobby: fly fishing.

RODGERS, Clodagh
Singer b. 5.3.47 Warrenpoint, Co Down. Began to sing professionally when 15 on the Irish ballroom circuit. Within a year she had moved to London with the family but it was eight years before her first disc hit, Come Back and Shake Me. Other successes have followed: Goodnight Midnight; Jack in the Box; Save Me; Love is Deep Inside of Me. Pantomimes, tours, summer seasons and TV spectaculars such as When Irish Eyes Are Smiling. Education: Poor Clares Convent, Newry, N Ireland. m. manager John Morris, 1 s. Matthew. Address: c/o Clomar Enterprises Ltd, London NW10. Starsign: Pisces. Hobbies: cooking, collecting antiques, horse riding. Unfulfilled ambition: to star in a musical on stage and screen.

RODGERS, David
Presenter b. 25.5.52 Yealmpton, Devon. After

three years' training in film and TV production, joined BBC as presenter of morning radio show. Worked on American radio and TV before joining Westward TV; presenter of Westward Diary and Treasure Hunt. Education: Tavistock Comprehensive; Plymouth Art College. Address: Lipson, Plymouth. Starsign: Gemini. Hobbies: sailing, food and wine, cinema. Unfulfilled ambition: to present the first TV programme from outer space.

ROËVES, Maurice
Actor/theatre director b. 19th March, Sunderland, Co Durham. Trained at the Royal College of Drama, Glasgow and has since had much experience both as actor and director. Stage incl: Macbeth; Romeo and Juliet; Othello; Tunes of Glory (world premiere); Carnegie; There Was a Man (one-man play at Edinburgh Festival 1977). Directed Little Boxes; Exit the King; City Sugar; Jacques Brel is Alive and Well and Living in Paris; Doo Lally Tap (Edinburgh Festival 1979). Films incl: The Fighting Prince of Donegal; Ulysses; Oh What a Lovely War; Young Winston; A Day at the Beach; The Eagle Has Landed; Transfusion; When Eight Bells Toll; SOS Titanic. TV incl many guest roles in series such as The Sweeney; Target; Oil Strike North. Also Danger UXB; Twelfth Night. Education: Church St Patrick, Hyndland Secondary School,

Glasgow. 1 d. Sarah. Address: c/o ICM Ltd, London W1. Starsign: Pisces. Hobbies: five-mile early morning runs, seven-card stud poker, girls, writing. Unfulfilled ambitions: to get married; to go to the moon; to sell a script or book.

ROGERS, Ted
Comedian b. 20.7.35 London. Started in bookshops and reached present status the hard way after touring, guest appearances, cabaret and one-night stands. Started by winning talent contest. After National Service in the RAF became a Butlin's Redcoat and in 1963, appeared in Billy Cotton's Band Show and had his own TV series, And So To Bed. Other TV incl: Sunday Night at the London Palladium; 3-2-1; a one-hour special, Ted on the Spot. On stage he has played the London Palladium 11 times and is the only British comedian to have worked with Bing Crosby both in Britain and America, being recommended to Crosby by Perry Como after meeting him during the Royal Variety Show in 1974. Has appeared on stage in Las Vegas, New York and Toronto and in cabaret in Hong Kong and Sydney and 11 times at London's Savoy Hotel. Also entertained at the Prime Minister's Euro Rally. First radio series in 1979. Education: St Mary's Secondary, Kennington, London. m. Margie (dis),

2 d. Dena, Fenella. Address: c/o Yorkshire TV, Leeds. Starsign: Cancer. Hobbies: polo, riding. Unfulfilled ambition: to receive fewer buff envelopes.

ROLFE, Guy
Actor b. 27.12.11 Lowdon, Essex. Wide stage, film and TV experience after a sound training in fit-ups in Ireland with Anew Macmaster. Claims to have gained his education from the backs of cigarette cards. m. actress Jane Aird. Address: c/o Eric Glass Ltd, London W1. Starsign: Capricorn. Unfulfilled ambitions: to ride the winner of the Grand National; to be able to tell butter from margarine; to live until tomorrow.

ROPER, David
Actor b. 20.6.44 Bradford, Yorks. Was an accountant for 8 years before leaving to take up acting, training at Bristol Old Vic Theatre School. TV incl: Country Tales; Churchill's People; Crown Court; Coronation Street; My Brother's Keeper. Starred in The Cuckoo Waltz and Leave It To Charlie. Education:

Bradford Grammar School.
m. Jacqui. Address:
Alphinston, Devon. Starsign:
Gemini. Hobbies: squash,
writing. Unfulfilled ambition:
to beat Leonard Rossiter at
squash.

ROSE, Clifford
Actor b. 24.10.29 Hamnish,
Herefordshire. Started with
Elizabethan Theatre
Company, followed by rep at
Ipswich, Nottingham, Bristol,
Royal Shakespeare
Company before West End,
films and TV. Films incl: The
Marat/Sade; Work is a
Four-Letter Word. TV incl:
Roads to Freedom; Callan;
The Pallisers; How Green
Was My Valley; The Lady
From The Sea; The Devil's
Crown; Richard II; Secret
Army. Education: King's
School, Worcester; King's
College, London. m. actress
Celia Ryder, 1 d. Alison,
1 s. Jonathan. Address: c/o
ICM Ltd, London W1.
Starsign: Scorpio. Hobbies:
music, travel, Russian.

ROSE, David
TV reporter b. 11.2.41
London. Journalistic training
on The Scotsman and then
worked for Border TV on

Lookaround; BBC Scotland
and Current Account and
Southern TV Day By Day.
Joined ITN as a reporter
1972; has been their political
correspondent since 1974.
Education: Dalhousie
School; Merchiston Castle
School. m. Rosalind,
1 d. Isobel, 2 s. Jeremy,
Christopher. Address: c/o
ITN, London W1. Starsign:
Aquarius. Hobbies: sport,
gardening. Unfulfilled
ambition: to win Wimbledon.

ROSS, Annie
Actress/singer b. 25.7.30
Mitcham, Surrey. Born into
famous show business family
(comedian Jimmy Logan
her brother, jazz singer Ella
Logan her aunt, with whom
she lived in America). She
was taken to Hollywood when
five to be in Our Gang
comedy film and a few years
later was Judy Garland's
sister in Presenting Lilly Mars.
Starred in London production
of Vaudeville and, after
cabaret dates in London and
on the Continent, returned to
West End in Cranks. Teamed
in America with jazz singers
Lambert and Hendricks to
form a trio. Came back to
England with Count Basie
Band in the early 1960's and
went solo to become one of
Britain's foremost revue and
cabaret stars and jazz
vocalists. Also a songwriter
(Twisted); actress
(Kennedy's Children; The
Seven Deadly Sins; The
Threepenny Opera); writer of
a cookbook, Annie Ross Says
Come On In; and involved in
jazz club venture . TV incl:

Not So Much a Programme;
The Caledonian Cascade;
Charlie Endell; The Ghosts of
Motley Hall; Send in the Girls.
Education: Hawthorne
Grammar; Beverly Hills High,
California. m. actor Sean
Lynch (dis). Address: c/o
Peter Campbell, London W1.
Starsign: Leo. Hobbies:
cooking, fishing. Unfulfilled
ambition: to sail round the
Western Isles of Scotland.

ROSS, Nick
Reporter/presenter/ director
b. 7.8.47 London. Worked for
BBC in Northern Ireland prior
to leaving university before
joining them as a reporter
1971. Radio and TV
experience. Radio incl:
Round-up Reports; Speaking
Personally (both N Ireland);
The Price of Violence;
Newsdesk; The World
Tonight; Today; The World At
One; PM; Time For Action;
Checkpoint. TV incl: In
Question; Scene Around Six
(both N Ireland); Man Alive
Report; Out of Court; The
Editors; Play For Today;
Tuesday documentaries;
Portrait of A 'Terrorist';
various schools
programmes; various
documentaries. Education:
Wallington County Grammar
School, Surrey; Queen's
University, Belfast. Address:
c/o Jon Roseman
Associates, London W1.
Starsign: Leo. Hobbies: will
try anything. Unfulfilled
ambition: to try everything.

ROSSINGTON, Jane
Actress b. 5.3.43 Derby.
Amateur acting experience
before joining The Archers as
Monica Downs. Rep at
Sheffield and York, then
Nurse Ford in Emergency –
Ward 10 and Jill Richardson
in Crossroads since it
started. Education: Sutton
Coldfield Grammar; Rose
Bruford College of Speech
and Drama. m. (1st) TV
director Tim Jones (dis),
(2nd) estate agent David
Dunger, 1 d. Sorrel.
Address: Birmingham.
Starsign: Pisces. Hobbies:
collecting clocks, crochet,
wine-making.

ROSSINGTON, Norman
Actor b. 24.12.28 Liverpool.
Originally an office boy at
Liverpool Docks, but started
acting as an amateur and
trained at Bristol Old Vic
Theatre School. An original
member of the cast of Salad
Days. London plays incl:
Tiger at the Gates; The
Changeling; Progress to the
Park; Royal Shakespeare
Co; In the Red. Joined
London Old Vic to tour USA
in A Midsummer Night's
Dream 1954. Supporting
roles in scores of films and
on TV. Films incl: Saturday
Night and Sunday Morning;
The Longest Day; A Hard
Day's Night; Tobruk; Double
Trouble; The Charge of the
Light Brigade; Digby the
Biggest Dog in the World;
Man in the Wilderness;
Young Winston. TV incl;
Tracy and Me; The Army
Game; Our House; Curry
and Chips; The Misfit; Roads
to Freedom; The Search for
the Nile; Casanova; Hamlet;
Lenin; Hunter's Walk; Crime
of Passion; Comedy
Playhouse; Armchair
Theatre; Village Hall; Budgie;
Follow That Dog; Spooner's
Patch. Education: Sefton
Park Elementary; Liverpool
Technical College. divorced.
Address: c/o Peter
Charlesworth Ltd, London
SW7. Starsign: Capricorn.
Hobbies: woodwork, skiing,
golf, languages.

ROSSITER, Leonard
Actor b. 21.10.26 Liverpool.
Unable to afford to go to
university to study
languages, worked in an
insurance office for six years
before joining Preston Rep.
Became assistant stage
manager and then went to
Wolverhampton and
Salisbury. In Free As Air
1957-58 and a tour of The
Iceman Cometh. Joined
Bristol Old Vic 1959 and was
there two years. Followed by
great activity on stage, in
films and on TV. Stage incl:
Arturo Ui; The Strange Case
of Martin Richter; Disabled;
The Heretic; The Caretaker;
Semi-Detached (in New
York). Films incl: A Kind of
Loving; Billy Liar; This
Sporting Life; King Rat; 2001
– A Space Odyssey; Otley;
Deadlier Than The Male;
Oliver!; Luther; Barry Lyndon.
TV plays and series incl:
Z Cars; Thick as Thieves;
Loch Lomond; The
Magistrate; The Baby's
Name Being Kitchener; If
There Weren't Any Blacks,
You'd Have To Invent Them;
Rising Damp (he was also in
The Banana Box, the play on
which the series was based);
The Fall and Rise of Reginald
Perrin; The Loser. Education:
Liverpool Collegiate.
m. (1st) actress Josephine
Tewson (dis), (2nd) actress
Gillian Raine, 1 d. Camilla
(from 2nd m). Address:
Fulham, London. Starsign:
Libra. Hobbies: squash,
football.

ROUTLEDGE, Patricia
Actress/singer b. 17th
February, Birkenhead,
Cheshire. Studied at Bristol
Old Vic Theatre School and
first stage appearance at
Liverpool Playhouse 1952 as
Hippolyta in A Midsummer
Night's Dream. Wide rep
experience incl Guildford,
Worthing, Windsor before
London debut in The Duenna
1956. London stage also
incl: Zuleika; The Love
Doctor; Follow That Girl;
Out of My Mind (revue); Little
Mary Sunshine; Virtue in
Danger; How's the World
Treating You?; The
Magistrate; Cowardy
Custard; Dandy Dick; And a

Nightingale Sang. Also Chichester Festival 1969, 1973, 1975; Bristol Old Vic. Broadway debut 1966 in How's the World Treating You? and later in Darling of the Day for which she received a Tony for Best Musical Actress 1967. Appeared in Offenbach's opera Grand Duchess of Gerolstein at Camden Festival 1978. Films incl: To Sir, With Love; Pretty Polly; The Bliss of Mrs Blossom; 30 is a Dangerous Age Cynthia; Don't Raise the Bridge, Lower the River; If It's Tuesday This Must Be Belgium; Lock Up Your Daughters; etc. Many TV appearances incl: Hobson's Choice; Victoria Regina; Z Cars; Samson and Delilah; Sense and Sensibility; Tartuffe; David Copperfield; When We Are Married; Nicholas Nickleby; Plain Jane; A Visit From Miss Protheroe; the Years Between; Doris and Doreen. Education: Birkenhead High School; Liverpool University. Address: c/o Larry Dalzell Associates Ltd, London WC2. Starsign: Aquarius.

ROWE, Pippa
Actress b. 16th October London. Always wanted to be an actress and worked as a secretary to pay her way through Guildhall School of Music and Drama. Seasons at Kilarney and Bangor before understudying in London in Boeing-Boeing. Rep at Liverpool, Bromley and Crewe. TV incl: Softly,

Softly; Family at War; Whodunnit?; Dixon of Dock Green; General Hospital. Education: private school for girls. m. (dis), 1 s. Matthew. Address: c/o Roger Carey, London WC2. Starsign: Libra. Hobbies: gardening, touring. Unfulfilled ambitions: to do a TV comedy series; to go to America and Australia.

ROWLANDS, Patsy
Actress b. 19.1.40. Always wanted to be an actress and after training at the Guildhall School of Music and Drama, made her first professional appearance in the chorus line of a London West End musical. Toured and did a season with the Fol-De-Rols before her big break in Valmouth. Stage includes revue, plays and recently, Shut Your Eyes and Think of England; Find the Lady. Films incl: Polanski's Tess. TV incl: The Gamblers; The Memorandum; Public Eye; Bless This House; The Squirrels; My Son, My Son; Ladies; The History of Mr Polly. Convent educated in London. m. (dis.), 1 s. Alan. Address: c/o David White Associates, London SW1. Starsign: Capricorn/ Aquarius. Hobbies: gardening, cooking. Unfulfilled ambitions: to go to America; to be in a long-running US TV series.

RUSHTON, William
Actor/writer/comedian b. 18.8.37 London. After National Service in the army he joined a solicitor's office

as an articled clerk, opted out to become a freelance cartoonist and helped to found and edit Private Eye. Came to the stage by joining Canterbury's Marlowe Theatre at the invitation of friends. Other stage incl: The Buxom Muse (at the Mermaid); Nights at the Comedy; The Private Eye Revue; Treasure Island; Gulliver's Travels. Films incl: Flight of the Doves; Pig Sticking; Those Magnificent Men in Their Flying Machines; The Bliss of Mrs Blossom; Adventures of a Private Eye. Came to fame with TV programmes That Was the Week That Was and Not So Much a Programme. Other TV incl: Don't Just Sit There; Up Sunday; Jackanory; Grubstreet; Any Questions; When Santa Rode the Prairie (which he wrote); Celebrity Squares; Dawson and Friends; You Can Make It; Those Wonderful TV Times; Ask a Silly Answer; Open House; Parkinson; Star Turn Challenge; Blankety Blank; You Can Make It; I'm Sorry I Haven't a Clue; Wake Up Wizzy; The Day of the Grocer. Books: William Rushton's Dirty Book (!!!); Super Pig. Education: Shrewsbury School. m. singer/dancer Arlene Dorgan, 1 s. Tobias, 2 step-s. Matthew, Sam. Address: c/o Kismet, London W1. Starsign: Leo. Hobbies: ping-pong, cricket, going to the pub. Unfulfilled ambition: to be a movie star.

RYCART, Patrick
Actor b. 9.5.52 Leamington.
Trained at Webber Douglas
Academy of Dramatic Art. TV
incl: General Hospital; The
Cedar Tree; Many Wives of
Patrick; Lillie; Dame of Sark;
Romeo and Juliet; My Son,
My Son. Education: Bloxham
School, Banbury, Oxon.
m. actress Marsha Fitzalan.
Address: c/o CCA, London
SW6. Starsign: Taurus.
Hobbies: tennis, holidays.
Unfulfilled ambition: to see
The Mousetrap.

S

SACHS, Andrew
Actor/writer b. 7.4.30 Berlin,
Germany. Came to England
just before the war. Began
working in the theatre after
leaving school. Rep at
Worthing and Liverpool and
with Brian Rix on tour and
London's West End. Other
stage incl: A Voyage Round
My Father; Habeas Corpus;
No Sex Please – We're
British. Probably best known
for his role as Manuel in
Fawlty Towers (it won him the
Variety Club Award as the
Most Promising Artist in
1977), though he has many
TV credits incl: Krek Bristle;
Took and Co; Crown Court;
James and the Giant Peach;
Tommy Cooper Show; Ask
Aspel; Celebrity Squares;
Star Turn; Strangers; Les
Dawson Show; Lovely
Couple; Rising Damp; The
Tempest; The History of Mr
Polly. Written several stage
plays incl: Made in Heaven.
Education: William Ellis
School, Highgate, London.
m. actress Melody Lang,
1 d. Kate, 2 s. Bill, John.
Address: c/o Richard Stone,
London WC2. Starsign: Aries.
Hobbies: wildlife,
photography, art. Unfulfilled

ambitions: to write a successful play, to become a Harlem Globetrotter.

SACHS, Leonard
Actor b. 26.9.09 Roodeport, Transvaal, S Africa. First appearance on the stage in South Africa 1926 and in London three years later. Has since had wide theatre experience as actor and director. With Peter Ridgeway founded the Players' Theatre 1936 and, except for Army service, directed and produced at that theatre till 1947. Probably best known for his role as chairman of The Good Old Days (which started in 1953), but other TV incl: Family at War; Coronation Street; The Man From Haven; Crown Court; The Glittering Prizes. Education: Jeppe High School, Johannesburg; Witwatersrand University. m. actress Eleanor Summerfield, 2 s. Robin, Toby. Address: c/o Miller Management, Teddington, Middx. Starsign: Libra. Hobbies: walking, swimming.

SADLER, Brent
TV reporter/ presenter

b. 29.11.50 Manchester. After training at the National Council for the Training of Journalists College in Preston, had newspaper experience on the Harrow Observer and Reading Evening Post before going into TV. TV incl: reporter/ news producer, Southern TV; reporter/ presenter, Westward TV; and since 1978 reporter/ presenter HTV's Report West and Report Extra. Education: Royal Masonic Boys' School, Bushey, Herts. Address: c/o HTV, Bristol. Starsign: Sagittarius. Hobbies: sailing (he owns a motor-boat and dinghy), tennis, riding, squash, angling, rugby, basketball, travel, cinema. Unfulfilled ambitions: to direct a film; to make a documentary; to be an ITN reporter.

SALLIS, Peter
Actor b. 1.2.21 Twickenham. Formerly a bank clerk. Came to acting through an amateur group during war service in the RAF. Studied at RADA, first professional appearance in London 1946. Rep and touring for a number of years before returning to London. Recent stage incl: Zoo Story; Cabaret. Films incl: Sarah; Julie; The VIPs; The Mouse on the Moon; Anastasia; Full Circle; Someone is Killing the Great Chefs of Europe. Radio incl: End of Term, a play he wrote himself. Much TV, but perhaps best known as Cleggy in The Last of the Summer Wine. Other TV incl:

Into the Dark; How to Murder Your Wife; The Big Eat; Public Eye; Spyder's Web; The Moonstone; The Diary of Samuel Pepys; Barlow; The Pallisers; Softly, Softy: Task Force; The Flaxborough Chronicles; Yanks Go Home; A Crowded Room; Leave it to Charlie. Education: Minchenden Grammar School, Southgate. m. actress Elaine Usher (divorced and re-married), 1 s. Crispian. Address: c/o London Management, London W1. Starsign: Aquarius. Hobbies: painting, gardening.

SANDERSON, Joan
Actress b. Bristol. Trained at RADA, first professional appearance at Stratford Memorial Theatre where she returned in 1953 to play leads. Rep career started 1940; first West End appearance in See How They Run just after World War II. Since appeared in numerous plays (Habeas Corpus; Popkiss; Banana Ridge) and many TV appearances incl: Crown Court; Upstairs, Downstairs; Wodehouse Playhouse; Please Sir! Holds LRAM and LGSM (Elocution) teaching diplomas. Education: Northumberland House, Bristol. m. actor Gregory Scott. Address: c/o Bryan Drew Ltd, London W1. Starsign: Sagittarius. Hobbies: reading, cooking, driving. Unfulfilled ambition: to retire and live in the country.

SAUNDERS, Alan
Reporter b. 8.8.39 Glasgow.
Newspaper experience on
Daily Record, Sunday
Express. TV: Sportscall;
Grampian Today. Education:
Portobello High School,
Edinburgh. m. Margaret,
3 s. Keith, Gordon, Brian.
Address: Dundee. Starsign:
Leo. Hobbies: golf, table
tennis, sport in general.
Unfulfilled ambitions: to play
professional football and to
win a golf tournament of note.

SAVALAS, Telly
Actor b. 21.11.22 Garden
City, New York. After three
years in the army, he
graduated as a psychologist
from Columbia University.
Then he joined the American
Broadcasting Company,
rebelled against the
discipline and, at 36, became
an actor, gaining an Oscar
nomination for a supporting
role in his first film, Birdman of
Alcatraz. Other films incl: The
Interns; Cape Fear; Man from
the Diner's Club; The
Greatest Story Ever Told;
Beau Geste; The Dirty Dozen;
Capricorn One; Kelly's
Heroes; McKenna's Gold; On
Her Majesty's Secret Service;

Diamond Mercenaries;
Escape to Athena. TV incl:
The Marcus Nelson Murders
(in which the Kojak character
first appeared); Kojak.
m. (1st) Catherine (dis),
(2nd) teacher Marilyn (dis),
(3rd) actress Sally Adams,
3 d. Christine (from 1st m),
Candice, Penelope (both
from 2nd m), 1 s. Nicholas
(from 3rd m). Starsign:
Scorpio.

SAVILE, Jimmy OBE
Disc jockey/entertainer
b. 31.10.26 Leeds. Fitness
fanatic and millionaire noted
for his untiring efforts for
charity, for which he claims to
have raised more than
£3,000,000. Left school at 14
years old. Began as a miner,
also managed a dance hall.
TV incl: Savile's Travels; Top
of the Pops; safety-belt
commercials, Clunk Click;
Jim'll Fix It. Books: As It
Happens (autobiography);
Love is an Uphill Thing; God'll
Fix it. Address: c/o Leeds
General Infirmary. Starsign:
Scorpio, Hobbies: cycling,
walking.

SCALES, Prunella
Actress b. 22nd June Sutton
Abinger, Surrey. Trained at

the Old Vic Theatre School
and with Uta Hagen in New
York. Made her name as Kate
Starling in TV comedy series
Marriage Lines. Stage incl:
Prospect Theatre; Royal
Shakespeare Company;
Chichester Festival Theatre;
The Old Vic. London West
End plays incl: The Promise;
The Wolf; Hay Fever;
Breezeblock Park. TV incl:
Coronation Street; Country
Matters; Seven of One;
Fawlty Towers; Mr Big; Lucky
Feller; Whodunnit?; Doris and
Doreen. Education: Moira
Havers School, Eastbourne.
m. actor Timothy West,
2 s. Samuel, Joseph.
Starsign: Cancer. Hobbies:
growing vegetables,
listening to music, reading.
Unfulfilled ambitions: to play
Rosmersholm and be in Play
for Today.

SCOTT, Brough
Sports presenter b. 12.12.42
London. Was amateur and
then professional National
Hunt jockey 1962-71 riding
exactly 100 winners before
giving up in an ambulance en
route to Warwick Hospital.
Had started racing TV and
journalism during previous
injury spells. Joined ITV
commentary team 1977. On
radio presented The
Thoroughbred 1978. On TV
produced Something to
Brighten the Morning, a
biography of Mill Reef 1973,
and was presenter and writer
of The Derby Stakes in 1979.
Other TV incl: BBC racing
commentaries July/August
1970; The Challenge of the

Sexes (Southern TV);
Sporting Chance (Tyne
Tees); Thames Sport
magazine, 1977-79.
Education: Radley and
Oxford (history). m. former
British skier Susie McInnes,
1 d. Sophie, 2 s. Charlie,
Jamie. Address: Ewhurst,
Surrey. Starsign: Sagittarius.
Hobby: making bonfires.
Unfulfilled ambitions: to finish
his best-seller, to walk across
South America.

SCOTT, Jack
Senior BBC weatherman b.
9.11.23 Co Durham. Joined
the weather service as
meteorological assistant in
1941 straight from school.
Celebrates 11 years as BBC
weatherman in May 1980.
Estimates he has televised
3,000 weather forecasts.
Education: Spennymoor
Grammar School, Co
Durham; Nottingham
Technical College. married.
Address: c/o London
Weather Centre, London.
Starsign: Scorpio. Hobbies:
golf, collecting weather
cartoons.

SCOTT, Terry
Comedian b. 4.5.27 Watford.
Was studying accountancy,
but after war service in the
Royal Navy, went into rep at
Grange-over-Sands. Then
years of work in clubs, pubs,
pantomime and summer
shows before teaming up
with Bill Maynard for Great
Scott, It's Maynard. Stage
incl: The Mating Game; A
Bedful of Foreigners. Films
incl: The Bridal Path; Carry

On Up the Khyber; Carry On
Camping; Carry On Henry;
Carry On Up the Jungle;
Carry On Loving. TV incl:
Hugh and I; The Gnomes of
Dulwich; The Scott On ...
series; Son of the Bride;
Happy Ever After; Terry and
June. Education: Watford
Grammar School.
m. (1st) dis, (2nd) former
ballet dancer Margaret
Pollen, 4 d. Sarah, Nicola,
Lindsay, Alexandra.
Address: Godalming, Surrey
Starsign: Taurus. Hobbies:
gardening and chickens.
Unfulfilled ambition: to return
to 'straight' theatre.

SEABROOK, Peter
Horticulturalist b. 2.11.35
Chelmsford, Essex. Trained
in commercial horticulture
production and marketing.
Joined BBC 1974, first to
present Dig This! and, since
1976, Gardeners' World as
well. Author of several books,
including Peter Seabrook's
Complete Vegetable
Gardener and Peter
Seabrook's Book of the
Garden. Education: King
Edward VI Grammar,
Chelmsford; Essex
Agricultural College.
m. Margaret, 1 d. Alison,

1 s. Roger. Address: c/o
BBC, Pebble Mill,
Birmingham. Starsign:
Scorpio. Hobby: gardening.
Unfulfilled ambitions: to learn
French; to learn to play the
piano to one's own
satisfaction; to visit
Wimbledon finals and the last
night of the Proms.

SEATON, Stuart
TV presenter/journalist
b. 12.4.27 Caergwrle,
N Wales. A journalist all his
working life, specialising in
agricultural journalism since
leaving the RAF 30 years
ago. Now managing editor
Farmers Guardian.
Presenter/ commentator/
consultant The Other Man's
Farm 1960-65; presenter/
script-writer Farming
Comment 1961-65;
presenter/ script consultant
Farming Outlook (Tyne Tees
TV) 1965-67 and since 1970.
Also contributor to BBC's
radio farming programmes,
commercial film script-writer
and narrator. Education:
grammar school. m. Audrey,
1 d. Val. Address: c/o Tyne
Tees TV, Newcastle upon
Tyne. Starsign: Aries.
Hobbies: film-making,
photography.

SECKER, Cathy
Announcer b. 18.2.50
Bedlington, Northumberland.
Originally worked in a bank,
but encouraged by her
husband when she married,
became a photographic and
fashion model until she
started a family. Has also

done TV commercials. Joined Tyne Tees TV as an announcer 1978. Education: The Gregg High School for Girls. m. Wally Secker, 1 d. Jayne, 1 s. David. Address: c/o Tyne Tees TV, Newcastle upon Tyne. Starsign: Aquarius. Hobbies: photography, reading, gardening. Unfulfilled ambition: to be involved in a networked children's TV programme.

SECOMBE, Harry CBE
Actor/comedian/ singer b. 8.9.21 Swansea. Originally a clerk in a steel mill, but began entertaining at church socials when a child. Forces shows during wartime service in the army and the Windmill Theatre on demob 1946. First break on radio in Variety Bandbox, then Welsh Rarebit and Educating Archie before The Goon Show. Numerous variety shows; stage musicals (The Four Musketeers; Pickwick); TV and guest appearances (Stars on Sunday). Books: Twice Brightly; Goon For Lunch; Welsh Fargo. Education: St Thomas Junior; Dynevor School, Swansea. m. Myra, 2 d. Jennifer, Katy,

2 s. Andrew, David. Address: Cheam, Surrey. Starsign: Virgo. Hobbies: reading, photography, golf, cricket.

SERLE, Chris
Reporter b. 13.7.43 Bristol. Former actor (Bristol Old Vic), radio producer (Petticoat Line, Brain of Britain) and TV director. Now one of Esther Rantzen's 'boys' on That's Life. 6ft 5ins tall. Education: Clifton College and Trinity College, Dublin. Address: c/o BBC, London W12. Starsign: Cancer. Hobbies: gliding, jazz drumming. Unfulfilled ambition: 'to do today what I nearly always put off till tomorrow'.

SHALLCROSS, Brian
Political correspondent/ interviewer b. 27.12.37 Cheshire. Journalist on northern morning papers. TV incl: Tyne Tees TV's children's programmes; Southern TV's Day by Day and political programme. Live commentaries on political party conferences for ITV network. Education: Newcastle Royal Grammar; University of Durham.

President of the University Debating Society and after political discussion programmes for Tyne Tees, joined their current affairs dept. m. Maureen, 2 d. Joanne, Rebecca, 1 s. Daniel. Address: Hedge End, Hants. Starsign: Capricorn. Hobbies: drawing with a felt pen, wine making, breeding goldfish, swimming. Unfulfilled ambition: to present live commentary on the full TV coverage of Parliament.

SHATNER, William
Actor b. 22.3.31 Montreal, Canada. Started career in summer stock theatre. Radio plays and work at National Rep Theatre, Ottawa, and Stratford Festival Theatre, Ontario. On Broadway he was in The World of Suzie Wong for 18 months. Films incl: The Brothers Karamazov; Judgment at Nuremberg; The Intruder; Sole Survivor; Big Bad Mama; Star Trek. Many TV plays and series incl: Dr Kildare; Hawaii Five-O; A Man Called Ironside; Capt Jim Kirk in Star Trek; Barbara Coast. Education: McGill University, Montreal (BA). m.(1st) actress Gloria Rand (dis), (2nd) actress Marcie Lafferty, 2 d. Lesley, Lisabeth. Address: c/o Desilu Productions Ltd, Hollywood. Starsign: Aries. Hobby: writing.

SHAW, Clem
Announcer b. 7.2.43 London.
Trained at Central School of
Speech and Drama before
joining BBC2 as an
announcer and director of
Network in 1971. Was in turn
announcer for Anglia and
Tyne Tees before moving to
Border TV in 1975. Educated
in London. m. poet Jane
O'Leary, 1 d. Rebecca, 1 s.
Shane. Address: c/o Border
TV, Carlisle. Starsign:
Aquarius. Hobby: music.
Unfulfilled ambition: to finish
cultivating his garden.

SHAW, Martin
Actor b. 21.1.45
Birmingham. Became a sales
clerk when he left school.
Trained at LAMDA, rep at
Hornchurch, Bromley and
Bristol Old Vic. Then a
leading part in TV play
Travelling Light; a spell in the
Doctor at Large series; Helen
– A Woman of Today; Electra;
The Professionals. Stage incl:
Look Back in Anger; The
Contractor; Cancer; The
Battle of Shrivings; National
Theatre for The Baachae;
Saturday, Sunday, Monday;
A Streetcar Named Desire;
Miss Julie; Teeth 'n' Smiles.
Films incl: Polanski's

Macbeth and Operation
Daybreak. Education: Great
Barr Comprehensive,
Birmingham. m. Jill, 1 d.
Sophie, 2 s. Luke, Joseph.
Address: c/o Hutton
Management Ltd, London
SW5. Starsign: Aquarius.
Hobbies: walking, reading,
strumming the guitar.

SHAW, Roger
Announcer/newscaster/
straightman b. 8.9.31
Penzance, Cornwall. Variety
of jobs before joining
Westward TV in 1961 – lorry
driver, barman, policeman
(England and Malaya). Did
his National Service in the
RAF as a physical training
instructor and for two years
was the RAF's high jump
champion. Education:
Humphrey Davy School;
Loughborough College.
m. Vivianne Mary, 1 d. Karen
Jane, 1 s. Guy Conrad.
Address: c/o Westward TV,
Plymouth. Starsign: Virgo.
Hobby: omniverous reading,
particularly Ancient History.
Unfulfilled ambition: a
lengthy tour of the Wild West
visiting the famous and
notorious cowtowns – on
horseback, in cowboy gear.

SHENTON, Joan
Presenter b. 16.3.43 Chile.
Started as governess to
ex-King of the Belgians' two
daughters while on a
vacation from Oxford, then
became a waitress and went
into radio on a programme for
BBC World Service, Latin
American Section. Moved to
COI and did a weekly TV film

for Latin America. Joined
Anglia TV as interviewer for
About Anglia, then worked as
a reporter on BBC's
Nationwide for its first three
years. Had her own show,
Person to Person, on Capital
Radio and works for Thames
TV presenting Money-Go-
Round and Help! Education:
Santiago, Buenos Aires;
Guatemala; Guildford,
Surrey, and St Anne's
College, Oxford (Modern
Languages). m. TV producer
Jack Crawshaw. Address:
c/o Thames TV, London
NW1. Starsign: Pisces.
Hobbies: Latin American folk
singing, tennis. Unfulfilled
ambitions: to be an airline
stewardess, to learn
patience.

SINDEN, Donald CBE
Actor b. 9.10.23 Plymouth.
Fellow of the Royal Society of
Arts. Trained at Webber
Douglas School of Dramatic
Art and first appeared on TV
in 1948 in Bullet in the Ballet.
Wide stage and film
experience, following his first
appearance with Charles
F Smith's company, MESA
(Mobile Entertainments
Southern Area) in 1941. TV:
numerous plays and guest

appearances, three series of Our Man From St Mark's; The Organisation; Two's Company. m. Diana Mahony, 2 s. Jeremy, Marcus. Address: c/o John Cadell Ltd, London N6. Starsign: Libra. Hobbies: theatrical history, collecting theatricalia, ecclesiology, reading history, serendipity, London. Unfulfilled ambition: 'to play cricket for England and to score a century in my first innings'.

SINDEN, Jeremy

Actor b. 14.6.50 London. Trained for the stage at LAMDA. Stage incl: Chichester, Bristol Old Vic and Royal Shakespeare Company; The Mating Game (Bournemouth); The Chiltern Hundreds (tour); London West End – Journey's End; Lady Harry. Films incl: Star Wars; Rosie Dixon, Night Nurse. TV incl: The Sweeney; Bass Player and the Blonde; The Expert; Crossroads; Danger UXB; School Play; Soldiers Talking Cleanly; Brideshead Revisited. Education: Lancing College. m. actress Delia Lindsay. Address: c/o Richard Stone, London WC2. Starsign: Gemini. Hobbies: walking, climbing, driving, travel, photography.

SINGLETON, Valerie

TV journalist b. 9.4.37 Hitchin, Herts. Won a scholarship to RADA, went into rep and worked on TV advertising magazines before going to the BBC as

an announcer. Joined Blue Peter 1962. Other TV incl: Blue Peter Special Assignments series on capital cities, islands and homes; Blue Peter Royal Safari (Princess Anne's visit to Kenya, 1971); Val Meets the VIPs; Nationwide's consumer desk; Tonight. Records incl: Solomon Centipede. Education: arts educational school. Address: c/o BBC TV, London W12. Starsign: Aries. Hobbies: looking at London, riding, skiing (snow and water), prowling round sale rooms, photography, travel, reading. Unfulfilled ambition: to spend a year wandering round Greece – and doing very little.

SISSONS, Peter

Newscaster b. 17.7.42 Liverpool. Joined ITN as trainee 1964, reporting since 1967, covering Middle East War. Wounded during Nigerian civil war 1968. Industrial editor 1974. Presenter of News At One, April 1978. Education: Oxford. m. former teacher Sylvia, 2 s. Michael, Jonathan. Address: c/o ITN,

London W1. Starsign: Cancer. Hobbies: clearing woods, his old Bentley car.

SLEEP, Wayne

Ballet dancer/actor born in Plymouth, but brought up on Tyneside. Won a scholarship to the Royal Ballet School when he was 12, joined the Royal Ballet in 1966 and became a principal dancer in 1973. Because of his height (5ft 3ins) he felt he had to diversify, so he combines stage, film and TV work with ballet and choreography. Stage incl: The Tempest; Winnie the Pooh; The Servant of Two Masters; The Point; London Palladium pantomime Aladdin. Films incl: Virgin Soldiers; Tales of Beatrix Potter; The First Great Train Robbery. On radio he has appeared in She Stoops to Conquer while his TV incl: The Dickie Henderson Show; The Eamonn Andrews Show; Showtime; Lena Zavaroni; The Michael Crawford Special; The Cilla Black Show. He devised, choreographed and danced in a jazz ballet, Adam's Rib, for BBC TV. Was in the Royal Variety Show 1978 and in Record Breakers on TV in January 1963 performed entre chats douze, beating Nijinsky's record of entre chats dix and thereby getting into the Guinness Book of Records. Education: Royal Ballet School, London. Address: c/o London Management, London W1.

SLEIGHTHOLME, Dorothy
TV cookery presenter b. 28th June, Norton Malton, Yorks. Interested in cookery since she was at school. Self-taught, largely through women's organisations including Women's Institute of which she is a member. Well-known to afternoon TV viewers through her Farmhouse Kitchen programmes; she has now done 10 series. Education: grammar school. m. William Sleightholme, 1 d. Judith, 2 s. Christopher, Bruce. Address: c/o Yorkshire TV, Leeds. Starsign: Cancer. Hobbies: show judging, cookery, knitting.

SLOMAN, Patricia
Reporter b. 29th August, Sandy, Beds. Trained at Leeds Business Training Centre, and as reporter, Bournemouth Evening Echo. TV: Home at 4.30 1964; Friday at Ten 1964-65; Day by Day 1965-68; regional reporter for Southern TV since 1968. Education: St Mary's Convent, Romford, Essex; Notre Dame Convent, Leeds. m. (dis), 2 s. Richard, Brian. Address: Wimborne, Dorset. Starsign: Virgo.

Hobbies: playing the piano, reading non-fiction, world travelling, Soroptimist International. Unfulfilled ambition: to have her own chat show.

SMITH, Delia
TV cook b. 18.6.41 Woking. Worked in hairdresser's and travel agency before working behind the scenes at a London restaurant where she learnt the art of cookery. Never had any formal tuition. Started preparing food for TV commercials and the occasional appearance on TV programmes before writing a cookery column for a national Sunday newspaper, then the London Evening Standard and now the London Evening News. Chosen to present and demonstrate the first every cookery course on TV spread over three years; now in its second year. Other TV incl: Family Fare; Multi-Coloured Swap Shop; Nationwide. Books incl: Recipes from Country Inns and Restaurants; How to Cheat at Cooking; Frugal Food; Delia Smith's Book of Cakes; Delia Smith's Cookery Course, Parts 1, 2 and 3. Educated at Bexley Heath. m. writer Michael Wyn Jones. Address: c/o BBC, London W12. Starsign: Gemini. Hobbies: cookery, football.

SMITH, Giles
ITN industrial editor b. 23.5.44 Beaconsfield, Bucks. Started in journalism on the Harrow Observer (at

£8 a week). Specialising in industrial matters, he became industrial correspondent of the Western Mail, Cardiff, and later joined The Times as industrial reporter and then BBC in same capacity before moving to ITN 1974. Education: Merchant Taylors School, Northwood. m. Gladwyn, 3 d. Sian, Georgia, Alex. Address: c/o ITN, London W1. Hobbies: cricket, squash. Unfulfilled ambition: to play cricket for England.

SMITH, Jaclyn
Actress b. 26.10.47 Houston, Texas. Started dancing at the age of three and acting since school days and studied drama at Trinity University, San Antonio, Texas. Moved to New York to study ballet but ended up doing TV commercials which led to parts on TV programmes and Charlie's Angels. TV incl: The Rookies; McCloud; Get Christy Love; a World of Disney film. Films incl: Bootleggers; The Adventurers. Education: Pershing Junior High; Lamar High. m. (1st) Alias Smith and

Jones actor Roger Davis (dis), (2nd) actor Dennis Cole. Address: Beverly Hills, California. Starsign: Scorpio. Hobbies: love of animals (her own poodle, Albert, appears in Charlie's Angels), water skiing, swimming, horse-riding, reading, listening to music (principally classical).

SMITH, Ray
Actor b. 1.5.36 Trealaw, Rhondda, Glam. First job was as a building labourer, then National Service in the Army before joining the London Players in Cardiff. Five years in rep in Channel Islands, Scotland and London before TV break in Shadows of Heroes. Other TV incl: Stella; Company of Five; Callan; A Family at War; Six Days of Justice; Public Eye; Sam; Country Matters; The Mill on the Floss; Second City Firsts; End of Season; The Beast. Films incl: Seven Men at Daybreak; Made; The Painted Smile. Radio incl: Some Trust in Chariots; Rape of the Fair Country; Story Time; Candida. Education: Trealaw Mixed Infants; Rhondda Technical College. m. Gale, 1 d. Branwen, 1 s. Justin. Address: c/o Felix de Wolfe, London WC2. Starsign: Taurus. Hobbies: women, whippets, whisky, reading the occasional poem. Unfulfilled ambition: 'to rid myself of the need to succeed'.

SMITH, Sally
Actress b. 19.4.42 Godalming, Surrey. Modelling and acting since she was five. Trained at Aida Foster Stage School. Wide stage and TV experience. Played the lead in Marigold when she was 16. Since then has been in pantomimes (including London Palladium) and stage work incl: Little Darlings; Roar of the Greasepaint, Smell of the Crowd (and Broadway); Arms and the Man; Lock Up Your Daughters; Listen to the Wind; Honour Bright; Something Afoot. Films incl: The Trouble With Eve; She Always Gets Her Man; A Tale of Two Ships; Father Came Too. TV incl: The Human Jungle; The Avengers; No Hiding Place; The Subtle Man; Life of Bliss; The Beryl Reid Show. Education: Aida Foster Stage School. m. musical writer Gordon Haskell. Address: c/o Aida Foster Ltd, London NW8. Starsign: Aries. Hobbies: painting, breeding dogs, riding, swimming, badminton.

SMYTH, Terry
Reporter/presenter b. 11.1.48 Belfast. With Belfast News Letter and Belfast Telegraph newspapers before joining Ulster TV 1973. Education: Rosetta Primary School; Annandale Grammar School. m. Margaret, 1 d. Joanna, 2 s. Gareth, Christopher. Address: c/o Ulster TV, Belfast. Starsign: Capricorn.

Hobbies: squash, show-jumping, hunting, rugby, hockey. Unfulfilled ambition: to become a public relations executive for a multi-national firm.

SNOW, Peter
Reporter b. 20.4.38 Dublin. 6ft 5ins tall. Joined ITN 1962 and was successively sub-editor, reporter, newscaster. Diplomatic correspondent 1966. Education: Wellington College and Balliol College, Oxford (studying classics). m. (1st) Alison (dis), (2nd) Ann, 1 d. Shuna, 1 s. Shane. Address: c/o ITN, London W1. Starsign: Aries. Hobbies: sailing, writing books, photography.

SOPER, Tony
Director/cameraman, writer/presenter b. 10.1.39 Southampton but brought up in Plymouth. Joined BBC straight from school. Studio manager and then film producer with BBC Natural History Unit; now freelance. TV incl: Look; Adventure with Hans Hass; documentaries on the fulmar, shelduck, etc; Out of the Blue; Plapp; Soper

215

at Large; Animal Marvels; Animal Stars; Animal Design; Beside the Sea; Wildtrack; World About Us. Education: Devonport High School. m. Hilary, 1 s. Timothy. Address: c/o BBC, Bristol. Starsign: Capricorn.

SOUL, David
Actor b. 28.8.44 Chicago. Originally wanted to be a teacher; then music became an obsession. Sang in clubs and cabaret – billed as The Covered Man, because, as a gimmick, he wore a ski mask. Eventually went to Hollywood and appeared in such TV series as Cannon; The Streets of San Francisco; Ironside; MacMillan and Wife; Here Come The Brides; Startrek; TV movie Little Ladies of the Night. Overnight success with Starsky and Hutch. Films incl: Johnny Got His Gun; Magnum Force; Doghound Shuffle (re-titled Spot in this country); The Stick-up. Records incl: Don't Give Up On Us; Going In With My Eyes Open; Silver Lady; Let's Have a Quiet Night In; It Sure Brings Out The Love In Your Eyes. Education: Minnesota. m. (1st) college sweetheart

(dis), (2nd) actress Karen Carlson (dis), 2 s. Kristofer (from 1st m), Jon (from 2nd m). Address: Hollywood Hills, Los Angeles. Starsign: Virgo.

SOUTHGATE, Robert
Reporter b. 20.1.34 Preston, Lancs. Russian speaking (he learnt the language while commissioned into the RNVR during National Service), he was on various local and national papers before joining ITN 1967 as reporter. Education: grammar school. m. Elizabeth, 4 s. Paul, Mark, Jonathan, Andrew. Address: Tunbridge Wells, Kent. Starsign: Capricorn. Hobbies: travel, music.

SPANKIE, Jimmy
Broadcaster b. 15.1.36 Dundee. Started in jute industry and amateur dramatics. Presenter, various programmes incl: sports quizzes, panel games, light entertainment, news and magazine programmes. Education: High School, Dundee; Dundee School of Economics. Address: c/o Grampian TV, Aberdeen. Starsign: Capricorn. Hobbies: amateur damatics,

sport. Unfulfilled ambition: to get married.

SPEED, Doris MBE
Actress b. 3.2.14 Manchester. Spent childhood mainly on tour with parents, both musical comedy artists. Professional training in rep. Annie Walker in Coronation Street since the first episode in 1960. Address: Manchester. Starsign: Aquarius. Hobbies: walking, reading, bridge, foreign travel. Unfulfilled ambition: to play with the National or Royal Shakespeare Companies.

SPIERS, Judi
Actress b. 15.3.53 Plymouth. Speech and drama specialist, Westward TV announcer. Trained at Rose Bruford College of Speech and Drama and qualified as a teacher. Stage incl: the Bush Children's Theatre; The Belgrade, Coventry; Plymouth Lunchtime Theatre. TV incl: Summer Scene; Down the Line; Gus Honeybun; Spytrap. Education: Notre Dame Convent, Plymouth. Address: c/o Westward TV, Plymouth.

Starsign: Pisces. Hobbies: reading, travelling, dance/movement, designing jewellery, collecting potted plants, watching old movies. Unfulfilled ambitions: to act in films (if they make the old Hollywood-type again); to travel the world.

SPINETTI, Victor

Actor b. 2.9.33 Cwm, S Wales. One-time waiter and factory worker. Trained for the stage at Cardiff College of Music and Drama. Career started in Welsh concert party. Stage since incl: Expresso Bongo; many plays at Theatre Royal, Stratford East incl: Make Me an Offer; Every Man in His Humour; The Hostage (and in America); Fings Ain't Wot They Used T' Be; Oh, What a Lovely War (also film and in America); Jesus Christ Superstar. Also a stage director incl: Pyjama Tops; Deja Revue; Don't Bother to Dress; Let's Get Laid; Yes, We Have No Pyjamas. Films incl: A Hard Day's Night; The Taming of The Shrew; The Pink Panther. TV incl: Two in Clover; Take My Wife; The Sea; appearances ('enjoyable experiences' he calls them) with Tommy Cooper, Bernie Winters, Kelly Montieth, David Frost, Eamonn Andrews, Russell Harty and Mavis Nicholson; Jackanory Playhouse (The Magic Poltergeist). Education: Monmouth School. Address: c/o Fraser and Dunlop, London W1. Starsign: Virgo. Hobbies:

writing, reading, talking. Unfulfilled ambitions: too numerous.

STACK, Robert

Actor b. 13.1.19 Los Angeles, Calif. Comes from a theatrical family and as a youngster travelled Europe with his mother. Studied acting at the Henry Duffy School of Theatre where he was spotted by a talent scout and his first film was First Love opposite Deanna Durbin. During the war was commissioned in the US Navy and afterwards spent 15 years in Hollywood in every type of movie before fame in The Untouchables as Eliot Ness, a part which Van Johnson turned down and for which Stack won an Emmy. Other TV incl: The Name of the Game; Most Wanted. Films incl: To Be or Not To Be; Eagle Squadron; Date with Judy; Bullfighter and the Lady; Bwana Devil; High and the Mighty; Good Morning Miss Dove; Written on the Wind (Oscar nomination); Tarnished Angels; John Paul Jones; Last Voyage; The Story of a Woman. Education: France, Italy and University of Southern California. m. former actress Rosemarie Bowie, 1 d. Elizabeth, 1 s. Charles. Address: Bel Air, Calif. Starsign: Capricorn.

STAMPE, Will

Actor/comedian/musician b. 7.10.20 London. Experience with amateur Gilbert and Sullivan societies, army shows, Tower

and Unity Theatres, comedy musical variety act. Stage incl: Rhinoceros; Blitz; Twang; old-time music hall, Players' Theatre. Films incl: The Main Chance; Go to Blazes; Mel Brooks' Twelve Chairs. TV incl: Diary of a Young Man; Three Clear Sundays; Cathie Come Home; Up the Junction; Coming Out Party; Pennies From Heaven; Country Party; Till Death Do Us Part; People Like Us; A Horseman Riding By; The Professionals; Crime and Punishment; The Fox; Bernie Winters Shows. Education: Northwold Elementary; Upton House Central, London – and the wartime army! m. actress Julie May with whom he has appeared as her husband in many TV productions. Address: c/o Ann Zahl, Sonny Zahl Associates Ltd, London W1. Starsign: Libra. Hobbies: antiques dealing and restoration, writing musicals and plays, watching TV. Unfulfilled ambitions: 'to choke the throat of that tall, slim man trying to get out of little fat me; to see both my musicals produced in the West End; to earn enough money to become a tax exile, then calmly state "I cannot leave Hertfordshire for mere money". Or, failing these – to win the pools and build my own theatre, thus keeping my friends in work!'

STANDING, John
Actor b. 16.8.39 London.
Real name Sir John Leon, the
fourth baronet. Acting in his
family goes back five
generations (his mother is
actress Kay Hammond), but
he originally wanted to be an
artist. After two years in the
army with the 60th Rifles,
studied at art school.
Decided he was not good
enough to become an artist
and set out to become an
actor. Began carrying a
spear in Royal Shakespeare
production of Titus
Andronicus at Stratford; then
rep at Birmingham and
Bristol. London stage
appearances incl: The
Importance of Being Earnest;
Ring Round The Moon; The
Fighting Cock; The Irregular
Verb to Love; Private Lives;
Popkiss; A Sense of
Detachment and, for the
National Theatre, Plunder
and The Philanderer. Films
incl: Psychopath; King Rat;
Walk, Don't Run; All the Right
Noises; The Legacy. TV incl:
Arms and the Man; The First
Churchills; Charley's Aunt;
Love Story; Tartuffe, Rogue
Male; Sinking of HMS
Victoria; Home and Beauty;
Ms or Jill and Jack.
Education: Eton and Millfield.
m. actress Jill Melford (dis),
1 s. Alexander. Address: c/o
William Morris Agency,
London W1. Starsign: Leo.
Hobbies: travelling, painting.
Unfulfilled ambition: to own
the Gare Saint Lazare by
Monet.

STAPLETON, John
TV presenter/reporter b.
24.2.46 Oldham, Lancs.
Newspaper training on local,
regional and national papers
before going to Thames TV's
Today programme.
Presenter of other TV incl:
Nationwide; Medical
Express; Miss United
Kingdom; Miss England;
Time to Talk (BBC North West
chat show); This Week
Special (The Confait Case).
Education: Hulme Grammar
School and St John's College
of Further Education,
Manchester. m. journalist
Lynn Faulds Wood. Address:
c/o BBC TV, London W12.
Starsign: Pisces. Hobbies:
watching sport and TV.

St CLAIR, Isla
TV personality b. 2.5.52
Buckie, Banffshire. Started
singing with the Aberdeen
Folk Singing Club when she
was 10, was regularly on
radio and TV while still at
school and had her own
radio series when she was
13. Has since travelled
extensively with folk concerts
as a hostess. Radio incl:
Hootin' Annie; Stories Are For
Singing. Though well-known
in Scotland, big break came
when she was chosen as
hostess for The Generation
Game in 1978. Other TV incl:
Isla's Island; Celebrity
Squares; Feeling Great;
Disney Time; Saturday Night
at the Mill; Juke Box Jury; The
Farm. Records incl: Isla
St Clair Sings Scottish
Traditional Songs; Isla
St Clair. Writers Guild of
Great Britain Award as Best
Newcomer in 1979.
Education: Aberdeen
Academy. m. folk singer
Hamish Bayne (dis.).
Address: c/o Peter Pritchard
Ltd, London SW1. Starsign:
Taurus. Hobbies: horses,
cats, horses, dogs, horses.

St CLAIR, Tony
Professional wrestler
b. 28.3.51 Redruth, Cornwall.
Left school at 15 to play for
Manchester Utd FC.
Switched to wrestling
following ankle injury.
Trained by father and
brother, both professional
wrestlers. First man to beat
Mick McManus on TV.
Currently British heavyweight
champion, youngest and
lightest wrestler ever to hold
the belt. Education:
secondary school in
Manchester. m. cabaret
singer Talli Halliday (sep),
1 s. Justin. Address:
Altrincham, Cheshire.
Starsign: Aries. Hobbies:
cooking, eating out, music,
fashion, making Giant
Haystacks grovel. Unfulfilled
ambition: to win world
heavyweight title, then retire
and open own restaurant.

STEAFEL, Sheila
Actress b. 26.5.35
Johannesburg, S Africa.
Trained for the stage at
Webber Douglas Academy
of Dramatic Art then rep at
Blackpool and the Players'
Theatre, London. Stage incl:
Billy Liar; Jump; How the
Other Half Loves; Bristol Old
Vic; Salad Days revival; A
Day in Hollywood, A Night in
the Ukraine. Films incl: Baby
Love; Some Will, Some Won't;
Otley; Goodbye Mr Chips;
Tropic of Cancer; Percy;
SWALK; The Waiting Room.
Main TV credits incl: The
Frost Report; Illustrated
Weekly Hudd; Horne-a-
Plenty; Beachcomber; How's
Your Father?; The Good Old
Days; Ghosts of Motley Hall;
Diary of a Nobody. Also has a
regular weekly radio
programme Week Ending.
Education: Johannesburg
Girls High School;
Witwatersrand University. m.
(dis). Address: c/o Jan
Dutton Management,
Richmond, Surrey. Starsign:
Gemini. Hobbies: cooking,
dressmaking, drinking wine.
Unfulfilled ambition: to have
her own one-woman show.

STEEL, Bill
Broadcaster b. 20.5.39
Newcastle upon Tyne. Wide
experience as TV announcer
with ABC, Thames, Border
and Tyne Tees. Has also
done 'voice over' for more
than 10,000 TV commercials.
On Metro Radio presented
The Bill Steel Breakfast Show
for three and a half years; on
BBC's Radio Newcastle had

his own show The Bill Steel
Show. Currently presenter of
Tyne Tees TV's Northern Life.
Other TV incl: presenter Miss
Tyne Tees TV; Songs for the
Singing Sixties; name part in
TV pantomime, Dick
Whittington. Recent stage
appearance in Side By Side
By Sondheim. Education:
Pendower Boys School;
Durham University.
m. Isabel, 1 s. Christian.
Address: c/o Tyne Tees TV,
Newcastle upon Tyne.
Starsign: Taurus. Hobbies:
jogging, sailing, squash,
reading, hill walking.
Unfulfilled ambition: to
present a TV talk show.

STEELE, Tommy
Actor b. 17.12.36
Bermondsey, London.
Started as bell-boy on a liner.
Decided to go into show
business and was
'discovered' while playing in
the Two I's Coffee Bar in
London. Within 10 weeks he
was famous and a teenage
idol. First stage appearance
in variety, Empire Theatre,
Sunderland 1956. London
debut, Dominion 1957; panto
in Liverpool same year.
Buttons in Rodgers and

Hammerstein's Cinderella at
London Coliseum following
year. Then She Stoops to
Conquer (Old Vic); Half a
Sixpence (London and New
York); The Servant of Two
Masters; Palladium panto
Dick Whittington; Meet Me in
London; Hans Andersen.
Films incl: Half A Sixpence.
TV appearances incl: The
Tommy Steele Show; Twelfth
Night; In Search of Charlie
Chaplin; A Special Tommy
Steele; Tommy Steele and a
Show. Education: Bacon's
School for Boys,
Bermondsey. m. former
dancer Ann Donoghue,
1 d. Emma. Address: c/o
Talent Artists Ltd, London
W1. Starsign: Sagittarius.
Hobbies: squash, painting.

STENNETT, Stan
Comedian b. 30.7.27 Cardiff.
Started singing and playing
guitar at local concerts.
Joined comedy act The
Harmaniacs. First big break
as resident comic on radio's
Welsh Rarebit. Then resident
comic with Cyril Stapleton's
Show Band and resident
comedy lead for seven years
with The Black and White
Minstrels on stage and TV. TV
incl: Stan at Ease; Road
Show; The Good Old Days;
Those Wonderful TV Times;
The Golden Shot; Celebrity
Squares; Top Town.
Appeared as a straight actor
in Crossroads; Coronation
Street. Stage: Leeds United;
Scully's New Year's Eve;
What a Performance; Cries
From A Watchtower.
Presents and appears in own

summer shows and pantomimes. Has starred in Cardiff's New Theatre panto for five consecutive seasons – a record for that theatre. Presented panto at Club Double Diamond; Caerphilly 1979-80. Education: secondary school. m. Betty, 2 s. Roger, Ceri. Address: c/o George Bartram Enterprises, Birmingham. Starsign: Leo. Hobbies: most sports, especially soccer (he's a director of Bridgend FC), flying (he pilots his own aircraft).

STEPHENS, Robert
Actor b. 14.7.31 Bristol. Studied for the stage at Bradford Civic Theatre School and started acting with Caryl Jenner Mobile Theatre Company. London debut at the Royal Court Theatre in The Crucible 1956. Stage since incl: The Entertainer; George Dillon (and in New York); Look After Lulu; The Kitchen; National Theatre at the Old Vic 1963-70 where he appeared in a wide variety of plays incl: Hamlet; Saint Joan; The Recruiting Officer; The Royal Hunt of the Sun; Hay Fever. Returned to National 1978. Also appeared in a revival of Private Lives; Zoo Story; Sherlock Holmes (the last two in New York); Regent's Park Open Air Theatre (Othello) and Chichester and Edinburgh Festivals. Many films incl: A Taste of Honey; Cleopatra; Morgan – A Suitable Case for Treatment; Romeo and Juliet; The Prime of Miss Jean Brodie; Travels With My Aunt; The Duellists; The Shout. TV incl: Vienna 1900; Gangsters; Softly, Softly; Holocaust; and more recently Eustace and Hilda; Voyage of Charles Darwin; Kean; Office Story; Friends in Space Society; Suez; Hesther For Example. Educated in Bristol. m. (1st) Nora Anne (dis), (2nd) actress Tarn Bassett (dis), (3rd) actress Maggie Smith (dis), 1 d. Lucy (by 2nd m), 3 s. Michael (by 1st m), Christopher, Toby (by 3rd m). Address: c/o Films Rights Ltd, London W1. Starsign: Cancer. Hobbies: cooking, gymnastics, swimming.

STEVENS, David
Presenter/newsreader b. 23.2.29 Worcester. Worked as actor (Old Vic, West End, rep and radio) and hotel receptionist and also in rag trade before joining BBC Midlands. Education: King's School, Worcester. Address: Harborne, Birmingham. Starsign: Pisces. Hobbies: music (listening), TV (watching), home (bruising fingers until they turn green). Unfulfilled ambition: to be a one-man concert pianist/ dancer/ opera singer/ athlete/ philosopher.

STEWART, Alastair
Industrial correspondent b. 22.6.52 Emsworth, Hants. Joined Southern TV's Day By Day team as editorial assistant 1976. Regular contributor to Your Men At Westminster and joint

presenter of People Rule. Also reports in Southern Report and Southerners. Education: St Augustine's Abbey School, Ramsgate; Bristol University. m. Sally. Address: Chandlers Ford, Hants. Starsign: Cancer/ Gemini cusp. Hobbies: riding, swimming, writing, aeroplanes. Unfulfilled ambition: to learn to fly.

STEWART, Allan
Comedian/singer/ impressionist b. 30.7.50 Garrow Hill, Glasgow. Began by making a record I'm Not Too Young at the age of 10. Played guitar and sang in Scottish clubs and theatres from the age of 11 and has been in show business ever since. TV incl: Celebrity Squares; Seaside Special; Hello, Good Afternoon, Welcome; The Allan Stewart Tapes. Education: Garrow Hill Primary School; Coatbridge High School. Address: c/o London Management, London W1. Starsign: Leo. Unfulfilled ambition: to own a Rolls-Royce.

STEWART, Ed (Stewpot)
Disc jockey/compere
b 23.4.41 Exmouth, Devon.
Started career as bass player
in Hong Kong jazz group.
Radio reporter/disc jockey in
Hong Kong 1961-65 when he
joined Radio London and
switched to the BBC two
years later for radio's Junior
Choice. TV incl: Anything You
Can Do; Stewpot; Edanzed;
Quizball; A Question of Sport;
Top of the Pops; We Want to
Sing; 2 G's and the Pop
People; Crackerjack;
Chipperfield's Circus; Play It
Again Stewpot; Celebrity
Squares; Runaround;
Celebrity Golf; The
Generation Game; Bruce's
Big Night; Star Turn.
Education: St Edward's
School, Oxford. m. Chiara,
1 d. Francesca, 1 s. Mario.
Address: c/o MAM Agency
Ltd, London W1. Starsign:
Taurus. Hobbies: football
(Everton), cricket, cycling,
golf.

STILGOE, Richard
Presenter/writer/ performer
b. 28.3.43 Camberley,
Surrey. A product of
Cambridge Footlights revue,
switched to music after

starting out on an
engineering course. Has
since had wide experience of
radio and TV incl: Pssst . . .;
Just Watch It; The Thumb of
Barnaby Locke; A Class by
Himself; Don't Ask Us;
Nationwide (Consumer Unit);
And Now the Good News.
Plays 14 instruments, sings in
opera and tours Britain with
his own one-man stage show.
Education: Liverpool
College; Monkton Combe
School; Cambridge
University. m. Annabel,
2 d. Jemima, Holly,
3 s. Rufus, Jack, Joe.
Address: c/o Noel Gay
Artists, London WC2.
Starsign: Aries. Hobbies:
sailing, do-it-yourself.
Unfulfilled ambition: to be
able to do a backflip.

STIRLING, Ian
Presenter b. 28.10.41 Leven,
Fifeshire. Originally a textile
buyer, then a display artist
before studying at the Royal
Scottish Academy of Drama
and Music, winning James
Bridie Gold Medal 1967.
Theatre and TV actor until
joined Westward TV as a
presenter 1974. Education:
Glasgow High School.
Address: c/o James Viccars
Management, London W1.
Starsign: Scorpio. Hobbies:
gardening, do-it-yourself,
listening to music. Unfulfilled
ambition: 'I regret never
having appeared in my
favourite TV programme,
Coronation Street'.

STOCK, Nigel
21.9.19 Malta. Wanted to be
a doctor and has been
haunted by this throughout
his career by his doctor roles:
a medical student in And No
Birds Sing; Dr Watson many
times; the title role in Owen
MD; The Doctors.
Discovered he liked acting
by competing with his sister's
party piece. Studied at RADA
and acted till the war, serving
first with the London Irish
Rifles and then the Assam
Regiment, Indian Army in
Burma. Major at 23. Many
stage and TV appearances
incl: Fall of Eagles;
Churchill's People; On the
Move; Wingate; London
Assurance; Van Der Valk;
Tinker, Tailor, Soldier, Spy; A
Man Called Intrepid; Flesh
and Blood.
Between 40 and 50 films incl:
The Lion in Winter; Cromwell.
Education: St Paul's School,
London
m. Sonia Williams (dis),
2 d. Penny, Polly, 1 s. Robin.
Address: c/o Derek Glynne
Ltd, London SW1. Starsign:
Virgo. Hobbies: ornithology,
stamps

STRANKS, Susan
Presenter b. 2.12.39 Trained
at RADA, St Martin's School
of Art in London, ballet,
modelling and 10 years as an
actress before becoming
Magpie presenter for six
years. Joined Nationwide
1974; also Hullabaloo on
Capital Radio and her own TV
programmes, Paperplay on
ITV and On Location on BBC.

Books incl: The Big Ideas Book. Educated privately in London and Sussex. m. actor/ presenter Robin Ray, 1 s. Rupert. Address: c/o Roger Hancock Ltd, London SW1. Starsign: Sagittarius. Hobbies: drawing, painting. Unfulfilled ambition: to visit India.

STRATTON, John
Actor b. 7.11.25 Clitheroe, Lancs. Rep in Dewsbury, Leeds, Hastings, service in Royal Navy during the war, more rep at Oxford and Dundee before West End. Films incl: The Cruel Sea; Man in the Sky. First TV 1948, many since incl: Letters from the Dead; When We Are Married; Forget Me Not; Backs To The Wall; Just William. Education: Royal Grammar School, Clitheroe. Address: Hampstead, London. Starsign: Scorpio. Hobbies: Staffordshire pottery, tennis, travel.

STRAULI, Christopher
Actor b. 13.4.46 Harpenden, Herts. Three-year stint at a teacher training college, qualifying as a maths and science teacher, before

going to RADA. Went to the Bristol Old Vic 1970. Other reps, London's West End (including The Licentious Fly). Many TV appearances, but his break came with the part of Bunny in Raffles. Other TV incl: Harriet's Back in Town; Owen MD; Family at War; Warship; Angels; For Tea on Sunday; Gentle Folk; Measure for Measure; Romeo and Juliet; Only When I Laugh; Edward the Seventh; Eustace and Hilda. Education: Felixstowe Grammar School. m. Lesley, 2 d. Belinda, Hanneli. Address: c/o Bryan Drew Ltd, London W1. Starsign: Aries. Hobbies: do-it-yourself, sports (tennis, badminton, squash), indoor games (board and otherwise), model making, his family.

STREET-PORTER, Janet
Presenter/reporter b. 27.12.46 London. Wide journalistic experience on magazines (Vogue, Harper's, etc) and national newspapers (Daily Mail, London Evening Standard, London Evening News, Observer) and commercial radio. Presenter of London Weekend Show, weekly

current affairs programme for young people and member of the Saturday Night People team. Education: state grammar school, Fulham; Architectural Association. m. (1st) photographer Tim Street-Porter (dis), (2nd) publisher Tony Elliott (dis), (3rd) film director Frank Cvitinovich. Address: c/o Jon Roseman Associates, London W1. Starsign: Capricorn. Unfulfilled ambition: 'not to have to explain things like this'.

STRIDE, John
Actor b. 11.7.36 London. Trained at RADA, professional stage debut at Liverpool Rep 1957 before joining the Army. On demob went to the Old Vic and within a year was playing leads. Five years with the National Theatre before TV's The Main Chance and Wilde Alliance. Films incl: Bitter Harvest; Brannigan; Macbeth; Juggernaut; The Omen; A Bridge Too Far. Education: Alleyn's School, Dulwich. m. (1st) actress Virginia Stride (dis), (2nd) actress April Wilding, 2 d. Philippa, Jane. Address: William Morris Agency, London W1. Starsign: Cancer. Hobby: music.

STRITCH, Elaine
Actress b. 2.2.27 Detroit, Michigan. Prepared for the stage by Irwin Piscator at the Dramatic Workshop of the New School, New York. Stage debut 1944. Since appeared in numerous plays,

mostly in America. London debut 1962 in Noël Coward's Sail Away. Many stage appearances since, incl: Company in 1970. TV in America and here, notably Two's Company with Donald Sinden. Education: Sacred Heart Convent, Detroit. m. John Bay. Address: c/o Felix de Wolfe, London WC2. Starsign: Aquarius. Hobby: people. Unfulfilled ambition: 'to win an Oscar just so I can write my acceptance speech'.

STUBBS, Una
Actress/dancer b. 1.5.37 London. Trained as a dancer at La Roche Dancing School, Slough, and made her stage debut in A Midsummer Night's Dream at the Theatre Royal, Windsor. Subsequent stage work incl: a Norman Wisdom spectacular at the London Palladium and a Folies Bergere revue, also in London. Since then has successfully combined stage and TV work in comedy, straight drama and musicals. Other stage work incl: Grab Me a Gondola; On the Brighter Side; Young Vic Company (The Knack; The Soldier's Tale) 1970; since

appeared in Cowardy Custard; Oh, Mr Porter; Irma la Douce; Baggage. TV started with Cool For Cats followed by Cliff Richard series; Till Death Us Do Part (over 10 years); Fawlty Towers; Give Us a Clue; Worzel Gummidge. Films incl: Summer Holiday; Wonderful Life. m. (1st) actor Peter Gilmore (dis), (2nd) actor Nicky Henson (dis), 3 s. Jason, Christian, Joe. Address: c/o Richard Stone, London WC2. Starsign: Taurus. Hobbies: embroidery, needlework. Unfulfilled ambition: to have her own TV dance spectacular.

SUGDEN, Mollie
Actress b. 21st July, Keighley, Yorks. Always wanted to be an actress. Eight years in rep and 'Mum' to a whole series of characters in successful comedy series on TV – Hugh and I; Please, Sir!; the Doctor series; For the Love of Ada; The Liver Birds – before her career really took off with Are You Being Served? Other TV incl: Coronation Street; Whodunnit?; Come Back Mrs Noah; Tea Ladies. Education: Keighley Girls Grammar School. m. actor William Moore, twins. Robin and Simon. Address: c/o Joan Reddin Ltd, London W11. Starsign: Cancer. Hobby: gardening. Unfulfilled ambition: 'to go on as I am – successfully'.

SUMMERFIELD, Eleanor
Actress b. 7.3.21 London. Studied for the stage under Lady Benson and at RADA. Numerous stage plays, incl: London's West End, films and TV. Most recent stage incl: Arms and the Man; The Rivals; A Murder is Announced. Films incl: A Watcher in the Woods. Lots of radio incl: Many a Slip (15th year); My Sainted Aunt. TV incl: My Wife's Sister, many plays and series, among most recent: Simon Fenton's Story; Kept on a String; chairman of Password; Shades of Greene; Overnight Bag; General Hospital; The Rather Reassuring Programme; Murder at the Wedding. Education: Essendine School, London. m. actor Leonard Sachs, 2 s. Robin, Toby. Address: c/o Miller Management, Teddington, Middx. Starsign: Pisces. Hobbies: horse-racing, photography. Unfulfilled ambition: to own a racehorse.

SURTEES, Allan
Actor b. 31.12.24 Liverpool. Jobs as rent collector, tea boy, tradesman, draughtsman, engineering executive, writer before going into show business. Films incl: The Adding Machine; Frankenstein Must Be Destroyed; The Reckoning; Goodbye Gemini; Ten Rillington Place; Get Carter. TV incl: Justice; The Flaxton Boys; Bill Brand; O'Holligan; A Story to Frighten the Children; The

Seagull; Rosie; The Professionals. m. Margaret. Address: c/o Peter Browne Management, London SW9. Starsign: Capricorn. Hobbies: woodwork, bonsai growing, guitar, gardening. Unfulfilled ambition: to design and make a piece of furniture as timeless as a Breuer chair.

SUZMAN, Janet
Actress b. 9.2.39 South Africa. Brought up in Johannesburg where she first wanted to become a doctor, but college theatricals changed that. Went to London to study at LAMDA. Rep at Windsor, Sheffield and Manchester before joining Royal Shakespeare Company 1963 for The Wars of the Roses. Stage productions incl: Much Ado About Nothing; Hamlet; As You Like It; The Relapse; The Taming of the Shrew; Antony and Cleopatra (and on TV); Hello Goodbye; The Three Sisters (and on TV); Hedda Gabler (and on TV); The Good Woman of Setzuan; Boo Hoo; Duchess of Malfi. Films incl: A Day in the Death of Joe Egg;

Nicholas and Alexandra; The Black Windmill; The Voyage of the Damned. TV incl: Family Reunion; St Joan; Macbeth; Miss Nightingale; Twelfth Night; Clayhanger; The Greeks. Education: Witwatersrand University (BA, English and French). m. stage director Trevor Nunn. Address: c/o William Morris Agency, London W1. Starsign: Aquarius. Hobby: eating but not cooking. Unfulfilled ambition: cooking but not eating.

SWIFT, Clive
Actor b. 9.2.36 Liverpool. Was interested in drama societies while at Cambridge University and after a year in rep at Nottingham, joined the Royal Shakespeare Company (1960-68). Also directed at LAMDA and RADA and toured America for RSC in The Hollow Crown. Films incl: Catch Us If You Can; Hitchcock's Frenzy; Jack Gold's The National Health; The Sailor's Return. Many TV plays and series incl: Dombey and Son; Clayhanger; Roll on 4 o'clock; Goodbye America; Waugh on Crime; Romeo and Juliet; Home Movies; Edward Gibbon; South Riding; Christmas Ghost Stories; A Case of Spirits; Henry IV Part 1; A Family Affair; In Loving Memory. Books incl: The Job of Acting. Education: Clifton College, Bristol; Caius College, Cambridge (BA Hons Eng Lit). m. writer Margaret Drabble (dis), 1 d. Rebecca, 2 s. Adam, Joseph.

Address: c/o ICM, London W1. Starsign: Aquarius. Hobbies: music, cricket, The Actors' Centre.

SYKES, Eric
Comedian/writer b. 4.5.23 Oldham, Lancs. Always wanted to be a comedian and started as a gag writer. Is now the only TV comic who writes his own situation comedies and one of the few TV writers who works alone, which he has done for 20 years and claims is a record. Wrote radio scripts for Educating Archie, Variety Bandbox and many comedians. Apart from his own shows on radio and TV (Sykes is celebrating its twentieth season), other TV incl: Saturday Spectaculars; Curry and Chips; Charley's Aunt. On stage he has toured with Jimmy Edwards in Big Bad Mouse and his own show, A Hatful of Sykes, in Hong Kong, Canada, Australia, Rhodesia, South Africa and seasons and tours in the United Kingdom. His many films incl: The Bargee; **One Way Pendulum; Those Magnificent Men in Their Flying Machines; Rotten to the Core; Spy With a Cold Nose; The Plank** (which he scripted, directed and acted in and has remade); **Shalako; Monte Carlo or Bust; Rhubarb; Theatre of Blood; Ghost in the Noonday Sun**. Education: Ward Street Central School, Oldham. m. Edith Milbrandt, 3 d. Catherine, Susan, Julie, 1 s. David. Address: c/o Paul Elliott, London WC2.

Starsign: Taurus. Hobbies:
golf, work. Unfulfilled
ambition: to keep people
laughing.

T

TAMES, Roger
Sports reporter/ presenter
b. 21.9.51 London.
Journalistic training with
Essex and East London
newspapers before joining
Tyne Tees TV in 1976 as
reporter/ presenter
Sportstime. Co-presenter
Shoot 1977-78 and that
programme's commentator
1979. Education: Brentwood
School, Essex; University of
Leicester (BA Hons English).
m. Tyne Tees TV presenter
Lyn Spencer, 1 d. Joanne.
Address: c/o Tyne Tees TV,
Newcastle upon Tyne.
Starsign: Virgo. Hobbies: all
sports, especially squash
and football, together with
usual accompanying
activities, music, cinema.
Unfulfilled ambition: to score
Arsenal's winning goal in a
European cup final.

225

TARBUCK, Jimmy
Comedian b. 6.2.40
Liverpool. Several jobs on
leaving school until some
friends pushed him into a
holiday camp talent contest
which he won. Compere for a
rock 'n' roll show, touring,
cabaret and clubs before
Comedy Bandbox; Saturday
Night At The London
Palladium; Royal Variety
Performance; his own TV
shows; summer seasons;
pantomime; records.
Education: Dovedale Road
and St Francis Xavier
Schools, Liverpool.
m. Pauline, 2 d. Cheryl, Lisa,
1 s. Jimmy. Address:
Kingston, Surrey. Starsign:
Aquarius. Hobbies: football,
golf.

TARPLEY, Edwina
Reporter b. 27.12.48
Sheffield. Newspaper
training in Sheffield and
London before joining
Yorkshire TV's Calendar
team. Education: Sheffield
High School for Girls.
m. Michael Janisch.
Address: Lincolnshire Wolds.
Starsign: Capricorn.
Hobbies: squash, tennis,
bridge, gardening,
decorating and maintaining a

200 year old house.
Unfulfilled ambition: to fly in
Concorde.

TAYLOR, Alan
Compere/presenter b. 6.8.24
Cardiff. Considerable radio,
theatre, pantomime, cabaret
and summer season
experience before TV as
newsreader and continuity
announcer. Then presenter
of current affairs
programmes, beauty
competitions and
entertainment shows, first for
Television Wales and West
then HTV, incl: Mrs and Mrs;
Try for Ten; Three Little
Words; Think of a Word;
Movie Magazine; Best in the
West; Tinker and Taylor;
Taylormade; Orbit; Help
Yourself; Funny You Should
Ask; Paint Along With Nancy.
Education: elementary
school, Cardiff; Technical
College; Cardiff College of
Dramatic Art. Address: Bath.
Starsign: Leo. Hobbies:
antiques, painting. Unfulfilled
ambition: to paint like
Caravaggio and to live like
Dali.

TAYLOR, Allan
Sports presenter/ reporter
b. 19.9.49 Glasgow.

Progressed from newspaper
journalism (more than four
years), to radio and television
including sports
correspondent on STV's
nightly magazine
programme Scotland Today.
Also sports presenter/
commentator on STV's sports
programmes and contributor
to World of Sport. Address:
c/o STV, Glasgow. Starsign:
Virgo. Hobbies: sport,
theatre, books, cinema, the
countryside. Unfulfilled
ambitions: to continue to be
successful and cover major
sports events throughout the
world.

TAYLOR, Shaw
Compere/presenter
b. 26.10.24 London. RADA
after service in RAF. Then
stage tours and London's
West End. Two years in ice
shows. Relief announcer ATV
1957. Quizmaster on This is
Your Chance; Tell the Truth;
Dotto; Pencil and Paper;
Password; commentator on
Remembrance Day Services,
ice skating, water skiing.
Presenter Police Five (since
1962) and Drive-In.
Education: council school.
m. Jane, 1 s. Richard.
Address: London W1.
Starsign: Scorpio. Hobby:
sailing. Unfulfilled ambition:
to skipper a merchantman.

TAYLFORTH, Gillian
Actress 14.8.55 London.
Trained as secretary before
taking up acting after
evening classes at Anna
Scher Children's Theatre.
First professional part was in

a BBC's Play For Today TV production. Then Zigger Zagger; The Rag Trade; Phyllis Dixey. Education: William Tyndale Junior School; Barnsbury Secondary School for Girls; Kingsway College of Further Education. Address: c/o Anna Scher Theatre Management, London N1. Starsign: Leo. Hobbies: any sport, swimming, reading, dancing. Unfulfilled ambitions: to play Calamity Jane or Jo in Little Women; to be a dancer.

THIRKETTLE, Joan
Reporter b. 14.9.47 Kent. Started with Associated-Rediffusion as a trainee researcher; left to work as a researcher for Radio Caroline. Later joined the Daily Mail, then Sunday Times. Next radio reporter for BBC and British Forces Broadcasting, and London Broadcasting before joining ITN 1976. Education: at school in Kent till 18; took an external degree in English at London University.
m. publisher Jonathan Wallace (grandson of thriller writer Edgar Wallace),
1 d. Daisy. Address: c/o ITN,

London W1. Starsign: Virgo. Hobbies: reading, writing short stories, natural history, politics and foreign affairs.

THOMAS, Brian
Comedian/instrumentalist/singer b. 27.7.51 Wolverhampton. Was at Royal Marine School of Music when 16 and later studied at Royal College of Music. TV incl: Crossroads; Johnny Carson Show (USA); host/presenter of The Wonderful World of Disney for nine months. Education: Wolverhampton Grammar School. Address: c/o Patricia Mackay, Wembley Park, Middx. Starsign: Leo. Hobbies: table tennis, riding, fencing. Unfulfilled ambition: to conduct and/or perform with the London Symphony Orchestra.

THOMAS, Gareth
Actor Trained at RADA followed by stage experience at the Yvonne Arnaud Theatre, Guildford; Liverpool Playhouse; Derby Playhouse; Royal Shakespeare Company and the Welsh Actors' Company. On TV, small parts in such series as

Z Cars and Coronation Street led to bigger things and his breakthrough came with the lead in Blake's Seven. Other TV incl: Parkin's Patch; Sutherland's Law; Topper's Copper; How Green Was My Valley; Children of the Stones; Fathers and Families; Gotcha; Who Pays the Ferryman?; Country Matters. Education: King's School, Canterbury. Address: c/o Leading Artists Ltd, London SW1. (Gareth Thomas refuses to give personal details for inclusion in his entry.)

THOMAS, Guy
Presenter/newsreader/interviewer b. 24.5.31 Swansea. Trained at RADA. Started broadcasting career on radio in Trieste, Italy. Joined Television Wales and West in Bristol as programme presenter 1959. Presenter/interviewer TWW Reports 1963-68; won Ambrose Fleming Television Award for work on that programme 1965. Freelance since 1968, appears regularly on BBC's Midlands Today. Other credits incl: Family Circle; profiles of Lord Bath and Vivian Ellis; sport documentary (Los Angeles); Behind the Scenes. Co-producer and presenter education cassettes for schools in this country and abroad. Education: Acton Grammar School, London. Address: London SW13. Hobbies: music, travel, theatre, swimming, American history. Unfulfilled ambition: to write another Chorus Line.

THOMAS, Terry
Angling correspondent, ATV
b. 9.1.20 Cardiff. Has been in
the fishing tackle industry
since leaving the army in
1946. Freelance contributor
on angling matters to various
journals; also broadcast on
the subject on radio and TV
before joining ATV as angling
correspondent 1967. Books
incl: Casting. Education:
Dulwich College; Frankfurt
and Caen Universities. m.
Anne Veronica, 2 d. Sybil,
Cathryn. Address: c/o ATV,
Birmingham. Starsign:
Capricorn. Hobby: music.

THOMPSON, Ron
Broadcaster b. 5.9.29
Dundee. Newspaper
experience incl: Daily Herald,
Sunday Express, Dundee
Courier. TV: Thompson at
Teatime; Ron Thompson
Reports; Grampian Today.
Author of Never a Dull
Moment. m. Mima,
1 s. Alistair. Address: c/o
Grampian TV, Dundee.
Starsign: Virgo. Hobby:
writing. Unfulfilled ambition:
to do a programme without
feeling nervous.

THOMSON, Kennedy
Senior announcer b. 4.4.36
Glasgow. Training in theatre
and teaching speech and
drama. Joined Grampian TV
in 1970 as announcer and
newscaster. Presenter
schools series Oil!, Granite,
Bricks and Mortar; children's
programmes Wonder
Weekly; 200M; Wings 'n'
Things. Also The Electric
Theatre Show. Education:
University of Glasgow; Royal
Scottish Academy of Music
and Drama. Address: c/o
Grampian TV, Aberdeen.
Starsign: Aries. Hobbies:
theatre, films and TV.
Unfulfilled ambition: to have
been actor/manager with a
rep theatre.

THORNTON, Frank
Actor b. 15.1.21 London.
Stage struck since boyhood.
Started his career in Sir
Donald Wolfit's company and
in recent years has returned
to Shakespeare on stage as
well as being foil to almost
every TV comedian. Now well
known as Captain Peacock in
Are You Being Served?
Served as RAF officer during
the war. Stage work incl:
Aldeburgh; Royal Court;
Royal Shakespeare

Company (Twelfth Night);
The Doctor's Dilemma; Play
By Play; Shut Your Eyes and
Think of England. TV incl: It's
a Square World; The World of
Beachcomber; Steptoe and
Son. Education: Alleyn's
School, Dulwich. m. actress
Beryl Evans, 1 d. Jane.
Address: c/o Max Kester,
Reigate, Surrey. Starsign:
Capricorn. Hobbies: music,
photography.

THORPE-BATES, Peggy
Actress b. 11.8.14 London.
Started at the Cone School of
Dancing and later at RADA.
First professional
appearance was walking on
in A Kiss for Cinderella at
Croydon Rep. Shakespeare
Memorial Theatre then rep at
Harrogate, Birmingham and
Bristol. West End debut in
The Country Wife. Countless
radio and stage
appearances since incl: The
Young Elizabeth in
Coronation year. Films incl:
Georgy Girl; The Mosquito
Squadon. TV: Oliver Twist;
The Franchise Affair; Kipling;
No Hiding Place; Riviera
Police; Our Man at St Marks;
Sanctuary; Richard II;
Timeslip; The Glittering
Prizes; Two's Company; The
Saint; Rumpole of the Bailey
(two series). Education:
Heathfield. m. actor Brian
Oulton, 1 d. Jenny,
1 s. Nicholas. Address: c/o
Patrick Freeman, London
W6. Starsign: Leo. Hobbies:
cooking, gardening, sewing,
home decorating. Unfulfilled
ambitions: to be an architect
and to speak French.

THROWER, Percy
Horticulturist b. 30.1.13
Winslow, Bucks. Started
gardening straight from
school when he was 14 at
Horwood House, Bucks,
where his father was head
gardener. Then worked in the
royal gardens at Windsor and
public parks at Leeds, Derby
and Shrewsbury. Has done
1300 gardening
programmes on radio and
1200 programmes on TV.
Awarded a National Diploma
in Horticulture 1945; Royal
Horticultural Society made
him an Associate of Honour
1962 and awarded him the
Victoria Medal of Honour
1974. Education: elementary
school. m. Constance,
3 d. Margaret, Susan, Ann.
Address: Bomere Heath,
Shrewsbury. Starsign:
Aquarius. Hobby: shooting.

TIMOTHY, Christopher
Actor b. 14.10.40 Bala,
Merioneth. Trained at Central
School of Speech and
Drama, then to New York for
Chips With Everything.
National Theatre for three
years. Films incl: The Virgin
Soldiers; Alfred the Great;
Here We Go Round The

Mulberry Bush; Olivier's
Othello. TV incl: Fly On The
Wall; Some Mothers Do 'Ave
'Em; Killers; The Moon Shines
Bright On Charlie Chaplin;
Kate; Three Sisters; Twelfth
Night; Murder Must
Advertise; Murder Most
English; The Kitchen; Z Cars;
The Two Ronnies; Hark at
Barker; All Creatures Great
And Small. Education:
schools in London and
Shrewsbury. m. (sep),
2 d. Tabitha, Kate,
4 s. Simon, Nick, Robin,
David. Address: c/o Plant
and Froggatt Ltd, London
W1. Starsign: Libra. Hobbies:
swimming, reading, writing,
pantomimes. Unfulfilled
ambitions: to direct for the
stage; to produce and play
Romeo and Iago; to do a
production of Night Must Fall.

TODD, Bob
Actor b. 15.12.21
Faversham, Kent. Formerly a
cattle breeder. Business
failed overnight through no
fault of his and at 42 turned
his hand to acting. First on TV
1963 in Citizen James with
Sid James. Has since been
foil to Benny Hill, Dick Emery,
Marty Feldman, Michael
Bentine, Des O'Connor and
has had his own series In For
a Penny. Other TV incl:
What's On Next? Education:
Kings, Canterbury.
m. Monica, 1 d. Anne,
2 s. John, Patrick. Address:
c/o International Artistes
Representation, London W1.
Starsign: Sagittarius. Hobby:
making people laugh.

Unfulfilled ambition: 'to stay
as I am'.

TOMLINSON, Peter
Announcer b. 4.4.43 Bristol.
Has a degree in English
Literature and was with the
De La Rue company for two
years before joining ATV.
Education: Bristol Grammar
School; Worcester College,
Oxford. m. Mary,
2 d. Belinda, Nicola.
Address: Wolverley, nr
Kidderminster. Starsign:
Aries. Hobbies:
motor-racing, shooting,
cricket, jazz. Unfulfilled
ambitions: to present a
network show and/or
become ITV's first full-time
motor-racing commentator.

TONG, Jaqueline
Actress b. 21.2.51 Bristol.
Got her first part in Between
the Wars while still at Rose
Bruford Drama School and
never went back. Spent a
year travelling between
leaving school and drama
studies. First job in the
theatre was as general
dogsbody at Bristol Old Vic.
Has since appeared in many
stage productions and a
horror movie, Tales From

Beyond the Grave. TV incl: Voyage in the Dark; Upstairs, Downstairs; Hard Times; Phyllis Dixey; Spearhead. Education: convent, primary school, girls grammar, technical college and art school. Address: c/o William Morris Agency, London W1. Starsign: Pisces.

numerous plays, films and TV programmes from the Alexandra Palace days. Has played Sam Pearson in Emmerdale Farm since the programme started in 1972. Educated in many schools in various parts of the country. Address: c/o Margery Armstrong, London SW1. Starsign: Scorpio. Hobbies: music (flute and recorder), reading. Fulfilled ambition by becoming an actor.

TROUGHTON, David
Actor b. 9.6.50 London. Son of Patrick Troughton. Trained with the Unicorn theatre for children and his first big TV role was in Dr Who. Other TV incl: The Regiment; Armchair Theatre; The Norman Conquests; Wings; Our Mutual Friend; Chips With Everything; David Copperfield; Wessex Tales; Backs to the Land; Crime and Punishment. Stage work incl: Parents' Day; The Fool; Loot; The Wedding Feast; The Changeling. Education: primary and Orange Hill Grammar. m. actress Alison Groves, 2 s. Sam, Jamie. Address: c/o David White Associates, London W1.

TONGE, Roger
Actor b. 30.1.46 Birmingham. One-time £8 a week GPO clerk before getting first professional acting job in Crossroads when serial started in 1964. Previous acting experience in amateur theatricals and studied drama in the evenings. Stage incl: Manchester Library Theatre; Belgrade Theatre, Coventry; tours. Film: Catch Me Going Back. TV incl: Z Cars; Nearest and Dearest; Detective. Education: Lordswood Technical Grammar. Address: c/o Peter Campbell, NEMS Management Ltd, London SW3. Starsign: Aquarius. Hobbies: used to be tennis and swimming, but his main interest is now his work and writing. Unfulfilled ambition: to write a book.

TOWNLEY, Toke
Actor b. 6.11.12 Margaret Roding, Essex. Born in the vicarage, his father being the local vicar at the time. Started as a clerk with acting as a spare-time interest. Did not become professional until joined Birmingham Rep when 32. Has since appeared in

Starsign: Gemini. Hobbies: cricket, board games, collecting books, squash. Unfulfilled ambitions: to be discovered as England's second all-rounder and to tour Australia as a member of the MCC.

TROUGHTON, Patrick
Actor b. 25.3.20 London. Trained at the Embassy School of Acting and won a scholarship to Leighton Rollin's Studio for Actors at Long Island, New York. After war service at sea joined the Old Vic and become a Shakespearean actor. Best known to TV viewers as the actor who took over from William Hartnell as Dr Who and played the part for three years. Many TV roles incl: The Six Wives of Henry VIII; Family at War; Little Women; Dr Finlay's Casebook; Churchill's People; Village Hall; Crown Court; Love Letters on Blue Paper; The Feathered Serpent; The Survivors; Lorna Doone, Angels; Space 1999; The Sweeney; Treasure Island; Yanks Go Home; The Old Curiosity Shop; The Main Chance; Colditz; Pathfinders; Jennie; Coronation Street. His films incl: Frankenstein; The Protector; Doomwatch; Scars of Dracula; Viking Queen; Sinbad and the Tiger; The Omen. Education: Mill Hill Public School. m. Shelagh, 2 d. Joanna, Jane, 1 step-d. Gill, 4 s. David, Michael, Peter, Mark, 1 step-s. Graham. Starsign: Aries. Hobbies: golf, sailing,

fishing. Unfulfilled ambition: to be able to play the piano.

TUCKERMAN, Ted
Angling reporter/ presenter b. 25.11.30 Weymouth. A lifetime angler; began as freelance reporter for angling press, local newspapers and radio before moving into TV. Catch '76, Catch '77 and Catch '79 series for Westward TV. Education: commercial college. m. Gwynneth, 1 d. Alison, 1 s. Keith. Address: Babbacombe, Torquay. Starsign: Sagittarius. Hobbies: fishing, photography, skiing, badminton. Unfulfilled ambition: to hold a world fishing record.

TURNER, Bridget
Actress b. 22.2.39 Cleethorpes, Lincs. Trained at RADA. Stage work incl: Time and Time Again; Absurd Person Singular; The Norman Conquests; The Fool; tours with Royal Shakespeare Company. TV incl: Slattery's Mounted Foot; Time and Time Again; Love Lies Bleeding; Resurrection; Two People. Education:

Wintringham Grammar, Grimsby. m. TV producer Frank Cox. Address: c/o Peter Browne Management, London SW9. Starsign: Pisces. Hobbies: walking, gardening. Unfulfilled ambition: 'to meet the most attractive man to have appeared on TV – Paul Tortelier'.

TUTIN, Dorothy CBE
Actress b. 8.4.30 London. Trained at RADA. First stage appearance at The Boltons Theatre, London. Since appeared with Bristol Old Vic, Old Vic, Royal Shakespeare Company and National Theatre. Wide experience in the classics. Stage appearances also incl: I Am A Camera; The Living Room; The Entertainer; Portrait of a Queen; Peter Pan (1971-72). Films incl: The Importance of Being Earnest; Beggar's Opera; Cromwell; Savage Messiah. TV incl: Victoria Regina; Six Wives of Henry VIII; South Riding; Mother and Son; Sister Dora; Ghosts; Willow Cabins. Education: St Catherine's, Bramley, Surrey. m. actor Derek Waring, 1 d. Amanda, 1 s. Nicholas. Address: c/o Peter Browne Management, London SW9. Starsign: Aries. Hobbies: music, boats, mountains.

TWIGGY
Actress b. 19.9.49 London. Hairdresser's assistant turned model; became bored with the fashion scene at 20 and decided to become an

actress. First screen role was in The Boy Friend. Other films incl: W; Shadow of Evil; There Goes the Bride. Stage debut in Cinderella pantomime at London Casino 1974. Other stage incl: concerts and cabaret. TV incl: Twiggs; Twiggy; The Frontiers of Science (Queen Victoria's Scandals); Bring on the Girls; Roller Coaster; The Muppet Show; The Val Doonican Music Show. Records incl: The Boy Friend; Twiggy; Here I Go Again; Please Get My Name Right; A Woman in Love; Tomorrow is Another Day. Books incl: Twiggy (autobiography). Voted World's Loveliest Woman 1977. Education: Kilburn High School for Girls. m. actor Michael Witney, 1 d. Carly. Address: c/o BBC, London W12. Starsign: Virgo.

TYLER, Martin
Sports commentator/ reporter b. 14.9.45 Chester. Staff writer/ sub-editor for part work publishers. TV: editorial assistant for On The Ball/ Big Match. Football commentator, Southern TV 1974, Yorkshire TV 1976;

cricket commentator,
Southern TV 1976, Yorkshire
TV 1977; On The Ball reporter
1974; co-editor ITV's 1974
World Cup coverage; football
correspondent Yorkshire
TV's Calendar Sport 1977.
Author/editor sports books
incl: Skills and Tactics;
Encyclopaedia of Football;
Enjoying Soccer; Story of
Football. Education: Royal
Grammar School, Guildford;
University of East Anglia (BA
Hons, MA). Address: London
SW16. Starsign: Virgo.
Hobbies: playing football,
cinema, travel. Unfulfilled
ambition: to establish a
sports documentary series
on TV.

UNDERWOOD, John
TV journalist b. 8.11.53
London. Trained for
journalism on a post-grad
journalism training course at
University College, Cardiff,
and a BBC training scheme.
Was with the BBC 1976-78 as
reporter, scriptwriter for radio
and TV in London, Plymouth,
Birmingham and Cardiff.
Joined Westward TV 1978;
based in Taunton. Education:
Archbishop Tenison's
Grammar School, London;
Sheffield University.
Address: c/o Westward TV,
Plymouth. Starsign: Scorpio.
Hobbies: theatre, bridge.
Unfulfilled ambition: to write a
really awful but best-selling
paperback.

URQUHART, Robert
Actor b 16.10.22 Ullapool,
Scotland. Originally in the
Merchant Navy; studied at
RADA for the stage then rep
at Stratford-upon-Avon,
Edinburgh and Glasgow
Citizen's Theatre. London
debut in The Second Mrs
Tanquery and was Horatio to
Alec Guinness's Hamlet
1951. Has made numerous
appearances on stage, film
and radio. Films incl: You're
Only Young Twice; Knights of
the Round Table; The Curse
of Frankenstein; Yangste
Incident; The Dunkirk Story.
TV incl: Murder Stamp; Jango
Smith; The Planemakers; The
Pathfinders; The Simple Life;
Country Matters; The
Reporters; Helen – A Woman
of Today; The Awful Mr
Goodall; The Inheritors; The
Button Man; Happy Returns;
The Professionals; Man and
Boy. Education: Heriot's
School, Edinburgh. m. (1st)
actress Zena Walker (dis),
(2nd) Jean, 1 d. Alison,
1 s. Matthew. Address: c/o
Boyack and Conway, London
W1. Starsign: Libra. Hobby:
messing about in boats.

USTINOV, Peter
Actor/dramatist/director/
raconteur b. 16.4.21 London.
Studied at the London
Theatre Studio. Stage debut
at the Barn Theatre, Shere
1938 and first London
appearance following year at
Players' Club in his own
sketch, The Bishop of
Limpopoland. Rep at
Aylesbury, Richmond and
world-wide film and stage
appearances, many in his
own plays which incl: The
Love of Four Colonels; A
Fiddle at the Wedding;
Romanoff and Juliet; Photo
Finish; Halfway Up the Tree;
The Unknown Soldier and His
Wife. Films incl; The Goose
Steps Out; One of Our
Aircraft is Missing; The Way
Ahead; Vice Versa; Private
Angelo; Odette; Hotel
Sahara; Beau Brummel; The
Egyptian; We're No Angels;
The Sundowners; Sparticus
(Oscar); Topkapi (Oscar);
Lady L; Hot Millions; Big
Truck and Sister Clare; One
of Our Dinosaurs is Missing;
The Purple Taxi; Death On
The Nile; Double Murder;
Last Remake of Beau Geste.
Many TV guest
appearances. Books incl:
The Loser; Klop and the
Ustinov Family; We Were
Only Human; Dear Me
(autobiography). Education:
Westminster. m. (1st)Isolde
Denham (dis), (2nd)
Suzanne Cloutier (dis), (3rd)
Helene de Lau d'Allemans,
3 d. Tamara (by 1st m),
Pavla, Andrea. 1 s. Igor (all
by 2nd m). Address: c/o
William Morris Agency Ltd,
London W1. Starsign: Aries.
Hobbies: tennis, squash,
music.

V

VARNEY, Reg
Comedy actor b. 11.7.22
London. Started as a pianist
and singer in working men's
clubs, then army shows,
variety, revue, pantomime,
summer season, TV and
films. Films incl: Joey Boy; On
The Buses; Mutiny on the
Buses; Holiday on the Buses.
TV incl: Rag Trade; Valiant
Varneys; Beggar My
Neighbour; On The Buses;
Best Pair of Legs in the
Business; Down the Gate.
Education: elementary
school. m. Lily, 1 d. Jeanne.
Address: c/o London
Management, London W1.
Starsign: Cancer. Hobbies:
painting, decorating,
gardening. Unfulfilled
ambition: 'to achieve 100 per
cent perfection in my work'.

VALENTINE, Anthony
Actor b. 17.8.39 Blackburn.
Acting debut aged 10 in film
No Way Back. Several years
as child actor in BBC series,
Vice Versa; Children of the
New Forest; Whirligig; Billy
Bunter. Adult career began in
TV production of John
Gabriel Borkman. Small parts
in films and rep at
Nottingham, Guildford,
Leatherhead and Croydon
before stage appearances in
Two Stars for Comfort; The
Platinum Cat; Half a
Sixpence; No Sex Please –
We're British; Hans
Andersen. TV incl: An Age of
Kings; Armchair Theatre; The
Avengers; Callan;
Codename; Colditz; Justice;
Raffles; The Dancing Years.
Education: Valerie Glynn
School; Acton County
Grammar. Address: London
Management, London W1.
Starsign: Leo. Hobbies:
squash, riding, guitar, skiing.

VAUGHAN, Frankie OBE
Entertainer b. 3.2.28
Liverpool. Started career at
Kingston Empire 1950. First
TV appearance two years
later. Has been topping the
bill in theatres, cabaret and
TV shows in Britain and
America ever since. Many
films incl: These Dangerous
Years; The Lady is a Square
(with Anna Neagle); Let's

Make Love (with Marilyn
Monroe); It's All Over Town.
Education: Leeds College of
Art. m. Stella, 1 d. Susan,
2 s. David, Andrew.
Address: c/o Clifford Elson
(Publicity) Ltd, London W1.
Starsign: Aquarius. Hobbies:
charity work for boys clubs,
fishing, painting. Unfulfilled
ambition: to play in a stage
musical.

VAUGHAN, Norman
Entertainer b. 10.4.27
Liverpool. Stage debut at 14
with a boys troupe in Leigh,
Lancs. At 15 formed his own
trio, The Dancing Aces,
toured until military service at
18 and was in army shows
with Harry Secombe, Spike
Milligan and Ken Platt.
Variety, a two year stay in
Australia and seasons with
Twinkle at seaside resorts
and Bath and Cheltenham.
First TV 1954 followed by
Saturday Showtime 1955,
ITV's first light entertainment
series. Compere of The Cliff
Richard Show 1959 and 1960
and a season at Blackpool
led to him taking over from
Bruce Forsyth as compere of
Sunday Night at the London
Palladium 1962, and from
Bob Monkhouse on The
Golden Shot 1972. Other TV
incl: Pebble Mill Showcase;
Those Wonderful TV Times.
Stage incl: Boeing Boeing;
Play It Again Sam; The Happy
Apple; The Tempest; No, No,
Nanette; Once More Darling;
There Goes the Bride; Wizard
of Oz; Calamity Jane;
Chichester Festival 1977.
m. ex-dancer Bernice,

1 s. David. Address: c/o Richard Stone, London WC2. Starsign: Aries. Hobbies: driving, reading, golf. Unfulfilled ambition: to make a film in Hollywood.

VAUGHAN, Peter
Actor b. 4.4.24 Shropshire but brought up in Uttoxeter, Staffs. Joined Wolverhampton Rep on leaving school. Other reps all over country and army service before West End plays: Entertaining Mr Sloane; Portrait of a Queen. Films incl: Twist of Sand; The Naked Runner; The Bofors Gun; Hammerhead; Alfred the Great; Straw Dogs; The Man Outside; Eyewitness; The Pied Piper; Symptoms; The Blockhouse; Death in Rome; 11 Harrow House; The Mackintosh Man; The Savage Messiah; Valentine; Zulu Dawn; Porridge. Early TV role in Deadline Midnight he regards as landmark in his career. Other TV incl: The Gold Robbers; Treasure Island; Oliver Twist; Great Expectations; Citizen Smith and many plays. Education: Uttoxeter Grammar School. m. (1st) actress Billie Whitelaw (dis), (2nd) actress Lillias Walker, 1 s. David (from 2nd m). Address: Crawley, Sussex. Starsign: Aries.

VERNON, Richard
Actor b. 7.3.25 Reading, Berks. Trained at Central School of Speech and Drama. Much theatre experience incl: Peter Pan; A

Friend Indeed (also on TV); Hay Fever; Saturday, Sunday, Monday; The Passion of Dracula. TV incl: Man in Room 17; Sextet; Sarah; Upstairs, Downstairs; Edward the Seventh; The Duchess of Duke Street; Aren't We All?; The Sandbaggers; The After Dinner Joke; Ripping Yarns. Latest film: The Human Factor. Education: Leighton Park and Reading School. m. actress Benedicta Leigh, 1 d. Sarah, 1 s. Tom. Address: c/o Leading Artists, London W1. Starsign: Pisces. Hobby: sailing.

VINE, David
Sports commentator/ interviewer/ presenter b. 3.1.36 Barnstaple, Devon. Started on local weekly newspaper; writer and news and sport interviewer for Westward TV 1962, BBC 1966. Specialises in equestrian sport, winter sports, tennis, The Superstars. Commentaries incl: Olympic Games (winter and summer); Commonwealth Games; Horse of the Year Show; World Ski Cup; Wimbledon Championships. Education: Barnstaple Grammar School. Address: c/o BBC, London W12. Starsign: Capricorn.

W

WAGNER, Lindsay
Actress b. 22.6.49 Los
Angeles. Began dance
studies when 13, but
switched to acting. First
professional role was a small
part in an episode of Marcus
Welby MD. This led to parts in
films – Two People; Paper
Chase; Second Wind. Roles
in other TV series incl: The
FBI; Night Gallery; The
Rockford Files; The Six
Million Dollar Man. It was her
appearance in this series
(there was such a protest
when she was killed off that
somehow the producers had
to bring the character back)
that led to her becoming a
new star in The Bionic
Woman. Education: North
Hollywood High School;
Portland High School;
University of Oregon; Mt
Hood Community College.
m. (1st) music executive
Allan Rider (dis), (2nd)
actor/writer Michael
Brandon. Address: Malibu
Beach, California. Starsign:
Cancer.

WALDEN, Brian
Presenter b. 8.7.32 West
Bromwich, Staffs. University
lecturer; MP for All Saints and
Ladywood Division of
Birmingham 1964-77, when
took over presentation of
Weekend World from Peter
Jay. Education: West
Bromwich Grammar School;
Queens College, Oxford;
Nuffield College, Oxford.
m. (1st) Jane, (2nd) Hazel,
1 s. Benjamin (from 1st m).
Address: London W9.
Starsign: Cancer. Hobbies:
chess, gardening. Unfulfilled
ambition: 'to see England win
the World Cup just once more
before I die'.

WALE, Michael
Writer/performer b. 25th May
Banstead, Surrey.
Newspaper experience with
Northern Echo (Newcastle
and Darlington) and Daily
Express (Dublin and Fleet
Street). Writing credits,
mainly on radio, incl: Five
Nights With The Osmonds;
The Roy Hudd Show; The
Frost Report; Hancock in
Australia; Death of a Rolling
Stone; Donovan; The Petula
Clark Story; Rockspeak;
Scene and Heard; The Betty
Witherspoon Show. TV incl:
London Bridge; Today
(1975-77); Thames at 6
(1977); various half-hour
specials. Books incl: Voxpop;
The Bay City Rollers Story.
Education: Bedales, Hants.
Address: c/o Thames TV,
London NW1. Starsign:
Gemini. Hobbies: working
with racehorses, gardening.
Unfulfilled ambition: to ride
the winner of the Epsom
amateur riders' Derby and
win the Möet and Chandon
Silver Magnum.

WALKER, Nancy
Actress/director b. 10.5.22
Philadelphia, Pa. Diminutive
lady (4ft 11ins) of many
talents, who comes from a
vaudeville family and as a
child toured Europe with her
parents. Originally a dancer
and singer, comedy came
later when she made her
Broadway debut in Best Foot
Forward (also film). Other
stage incl: Girl Crazy (also
film); Broadway Rhythm
(also film); Meet The People;
On the Town; Fallen Angels;
Pal Joey; Wonderful Town;
Do Re Mi; A Funny Thing
Happened on the Way to the
Forum. Films incl: Lucky Me;
Stand Up and Be Counted;
The World's Greatest
Athlete; Forty Carats; Murder
By Death. Has appeared in
nearly every major American
TV show incl such series as
McMillan and Wife (Emmy
nomination for her role as the
uninhibited maid, Mildred);
Rhoda (as the Jewish
mother); The Mary Tyler

Moore Show. Has recently turned her attention to directing Broadway plays and a new film, Education: New York Professional Children's School. m. music coach David Craig, 1 d. Miranda. Starsign: Taurus. Hobby: work.

WALKER, Peter
Linkman/commentator b. 17.2.36 Bristol. Professional cricket with Glamorgan CCC 1955-72; three caps for England (v South Africa 1960). Began broadcasting with BBC Wales on radio programme Good Morning Wales 1963. Also presented BBC Wales Sports Parade on TV at that time. Frontman for John Player Sunday League cricket; also linkman for Test matches, international table tennis, golf and bowls. Sports correspondent for Times newspaper in Wales. Books incl: Cricket Conversations; Winning Cricket; The All-rounder. Educated in South Africa. m. (1st) dis, (2nd) Susan, 1 d. Sarah; 2 s. Justin, Daniel. Address: c/o BBC, Cardiff. Starsign: Aquarius. Hobbies: classical music, golf, squash, historical research. Unfulfilled ambition: to go round St Andrews golf course in par!

WALKER, Roy
Comedian b. 30.7.40 Belfast, N Ireland. Began as a boy soprano in a choir that toured Britain. Ventured into

comedy in Belfast and moved to England 1969. Soon made a name for himself in cabaret and northern clubs. London Palladium 1974. A New Faces winner in 1975 recording the highest ever marks for a comedian. Other TV incl: Seaside Special; Blackpool Bonanza; The Comedians. Education: Park Parade Secondary School, Belfast. m. Jean, 1 d. Joanna, 2 s. Mark, Philip. Address: c/o Mike Hughes Entertainments, Liverpool. Starsign: Leo. Hobby: golf. Unfulfilled ambitions: to appear in a Royal Variety performance; to play golf with Lee Trevino.

WALKER, Zena
Actress b. 7.3.34 Stratford-upon-Avon. Originally wanted to study stage design but became an actress at 17 at the Stratford Memorial Theatre and stayed with the company for three years, touring most of the world. Then to the Old Vic in London. Stage work has incl: 'Tis A Pity She's a Whore; Man and Superman; The Cherry Orchard; Macbeth;

The Fighting Cock; A Day in the Death of Joe Egg. Films incl: The Reckoning; Cromwell; The Hellions; The Traitors; Girl in the Headlines. TV incl: Albert and Victoria; Happy Ever After; Frenzy; House of Lies; The Citadel; The Doll's House; Man at the Top; Country Matters; Telford's Change; The Beast. Education: St Martin's School for Girls, Solihull; RADA. m. (1st) Robert Urquhart (dis), (2nd) Julian Holloway (dis), (3rd) John French, 1 d. Alison, 1 s. Matthew (both from 1st m). Address: c/o French's, London W1. Starsign: Pisces. Hobbies: gardening, driving.

WALLACE, Eric
Reporter b. 16.7.38 Carlisle. Started as a labourer, then two years in Royal Navy and three years at college. Two short films: Stage Company and I Can Lick Any Girl in the House. TV documentaries Border TV, etc. Education: Austin Friars; Bede College. m. Maureen, 1 d. Deborah, 1 s. John. Address: c/o Border TV, Carlisle. Starsign: Cancer. Hobbies: reading, physical fitness.

WANLESS, Neville
Continuity announcer b. 28.7.31 Wallsend- on-Tyne. Trained at LAMDA where he won the bronze, silver and gold medals for acting, verse-speaking and elocution. Was a radio newsreader for BBC's North Region 1972-76 before

joining Tyne Tees TV as announcer. Education: St Bees School, Cumbria. m. Patricia, 1 d. Melanie. Address: c/o Tyne Tees TV, Newcastle. Starsign: Leo. Hobbies: golf, amateur dramatics, hospital radio. Unfulfilled ambition: to host his own record programme or phone-in programme.

WARING, Derek
Actor. b. 26.4.30 London. Service in the Indian and British armies before training at RADA and five years in rep including Bath, Dundee and Amersham. On the London West End stage he has appeared with the Royal Shakespeare Company; as Prince Albert in Portrait of a Queen (with his wife as Queen Victoria); The World of Suzie Wong; Call It Love; Not to Worry; Cowardy Custard; Six of One. Films incl: Dunkirk; I Accuse; Last Days of Hitler; Battle of Britain. On TV he has played everything from a ringmaster to Sir Bernard Spilsbury (in The Killers). Other TV incl: Z Cars; Marked Personal; The Avengers; Carrington VC; Moody and Peg; Forget Me

Not; She; Crown Court; An Unofficial Rose; Flaxborough Chronicles; Hi-Summer; Wings; George and Mildred; Thundercloud. Brother Richard Waring (Not in Front of the Children; Marriage Lines; My Wife Next Door; and Mother Makes Five); water diviner; expert chef. Education: Dulwich College. m. actress Dorothy Tutin, 1 d. Amanda, 1 s. Nicholas. Address: c/o Peter Browne Management, London SW9. Starsign: Taurus. Hobbies: tennis, natural history, music, boats. Unfulfilled ambition: to visit the East and Far East.

WARING, George
Actor b. 20.2.27 Eccles, Lancs. Joined the RAF when 18 and began acting with RAF Rep Company on the Continent. Back in this country, joined the Century Theatre after a variety of jobs and toured Lancashire, Cheshire and Staffordshire. Also worked in rep at Manchester, Sheffield, Richmond and Birmingham. West End plays incl: Emil and the Detectives; Alfie; The 4th of June; The Bells. Hundreds of TV appearances incl: Z Cars; Mrs Thursday; Dr Who; Softly, Softly; Castle Haven; New Scotland Yard; Marked Personal; Rooms; Six Days of Justice; Coronation Street; Emmerdale Farm; Mixed Blessings. Education: Dulcie High School, Manchester. m. (1st) (dis), (2nd) actress Geraldine Gwyther, 1 d. Georgina, 1 s. Geoffrey. Address: c/o

Bernard Gillman Ltd, Tolworth, Surrey. Starsign: Pisces. Hobbies: listening to good music, interior decorating, cooking interesting meals. Unfulfilled ambition: to play Napoleon in the West End.

WATERMAN, Dennis
Actor b. 24.2.48 London. First acting appearance was in Night Train to Inverness when 11. By 16 he had been in The Music Man, done a season at Stratford-upon-Avon, starred as the original William in the first TV version of Just William and been to Hollywood to make the Fair Exchange series. Films incl: Up The Junction; The Sweeney; Sweeney 2. TV incl: The Sweeney; Give us a Kiss, Christabel; Dennis Waterman – With a Little Help From His Friends; The Minder. Also writes and sings songs and has made several successful records incl: Down Wind With Angels; Waterman. Education: Corona Stage School. m. (1st) Penny (dis), (2nd) actress Patricia Maynard, 2 d. Hannah, Julia. Address: c/o Boyack and Conway Ltd, London W1. Starsign: Pisces. Hobbies: playing guitar, writing songs.

WATERS, Alison
TV reporter b. 20.12.54 Baghdad, where her father was working for an oil company. Professional experience includes reporting for Radio Oxford and Radio Merseyside and

reporter/producer, Radio Bristol. Producer/presenter Best of Bristol and reporter for HTV's Report West; Gallery; Report Extra. Education: Ashford School, Kent; Maidstone Grammar; Exeter University; University College, Cardiff (BA Hons, English and American arts; Dip Journalism). Address: c/o HTV, Bristol. Starsign: Sagittarius. Hobbies: punk music, skiing, Florentine art, revue. Unfulfilled ambition: to be a singer in a sleazy night club.

WATFORD, Gwen
Actress b. 10.9.27 London. Started at Embassy, Swiss Cottage. Rep at Buxton, Croydon, Hornchurch, Salisbury, Old Vic. Stage plays incl: No Room at the Inn; Daddy Longlegs; A Lady Mislaid; Women of Twilight; The Queen and the Rebels; Time to Speak; The Woman on the Stair; Singles; Bodies. TV incl: Fate and Mr Brown; Mr Brown Comes Home; Till Time Shall End; A Woman of No Importance; Take Care of Madam; Dangerous Corner; The Waters of Babylon; Second Time Around; The

Train Now Standing . . .; A Bit of an Adventure; A Provincial Lady; A Suitable Case For Killing; Love Me to Death; Don't Forget to Write; Aren't We All?. Films incl: Never Take Sweets from a Stranger; The Very Edge; Cleopatra. Twice Actress of the Year. Education: St Leonard's on Sea. m. actor Richard Bebb, 2 s. Mark, Owen. Address: Hampstead Garden Suburb, London. Starsign: Virgo. Hobbies: playing the piano, gardening.

WATLING, Dilys
Actress b. 5.5.46 Fulmer Chase, Bucks. Studied art until 17 then decided to join the Italia Conti Stage School and more training at the Bristol Old Vic. Between spells in rep including Frinton and Hornchurch, she made her TV debut in Compact and appeared in two films. Her big stage break came in Pickwick (with Harry Secombe) followed by Our Man Crichton; Promises, Promises; Company; Fiddler on the Roof; Kings and Clowns; pantomime. On TV she has appeared with Tommy Cooper, Benny Hill, Dickie Henderson, Morecambe and Wise, Frankie Howerd, Terry Scott, the Two Ronnies and Mike Yarwood. Other TV incl: Coronation Street; United; The Alchemist; Tonight; Twice a Fortnight; The Likely Lads; Going For a Song; Celebrity Squares; Blankety Blank; 3-2-1. Education: St Mary's Convent, Woodford

Green, Essex. m. (dis). Address: c/o London Management, London W1. Starsign: Taurus. Hobby: watching the ITV Seven with a glass of Buck's Fizz. Unfulfilled ambition: 'having just played Principal Boy at the London Palladium, I would now like to appear there as myself!'

WATLING, Jack
Actor b. 13.1.23 London. First appearance in Where the Rainbow Ends 1935 at Holborn Empire. Apart from three years in the RAF has been employed continuously in stage, film and TV work ever since. TV incl: The Planemakers; The Power Game; The Cedar Tree. m. actress Patricia Hicks, 3 d. Dilys, Deborah, Nicola, 1 s. Giles. Address: Loughton, Essex. Starsign: Capricorn.

WATSON, Jack
Actor b. 15th May London. Started as stooge (Hubert) to his father, comedian Nosmo King, and was in variety for 15 years before becoming a straight actor after a part in Z Cars. Numerous film and TV

parts since. Films incl: The Hill: The Idol; Tobruk; Grand Prix; Red Gauntlet; Every Home Should Have One; Three Musketeers; Juggernaut; Schizo; The Purple Taxi; Wild Geese. TV incl: Troubleshooters; Arthur of the Britons; Upstairs, Downstairs; The Hanged Man; The Charges; Sky; The Georgian House; Onedin Line; Killers; Goodbye America; Warship; Rob Roy; Who Pays the Ferryman?; Treasure Island; All Creatures Great and Small; The Cost of Loving; Kidnapped. m. Betsy, 2 d. Penelope, Fiona, 1 s. Alastair. Address: c/o Joseph and Wagg, London W1. Starsign: Taurus. Hobbies: sailing, surfing, water skiing, golf, tennis.

WATSON, Moray
Actor b. 25.6.30 Sunningdale, Berks. Trained at the Webber Douglas Academy of Dramatic Art, then rep at Leatherhead, Nottingham and Liverpool before London's West End and his first hit The Grass is Greener (also the film version with Cary Grant and Robert Mitchum). Other stage incl: The Public Eye and the Private Ear (Broadway); Don't Just Lie There, Say Something; On Approval; The Incomparable Max (his one-man show as Max Beerbohm). Films incl: Operation Crossbow; The Valiant; Every Home Should Have One. TV incl: Compact; The Borderers; On Approval;

Quiller; Upstairs, Downstairs; A Place in the Sun; The Pallisers; Murder Most English; Rumpole of the Bailey; Company and Co; Pride and Prejudice. Education: Eton. m. actress Pam Marmont, 1 d. Emma, 1 s. Robin. Address: c/o Leading Artists, London SW1. Starsign: Cancer. Hobbies: gardening, philately.

WAUGH, Eric L
Industrial and economics correspondent b. 1.7.29 Londonderry, N Ireland. After gaining a history and politics moderatorship at Trinity College, Dublin, went to Northwestern University, Illinois, as research fellow 1953 and the University of Chicago 1954. During that time was producer and commentator, foreign news features for Station WNMP, Chicago. Became Belfast Telegraph staff writer 1955-61 and BBC staff correspondent in N Ireland 1962. Education: Methodist College, Belfast. m. Mattie, 2 d. Address: Cultra, Co Down and c/o BBC, Belfast. Starsign: Cancer.

WEAVER, Dennis
Actor b. 4.6.25 Joplin, Missouri. Always wanted to be an actor, but many jobs and service in the Naval Air Force before going to Oklahoma University in 1946 where he became a top athlete, setting up many track and field records, and

a leading light in the dramatic society. Broadway stage debut 1951. Big TV break came in 1954, when he was chosen to play Matt Dillon's limping side-kick Chester in Gunsmoke, a part he played for 10 years and for which he was awarded an Emmy. Other TV incl: Kentucky Jones; Gentle Ben; McCloud; Centennial. Also several TV movies incl: The Islander; The Ordeal of Patty Hearst. Films incl: Horizon's West; The Redhead from Wyoming; Column South; Mississippi Gambler; Law and Order; Man from the Alamo; Dangerous Mission; Dragnet; The Bridges of Toki-Ri; Ten Wanted Men; Seven Angry Men; Touch of Evil; The Gallant Hours; Duel at Diabalo; A Man Called Sledge; What's the Matter With Helen?; Duel. Talented writer of songs and has cut a number of LP's and singles. Education: Joplin Junior College; Oklahoma University. m. former actress Gerry Stowell, 3 s. Richard, Rob, Rustin. Address: West San Fernando Valley. Starsign: Gemini. Hobby: song-writing.

WEBB, Marylyn
Reporter/presenter b. 20.9.47 Brighton. Started on provincial newspapers. TV: Calendar; Who is the Ripper? (Calendar special); Sandringham Sydney and Co (documentary on Queen's gun dogs). Education: state school. m. journalist Peter Charlton. Address: c/o

Yorkshire TV, Leeds. Starsign: Virgo. Hobbies: wildlife conservation, walking, cooking, gardening (window box), tennis, table tennis, reading non-fiction. Unfulfilled ambitions: to write a best seller; to own a house in the country with enough land to cultivate and keep animals; to beat her husband at tennis; to cuddle a lion; to visit Canada.

WEBB, Rita
Actress. Born in London but declines to divulge her age because she says she is perpetually young. Vital statistics: 48in bust, 46in waist, 52in hips; 4ft 10ins tall; weighs 15 stone; dyed red hair; all her own teeth. Husband's nickname for her: 'Podge'. Starsign: Pisces. Address: c/o Peter Campbell, NEMS Management, London SW3. (This is the only information about her that Rita Webb wishes us to include, despite the fact that she has worked with almost every comic on TV as well as in films with Gary Cooper (in his last picture), Elizabeth Taylor, David Niven, Michael York

and Nigel Davenport. She also has two other claims to fame: she signs her letters 'Dame' Rita Webb; and 'Did you ever hear of an actress refusing to be on This Is Your Life?' she asks. 'Well you have now, because I bleedin' well did!' – Editor.)

WEBBER, Christine
Announcer/presenter/newsreader b. Redhill, Surrey. Trained as a singer and has sung with Black and White Minstrels and in cabaret. Theatre work has also taken her on tours and in rep. On TV has been announcer for Southern TV, announcer/newsreader for Anglia TV, presenter of Watch Your Language and announcer/interviewer on British Forces TV. Education: Lady Edridge Grammar, Croydon; Guildhall School of Music and Drama. m. actor/writer Hugo Myatt. Address: c/o Pamela Juvenile New Management, London W1. Starsign: Aries. Hobbies: motor cycles, motoring, gardening, looking after an exigent ginger cat. Unfulfilled ambition: to own a Rolls-Royce.

WEEKS, Alan
Sports commentator b. 8.9.23 Bristol. First broadcast while serving in the Royal Navy (Midshipman to Lieutenant RNR) during the Second World War – over ship's radio in the corvette HMS Rushen Castle, giving nightly situation report to ship's company. Public

address announcer, Brighton Sports Stadium 1946-65. First commentary for BBC TV on ice hockey 1951. Has since commentated and presented most sports, including ice hockey (since 1958), gymnastics (1962), swimming (1970), Pot Black (1970), Olympic Games (1960, 1964), Summer Grandstand (1959-62), Winter Olympics (1964-76), Olympics (1968-76), World Cup (1966-78), Commonwealth Games (1970-78). Education: Brighton, Hove and Sussex Grammar. m. Barbara Jane, 1 d. Beverly, 2 s. Nigel, Roderick. Address: c/o The Bagenal Harvey Organisation, London W1. Starsign: Virgo. Hobbies: swimming, football. Unfulfilled ambition: to see ice hockey return as a major sport in Britain.

WEIR, Molly
Actress b. Glasgow. First public appearance at age of five in her local cinema. Trained as a secretary and became a champion shorthand typist with a shorthand speed of 300 wpm. Made her name in

London playing Tattie McIntosh in Tommy Handley's series Itma. Then came the part for which she is probably best remembered – Aggie in Life With The Lyons. Stage work incl: A Play For Ronnie; The Happiest Days of Your Life. Much TV work incl: Short Story; The Andy Stewart Show; Oil Strike North; The Root of All Evil; Within These Walls. Frequently seen on TV in a well known detergent commercial. Has also written five volumes of her autobiography. m. Sandy. Address: Pinner, Middx. Hobbies: gardening, knitting, cooking.

WELFARE, Simon
Reporter/producer
b. 21.11.46 Cambridge. TV incl: Calendar reporter 1968; The Scientists; Discovery; Don't Ask Me; The Boy in the Bubble. Education: Harrow; Magdalen College, Oxford. m. Mary, 2 d. Hannah, Alice, 1 s. Toby. Address: N Yorkshire. Starsign: Scorpio. Hobbies: driving my lawnmower, reading old newspapers. Unfulfilled ambition: to limbo as well as Kermit.

WELLAND, Colin
Actor/writer b. 4.7.44 Leigh, Lancs. Worked for five years as an art teacher before being taken on at Manchester's Library Theatre. Briefly compere of BBC's North at Six and an appearance in The Verdict is Yours before becoming PC

Graham in Z Cars for three years. Took to writing and hasn't looked back since with awards both for acting and writing. TV plays incl: Bangelstein's Boys; Slattery's Mounted Foot; Roll On Four O'Clock; Say Goodnight to Grandma (stage version marked his London West End debut as actor and playwright); Catherine Wheel; The Hallelujah Handshake; A Room Full of Holes; Leeds United; Kisses at Fifty; The Wild West Show; Your Man From Six Counties; Yanks (film script). TV appearances in addition to many of his own plays and Z Cars, incl: Man at the Top; Left; Passage to England; The Cost of Loving; Blue Remembered Hills; Jack Point. Also presenter of How to Stay Alive and sports commentator. Films incl: Kes; Villain; Straw Dogs; The Sweeney. Education: Grammar School, Newton-le-Willows. m. former teacher Pat, 3 d. Genevieve, Catherine, Caroline, 1 adopt. s. Christie. Address: c/o Peter Charlesworth Ltd, London SW7. Starsign: Cancer. Hobbies: cricket, rugby, singing.

WELSH, John
Actor b. 7.11.14 Wexford. Regards five years at the Gate Theatre, Dublin (1945-50) as his training before moving to London. Has since had wide experience in the theatre, films and TV. Subsequently

joined the Royal Shakespeare Company and was in their Wars of the Roses 1964. Other stage incl: The Party; Look Back in Anger; Too True to be Good; Measure For Measure. Films incl: The Man Who Haunted Himself; Cromwell; The Pied Piper of Hamelin. Much TV incl: The Forsyte Saga; Mr Rose; Uncle Silas; Paper Dolls; Flower Dew; Raj; Trials of Marshal Petain; Oh, Brother; Footprints in the Jungle; Codename; Little Women and Good Wives; Last Wishes; Duchess of Duke Street; Affairs of the Heart; Diary of a Nobody; The Recruiting Officer. Education: Christian Brothers, Wexford. m. Audrey, 1 d. Lucy, 2 s. Simon, John. Address: c/o Joy Jameson Ltd, London SW1. Starsign: Scorpio. Hobbies: golf, music. Unfulfilled ambition: to be happy.

WEST, Adam
Actor b. 19th September, Walla Walla, Washington. Born on a ranch and grew up with a liking for the active life. Been interested in show

business since the age of six, but worked in radio and TV and in journalism before winning an audition as writer/producer/director/announcer for a small broadcasting network. A year later he was called up for the Army for which he set up a TV station. On discharge he walked through Europe, working as a milkman, singing in clubs and doing TV to pay for the trip. TV debut in Colt 45 and before The Detectives and Batman, TV also incl: 77 Sunset Strip; Sugarfoot; Cheyenne; Lawman; Maverick; Perry Mason; Bonanza. Films incl: Tammy and the Doctor; Soldiers in the Rain; Petticoat Junction; Bewitched; Geronimo; The Specialist; The Outlaws is Coming. Starsign: Virgo.

WEST, Peter
Commentator b. 12.8.20 Addiscombe, Surrey. Specialised in many sports including rugby, tennis and cricket, and for 15 years (1957-72) was commentator for Come Dancing. Also compered talent shows and chaired a panel game (Guess My Story). Now heads a firm of public relations consultants. Education: Cranbrook School, Kent. m. Pauline, 1 d. Jacqueline, 2 s. Simon, Stephen. Address: c/o West Nally Group, London W1. Starsign: Leo.

WEST, Timothy
Actor b. 2.10.34 Bradford. Studied modern languages at London Polytechnic 1951-53, but neglected studies to act Shakespeare in pubs with a group called The Taverners. Short spells as furniture salesman and recording engineer before making the stage his career. Worked with various reps including Northampton, Canterbury, Bath, Bristol and Salisbury leaving there 1959 to make his London debut in Caught Napping. Stage work since includes leading roles in West End and with Royal Shakespeare and Prospect Companies, in UK and abroad. Films incl: Twisted Nerve; Looking Glass War; Nicholas and Alexandra; The Day of the Jackal; Joseph Andrews; The Devil's Advocate; News from Nowhere; Agatha; The Thirty-Nine Steps. TV incl: Joy; Horatio Bottomley; Edward the Seventh; The After Dinner Game; Hard Times; Henry VIII; Crime and Punishment; Churchill and the Generals. Education: 13 schools (his actor father, Lockwood West, and mother were frequently on tour) incl: John Lyon School, Harrow. m. (1st) Jacqueline Boyer (dis), (2nd) Prunella Scales, 1 d. Juliet (from 1st m), 2 s. Sam, Joe. Address: London SW18. Starsign: Libra. Hobbies: listening to music, exploring old railway lines. Unfulfilled ambition: to be as good as the Muppets.

WESTWOOD, Barry
Presenter/interviewer/producer b. 7.9.27 Birmingham. Originally articled to a Birmingham firm of chartered accountants. After qualifying, moved to Southampton 1954 where he lectured in Accountancy, Taxation and Company Law etc, and became senior lecturer in charge of Professional Studies at Southampton Tech College. Met Roy Rich, then Southern TV's Programme Controller, while presenting prize in best secretary competition 1959 and within 12 days was introducing his own TV programme. Has since appeared in and/or introduced more than 3,500 programmes incl: Southern TV's award-winning Day By Day (since 1969); Sunday Break; Background; ABC Weekend; Your Point of View; Afloat; General Election outside broadcasts and numerous adult education programme series. Education: Solihull School. Address: Fareham, Hants. Starsign: Virgo. Hobbies: caravanning, wine, music. Unfulfilled ambition: to be full of ambition!

WHEELER, Charles
TV correspondent b. 26.3.23 Bremen, Germany. Joined the old Daily Sketch from school and a year later was doing war service in the Royal Marines (1941-46). Then he joined the BBC. Was co-producer of Panorama 1956-58. Has become one of

the most respected foreign correspondents on TV having been BBC correspondent in India, Berlin and Washington and chief correspondent in America and Europe, based in Brussels. Became a freelance broadcaster in 1976 since when he has presented Newsday and Panorama. Education: Cranbrook School, Kent. m. Dip Singh, 2 d. Shirin, Marina. Address: c/o BBC TV, London W12. Starsign: Aries.

WHICKER, Alan
Journalist b. 2.8.25 Cairo, Egypt. Came to England at the age of five with his mother after the death of his father. TV's most travelled reporter. Many world-wide reports and documentaries on numerous subjects have earned him many awards. After 12 years with BBC, switched to ITV and especially Yorkshire TV of which he is largest private shareholder. Army service in Second World War; war correspondent for Fleet Street news agency and visited almost every country in the world. First Whicker's World series began 1958.

Education: Haberdashers' Aske's School, Hampstead, London. Address: Jersey, Channel Islands. Starsign: Leo.

WHITE, Sheila
Singer/dancer b. 18.10.50 Highgate, London. Started with Terry's Juveniles when she was 12 before training at the Corona Stage School. Early stage work incl: The Sound of Music; Roar of the Greasepaint, Smell of the Crowd; On the Level; Dames at Sea (also in France where it was a huge success and Sheila became the toast of Paris); pantomimes and Queen Daniella; tours. Films incl: Here We Go Round the Mulberry Bush; Ghost Goes Gear; Stranger in the House; Oliver!; Confessions of a Window Cleaner; Confessions of a Pop Star; Confessions of a Driving Instructor; Mrs Brown You've Got a Lovely Daughter; The Spaceman and King Arthur; The Silver Dream Racer. Many TV plays and series both here and in France where through, TV, films, cabaret and records she was regarded as a superstar. TV here incl: appearances with Cliff Richard and Bill Dainty; such series as Z Cars; Emergency-Ward 10; Oranges and Lemons; Dear Mother . . . Love, Albert; Poldark; Love School; The Songwriters. Also Alice in Wonderland; I Claudius; Ladies of Ridgemead; Minder; Pickwick Papers; Tiptoes; Jazz Age.

Education: Woodberry Down Primary; Woodberry Down Comprehensive; Campbell's Private School, Muswell Hill. Address: c/o Peter Charlesworth Ltd, London SW7. Starsign: Libra. Hobbies: riding, tennis, swimming, cooking, country walks, singing, listening to records with headphones very loud, driving, gardening.

WHITEHEAD, Geoffrey
Actor b. 1.10.39 Sheffield. RADA trained, followed by work in Canterbury, Coventry and Sheffield Reps. TV incl: Bulldog Breed; Z Cars; Last of the Best Men; Robin's Nest; The Foundation. Education: Westbourne Road Prep; Trent College, Nottingham. m. actress Mary Hanefey, 1 d. Clare, 2 s. Ben, Jonty. Address: Wraysbury, Middx. Starsign: Libra. Hobbies: football, cricket.

WHITELEY, Richard
Presenter b. 28.12.43 Bradford, Yorkshire. TV trainee with ITN 1965, joined Yorkshire TV 1968. Presenter of Calendar and associated programmes, incl: Calendar

Sunday; Calendar Tuesday; Calendar People; Calendar Forum; Election Calendar; Good Morning Calendar (breakfast programme); Goodnight Calendar; Calendar Profile; Country Calendar; Calendar Specials. Education: Giggleswick School, N Yorks; Christ's College, Cambridge. Address: Fearby Cross, Masham, N Yorks. Starsign: Capricorn. Hobbies: walking, watching TV. Unfulfilled ambition: to have a numbered bank account in Barnsley.

WHITFIELD, June
Comedy actress b. 11th November, London. After training at RADA and such stage shows as Love From Judy, came to the fore as Eth in the radio series Take It From Here (1953). On TV she has been foil to the best funny men in the business incl: Morecambe and Wise, Jimmy Edwards, Frankie Howerd, Terry Scott, Dick Emery, Stanley Baxter, Arthur Askey, Eric Sykes and Tony Hancock. Films incl: Carry On Abroad; Bless This House; The Spy With the Cold Nose. TV incl: Beggar My Neighbour; The Best Things In Life; Hancock's Half Hour; Scott On . . .; Happy Ever After; Terry and June. Education: Streatham High. m. surveyor Tim Aitchison, 1 d. Susan. Address: Wimbledon, London. Starsign: Scorpio. Hobby: cooking. Unfulfilled ambition: just to keep working.

WHITTAKER, Roger
Singer/entertainer/ songwriter b. 22.3.36 Nairobi, Kenya. Called up at 18 into the Kenya Regiment. Afterwards became a schoolmaster, singing in clubs at night. Came to Britain, got a biochemistry degree but decided to try show business. By the end of 1963 he had a small late night TV series. Has since appeared in concerts, cabaret and clubs all over the world as well as his own TV programmes. Prolific songwriter incl: Durham Town; I Don't Believe In If Anymore; New World in the Morning; Why; The Last Farewell. Education: Capetown and Bangor Universities (BSc). m. Natalie, 3 d. Emily, Lauren, Jessica, 2 s. Guy, Alexander. Address: c/o Tembo Entertainments Ltd, London NW1. Starsign: Aries. Hobbies: photography, flying aeroplanes, collecting antiques. Unfulfilled ambition: to write a successful musical.

WILCOX, Paula
Actress b. 30th December,

Manchester. Applied for a job with National Youth Theatre while still a schoolgirl. Played the part of a factory girl in their production of Apprentices which led to her being spotted for her TV role in The Lovers, 1970. Other TV incl: Coronation Street; The Dustbinmen; The Liver Birds; On Her Majesty's Pleasure; Man About the House; Miss Jones and Son; The Cost of Loving; episodes of Kate and Hadleigh. In the theatre she has appeared with Bristol Old Vic and at Harrogate and in London's West End in Bedroom Farce. Toured Australia in My Fat Friend and British tours in Touch of Spring; Time to Kill. Education: Hollies Convent, Manchester. m. actor Derek Seaton (dec). Address: c/o Larry Dalzell Associates Ltd, London WC2. Starsign: Capricorn.

WILKIE, David MBE
Sports commentator/ swimmer b. 8.3.54 Colombo, Sri Lanka. Swimmer extraordinary, contracted to London Weekend Television to commentate on the 1980 Moscow Olympics. Retired undefeated in summer 1976 as Olympic, World, European and Commonwealth champion and record holder of 200 metres breaststroke. Held 30 major records (three World, nine European and 18 Commonwealth) and won 15 major swimming medals (eight gold, four silver and three bronze). Britain's only gold medallist at the 1976

Montreal Olympics for 200 metres breaststroke. Swimmer of the Year 1970/72/73/74/75. Scotland's Sportsman of the Year 1972 and Sports Writers' Association of Great Britain Sportsman of the Year 1975. Europe's swimming Man of the Year 1975. Awarded full scholarship 1973 to study marine biology at the University of Miami, Florida, but later transferred to Broadcasting and Communications. Education: boarder at Daniel Stewart's College, Edinburgh; reluctant member of Warrender Bath's Swimming Club, Edinburgh. Address: c/o MSW Management Ltd, London WC2. Starsign: Pisces. Hobbies: scuba diving, tennis, reading. Unfulfilled ambitions: 'to be successful in my work for television; to raise money (a) for youngsters through sponsored 'swim-a-longs', (b) for British sport.'

WILLIAMS, Alun
Commentator b. 26.8.20 Port Talbot, S Wales. War service in Royal Navy and Royal Volunteer Reserve before joining BBC 1946. Since commentated in English and Welsh at Olympic and Empire Games; covered rugby tours in New Zealand, Australia, South Africa and South America. Also commentated on many royal occasions incl: the Coronation. Education: Llandeilo and Pontypridd Grammar Schools; University College, Cardiff. m. Perrie,

2 d. Elinor, Nia, 1 s. Rhys. Address: Cyncoed, Cardiff. Starsign: Virgo. Hobbies: golf, walking, all kinds of music. Unfulfilled ambition: to find a house five minutes from the golf course, the sea and Broadcasting House.

WILLIAMS, Dorian OBE
Equestrian commentator. Began his long career as announcer over the public address system at big horse shows, which he soon combined with commentating for the BBC. Is now the best known voice in show-jumping, covering such events as Royal International Horse Show, the European Show-jumping championships and the Montreal Olympics. Founder and director of a residential adult education college near Tring, Herts. Books incl: The Horse of the Year Show; Master of One. Education: Harrow. married. 1 d. Carola, 1 s. Piers. Address: c/o BBC, London W12. Hobbies: hunting – he is Master of Foxhounds. Also chairman of the British Horse Society and founder of National Equestrian Centre.

WILLIAMS, Guy
Reporter b. 28.10.47 Eccles, Lancs. BBC news training scheme and wide experience in local radio in Hull, Leicester, Middlesbrough, Sheffield. Worked for BBC local radio in House of Commons. Hull reporter for Yorkshire TV. Education: Giggleswick

School, Yorks; Liverpool University. m. Lindy, 1 s. Thomas. Address: Beverley, Yorks. Starsign: Scorpio. Hobbies: squash, cricket, reading sports books and autobiographies of politicians. Unfulfilled ambition: to read the news regularly on television.

WILLIAMS, Peter
TV journalist b. 21.9.33 Bristol. Newspaper experience – Bristol Evening Post (10 years) and TV journalism with Television Weekly – before freelancing with TWW and BBC Radio and joining Southern TV as a reporter on Day By Day. Switched to This Week 1966 and has since done some notable documentaries incl: The American Space Programme; Everyone's Gone to the Moon; Manhunt on the Cannock Chase Murders; The Test-tube Baby; DC10 Air Crash; The Guinea Pig Club. Joined BBC 1979. Education: King Edward School, Totnes, Devon; Cotham Grammar School, Bristol. m. Ann, 3 d. Deborah, Jacqueline, Claire, 2 s. Mark, Gareth.

Address: Chesterfield, Kent. Starsign: Virgo. Hobbies: conservation of environment – and self, cricket (watching and discussing).

WILLIAMS, Robin
Comedy actor b. 1943, Edinburgh. Was a year old when his family moved to America. Originally wanted to study political science but developed an interest in acting while at college. Won a three year acting scholarship to the Juilliard School, New York, and became a stand-up comic working in clubs and cabaret when he couldn't get work. First TV was Laugh-In, but it was his appearance as Mork in the episode of Happy Days that led to the successful spin-off series Mork and Mindy. Album: Reality – What A Concert. Education: Redwood High, San Francisco; Claremont Men's College; College of Marin, California. m. former dancer Valerie Velardi. Hobbies: cross-country running, yoga, roller skating and dance exercise.

WILLIAMS, Simon
Actor b. 16.6.46 Windsor,

Berks. One of the tallest actors in the business (he stand 6ft 4ins in his socks), he started in pantomime in 1965, followed by rep at Worthing, Birmingham and Croydon. London West End appearances incl: A Friend in Need; Hay Fever; His and Hers; No Sex Please – We're British; Gigi. Films incl: Joanna; The Touchables; The Incredible Sarah; Jabberwocky; No Longer Alone; The Fiendish Plot of Dr Fu Manchu. TV breakthrough was as Captain Bellamy in Upstairs, Downstairs. Other TV incl: The Regiment; Man in a Suitcase; Romance; Wodehouse Playhouse; Mr Big; Liza; Agony; Company and Co. Education: Harrow. m. actress Belinda Carroll, 1 d. Amy, 1 s. Tamlyn. Address: c/o Leading Artists, London SW1. Starsign: Gemini. Hobbies: riding, reading, writing. Unfulfilled ambition: to complete writing a stage play.

WILSON, Anthony
TV journalist b. 20.2.50 Salford. After leaving Cambridge (Jesus College) with an hons degree in English and having edited Varsity, received his training in TV journalism with ITN. Joined Granada TV and was involved with Granada Reports; Powerpoint; What's On; writer/ presenter of So It Goes. Education: St Mary's Primary School, Marple, Cheshire; De La Salle College. Salford; Jesus

College, Cambridge. m. Lindsay. Address: c/o Granada TV, Manchester. Starsign: Pisces. Hobbies: music, reading, indoor gardening, films. Unfulfilled ambitions: to do a third series of So It Goes; to have lunch with Johnny Rotten; to make half-hour films.

WILSON, Arnold
Reporter b. 14.2.44 Ruislip, Middx. Journalist with Kent Messenger, Daily Mirror, Sunday People, Anglia TV, ITN. Reporter with Radio Sheffield and, since 1975, reporter for Southern TV (Day By Day). Education: Simon Langton Grammar, Canterbury; Friends School, Saffron Walden. m. Veronica, 4 d. Melissa, Samantha and twins Amber and Lara. Address: Smarden, Kent. Starsign: Aquarius. Hobbies: skiing, travel, football, jogging, music. Unfulfilled ambitions: to play (and score a hat trick) for Nottingham Forest; to beat Klammer in the downhill ski race; to be the first reporter on the moon.

WILSON, Bob
Sports presenter b. 30.10.41 Chesterfield, Derbys. Former Arsenal and Scotland goalkeeper. Joined the club 1963 from Loughborough College where he was a teacher of physical education. Joined BBC 1974 to present football spot Football Focus in Grandstand. Education: Chesterfield Grammar. m. Margaret (Megs),

1 d. Anna, 2 s. John, Robert. Address: Brookman's Park, London. Starsign: Scorpio. Hobbies: squash, golf.

WILSON, Jennifer
Actress b. 25th April London. Wanted to be a dress designer but changed her mind when successfully auditioned for RADA. Rep, then Regent's Park Open Air Theatre, the Old Vic, a tour of America and Canada with them, Shakespearean tour of India. Two years in Spring and Port Wine in London's West End. Other stage incl: Lend Me Five Shillings; It Happened in Harrods; Pygmalion; Most Gracious Lady; Travesties; The Four Poster; Hong Kong Festival; Bedroom Farce; The Complaisant Lover; The Grass Is Greener. Starred in dozens of TV plays and series but is probably best known as Jenny Hammond in The Brothers for six years. Other TV incl: Nicholas Nickleby; You Never Can Tell; Time and the Conways; The Widowing of Mrs Holroyd; Antigone; A Doll's House; Man of Our Times; The Second Mrs Tanquery; The Befrienders. Educated in the Cotswolds and London College. m. (1st) S Swain (dis), (2nd) actor/director Brian Peck, 1 d. Melanie (by 2nd m). Address: c/o NEMS Management, London SW3. Starsign: Taurus. Hobbies: collecting pictures, cooking. Unfulfilled ambition: 'to work until I'm 90 years old in relative comfort'.

WILSON, Lee
Comedian b. 31.7.38 Wednesbury, Staffs. Started in show business as a guitarist/vocalist before joining the army. While serving overseas with the Cheshire Regt. toured with a group entertaining the troops. After completing his service set about a show business career in earnest, winning many talent competitions. Later added comedy between his songs and this now forms the basis of his act. Was a New Faces winner in September 1976, followed by two seasons at Pontins where he was voted top comedy act. Midlands Club Award as Comedian of the Year 1978. TV incl: The Comedians; The Lee Wilson Show. Education: King's Hill School, Wednesbury. m. Shelia, 2 d. Tracy, Debbie, 1 s. Lee. Address: c/o International Artistes Representation, London W1. Starsign: Leo. Hobbies: salmon fishing (he once landed a 30-pounder), football (West Bromwich Albion). Unfulfilled ambition: to continue to enjoy life.

WILSON, Malcolm
Newscaster/writer/ broadcaster b. 25.7.50 Ayr, Scotland. Newspaper background with The Scotsman and in Edinburgh and Glasgow. Joined Scottish TV 1973 and moved to BBC Scotland 1976. TV incl: Scotland Today; Crimedesk (both for STV); Reporting Scotland; Sportscene (both for BBC). Education: Ayr Academy; Edinburgh University. m. Irene, 2 s. Jamie, Louis. Address: c/o BBC, Glasgow. Starsign: Leo. Hobbies: crosswords, literature, losing charity football matches. Unfulfilled ambitions: to work abroad; to play good piano.

WILSON, Richard
Actor/director b. 9.7.36 Greenock, Renfrewshire. Originally a research scientist in Scotland but gave it up to study for the stage when he was 27. Trained at RADA then rep at Glasgow, Edinburgh (Traverse) and Manchester (Stables). Frequently seen on TV in a variety of roles and programmes incl: Dr Finlay's Casebook; The Revenue

Men; My Good Woman; Crown Court; Big Boy Now; Cilla's World of Comedy; Pickersgill People; A Sharp Intake of Breath; Through the Night; Some Mothers Do 'Ave 'Em; In Loving Memory; Chalk and Cheese; Only When I Laugh. Also directs in the theatre being an associate director at Oxford Playhouse and an assistant director at the Stables Theatre, Manchester. Most recently directed The House for the Joint Stock Company. Educated at Greenock. Address: c/o Green and Underwood Ltd, London WC2. Starsign: Cancer. Hobby: squash.

WINDING, Victor
Actor b. 30.1.29 London. Trained as a draughtsman, but in evenings was acting in amateur dramatics and teaching drama in LCC night schools. At 29 he got a job with Farnham Rep and three years later went to London Old Vic. Then Malvern Festival and London's West End incl: Next Time I'll Sing to You; Poor Bitos; Merchant of Venice. Films incl: The System. Much TV incl: Emergency – Ward 10; Probation Officer; No Hiding Place; The Informer; The Saint; Dr Who; The Expert; The Flaxton Boys; Warship; Crossroads. Education: Westminster Technical Institute. m. Rosalind (dis), 3 d. Celia, Kay, Jane, 1 s. Julian. Address: c/o Richard Stone, London WC2. Starsign: Aquarius. Hobbies:

sport, gardening. Unfulfilled ambitions: to be fulfilled; to farm.

WINDSOR, Frank
Actor b. 12.7.27 Walsall, Staffs. Started in radio 1946 after RAF station shows. Founder member of the Oxford and Cambridge Players, later the Elizabethan Players and before going into TV was a classical actor. London stage incl: Androcles and the Lion; Brand; Travesties (with Royal Shakespeare Co); the Old Vic. Films incl: This Sporting Life; Spring and Port Wine; Bloody Sunday; The Drop Out; Assassin; Someone is Killing Off the Great Chefs of Europe. Best known on TV for his role as Sergt Watt in Z Cars and in Softly, Softly. Other TV incl: An Age of Kings; A for Andromeda; Call My Bluff; Whodunnit?; Jack the Ripper; Headmaster; Crown Court; Kidnapped. Education: St Mary's School, Walsall. m. former dancer Mary Corbett, 1 d. Amanda, 1 s. David. Address: c/o Boyack and Conway Ltd, London W1. Starsign: Cancer. Hobbies: tending his grapevine to make his own wine, dogs, working for World Wildlife Fund and Variety Club of GB.

WINKLER, Henry
Actor b. 30.10.45 New York City. Alias Fonzie of Happy Days. Always wanted to be an actor. Gained a Master of Arts degree at Yale School of

Drama where he appeared in more than 30 plays as a student. On graduation stayed on as professional actor. After a brief spell with the Arena Theatre in Washington (he was sacked after three weeks) found work in radio, TV commercials and acted with a children's group in New York. Started in Happy Days 1972. Films incl: Heroes; The One and Only. Education: McBurney Prep School; Emmetson College, Boston; Yale University. m. public relations executive Stacey Weitzman. Address: Beverly Hills, California. Starsign: Scorpio. Hobbies: listening to music, watching TV, reading, jogging. Unfulfilled ambition: to act in Britain's National Theatre in Shakespeare.

WINTERS, Bernie
Comedian b. 6.9.32 Islington, London. Went straight into show business on leaving school. Later formed a double act with his brother Mike, then joined the Merchant Navy to see the world. Resumed partnership with brother 1949 and appeared in numerous

variety, musical and TV shows incl: Six-Five Special; Big Night Out; Blackpool Night Out. Went solo 1978 and his own series Bernie. Education: Crowland Rd School, Tottenham; Vartry Rd, Seven Sisters, London. m. ex-dancer Siggi Heine, 1 s. Ray. Address: c/o Joe Collins Ltd, London NW1. Starsign: Virgo. Hobbies: football, tennis. Unfulfilled ambitions: to tour the world in a successful play and follow it up with a film made in America.

WISE, Ernie OBE
Comedian b. 27.11.25 Leeds. Child entertainer with his father in working men's clubs. Theatre debut at Bradford 1936; London debut in Band Waggon 1939 then toured in Bryan Michie's Youth Takes a Bow in which he met Eric Morecambe 1941. Formed a double act but touring was interrupted by National Service in Merchant Navy. After the war both booked for Lord John Sanger's Variety Circus and partnership resumed. Radio breakthrough on Worker's Playtime and own radio series, You're Only Young Once. TV incl: Running Wild; Sunday Night at the London Palladium; The Morecambe and Wise Show (BBC and ITV). Numerous variety, pantomimes, summer and royal shows, tours of Australia and Canada and Ed Sullivan Show in America. Films: The Intelligence Men; That Riviera Touch; The

Magnificent Two. Freeman City of London 1976. Education: elementary schools. m. Doreen. Address: c/o Billy Marsh, London Management, London W1. Starsign: Sagittarius. Hobbies: cricket, writing, boating, gardening, tennis, swimming. Unfulfilled ambition: to break into American showbusiness—films, TV, theatre.

WITTY, John
Actor/broadcaster/interviewer b. 17.9.15 Bristol. Trained at Webber Douglas Academy of Dramatic Art before army service, then rep, including Oxford and Colwyn Bay, and London West End. In films since 1944 (most recent: Vault of Horror), and TV films and series since 1946; most recent TV: Q9. More than 6000 broadcasts and 1000 film and audio-visual commentaries in UK and abroad. Also regularly voicing TV and radio commercials. Education: Clifton College and Exeter College, Oxford (BA) where he was president of the Oxford University Dramatic Society. m. Susan, 1 d. Sara Jane, 1 s. Jonathan. Address: Highgate, London N6. Starsign: Virgo. Hobbies: family, philately, archaeology, travel. Unfulfilled ambition: to be able to speak six foreign languages really well.

WOGAN, Terry
Broadcaster b. 3.8.38 Limerick, Ireland. Claims his training and background were 'bourgeois Irish'. Collected many awards for his radio work, including Radio Industries Club award for Radio Personality of the Year 1974, 1976, 1978. Radio incl: Terry Wogan Show; Pop Score; Punchline; Twenty Questions. TV incl: Lunchtime With Wogan; Come Dancing; Miss World; Eurovision Song Contest; Song For Europe; Variety Club Awards; Carl-Alan Awards; Disco; Startown; Blankety Blank. Education: Crescent College, Limerick; Belverdere, Dublin. m. former model Helen Joyce, 1 d. Katherine, 2 s. Alan, Mark. Address: c/o Jo Garnett Personal Management, London SW7. Starsign: Leo. Hobbies: family, reading, golf.

WOODS, Peter
Newsreader b. 7.11.30 Essex. Started on local newspapers including The Yorkshire Post before military service in the Royal Horse Guards in which he was

commissioned. Spent 10 years in Fleet Street, first on the Daily Mail, then as special correspondent on the Daily Mirror. Was parachuted into Suez as a reporter for an exclusive on the 1956 attack. Joined BBC in 1959 as a reporter but left in 1963 to join ITN as their first American correspondent, based in New York. Rejoined BBC in 1967 as foreign correspondent. Also wrote for and presented Newsroom on BBC2. Subsequently became newsreader. Education: Hull Grammar School; Imperial Services College, Windsor. m. (1st) Kathleen (dis), (2nd) Esma, 1 d. Susan; 1 s. Guy (both by 1st m). Address: c/o BBC TV, London W12. Starsign: Scorpio.

WOODWARD, Edward OBE
Actor b. 1.6.30 Croydon. Wanted to be a journalist but started work in a sanitary engineer's office. Trained at RADA, then years in rep before London debut in Where There's a Will. Other stage productions incl: Rattle of a Simple Man; A Tale of Two Cities; High Spirits (in America); The Wolf; Male of the Species; On Approval; The Dark Horse. Many radio plays. Films incl: Becket; File on the Golden Goose; A Fine and Private Place; Callan; Hunted; Young Winston. TV incl: Emergency – Ward 10; Skyport; Sword of Honour; Au Pair Swedish Style; Entertaining Mr Sloane; Murders in the Rue Morgue;

Night of Talavera; Julius Caesar; The Listener; Callan; Saturday, Sunday, Monday; The Bass Player and the Blonde. Records incl: Grains of Sand; This Man Alone; Love is the Key. Education: Eccleston Road and Sydenham Road Schools, Croydon; Elmwood School, Wallingford; Kingston Commerical School. m. actress Venetia, 1 d. Sarah, 2 s. Timothy, Peter. Address: c/o Eric Glass Ltd, London W1. Starsign: Gemini. Hobbies: collecting swords, gem polishing.

WORSNIP, Glyn
Reporter b. 2.9.38 Highnam, Gloucestershire. Trained as actor in rep and as writer/journalist in theatre, radio and TV. Photographic Intelligence Officer in RAF 1956-58. Stage incl: everything from farce with Frankie Howerd to Pirandello with Albert Finney and from revue to the Royal Shakespeare Company, incl: roles in London West End musicals Our Man Crichton; Oliver!; Canterbury Tales. TV incl: That's Life 1974-78; Nationwide (since 1976) especially Pigeonhole; Omnibus; Arena; Help Yourself; Joint Account. Education: Highnam C of E; Monmouth School; St John's College, Oxford (BA Hons English). m. Jo Glanville, 1 d. Elinor. Address: c/o Jeanne Griffiths Agency, London NW6. Starsign:

Virgo. Hobbies: walking, gardening, watching rugby and cricket. Unfulfilled ambition: to have an ambition.

WORTH, Harry
Actor/comedian b. 20th November, Tankersley, near Barnsley. Early in his career spent two years touring with Laurel and Hardy, but appearances in Royal Command Performances turned him into a household name. Stage incl: Harvey; Norman Is That You?; Send Me No Flowers (Windsor); Pardon Me, Prime Minister (on tour). Stage success led to TV including over 100 episodes of Here's Harry. TV also incl: Thirty Minutes' Worth; My Name is Harry Worth; How's Your Father?; Scoop. Married with one daughter. Address: c/o London Management, London W1. Starsign: Scorpio.

WRIGHT, Jenny Lee
Actress b. London. Left school at 16 to train with the Ballet Rambert. By 17 she was touring the world with a French cabaret group. On

return to Britain joined Lionel Blair's group of dancers. She has played stooge to many comedians incl: Morecambe and Wise, Jimmy Tarbuck, Benny Hill, Frankie Howerd, Mike and Bernie Winters and Les Dawson. Other TV incl: The Protectors; The Golden Shot; Paul Temple; Public Eye; General Hospital; Beryl's Lot; The Generation Game; The Masterspy (in which she plays Miss Moneypacker). Films incl: Husbands; The Triple Echo; The Revenge of Dr Death. Address: Cobham, Surrey. Hobbies: water skiing, driving, antique hunting.

WYATT, Richard
Presenter b. 25.7.49 Weston-super-Mare. Newspaper and radio experience before joining HTV. Presenter weekly entertainment programme What's On and gardening spot. Country Crafts documentaries The Thatcher; Withies and Weavers; Forest of Dean Miners. Other TV incl: children's programmes Ten on Saturday; Wyatt's Place; presenter HTV's programme for unemployed youngsters Jobline; I Think We'll Call Him Georgie Fame; The First Robin Cousins (Royal Television Society award). Education: 'still continuing' he says. Address: c/o HTV, Bristol. Starsign: Leo. Hobby: work. Unfulfilled ambition: that the right producer reads this.

WYATT, Tessa
Actress b. 23.4.48 Woking, Surrey. Studied ballet and appeared in rep in school holidays. Rep at Cheltenham, Leatherhead, Bromley. TV debut at 14 in a Mr Pastry series. Stage: Minor Murder. Films: Wedding Night; I Think You'll Die Young Man; Spy Story; but mainly TV incl: The Tempest; The Black Tulip; Z Cars; Dixon of Dock Green; Sanctuary; Out of the Unknown; The Main Chance; Love Story; The Goodies; Within These Walls; Seaside Special; Celebrity Squares; Robin's Nest. Education: Elmhurst Ballet School, Camberley. m. disc jockey Tony Blackburn (dis), 1 s. Simon. Address: Datchet, Berks. Starsign: Taurus.

WYMARK, Jane
Actress b. 31.10.52 London. Always wanted to be an actress, though warned about the hardships by her father, the late Patrick Wymark. Rep in Bristol, Derby, Birmingham, Nottingham. TV incl: Rooms; The Future Ghost; Beasts; Poldark; The Bass Player and the Blonde. Education: Birmingham University Drama Faculty (hons degree). Address: c/o Larry Dalzell Associates, London WC2. Starsign: Scorpio.

WYNTER, Mark
Actor b. 29.1.43 Woking, Surrey. Former choirboy (at Downham, Kent) who sang in Canterbury Cathedral and Royal Albert Hall. After a variety of jobs became one of Britain's best-known and highest paid singing stars with such hits as Image of a Girl; Venus in Blue Jeans and Go Away, Little Girl. Singing engagements took him seven times around the world, but he now concentrates on acting with leading rep companies and in London's West End (Conduct Unbecoming and Phil the Fluter). Stage also incl: Side By Side By Sondheim (Britain and Canada); Charley's Aunt. Films incl: The Haunted House of Horror; Red; Superman; The Jealous Mirror. Radio incl: It's Mark Time. TV incl: Call In On Wynter; Tale of Two Rivers; According to Dora; Tribute to Terence Rattigan; The Cedar Tree; Sally Ann. Education: Forest Hills Comprehensive. Address: c/o CCA, London SW6. Starsign: Aquarius. Hobbies: squash, swimming, reading, theatre, running, cycling. Unfulfilled ambition: to cycle through the outback of Australia.

YATES, Marjorie
Actress b. 13.4.41
Birmingham. Trained at
Guildhall School of Music of
Drama then rep at Liverpool.
London stage incl: Royal
Court Theatre (Sea Anchor;
Small Change; Inadmissible
Evidence) and the National
Theatre (incl: A Fair Quarrel;
As You Like It). TV incl: Kisses
at Fifty; Connie; All Day on the
Sands; Lovely Day
Tomorrow; Marya; Couples;
The Sweeney. Films incl:
Black Panther. State school
education. m. London
University official and local
councillor Michael Freeman,
1 d. Polly, 1 s. Carl. Address:
c/o Boyack and Conway,
London W1. Starsign: Aries.
Hobbies: birdwatching,
tennis.

YARWOOD, Mike OBE
Impressionist b. 14.6.41
Stockport, Cheshire. Started
as entertainer by entering a
pub talent contest. Appeared
in pubs and clubs at night
while still a traveller.
Warm-up for Comedy
Bandbox led to
engagements throughout the
country, the London
Palladium, Royal Variety
Performances and TV incl:
Will the Real Mike Yarwood
Stand Up?; Look – Mike
Yarwood; The Best of Mike
Yarwood; Mike Yarwood in
Persons. Autobiography:
And This Is Me. Education:
secondary modern school.
m. ex-dancer Sandra
Burville, 2 d. Charlotte,
Clare. Address: Prestbury,
Cheshire. Starsign: Gemini.
Hobby: football. Unfulfilled
ambition: to top the bill at the
London Palladium.

YATES, Pauline
Actress b. 16th June
Liverpool. No academic
training for the stage; went to
Oldham Rep straight from
school. Also experience at
Liverpool Rep but has
worked mainly on TV, incl:
Hancock; The Second
Interview; Harriet's Back in
Town; Nightingale's Boys;
Going, Going, Gone Free;

Rooms; My Honourable Mrs;
Crown Court; The Fall and
Rise of Reginald Perrin;
England's Green and
Pleasant Land; Keeping It in
the Family. Film: The Four
Feathers. Education:
Childwall Valley High School
for Girls, Liverpool.
m. actor/writer Donald
Churchill, 2 d. Jemma, Polly.
Address: c/o Kate Feast
Management, London NW1.
Starsign: Gemini. Hobbies:
theatre, tapestry.

YORK, Michael
Actor b. 27.3.42. Became
interested in acting at school.
At 16 joined Michael Croft's
National Youth Theatre
touring Britain and the
Continent. Then rep in
Dundee, after which he
joined the National Theatre.
Left National Theatre to
concentrate on films. Stage
incl: Hamlet; Much Ado
About Nothing. First film part
in The Taming of the Shrew.
Other films incl: Romeo and
Juliet; Zeppelin; Accident;
Cabaret; England Made Me;
The Three Musketeers;
Logan's Run; Conduct
Unbecoming; Seven Nights
in Japan; The Island of Dr
Moreau; Riddle of the Sands.
TV incl: Rebel in the Grave;
The Forsyte Saga; True
Patriot; Jesus of Nazareth.
Education: Oxford University
(Literature). m. American
photographer Patricia
McCallum. Address: Monte
Carlo. Starsign: Aries.

YOUENS, Bernard
Actor b. 28.12.14 Hove,
Sussex. Acting training in
fit-ups, reps and tours. Stan
Ogden in Coronation Street
since 1963. Education:
Connaught Road School,
Hove; Rutherford College,
Newcastle upon Tyne.
m. Edna, 2 d. Ann, Diana,
3 s. Brian, Peter, Michael.
Address: c/o Elizabeth
Robinson, Hove, Sussex.
Starsign: Capricorn.
Hobbies: golf, bridge.
Unfulfilled ambition: to play in
London's West End.

YOUNG, Chris
Reporter/interviewer
b. 19.6.47 Devonport. Local
newspaper training and
news producer for BBC
Radio Brighton and as news
scriptwriter for BBC TV,
Norwich before joining Anglia
in 1971 (About Anglia).
Education: Plymouth
College. m. Karen,
2 d. Jessamy, Tammy,
1 s. Trystan. Address:
Saxlingham Nethergate,
Norfolk. Starsign: Gemini.
Hobbies: TV, radio, reading,
family, swimming, cricket,
jogging. Unfulfilled ambition:
'to top my village cricket
team's bowling average'.

Z

ZUCKERMAN, Nina
(Nina Francis)
Actress b. 14.1.52 London.
Became an actress on
leaving Arts Educational and
Aida Foster Stage Schools.
Stage incl: Ring Round The
Moon; Henry V – Ludlow
Festival; Come Blow Your
Horn – Windsor; Tonight We
Improvise – Chichester.
Films incl: The Man Who Had
Power Over Women; Assault;
Everything in Common;
Spanish Fly. TV incl:
Crossroads; Rasputin; The
Man in the Wood; The Prison;
Silhouettes; Signs and
Symbols; Are You Being
Served?; Well Anyway; The
Many Wives of Patrick;
Devil's Crown; Ghost Sonata.
Education: Queens College,
Harley St, London; Lycée
Camot, France. Address: c/o
Aida Foster Ltd, London
NW8. Starsign: Capricorn.
Hobbies: scuplting, painting,
music. Unfulfilled ambition: to
win an acting award.

ZAVARONI, Lena
Child entertainer b. 4.11.63
Isle of Bute. Discovered
singing with her parents in a
Rothesay pub, but achieved
instant stardom as five times
Opportunity Knocks winner,
singing Ma, He's Making
Eyes At Me! Since toured the
world, appeared in a Royal
Variety Performance and
starred with her friend Bonny
Langford in their own TV
show, Lena and Bonny.
Topped the bill at the London
Palladium for one week in
October 1978 and recorded
her first BBC series, Lena
Zavaroni and Her Music
(screened May/June 1979).
Education: local school in
Rothesay; Italia Conti Stage
School. Address: c/o Dorothy
Solomon, London W1.
Starsign: Scorpio. Hobbies:
swimming, reading, tennis.
Unfulfilled ambition: to make
a film.